Anthropology of C

History and Power in the Study of Law

NEW DIRECTIONS IN LEGAL ANTHROPOLOGY

EDITED BY

June Starr and
Jane F. Collier

Cornell University Press

Ithaca and London

LIBRARY SERVICES
UNIVERSITY OF SOUTHERN INDIANA
EVANSVILLE, IN

Copyright © 1989 by Cornell University

Chapter 7, "Thinking about 'Interests': Legislative Process
in the European Community," copyright © 1989 by Francis Snyder

All rights reserved. Except for brief quotations in a review, this book,
or parts thereof, must not be reproduced in any form without
permission in writing from the publisher. For information, address
Cornell University Press, 124 Roberts Place, Ithaca, New York 14850.

First published 1989 by Cornell University Press.

International Standard Book Number (cloth) 0-8014-2113-6
International Standard Book Number (paper) 0-8014-9423-0
Library of Congress Catalog Number 88-30258

Printed in the United States of America

Librarians: Library of Congress cataloging information
appears on the last page of the book.

The paper in this book is acid-free and meets the guidelines for
permanence and durability of the Committee on Production Guidelines
for Book Longevity of the Council on Library Resources.

LIBRARY SERVICES
UNIVERSITY OF SOUTHERN INDIANA
EVANSVILLE, IN

Contents

Contents

Preface

A conference called "Ethno-historical Models and the Evolution of Law" was held in Milan and at Bellagio, Lake Como, Italy, from August 10 to August 18, 1985. The Wenner-Gren Foundation for Anthropological Research and the Rockefeller Foundation provided funding. The conference was organized by June Starr of the Department of Anthropology, State University of New York at Stony Brook, and Jane F. Collier of the Department of Anthropology, Stanford University. The goal was to compare case studies of legal change in particular societies using historical frameworks in order to search for shared questions and methodologies to direct future research.

The twenty anthropologists, sociologists, and law professors from North America and Europe who attended devoted five half-days to discussing seventeen previously circulated papers and four half-days to a general consideration of conference issues. In their discussions, participants focused on the models they were using to analyze the development, change, decay, integration, and articulation of legal systems within specific social units. Professors Elizabeth Colson and William Twining served as commentators, Jessica Kuper was editorial adviser, and Longina Jakubowska and Richard Maddox were rapporteurs.

We soon settled down into a cheerful and sometimes argumentative group. Almost every idea offered was challenged, reanalyzed, and reconstituted. This aspect of the conference is covered in more detail elsewhere.[1] By the end of the conference we believed that we had developed new ideas and methods for studying the anthropology of law, and conference participants decided we should publish the papers as a unit in a volume.

Most of the chapters here have been reworked so that they relate to the major intellectual developments of the conference. Authors of six conference papers were offered the opportunity to rewrite their papers or submit different ones. Laura Nader and Francis Snyder submitted different papers, June Starr rewrote hers, and Philip Gulliver, Sally Humphreys, and Robert Hayden chose to publish their papers elsewhere.

We especially wish to thank Lita Osmundsen, past president and director of research at the Wenner-Gren Foundation, for her sustained support of our project. We are also indebted to Nina Watson, who made complicated administrative arrangements go smoothly. Susan Garfield of the Rockefeller Foundation, and the staff at Bellagio, gained our appreciation for creating a tranquil atmosphere in which the only surprises were culinary and intellectual. Linda Josephs quickly and efficiently retyped sections of the manuscript.

We also thank Peter Agree, our editor at Cornell University Press; Peggy Hoover, our copyeditor for the Press; and Roger Sanjek, the series editor, who helped us solve certain problems with the manuscript.

J.S. and J.F.C.

Stony Brook, New York
Stanford, California

[1]June Starr and Jane F. Collier, "Historical Studies of Legal Change," *Current Anthropology* 28/3(1987):367–372.

Contributors

SAID AMIR ARJOMAND, Associate Professor of Sociology, State University of New York, Stony Brook.

VILHELM AUBERT, Professor of Sociology, University of Oslo, Norway.

ANTON BLOK, Professor of Anthropology, Center for Mediterranean Studies, University of Amsterdam, The Netherlands.

JEREMY BOISSEVAIN, Professor of Anthropology and Director of the Center for Mediterranean Studies, University of Amsterdam, The Netherlands.

BERNARD S. COHN, Professor of Anthropology, University of Chicago.

GEORGE A. COLLIER, Professor of Anthropology, Stanford University.

JANE F. COLLIER, Associate Professor of Anthropology, Stanford University.

CAROL J. GREENHOUSE, Associate Professor of Anthropology, Cornell University.

HANNEKE GROTENBREG, Contract Research Coordinator for the Anthropological/Sociological Center, University of Amsterdam, The Netherlands.

SALLY FALK MOORE, Professor of Anthropology, Harvard University.

Contributors

LAURA NADER, Professor of Anthropology, University of California, Berkeley.

JUNE NASH, Professor of Anthropology, City College, City University of New York.

LAWRENCE ROSEN, Professor of Anthropology, Princeton University.

FRANCIS G. SNYDER, Reader in European Community Law, University College, London, formerly of the Law Faculty at the University of Warwick.

JUNE STARR, Associate Professor of Anthropology, State University of New York, Stony Brook.

JOAN VINCENT, Professor of Anthropology, Barnard College.

History and Power in
the Study of Law

Introduction: Dialogues in Legal Anthropology

June Starr and Jane F. Collier

Should social anthropologists continue to isolate the "legal" as a separate field of study?[1] In seeking explanations for legal change, most of the contributors to this volume have crossed the boundaries between legal anthropology and other subfields of social anthropology. By making asymmetrical power relations and world historical time essential to their analyses, the contributors reach conclusions that are different from those of social scientists working without temporal or power dimensions.

Several types of questions unite the chapters in this book: What legal resources are available to groups competing for state power? How do legal ideas privilege some at the expense of others? How do weaker groups overcome obstacles created by the legal order? What explains the lengthy continuities among certain legal ideas and social orders? Historical analysis thus becomes a dynamic aid in understanding the role law plays in changing asymmetrical power relationships among social groups, and how that role is limited. Instead of treating change and power differences as variables that complicate a structural or structural-functional analysis of dispute management, most of the contributors to this volume focus on power differentials to understand both the

[1]For criticisms and suggestions on and for this introduction, we thank William Arens, Beverly Birns, Elizabeth Colson, George Collier, Carol Greenhouse, Laura Nader, Roger Sanjek, William Twining, and two anonymous readers.

course of legal change and the persistence of certain legal ideas and processes through time. Rather than ask how societies achieve the peaceful resolution of disputes, most ask how individuals and groups in particular times and places have used legal resources to achieve their ends. Instead of focusing on either normative systems or dispute processes, the chapters analyze the relationship of law to wider systems of social relations. We have thus modified the field of legal anthropology in the process of revitalizing it.

Breaching subdisciplinary boundaries has allowed most of us to enlarge our vision of legal anthropology in a decade that finds some law researchers questioning the usefulness of a separate subfield of "anthropology of law." Several scholars have called for abolition of the anthropology of law, while others predict its demise (Comaroff and Roberts 1981; Snyder 1981a, 1981b; Chanock 1983; Francis 1984). Comaroff and Roberts, for example, doubt "the value of distinguishing 'the legal' as a discrete field of inquiry" (1981:243). Arguing that the aim of social anthropology is to study total social systems, they suggest that instead of isolating dispute processes or rule systems for separate study, anthropologists should study disputes and invocations of rules for what they reveal about systemic processes. Snyder also suggests that legal anthropology is too narrow: "The anthropology of law is a myth if conceived as the search for ahistorical or cross-culturally valid features of law, or alternatively, as the reduction of historically and culturally specific normative forms to ethnographic descriptions of individual behavior" (1981b:164). He also advocates redirecting anthropologists interested in legal issues toward the study of a total system, but his "system" is the historical expansion of Western capitalism. The future development of legal anthropology lies "not only in elucidating the relationships between social action and cultural ideologies, but also in grasping the extent to which these relationships and the wider social processes of which they form a part are the product of specific historical and economic conditions" (ibid., p. 164).

Questions about "usefulness" and predictions of demise have also been directed toward other subdisciplines in social anthropology (see, e.g., Schneider 1984; Ranger 1983; Smith 1985; Wolf 1982:21). Studies of kinship, anthropological economics, "tribal" politics, and the anthropology of religion have also been criticized for being too isolated from major integrative theory in social anthropology. Once "narrowness" was useful for theory-building at a particular stage in social anthropology's development. But many social anthropologists, viewing subdisciplinary study as too limiting in the 1980s, have returned to studying the interrelatedness of institutions and social action as they bring history and

[2]

political economy into their ethnographies. Eric Wolf has stated that we need to relate both the history and theory of the development of modern world markets "to processes that affect and change the lives of local populations," that we need "theoretically informed history and historically informed theory . . . to account for populations specifiable in time and space, both as outcomes of significant processes and as their carriers" (1982:21).

This volume grew out of a 1985 conference at Bellagio, Italy. Focusing on complex societies, all the contributors are concerned with aspects of how law changes over time, how conflict develops among groups that have different access to legal resources and different ideas about how conflicts should be resolved. The conference's focus on change within world historical time meant that all contributors studied societies marked by asymmetrical power relationships.

Each chapter addresses one or more overarching themes, such as the transmission of power relationships through time as these are embodied in particular social and legal forms; the role of law and legal ideas as contested metaphors for and determinants of social order; or the relationship between law and culture, with the latter defined as the production and reproduction of social forms, symbolic orderings, and hegemonic systems of domination. Some emphasize cultural form, others emphasize the person as a social agent. Some focus on the cultural construction of power relations and social hierarchies, others portray culture as less important than different access to material resources in separating the powerful from the powerless. Many of the chapters document ways that groups in power enable the law to change rapidly. But the law is not viewed as a seamless web, nor is it seen as neutral. All the chapters view law not as a natural occurrence, as in "natural law," but as a "thing" constructed by human agency that is advantageous to some at the expense of others. Most of the chapters treat legal rules as formulations that have been discussed, argued over, and arrived at through negotiated settlements among conscious agents.

A summary of recent developments in the subdiscipline of anthropology of law will show how this volume builds on and differs from previous and current research.

Developments in the Anthropology of Law in the 1960s and 1970s

Within the subdiscipline of legal anthropology, dispute management as a cultural system was the focus of two important conferences held in the 1960s and organized by Laura Nader (Nader 1965a, 1969b).[2] Before these conferences, anthropologists interested in law followed Malinowski (1926) to understand how social control was maintained through the interconnectedness of social institutions, or they followed Radcliffe-Brown (1933) in studying disputes to discover the rules (i.e., "laws") whose supposed enforcement by third parties was credited with maintaining order in particular societies (see also Llewellyn and Hoebel 1941). The two conferences marked the replacement of a concern for rules with a concern for processes.

The focus on disputing processes that dominated research in the 1960s and 1970s highlighted what had been slighted in the former concern for rules.[3] Anthropologists and others studying dispute management focused on litigants' use of law to attain their own ends, rather than on law's role in maintaining social order. They examined the political and economic interests of those who quarreled, instead of assuming that public disputes reflected a breach of norm by some wrongdoer; they focused on litigants, rather than on third parties or judges; and they emphasized the role of relative power in shaping outcomes, rather than assuming the impartiality of dispute-settlers or judges. In the process, rich case materials for analyzing the interplay of interest groups were discovered.[4]

But in focusing on processes rather than laws, interests rather than rules, litigants rather than judges, and power rather than order, anthropologists who studied dispute management found themselves limited by the analytic dichotomies their projects created. They realized that law has a limited autonomy, even as it is embedded in political and legal systems. In the process of examining litigants' options, they found they had to consider rules, if only to treat them as resources that litigants

[2]In 1964, Laura Nader organized a small conference of social anthropologists at the Center for Advanced Study in the Behavioral Sciences in Stanford, California. The goal was to discuss their work and current trends in the field (Nader 1965a:v). In 1966, Nader organized a larger conference, held for ten days at Burg Wartenstein, Austria, to stimulate more and better research in areas "the potential of which has not yet been well mined" (Nader 1969b:vii).

[3]Earlier anthropologists, studying peoples who might be said to lack "law," developed methodologies for finding the legitimate rules of particular peoples. See Llewellyn and Hoebel 1941; Gluckman 1955; Bohannan 1957; Pospisil 1958; Epstein 1954.

[4]Studies on disputing that flourished during the 1960s and 1970s are Collier 1973; Gibbs 1963; Gulliver 1963, 1971; Hamnett 1977; Nader and Todd 1978; Koch 1974; Lowy 1978; Merry 1981; Starr 1978; Todd 1978; Witty 1980; and Yngvesson 1976. Of course, other types of anthropological studies were influential too. See Moore 1978 and also Burman and Harrell-Bond 1979.

could use in pursuing private interests. Further, they found they had to consider how law maintained the powerful, even as they examined its role in aiding the powerless. Many anthropologists who studied dispute management in the 1960s and 1970s experienced a sense of paradigm crisis by 1980, as did most social anthropologists, because functionalist theory (the framework within which we previously worked) was increasingly criticized. Once functionalism was called into question, many legal ethnographers believed that the central questions and the organizing rationale of anthropological study was lost. What is kinship if it is not about reproduction? And what is the anthropology of law if we doubt that legal systems settle conflicts?

Although many social anthropologists turned to the study of structuralism and symbolism based on the notions of Claude Lévi-Strauss in the 1960s and 1970s,[5] this approach had little or no impact on anthropology of law. Faced with a crisis of paradigm, many legal anthropologists wondered where organizing ideas and theory might be found. Paradoxically, this occurred at a time when some legal scholars were looking to anthropologists for insights on dispute management,[6] just as earlier anthropologists searching for legitimate rules had looked to legal scholars for guidance.

New Formulations

Calls for abolition of the anthropology of law thus reflect an emerging idea that anthropological understanding of legal processes needs to be based on a broader vision. This means constructing research questions that return to issues, and research agendas that are important to social anthropology as a whole. Such questions might involve viewing dispute management procedures as affecting relations among kin, the production and distribution of goods, political hierarchies, and ideas of ultimate order. We certainly hope such studies will continue to emphasize, as this volume does, the importance of power relationships and historical contextualization in understanding legal and social change.

This volume begins the preliminary work of conceptualizing anthro-

[5]See Turner 1967; Dolgin, Kemnitzer, and Schneider 1977; and Leach's (1970) book on Lévi-Strauss.

[6]Abel (1974, 1981a, 1981b), Danzig and Lowy (1975), Galanter (1983), Felstiner, Abel, and Sarat (1980–81), Roberts (1979), and Trubek (1980–81a, 1980–81b) were directly influenced. Auerbach (1983) seems to have been influenced indirectly.

pology of law not as a subdiscipline "apart from" social anthropology, but as a theory-building "part of" social anthropology. Ideas from political economy especially have proved fruitful for several chapters, but other cross-fertilizations, from philosophy, sociology, and cultural analysis, are also in evidence. At the same time, this volume makes a strong argument for the value of maintaining orderly subdisciplinary discourse in anthropology of law. Although legal anthropology at some future point might well dissolve (along with other anthropological subfields) into a renewed social anthropology, that time has yet to come. There is still much to discover from subdisciplinary discourse as we reach better understandings of how all legal processes are embedded in social relations. Meanwhile, some contributors to this volume recognize the convergence between their interests and the interests of the Critical Legal Studies Movement. Both ask how law acts to legitimate particular ideologies and asymmetrical power relations, and both seek to analyze the mutual construction of legal and social orders in historical time (*Critical Legal Studies Symposium*, 1984).

Common Themes

Asymmetrical Power Relationships and Legal Change

Although the chapters in this book share common assumptions about the ways legal systems encode asymmetrical power relationships, they differ in the way they conceptualize power asymmetries and in the amount of attention they devote to power differences. Some focus directly on the antagonistic relationship between economic classes in emerging and developed capitalist societies. Vilhelm Aubert, Anton Blok, George Collier, and June Nash, for example, use class analysis as a way to conceptualize particular historical struggles or general trends in legal development. Although these contributors may recognize the role of legal orders in establishing property rules that motivate class antagonism, they treat economic classes as given, because they are analyzing not the creation of new legal orders, but only struggles within existing legal orders.

The contributors who analyze the creation of new legal orders focus, not unexpectedly, on ruling groups rather than on antagonisms between economic classes. Bernard S. Cohn, analyzing the development of British rule in India, and Said Amir Arjomand, analyzing the creation of an

Islamic theocracy in Iran, discuss rulers who were in the process of establishing legal systems that were clearly designed to grant special privileges to their own ethnic, national, or religious group over others. Ruling groups are not monolithic, however. Joan Vincent, for example, discusses how conflicts between factions of the British ruling class structured colonial legislation in Uganda. Francis G. Snyder, too, analyzes how legislative rules and legal structures of the European Economic Community create interest groups and organized coalitions.

Even those who do not focus directly on the power asymmetries established by particular legal systems share the assumption that legal orders incorporate inequality. Those who discuss subordinated groups may focus on social relations within these groups, but they accept implicitly the idea that the legal ideology of the wider political system puts constraints on the possibilities for subordinated peoples. For example, the power imbalance between colonizer and colonized is assumed by Laura Nader and Sally Falk Moore when they discuss actions localized groups took to preserve areas of autonomy. In discussing the problems of the Surinamese entrepreneurs in Amsterdam, Jeremy Boissevain and Hanneke Grotenbreg also recognize the asymmetry between Dutch residents and recent migrants who lack legal resources, legal knowledge, and kinship ties to the members of the parliament. Cultural systems also embrace inequalities, as revealed in Lawrence Rosen's analysis of the ways Moroccan courts incorporate popular understandings about the relative worth of the testimony of men and of women, and of the testimony of rich men and poor men.

Because all the contributors hold the view that legal orders create asymmetrical power relations, they also share the assumption that the law is not neutral. The legal system does not provide an impartial arena in which contestants from all strata of society may meet to resolve differences. For example, conflicts between factions of a ruling class may shape the possibilities open to subordinated groups.

The neutrality of law fitted well with an older ahistorical, functionalist view of a "timeless, classless, custom-ridden" Third World. It masked the restructuring of societies by the Spanish, British, French, German, and North Americans. As early as 1961 the concept of law as a neutral arena was directly challenged by the anthropologist J. A. Barnes, who in a pointedly titled article, "Law as Politically Active," illustrated the ways that African political elites passed new legislation and used it for their own purposes (Barnes 1961:178). Not only was the law not passive, but it was actively created by and for groups in power. In addition, complex legal situations existed within African societies themselves. Paul Bohannan had earlier criticized the idea of dual legal systems: "The mark of a colonial situation might be said to be a systematic misunderstanding between the two cultures within the single power system, with constant revolutionary proclivities" (1965:38–39).

A contemporary overview of precolonial societies in Africa has shown that the "closed corporate consensual system" that came to be accepted as characteristic of "traditional Africa" rarely existed (Ranger 1983:248). The boundaries of tribal polity and the hierarchies of authority within them did not define the horizons of Africans. Ranger notes that most Africans had multiple identities. An African might define himself "at one moment as subject of this chief, at another moment as a member of that cult, at another moment as part of this clan, and at yet another an initiate in that professional guild" (ibid.). In addition, nineteenth-century Africa "was *not* characterized by a lack of internal social and economic competition, by the unchallenged authority of the elders, and by an acceptance of custom which gave every person . . . a place in society which was defined and protected" (ibid.).

The finding that Africa was not "tribal" and "custom-bound" when Europeans began migrating there has opened up a new way of conceptualizing group relationships and the evolution of legal orders in Africa. Peter Fitzpatrick, for example, described ways in which colonists "created reserves and other enforced settlements; restricted mobility beyond the 'tribal' area; required a continuing attachment to that area in indenture, vagrancy and pass laws; confined people to the amount of land deemed adequate for 'subsistence' and appropriated so-called waste and vacant land; prohibited or restricted wide-ranging political activity and food gathering; and in varying forms, erected systems of so-called indirect rule." He argues that "with colonialism existing social relations were taken, reconstituted in terms of its imperatives and then, as it were, given back to the people as their own. In this, history was denied and tradition created instead" (1985:479).

Sharing the views of Fitzpatrick and Ranger that legal orders inevitably create conflict, the chapters here assume that conflict, and not consensus, is an enduring aspect of any legal order. In studying how changes in power relations between groups create changes in legal systems, the contributors do not assume the existence of static cultural traditions either. Instead, they explore how cultural concepts are used by people acting in particular times and places within particular systems of unequal power relations. Each author is careful to separate the concept of "indigenous law," defined as the reconstruction of precontact native law by an anthropologist, from "customary law," defined as the outcome of historical struggles between native elites and their colonial or postcolonial overlords.

The recognition that inequality inheres in legal systems, in combination with the idea of continuously evolving cultural traditions, has led the contributors to think beyond the concepts of legal pluralism and dual legal orders. No contributor uses the term "legal pluralism" or "dual legal system" when analyzing complex social systems. Both words, "pluralism" and "dual," carry connotations of equality that misrepresent the asymmetrical power relations that inhere in the coexistence of multiple legal orders. Various legal systems may coexist, as occurs in many colonial and postcolonial states, but the legal orders are hardly equal. A comparison of the chapters in this volume will show that legal ideas and processes maintained by subordinated groups are constrained in ways that the legal orders of dominant groups are not.

The above terms also imply that coexisting legal systems evolve independently after coming into contact with each other, a notion that misrepresents the contributors' collective view that coexisting legal orders evolve together. Moore, for example, observes that Chagga "customary law" is a product of long interaction between the Chagga people and those claiming to rule their country. Nader's chapter on the ideology of social harmony reveals that the legal orders maintained by Mesoamerican "closed corporate communities" evolved in relation to pressures from outside conquerors.

Thus, we share Kidder's observation that "the command model of law is inadequate. It oversimplifies the process known as law because it is static, treating imposition as a fait accompli rather than an interactional process affected by power differentials" (1979:291). A concept of imposed law also implies a false assumption of complete cultural incompatibility between the dominating and dominated peoples (ibid.), thus making it difficult to analyze the ways that subordinated peoples invoke wider legal orders to achieve their ends. Legal orders should not be treated as closed cultural systems that one group can impose on another, but rather as "codes," discourses, and languages in which people pursue their varying and often antagonistic interests.

Legal Ideas and Processes as They Shape and Change Dynamic Relations among Groups

The contributors avoid the terms "micro" and "macro" in conceptualizing group or geographic relationships. There are several reasons for this. First, the ruling groups may not be localized, and they may consist of coalitions of a number of different ethnic and interest groups. Second, complex disputes involving the interests of a number of groups may stretch outside a nation-state or may unite groups at different levels within a nation or empire. For example, nineteenth-century manufacturers in England had interests in common with plantation owners in Africa, and these interests differed from those of the British Crown (see the chapter by Vincent).

Legal ideas and processes emerge as important factors in upholding or changing systems of inequality when a society is studied in a historical context. The view that rules are systemic resources permits analysis both of the power of law to shape events and of the fact that legal rules do not exist except as invoked by people pursuing particular ends. The contributors came to accept the notion that transmission of legal ideas, embedded as they are in cultural and social processes, gives legitimacy to hegemonic groups (see Williams 1977).

As shared understanding grew among the contributors that legal and societal change evolved through changing power relationships between social groups and economic classes, we found ways to conceptualize the persistence of *some* legal ideologies in time and space. This perspective provided greater understanding of conflict between groups, as well as of conflicts between groups and "the law" itself (see Leach 1977). Thus, conflict is conceptualized as an interactional, ideological, and institutionalized process. Differing concepts of power and of legitimacy may explain why some groups look to the legal system and to changing the laws as a way to gain rights, while other groups shun national law, using banditry, violence, and revolution as a way to make their interests known and to legitimize their goals.

A unifying focus on the historical context in which legal ideas are shaped by groups, and how limits for changing laws are also set by dominant groups, became a way to illuminate systems of hegemony through time and across many societies. June Starr's reanalysis of selected Roman legal categories demonstrates that unchallenged ideas can dominate theoretical assumptions too. Thus, these chapters present a coherent view of an emerging interest within legal and political anthropology in history and power relations in the study of law.

By dividing history into transformational sequences, a researcher can understand why groups in power prefer and use certain sociolegal forms and institutions and neglect others. Once the contributors began to look at dominant groups and the cultural ideas embedded in a legal form, they were able to make generalizations about how certain countries exported and extended their colonial experience. For example, the British colonial experience began in Ireland and soon led to a movement of both administrators and ideas from Ireland to India. Later, Indian colonial officials brought many of their symbols of rule and administration (such as the concept of "customary law" and the institution of "district officers") with them when they moved to Africa. A historical framework allowed comparison of British ideas of how to rule "native peoples" with those held by the sixteenth-century Spaniards who debated how to govern ancient American civilizations.

Although not all the contributors would subscribe to Giddens's theory of structuration (Giddens 1976, 1979), three of his propositions are germane to our volume. First, the realm of human agency is bounded: people "produce society, but they do so as historically located actors, and not under conditions of their own choosing." Second, "structures must not be conceptualized as simply placing constraints upon human agency, but as enabling." And third, "the processes of structuration involve an interplay of meanings, norms and power" (1976:160–161).

Law as Culture

The concern in this volume is more with the continuities between legal orders and wider cultural systems than with differentiating law from custom or morality. Although several contributors might accept Bohannan's proposition that laws are customs that have been lifted out of daily life to be "reinstitutionalized within the legal institution" (1965:36), they focus on the ways in which legal ideas permeate daily life and how common-sense understandings of the person, time, and causality inform legal processes. Rosen, for example, traces the ways everyday concepts are used in Moroccan courtrooms, and other contributors stress that legal systems are part of wider cultural systems.

Not only anthropologists, but also the peoples they study, assume that legal systems are cultural systems. As a result, people treat legal orders as appropriate vehicles for asserting, creating, and contesting national identities. In the modern world, where the ideology of "nationhood" mandates a congruence between cultural and legal entities, legal orders and ethnic groups are mutually defining categories. To create a legal order is to write into law a sense of national unity and purpose, as Arjomand shows in his analysis of Iran's 1979 constitution and as revealed in Carol Greenhouse's tracing of key American cultural concepts

[11]

to the founding documents of the United States. Similarly, attempts by colonial powers to recognize "customary law" or grant limited autonomy to local groups foster ethnic identities among these enjoying such privileges or aspiring to them (see the chapters by Moore, Nader, Vincent, Cohn, and Boissevain and Grotenbreg).

Because legal and cultural orders are mutually defining, the contributors assume that the groups they study are not objective units that have endured through time or exist outside of time, but rather that they are conceptual entities produced by particular historical processes. For example, when Aubert writes about Norway, or Greenhouse writes about North America, or Starr writes about Roman legal categories, they refer to conceptual entities created by founding documents. A sense of history thus enters into the way the contributors constitute their objects of study.

The contributors also share the assumption that legal rules, procedures, and concepts exist only as they are invoked by people. Legal orders endure because people act as if they do, and people change legal orders by invoking new rules and abandoning old ones. As a result, the contributors understand legal continuities and changes by tracing the historical processes that shape people's actions by shaping their material interests and cultural understandings.

While recognizing the constraining effects of legal orders, especially the ways in which legal orders constrain weaker groups, the chapters focus on the enabling aspects of law. People and groups use legal rules to accomplish particular ends, even if such uses often have unintended consequences. Legal orders may embody asymmetrical power relations, but power is always an interactional process. Dominant groups enjoy legally protected privileges, but they are also constrained by the law. And subordinated groups that suffer under particular legal systems may find that law offers them, the less powerful, a measure of protection from the powerful, just as it sometimes offers them resources for action (Thompson 1975:262–263).

When subordinated groups use the laws of more powerful groups for personal or group gain, however, they tend to find themselves in the position of endorsing, both materially and symbolically, social orders that they might prefer to change. The Surinamese migrants described by Boissevain and Grotenbreg who applied for licenses to do business in Holland granted legitimacy to licensing laws designed to protect Dutch businessmen. And even migrants who sought to change the laws nevertheless granted legitimacy to Dutch legislative procedures. To use

[12]

laws is to admit membership in the group regulated by that legal order. To refuse to participate in legal activities—like the Baptists described by Greenhouse or the Bokkerijder bands described by Blok—is to declare symbolically one's estrangement from a legal order.

Legal Change

The contributors implicitly define legal change as a change in the way power and privilege are distributed through legal means. Because they share the assumption that legal orders invariably create inequality, changes in asymmetrical power relations among groups are treated as the defining feature of legal change.

Some contributors focus on actual changes in legal rules or procedures, arguing that such changes signal or cause a change in power relations. Blok, for example, suggests that the change from theatrical punishments to imprisonment in eighteenth-century Europe indicated an increase in the power of elites to control the population, while George Collier discusses a situation in which previously deprived groups in a Spanish village were empowered by new legislation. Cohn and Arjomand write about elites who created new legal orders giving controlling power to their own groups. Vincent and Snyder, by contrast, focus less on how legal changes empower already recognized groups and more on the role of law in structuring interests and in organizing the alignments of groups and individuals.

Others focus on continuities that are apparent or actual. For example, Aubert, Starr, and Moore argue that apparent continuities in key legal concepts—such as "the rule of law" in Norway, or the early occurrence of "private property" under Roman law, or "customary law" in Tanzania—can in fact mask changes both in power relations and in the substance of legal rules. Nash, Nader, and Boissevain and Grotenbreg are less concerned with changes than with analyzing struggles for power within existing legal frameworks. Rosen and Greenhouse focus on continuities. They write about those central cultural concepts that people continue to invoke despite historical changes in power relations.

Because the contributors to this volume focus on both change and continuity, they choose processes, rather than entities defined in space and time, as the units of their analyses. Instead of focusing on "societies," communities, or institutions abstracted from time, they tend to choose a process, an extended case, or a set of concepts to follow across spatial and temporal boundaries.

[13]

Some contributors focus on specific historical events. Cohn, Arjomand, Blok, and George Collier, for example, take particular happenings, such as the writing of constitutions, the passing of legislation, or specific trials, as points of entry for studying ongoing processes. Other contributors focus on the processes themselves. Aubert, Vincent, Moore, Nader, and Nash seldom mention specific historical events, preferring instead to chart ongoing processes. Finally, Greenhouse, Boissevain and Grotenbreg, Rosen, and Starr refer to specific historical events, but treat them less as points of entry than as evidence of ongoing processes.

Just as the contributors treat historical events as indicators of larger historical processes, so they treat specific field sites as embedded in wider spatial units. When such contributors as George Collier, Nash, Nader, Boissevain and Grotenbreg, Greenhouse, and Moore write about the villages, towns, and cities they studied, they do so not to focus on local customs and events, but to treat such customs and events as examples of wider regional, national, and international processes.

Organization of the Chapters

Although such diverse chapters may be grouped in several ways, we decided to divide them into four sections that highlight shared interests in understanding inequality and historical processes of change and continuity in legal systems. After discussing how the chapters in each section relate to one another, we discuss themes that divide the contributors to the volume—that is, things they disagreed about, sometimes vehemently.

In Part I, "Resisting and Consolidating State-Level Legal Systems," the chapters are arranged chronologically to emphasize the importance of understanding the historical moment and the historical sequence for analyzing legal changes. Blok, Aubert, and Nash chronicle developments in Western legal systems in the eighteenth, nineteenth, and twentieth centuries, and Arjomand picks up this thread by tracing recent efforts by Iran's Islamic rulers to create a constitution (a Western legal idea) for the return to an Islamic state.

At the end of the eighteenth century in Europe, there was a transition from public executions to imprisonment, and Blok highlights changes in legal and social thought that accompanied this transition. He analyzes court records of sentences imposed on more than 500 members of robber bands in the Lower Meuse between 1741 and 1778 and discusses the

[14]

change from public spectacles of torture and execution to confinement of wrongdoers in workhouses and prisons. Blok suggests that attacks began as a form of social protest by marginalized members of a politically fragmented rural society. These night raiders attacked large farms and church institutions. The court records chronicling the trials and sentences of robber bands reveal a steady decline in the theatricality of executions. In the 1740s, robbers were executed in public spectacles of torture, but by the 1770s the condemned were no longer burned or dismembered before being hanged, and several convicted robbers were merely jailed or banished. Blok suggests that both the decline of public executions and the decline of robber bands were due to the state's development of more efficient means for controlling the population.

Blok's analysis of state control is extended by Vilhelm Aubert's attempt to make sense of legal changes in nineteenth-century Norway. When the Norwegian state adopted the Enlightenment idea of the "rule of law," which was prevalent at the end of the eighteenth century, the concept meant only the state's commitment to provide its citizens with access to legal remedies against unlawful exertions of state power. The state relied on penalties to discourage unwanted behaviors. But by the twentieth century Norway used the concept of the "rule of law" differently. It meant the state's attempts to encourage desired behaviors through fiscal allocations. Aubert suggests that the state's wealth may have been a determining factor in the change from a liberal state protecting individual rights to a modern welfare state. A poor state can only use punishment for those whose behaviors violate the rights of others. A rich state can afford to reward those who perform desired acts through the selective allocation of economic rewards.

Nash also seeks a way to understand the role of state power in allocating the products of social production. She argues that one myth of twentieth-century North America is that we have "free enterprise." In fact, what are often treated as simple economic transactions have a political dimension because of the complex intermingling of government interventions, promoted by corporations through laws designed to protect individuals from the centralization of economic power. Such laws also prevent the polarization of wealth inherent in unfettered capitalist accumulation. By focusing on "redistributive processes" enacted into law, Nash develops a way of analyzing the policies of a modern state at work in the households, factories, and public agencies of a small industrial city in New England.

Consolidation of state power in twentieth-century Iran is reflected, although not actually discussed, in Said Arjomand's analysis of the drafting of Iran's 1979 constitution. The state's right and ability to control the population is a premise underlying the attempt of the Ayatollah Khomeini and his followers to replace the defeated Shah's Western-based system of law and order with a Shi'ite theocracy. Arjomand focuses on the revolutionary character of the constitution-drafters' task. Because the Arab and Ottoman empires were built on Sunni ideas of statehood, and the Shah's Western advisers had advocated a separation of "church" and state, Iran's new rulers had no models to follow in adapting Shi'ite law to what they perceived as the needs and prerogatives of a modern Islamic nation. Drawing on Weber's concept of rationalization, Arjomand analyzes the mode of reasoning that Iranian lawmakers used to elaborate the Shi'ite tradition.

The chapters in Part II, "Exporting and Extending Legal Orders," demonstrate how European notions of the rule of law are brought into new continents. Once again the chapters are arranged in rough chronological order.

Noting the unprecedented situation, Cohn documents the huge task facing the British when they set out to find a way to govern India. Earlier British colonies had been treated as extensions of the home country, to be governed by English law, but British officials recognized that India was an ancient civilization, with its own complex political hierarchies and customs. Hoping simply to replace India's rulers, the British first sought to rule through Indian law. Academic disciplines for translating Sanskrit, Persian, and Arabic texts developed out of British attempts to find an authentic, "ancient" Indian constitution, which they could use as the law for governing India. However, what started as a search for authentic ancient codes ended within a century as Hindu law was transformed into English case law.

Vincent's analysis of colonial legislation in Uganda reveals the complex forces at work in the creation of a new legal order too. Arguing that laws imposed by colonial rulers serve the general interests of the ruling class in maintaining its hegemony, the Ugandan case reveals that legislation is rarely a simple reflection of ruling-class interests. Further, it is the outcome of struggles between different factions of that class. Legislation always bears the traces of continually renegotiated disputes and compromises. Many of the laws passed in colonial Uganda reflect not local interests but the interests of Manchester manufacturers, missionary societies, planters in Kenya, and so forth.

In a paper on lawmaking in the supranational European Economic Community, Snyder illustrates the complexity of the legislative process by focusing on what seems to be a paradox—the apparent visibility of legislative activity and the surprising opacity of the issues and interests involved. Snyder uses this paradox to challenge the idea that interests and coalitions antedate the legislative process. He demonstrates how interests and new affiliations emerge in the negotiations to create new law.

The chapters in Parts III and IV have to do with local-level attempts to use, engage, confront, resist, ignore, and shape the laws that affect people's lives. The authors consider how people at particular times and places have used, or avoided, the legal resources available to them.

In Part III, "Receiving and Rejecting National Legal Processes," George Collier's chapter illustrates Snyder's point that legislative processes may conjure up new interests and affiliations. Collier analyzes how national decrees that were intended to reform agrarian employment led to polarization of a Spanish village in the years between 1930 and 1936. A class analysis reveals a prior conflict of interest between day laborers and proprietors of large estates, but the structures set up by the new legislation created a situation in which intermediate groups of tenant farmers and small landholders were forced to choose sides. The village became split between "workers" and "owners." Although over-arching state processes conditioned the possibilities for local action, local economic concerns and cultural understandings of male honor affected the unfolding of events.

In George Collier's revolutionary situation, opposing individuals understood each other only too well; in Boissevain and Grotenbreg's non-revolutionary situation there are notable cultural misunderstandings. The plight of recent Surinamese migrants to the Netherlands as they tried to establish small businesses is documented in detail. Many of these small entrepreneurs expected Dutch laws regulating small businesses to be the same as those in Surinam. Many did not understand Dutch. All lacked information about the maze of laws governing small businesses in Holland. The degree of compliance varied. Some entrepreneurs operated completely outside the law. Among these who did comply with some regulations, the researchers found many who were seeking ways to further legitimize their operations. They conclude that although many Surinamese entrepreneurs have managed to establish businesses that survived for several years in spite of the law, the overwhelming power of the Dutch state, combined with the fragmented nature of the Surinamese community, will lead Surinamese entrepreneurs who do continue in business to ever greater conformity with the law.

Greenhouse analyzes people who actively reject the local and regional legal system. Asking why North Americans accuse themselves of having a "litigious" society, she provides answers on two levels. First, the historical situation of Baptists in a Southern town reveals the equation between disputing and unchristian behavior. Then the wider cultural context that provided the Baptists with the symbolic resources they used to formulate their ban on pursuing legal remedies is analyzed. To invoke "outside" authority is to negate the principle of equality enshrined in the American Declaration of Independence. Greenhouse's discussion of North American cultural concepts complements Nash's discussion of conflict over redistributive processes in a New England town. Greenhouse suggests a reason for the difficulty North Americans have in perceiving the state's role in the transactions of daily life.

In contrast to the chapters documenting rejection of the wider legal system, the chapters in Part V, "Constructing and Shaping Law," discuss the ways local people use law to shape the legal orders that affect their lives. In comparing North American conceptions of courts with Moroccan ones, Rosen extends Greenhouse's theories concerning American cultural conceptions of litigiousness, asserting that Americans consider courts as esoteric arenas outside of ordinary social interaction. This has discouraged American anthropologists from analyzing the ways legal concepts in other societies pervade daily life and how ordinary common sense informs legal rules. Arguing that courts are as good a place as any to study a people's world view, in addition to their economic exchanges, religious rituals, or political struggles, Rosen proceeds to show that the mode of fact-finding and the form of judicial reasoning used in Islamic courts in Morocco express conceptions of the person, truth, and social order that are also apparent in the marketplace and other cultural contexts. Over the years, Morocco has adopted a new legal code and reorganized the courts, but the concerns and understandings of ordinary Moroccans continue to shape the way courts operate.

In contrast to Rosen's emphasis on cultural continuities, Moore's historical study of legal change among the Chagga of Tanzania (1986) allows her to argue that "customary rules" are not survivals of a traditional past, but are continually renegotiated as conditions change. Certain aspects of customary forms may appear enduring, such as the concept of "customary law" itself, but the content of customary rules reflects the political and economic circumstances in which they are negotiated. Moore thus suggests that any attempt to understand customary rules in terms of an ahistorical cultural system is doomed to misinterpret them unless it is supplemented by a historical analysis of the political and economic contexts in which the rules are invoked, challenged, and restated.

Both the cultural continuities and the changing political contexts are considered by Laura Nader, who explains how the ideology of community harmony developed among native peoples. Christian missionaries working actively in the Philippines, in Mexico, in Central America, and in parts of Africa taught colonized people that God's will was Christian submission. Local leaders used this notion in trying to maintain control over local affairs. Anthropologists learned the harmony model from their informants, who were actively using the concepts of their conquerors to preserve some measure of local autonomy. Focusing on the history of a Zapotec village in the mountains of Oaxaca, Mexico, Nader discusses how the political structures introduced by Spanish conquerors and the religious beliefs introduced by Catholic priests in the sixteenth century provided the concepts that villagers continually used and that continued to pervade the village legal processes that she studied in the 1960s. In writing about how anthropologists have used the idea of harmony, Nader concludes that "anthropology was never meant *only* to be the study of other cultures."

Sometimes ethnographic information is available to us only through anthropological models. Yet, if knowledge is both cumulative and "situated" in a historical time, as our contributors assume, then we need strategies that "disengage" data from its theoretical use. Starr's essay attempts to open up a gap between a literal understanding of nineteenth-century theory (concerning early and classical Roman society) and the "ethnographic sources" used by nineteenth-century intellectuals. Focusing on the legal ideas and practices concerning the ability of elite married women to hold and manage their own property, Starr reexamines Sir Henry Maine's major source of information to correct certain of Maine's ideas that have been important touchstones for anthropological theory. Starr uses knowledge accumulated by scholars of Roman law to suggest that Roman women were more free in some contexts than Sir Henry Maine imagined, and less free in others. Implicit in this study is the idea that we need to understand each society's legal ideas and resources in the context of its own time.

Divergent Themes

The chapters in this volume are grouped to highlight the contributors' shared interests in historical processes and asymmetric power relations, but the contributors also disagree over several issues. Many exchanges at the conference were confrontational. Contributors argued, sometimes vehemently, over concepts, ideas, strategies of research, and the nature of knowledge itself. In retrospect, we believe these confrontations were necessary to dislodge accepted assumptions and to open the way to rethinking the anthropology of law.

Cultural vs. Social Analysis

The contributors are divided over the issue of whether power and interests can be analyzed without an examination of cultural concepts. Rosen, Greenhouse, and Cohn, for example, emphasize the role of cultural constructions of reality in shaping social practice. They suggest that ethnographers cannot understand what their research subjects are doing unless they analyze the cultural system that informs subjects' actions. Other contributors, such as Moore, Nader, and Boissevain and Grotenbreg, treat power asymmetries and differences in access to resources as factors that ethnographers can understand and use in their analyses without reference to the cultural categories of their informants.

This division among contributors reflects a deep division among anthropologists over the methods and aims of their discipline, a division that in turn reflects differing views on the possibility and purposes of knowledge. Geertz, for example, suggests that many anthropologists have turned "from trying to explain social phenomena by weaving them into grand textures of cause and effect to trying to explain them by placing them in local frames of awareness" (1983:6). Having become disillusioned about the possibilities of discovering laws of cause and effect for social occurrences and processes, these anthropologists have abandoned the premise that social systems are rule-governed. Instead, they treat cultural phenomena as "significative systems" in need of interpretation (ibid., pp. 3, 10).

This division among the contributors reflects a deep chasm over the nature of knowledge. Superficially, it resembles the argument that came to be known in legal anthropology as "the Bohannan-Gluckman controversy" (Nader 1969a:5). Like the earlier argument, it appears on the surface to be an argument concerning whether Western conceptual categories are appropriate tools for analyzing another culture. Moore once suggested that the disagreement between Bohannan (1957) and Gluckman (1955) was less over methodology than "over the *significance* of legal categories" (1969:346). Bohannan (1969) thought an analysis of native legal categories could reveal the natives' "system." Gluckman (1969) thought that legal categories did not form such a system because social processes inevitably produced contradictory understandings. Gluckman also suggested that there were universally sound legal ideas, and some legal systems pushed toward these fundamental notions. In sum, the earlier controversy was based on fundamental differences in attitudes about knowledge and about definitions of the object of study.

Although there are resemblances to the earlier debate, this is in fact a new controversy. Some contributors to this volume seek social order in cultural understandings. Others find social order in social processes. There seems to be no way to resolve these fundamentally different stances toward how "objective" reality is constituted.

Differing Perspectives on Law

Different aspects of law and legal systems are emphasized by the contributors. Although there is considerable overlap, three different approaches can be identified: the interactional, the cultural, and the institutional. The contributors who adopt an interactional approach focus on individuals and groups who use laws and legal processes for pursuing their own ends. They take an instrumental perspective and tend to examine particular behaviors. Nader, for example, discusses colonized groups in the Americas who used the ideology of harmony to preserve local autonomy, and Boissevain and Grotenbreg write about how Surinamese entrepreneurs in Holland have either avoided or used Dutch laws regulating small businesses.

The contributors who use a cultural approach tend to treat laws and legal systems as elements of a discourse. They focus on the communicative dimension of law. Rosen, for example, discusses how the concepts and procedures used in Moroccan courts inform and reinforce the common-sense understandings that Moroccans draw on in everyday life. Greenhouse treats North American cultural concepts as resources that people use in their conversations with others to communicate their intentions and positions. Cohn writes about British efforts to find a legal system for India that would communicate the concepts of order that the British wanted to enforce.

The institutional approach used by some contributors leads to a focus on economic and political processes, treating individuals as representatives of particular economic interests or social groups, and laws as representing particular ideological positions. Moore, for example, carefully identifies the institutional and class forces affecting Chagga use of "customary law." Vincent and Snyder try to identify the interest groups that both create and are created by legislation. Blok identifies the class positions of the eighteenth-century bandits he studied and of their victims and prosecutors. These writers focus on the ordering dimension of law, emphasizing the role of legal processes in preserving or changing established power asymmetries.

Different Problems

The contributors also define their problems differently. Some try to understand major legal watersheds. Blok analyzes the eighteenth-century transition from theatrical punishments to imprisonment. Aubert discusses the nineteenth-century transition from law as repressing undesired behaviors to law as encouraging desired ones. Arjomand, Cohn, and Vincent all focus on the establishment of new legal orders. Other focus less on explicit watersheds than on long-term processes. For example, Moore analyzes the survival of "customary law" in changed form. Nader traces the spread and use of an ideology of community harmony. Starr focuses on the inheritance of legal ideas from nineteenth-century social theory and their need to be "exhumed" from that cultural context and placed back into the context of Roman society, where they originated. Still others focus on the impact of certain pieces of legislation. George Collier analyzes the effects of reformist legislation on a Spanish village before the civil war, while Boissevain and Grotenbreg ask how Surinamese entrepreneurs in Holland cope with the many laws designed to regulate small businesses.

Some contributors are concerned less with analyzing particular historical shifts or continuities and more with building theoretical frameworks to understand legal processes. Snyder seeks a framework for understanding how interests are created by legislation, as well as how interests can be contributors to the creation of legislation. Nash proposes the concept of redistribution as an analytical tool for understanding the role of legal orders in advanced capitalist societies.

Finally, Rosen and Greenhouse want to understand particular cultural concepts. Rosen shows how the assumptions of everyday life enter into Moroccan courts even as legal ideas permeate common-sense understandings. Greenhouse seeks a framework for understanding modern North Americans' fear and condemnation of "litigiousness."

Conclusion

The anthropologists convened by Laura Nader in 1966 welcomed the proliferation of subdisciplines and hoped that creating an "anthropology of law" would allow scholars "to make some systematic progress in data accumulation and theory building" (Nader 1969a:1). These anthropologists encouraged the borrowing of ideas and insights from neighboring subdisciplines, but still hoped that a shared focus on the theme of disputing would allow them to build on one another's work. They were successful. The focus on disputing processes that characterized the subdiscipline for many years did foster a sense of cumulative knowledge and deepening understanding. But the recent questioning of subdisciplinary boundaries and the use of divergent theoretical frameworks has broken down a sense of shared purpose.

The anthropologists who met in 1985 to share the papers that became chapters in this volume and to exchange and defend ideas came to recognize by the end of the conference that a new integrative framework was available even as we agreed to differ over the use of social or cultural categories as primary modes of research. World history emerged as the relevant integrative framework. Moore proposed that anthropologists should study and compare transformational sequences, such as the changes experienced by small landholding farmers under population pressure. Here we might seek regularities in transformational processes. Cohn and Greenhouse, in contrast, wanted to understand the logic of cultural systems by examining the specific historical conditions in which concepts were developed and used.

When conference participants began putting their studies end to end in historical time, we began to recognize recurring sequences, such as the usefulness of the "harmony" model for local groups attempting to maintain some autonomy from state power. We also recognized the multiple cultural logics occurring and spreading in world history. Thus, we did develop a framework for cumulative knowledge despite our divergent philosophies. Also, we found we could use each other's work constructively in our own projects by conceptualizing law and social change as categories that shape and are shaped by asymmetrical power relationships. This allowed us to build a more powerful image of the spread and consolidation of legal ideas and legal forms in the British Empire (see above).

Thus, the chapters in this volume expand the concerns that characterized the decades of anthropology of law since the 1960s. Rather than

[23]

embracing the idea that law creates order in a society, the chapters treat law as the symbolic representation of interests of particular groups, especially groups in power. Rather than assuming a functionalist, legal-evolutionary bias in attempting to understand the growth of legal institutions, law and legal forms are considered as rising from particular historical negotiations between and among groups, or as resulting from particular systems of hierarchy and domination. In writing about legal forms, J. A. Barnes argued that social anthropologists should take the political struggle as given and examine how in that struggle various institutions, including the law, are used (1961:194). The chapters in this volume do that. Law is conceptualized as a historical product rather than as a universal category. Some of the chapters present law as dependent on social agents and social groups rather than as an institution existing above the concerns of human actors. Others view law as dependent on economic and political processes of a more global nature.

When law and legal forms are viewed as historical products, we no longer assume the "essential comparability" of law per se. Law and lawlike forms are analyzed as embedded in and created both by particular historical circumstances and by interrelationships between local, national, and international events. From local "tribal law" to the law of modern industrial states, the chapters express concern with understanding the specific historical form, which is shaped by cultural and interest-group configurations.

By separating law from the study of disputes, the chapters in this volume have demonstrated the view of E. P. Thompson (1978:96) and Robert Gordon (1984:123) that law has a tendency to intrude into all kinds of relationships, from those of economic production to those of philosophical treatises where it hides in the guise of ideology. Although elites may exercise a disproportionate influence on the forms that go into the making of legal relationships, "the forms are manufactured, re-produced, and modified for special purposes by everyone, at every level, all the time" (ibid.).

In analyzing systems of hierarchy and domination, we have not used the concepts of "legal pluralism" and micro- or macro-analysis. Fresh looks at "pluralistic" situations and how these situations have developed through time have led to a new recognition of the place of history, power, and domination in shaping the role of law in society. As Peter Fitzpatrick (1985:6) remarked, in assessing any data base, there is the need to know history and to assess the relevant forms and traditions of knowledge that inhere in its collection.

Some of the chapters attempt a general historical understanding of the development of legal forms and ideas and of the transmission of power relationships within a given society (Cohn, Moore, Vincent, Aubert, Nash), but some view law as a contested metaphor that represents and reproduces a social and symbolic ordering system and that changes as groups of human agents seek new social forms (Blok, Greenhouse) or even a new society (Arjomand, G. Collier).

In answer to the question "How autonomous is law in the last instance?" E. P. Thompson wrote:

> Well, for most of the time when I was watching, law was running quite free of economy, doing its errands, defending its property, preparing the way for it, and so on. . . . But . . . I hesitate to whisper the heresy . . . on several occasions, while I was actually watching, the lonely hour of the last instance *actually came.* The last instance like an unholy ghost, actually, grabbed hold of law, throttled it, and forced it to change its language and to will into existence forms appropriate to the mode of production, such as enclosure acts and new case-law excluding customary common rights. But was law "relatively autonomous"? Oh, *yes.* Sometimes. Relatively. *Of course.* (1978:96)

Like Thompson, most of the contributors to this volume also view law as having limited autonomy and in the "last instance" as responsive to economic forces.

Thus, we have moved from a focus on dispute-processing to an attempt to understand situations where legal forms and legal understandings are called into existence. We find legal activity at every level but within systems of domination. And we have moved from a focus on disputes and disputants to a view that treats elites and less powerful groups as active agents in legal change.

The anthropologist I. M. Lewis argued that "time-centred historical inquiry" needed to take its place alongside timeless structural analysis before social anthropology could satisfactorily analyze social change (1968:xxii). In the present volume, dedicated to the understanding of legal change, we present new ways of looking at law, society, legal ideas, legal institutions, and culture, using historical analysis and the study of power as important dimensions. The chapters indicate a continuing vitality in legal anthropology as we move into the next decade with fresh views of ways to study and conceptualize legal, societal, and cultural change.

REFERENCES

Abel, Richard L. 1974. "A Comparative Theory of Dispute Institutions in Society." *Law and Society Review* 8(2):218–347.

[25]

―――. 1981a. *The Politics of Informal Justice: The American Experience.* New York.

―――. 1981b. *The Politics of Informal Justice: Comparative Studies.* New York.

Auerbach, Jerold S. 1983. *Justice without Law? Resolving Disputes without Lawyers.* New York.

Barnes, J. A. 1961. "Law as Politically Active: an Anthropological View." In Geoffrey Sawer, ed., *Studies in the Sociology of Law,* pp. 167–196. Canberra.

Bohannan, Paul. 1957 *Justice and Judgment among the Tiv.* London.

―――. 1965. "The Differing Realms of the Law." *American Anthropologist* 67(6), part 2, pp. 33–42.

―――. 1969. "Ethnography and Comparison in Legal Anthropology." In Laura Nader, ed., *Law in Culture and Society,* pp. 401–418. Chicago.

Burman, Sandra B., and Barbara E. Harrell-Bond. 1979. *The Imposition of Law.* New York.

Chanock, Martin. 1983. "Signposts or Tombstones? Reflections on Recent Works on the Anthropology of Law." *Law in Context* 1:107–125.

Collier, Jane F. 1973. *Law and Social Change in Zinacantan.* Stanford, Calif.

Comaroff, John L., and Simon Roberts. 1981. *Rules and Processes: The Cultural Logic of Disputes in an African Context.* Chicago.

Critical Legal Studies Symposium. 1984. *Stanford Law Review* 36(1–2).

Danzig, Richard, and Michael Lowy. 1975. "Everyday Disputes and Mediation in the United States: A Reply to Professor Felstiner." *Law and Society Review* 9(4):675–694.

Dolgin, Janet L., David S. Kemnitzer, and David M. Schneider, eds. 1977. *Symbolic Anthropology: A Reader in the Study of Symbols and Meanings.* New York.

Epstein, A. L. 1954. *Judicial Techniques and the Judicial Process.* Rhodes-Livingstone Papers 23. Manchester, Eng.

Felstiner, William, R. L. Abel, and Austin Sarat. 1980–81. "The Emergence and Transformation of Disputes: Naming, Blaming, Claiming." *Law and Society Review* 15(3–4):631–654.

Fitzpatrick, Peter. 1985. "Is It Simple to Be a Marxist in Legal Anthropology?" *Modern Law Review* 48(4):472–485.

Francis, Paul. 1984. "New Directions in the Study of African Law." *Africa* 54(4):81–88.

Friedman, Lawrence, and Stewart Macaulay. 1969. "Preface." In *Law and the Behavioral Sciences,* pp. xiii–xvii. First edition. Indianapolis. Second edition 1977.

Galanter, Marc. 1983. "Reading the Landscape of Disputes: What We Know and Don't Know (and Think We Know) about Our Allegedly Contentious and Litigious Society." *UCLA Law Review* 31(1):1127.

Geertz, Clifford. 1983. *Local Knowledge: Further Essays in Interpretive Anthropology.* New York.

Gibbs, James Lowell, Jr. 1963. "The Kpelle Moot: A Therapeutic Model for the Informal Settlement of Disputes." *Africa* 33:1–11.

Giddens, Anthony. 1976. *New Rules of Sociological Method.* London.

————. 1979. *Central Problems in Social Theory: Action, Structure, and Contradiction in Social Analysis.* Berkeley and Los Angeles.

Gluckman, Max. 1955. *The Judicial Process among the Barotse of Northern Rhodesia.* Manchester, Eng.

————. 1969. "Concepts in the Comparative Study of Tribal Law." In Laura Nader, ed., *Law in Culture and Society*, pp. 349–373. Chicago.

Gordon, Robert. 1984. "Critical Legal Histories." *Stanford Law Review* 36(1–2):57–125 (January).

Gulliver, Philip H. 1963. *Social Control in an African Society.* Boston.

————. 1971. *Neighbours and Networks.* Berkeley and Los Angeles.

————, ed. 1978. *Cross Examinations: Essays in Memory of Max Gluckman.* Leiden.

Hamnett, Ian, ed. 1977. *Social Anthropology and Law.* New York.

Kidder, Robert L. 1979. "Toward an Integrated Theory of Imposed Law." In S. E. Burman and B. Harrell-Bond, eds., *The Imposition of Law*, pp. 289–306. New York.

Koch, Klaus F. 1974. *War and Peace in Jalemo.* Cambridge, Mass.

Leach, Edmund. 1970. *Lévi-Strauss.* London.

————. 1977. *Custom, Law, and Terrorist Violence.* Edinburgh.

Lévi-Strauss, Claude. 1969. *The Elementary Structures of Kinship.* London. First published in France in 1949.

Lewis, I. M. 1968. "Introduction." In *History and Social Anthropology.* London.

Llewellyn, Karl, and E. A. Hoebel. 1941. *The Cheyenne Way.* Norman, Okla.

Lowy, Michael. 1978. "A Good Name Is Worth More Than Money: Strategies of Court Use in Urban Ghana." In L. Nader and H. Todd, eds., *The Disputing Process: Law in Ten Societies*, pp. 181–208. New York.

Malinowski, Bronislaw. 1926. *Crime and Custom in Savage Society.* London.

Merry, Sally Engle. 1981. *Urban Danger: Life in a Neighborhood of Strangers.* Philadelphia.

Moore, Sally Falk. 1969. "Introduction" to section on "Comparative Studies." In Laura Nader, ed., *Law in Culture and Society*, pp. 337–348. Chicago.

————. 1978. *Law as Process.* London.

————. 1986. *Social Facts and Fabrications: "Customary" Law on Kilimanjaro, 1880–1980.* Cambridge, Eng.

Nader, Laura, ed. 1965a. *The Ethnography of Law. American Anthropologist* 67(6), part 2. (Special issue).

————. 1965b. "The Anthropological Study of Law." *American Anthropologist* 67(6), part 2, pp. 3–32.

————. 1969a. "Introduction." In Laura Nader, ed., *Law in Culture and Society*, pp. 1–10. Chicago.

————, ed. 1969b. *Law in Culture and Society.* Chicago.

Nader, Laura, and Harry Todd, eds. 1978. *The Disputing Process: Law in Ten Societies.* New York.

Ortner, Sherry. 1984. "Theory in Anthropology since the Sixties." *Comparative Studies in Society and History* 26(1):126–166.

[27]

Pospisil, Leopold. 1958. *Kapauku Pupuans and Their Law.* Publications in Anthropology 54. New Haven.

Radcliffe-Brown, A. R. 1933. "Primitive Law." In *Encyclopedia of the Social Sciences,* 9:202–206. New York.

Ranger, Terence. 1983. "The Invention of Tradition in Colonial Africa." In Eric Hobsbawm and Terence Ranger, eds., *The Invention of Tradition,* pp. 211–262. Cambridge, Eng.

Roberts, Simon. 1979. *An Introduction to Legal Anthropology.* Harmondsworth, Eng.

Schneider, David. 1984. *A Critique of the Study of Kinship.* Ann Arbor, Mich.

Smith, Carol A. 1985. "Local History in Global Context: Social and Economic Transitions in Western Guatemala." In B. R. DeWalt and P. J. Pelto, eds., *Micro and Macro Levels of Analysis in Anthropology,* pp. 83–120. Boulder, Colo.

Snyder, Francis. 1981a. *Capitalism and Legal Change: An African Transformation.* New York.

———. 1981b. "Anthropology, Dispute Processes, and Law: A Critical Introduction." *British Journal of Law and Society* 8(2):141–180.

Starr, June. 1978. *Dispute and Settlement in Rural Turkey: An Ethnography of Law.* Leiden.

Thompson, E. P. 1975. *Whigs and Hunters.* New York.

———. 1978. "The Poverty of Theory." In E. P. Thompson, *The Poverty of Theory and Other Essays.* New York.

Tigar, Michael E., and Madeleine R. Levy. 1977. *Law and the Rise of Capitalism.* New York.

Todd, Harry. 1978. "Litigious Marginals: Character and Disputing in a Bavarian Village." In Laura Nader and Harry Todd, eds., *The Disputing Process: Law in Ten Societies,* pp. 86–121. New York.

Trubek, David M. 1980–81a. *Dispute Processing and Civil Litigation* (Special Issue). *Law and Society Review* 14(3–4).

———. 1980–81b. "Studying Courts in Context." *Law and Society Review* 14(3–4):485–501.

Turner, Victor. 1967. *The Forest of Symbols: Aspects of Ndembu Ritual.* Ithaca, N.Y.

Williams, Raymond. 1977. *Marxism and Literature.* New York.

Witty, Cathie. 1980. *Mediation and Society: Conflict Management in Lebanon.* New York.

Wolf, Eric R. 1966. "Kinship, Friendship, and Patron-Client Relations in Complex Societies." In Michael Banton, ed., *Social Anthropology in Complex Societies,* ASA Monograph 4, pp. 1–22. London.

———. 1982. *Europe and the People without History.* Berkeley and Los Angeles.

Yngvesson, Barbara. 1976. "Responses to Grievance Behavior: Extended Cases in a Fishing Community." *American Ethnologist* 3(2):353–373.

PART I

Resisting and Consolidating State-Level Legal Systems

[1]

The Symbolic Vocabulary
of Public Executions

Anton Blok

One of the most dramatic changes in the history of European legal systems has been the transition from public executions to imprisonment, which took place at the end of the eighteenth century and the beginning of the nineteenth. Although this development has often been discussed (e.g., Foucault 1977) and much has been written on public executions in general, especially with regard to the German territories (e.g., Schild 1980; Dülmen 1984), one would like to know more about the meaning of these forms of punishment, and the reasons that they met with increasing resistance until they finally became intolerable. The sentences given well over 500 members of the robber bands in the Lower Meuse—the so-called Bokkerijders—between 1741 and 1778 may be of interest because they show a development that foreshadows the main transition from corporal punishment in public to confinement in workhouses and prisons. My sources are chiefly court records, which I have supplemented with the correspondence and published writings of contemporary judges, government officials, priests, and other notables. Seeking to decode the messages inscribed in the cultural forms of theatrical punishments, this chapter draws heavily on material I have collected for a forthcoming monograph on the social history of these robber bands.[1]

[1]Most of the archival sources I used are located in the Rijksarchief of Limburg in Maestricht, section "Landen van Overmaas, criminal procedures, 1741–1778." For more precise references, see Blok 1979, 1981a.

[31]

The Area

The robber bands operated on the east bank of the Meuse, in the rural districts enclosed by the towns of Maestricht, Aix-la-Chapelle, Gulick, and Roermond. Up to the early eighteenth century, this part of the Lower Meuse had suffered from frequent military operations. The rural population had to feed and lodge armies in transit and in winter camps if there was no chance to pay the military off through expensive sauvegardes. Worse still was the scourge of disbanded soldiers who indulged in looting and plundering villages and farms (see Wouters 1970; Gutmann 1980). Although virtually without protection (except flight), the inhabitants of this frontier area of the Dutch Republic and the Spanish (after 1713, Austrian) Netherlands succeeded in recovering from these afflictions. Between 1650 and 1750, the rural population remained fairly stable in this hilly, wooded, and relatively fertile region of mixed farming where large tenant farms dominated. As elsewhere in Europe, it was only after 1750 that the population of the Lower Meuse started to grow rapidly. Contemporary maps indicate a relatively dense population (about fifty inhabitants per square kilometer) grouped into many small, nucleated villages and towns. Most settlements fell into the pattern of what are customarily called "street villages"; of these, many had originated as *Waldhufendörfer;* place names ending in *-rode, -rade, -rath, -hage, -heide, -veld,* and so on, reveal the late-medieval foundation of these settlements as forest- and heath-clearing villages. Access to land was all-important. Broadly speaking, there were two main social classes, each defined in relation to control over land. Exclusion from ownership of land implied social exclusion too (see Slicher van Bath 1963; Roebroeck 1967; Philips 1975; Schrijnemakers 1984).

There were also several industries in the area, not only in the towns but also in the rural villages, which produced textiles, metal, and leatherwork. The entire region, in fact, formed an offshoot of the important industrial concentration around Liège. Apart from agriculture, therefore, people lived off several rural domestic manufacturers and commerce. We know, for example, of an ironworkers guild (*gilde van den eyseren*) in the district of Geleen that incorporated makers of locks, hinges, chains, harnesses, and scissors. In 1720 the guild numbered 109 members from several towns and villages in one of the Austrian enclaves in the Lower Meuse. Because of falling prices, the guild formed a cartel to fix prices and production quotas. Work stopped during the summer months to allow guild members to find employment in harvest work.

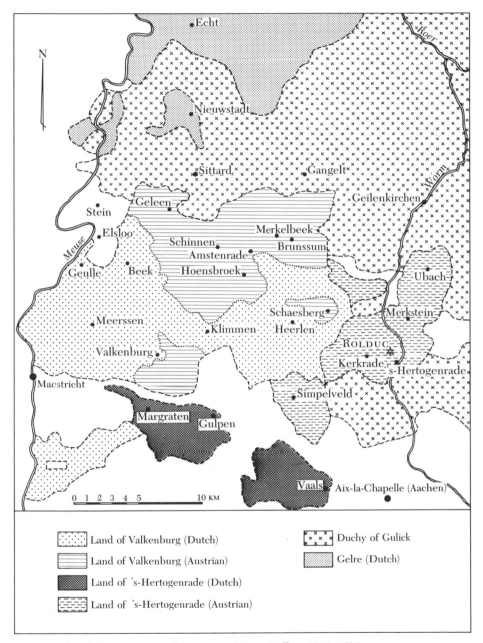

Map 1. Political fragmentation of the eastern Meuse Valley, 1715–1785

The cartel expanded to include ironworkers from other places in the area. By 1740 its membership had grown to 280 ironworkers (Thurlings and van Drunen 1960).

At the time this part of the Meuse valley was politically fragmented to a considerable extent (see Map 1). Including parts and enclaves of Dutch and Austrian territories, together with sections of the duchy of Gulick and various autonomous and semiautonomous seigneuries, it was in several respects a border area par excellence. Apart from the political frontiers, there were many different jurisdictions, and the boundary line dividing Protestants from Roman Catholics ran right across the area. The transitional character of the entire region was reinforced by its location on commercial and military crossroads. The Lower Meuse formed a bridgehead in a major European interaction zone—connecting Flanders with the Rhineland, and the Dutch Republic with the southern Netherlands and France. Finally, we should note the extremely peripheral location of the Dutch and Austrian territories with respect to their political centers—The Hague and Brussels. Disconnected from the other parts of the Dutch Republic and the Austrian Netherlands, respectively, these territories were true enclaves (Wouters 1970; Haas 1978).

The Bokkerijders: Background and Operations

Over a period of almost fifty years—from the late 1720s through the early 1770s—various bands of changing size and composition carried out more than one hundred attacks on inns, shops, breweries, and various Roman Catholic churches, rectories, wayside chapels, and in particular tenant farms. All the attacks took place in the area of the Lower Meuse. The size of the bands ranged from a dozen to well over 150 participants. The raids fell into three distinct periods, each of which came to an end with mass arrests, trials, and executions. The first phase, which lasted until the early 1740s, saw more than sixty operations, most of which were directed against churches, while at least ten raids involved massive attacks on farms and rectories. The second phase, which covered only the years 1749–50, included just two outings and was to some extent a short-lived revival of what had remained of the earlier bands. In the third phase, from the early 1750s onward, the ranks of the robbers swelled considerably. Various local bands participated in several large-scale attacks against at least a dozen farms, two rectories, one hermitage, one monastery, and one church. As in the early 1740s, a haphazard

[34]

outing not authorized by the leaders and carried out toward the end of 1770 led to the discovery and subsequent demise of the robber bands.

In the early stages of the Bokkerijder movement—if that is an adequate description of these sustained forms of brigandage—most of the robbers came from the easternmost enclaves of the Austrian Netherlands and the adjoining reaches of the duchy of Gulick. With the towns of Nieuwstadt and Heerlen, the Dutch territories were only modestly represented at that time. Later, large groups of people from neighboring Dutch districts joined in the raids, while certain Austrian territories and the land of Gulick stopped being important areas of recruitment. All attacks took place late in the evening or in the early morning. During these nightly ventures the robbers looked for money, jewelry, clothing, food, and other valuable goods. Victims were often maltreated (to make them talk first and to keep them quiet after), and a few of them lost their lives. But not all operations involved the same amount of violence, nor were they all equally successful. Several important outings failed—some because the victims or their neighbors managed to give the alarm; others because the robbers found only items of little value. And it is significant that on a number of occasions, most notably during the large-scale operations in 1770, the victims were conspicuously spared, if they woke up at all.

How many people actually participated in the operations of the robber bands we cannot possibly know. What we do know is that about 600 people were tried for being members of the "notorious band." In the early 1740s, about 170 people (including well over 20 women) appeared before local courts. About ten years later, 29 people were tried, including 5 men who had also been active in the first period. During the trials of the 1770s, close to 400 people (6 of them women) were convicted (see Table 1.1), so I could trace more than 500 verdicts—which were all

Table 1.1. Number of Bokkerijders Brought to Trial, 1741–1778

Outcome of Trial	1st Phase	2nd Phase	3rd Phase	Total
Tried and sentenced	113	27	371	511
Tried but sentence unknown	54	2	28	84
Unknown*	50	6	3	59
Total	217	35**	402	654

*All these people were mentioned as accomplices in the records. If they were tried, the trial records did not survive.

**Five of these people had also been active in the first period, which brings the total down from 654 to 649, including 36 women (30 of whom were active in the first period).

[35]

carried out. Most of these convictions involved death sentences. No less than 354 Bokkerijders were put to death one way or another (see Table 1.2). In most cases these executions took place near the robbers' home towns. Relatively few convicted robbers—12 after being flogged, and 2 after being flogged and branded—were banished (they were mostly women and young men). For lack of sufficient proof, 17 suspects were released from detention. Only 3 people were sent to houses of correction. As many as 46 died in prison; in most cases we know the circumstances under which they expired, partly because they can be read from the sentences that the local courts passed on their remains. Finally, because many suspects had fled before the trials got under way, at least 76 people were tried in absentia. (The actual number was probably over 100; we know of an additional 34 fugitives under trial for whom no sentences could be traced.) Most of the fugitives were banished, and we know that at least 11 of them were hanged in effigy (Table 1.2). In order to understand the particulars of all these sentences, we have to know

Table 1.2. Outcome of Trials against Bokkerijders, 1741–1778

Sentence/Outcome	1st Phase	2nd Phase	3rd Phase	Total
Death sentence not specified, but presumably gallows	4	—	45	49
Gallows	45	16	191	252
Gallows and additional punishments	1	1	1	3
Broken on the wheel	—	1	4	5
Broken on the wheel and additional punishments	5	—	1	6
Garroted	—	—	2	2
Garroted and additional punishments	27	—	—	27
Decapitated	6	—	—	6
Decapitated and additional punishments	4	—	—	4
Died in detention	11	4	31	46
Banishments	3	—	11	14
Convicted in absentia: banishment	1	—	64	65
Convicted in absentia: hanged in effigy	1	5	5	11
Confinement	—	—	3	3
Released from detention	5	—	12	17
Warrant for arrest refused	1	—	1	2
Total	114	27	371	512*

*These 512 sentences (verdicts) concern 511 persons because one person was tried and convicted two times: a woman from the first period was first banished after being flogged and branded, then later sent to the gallows and hanged.

what these people were punished for and what might have brought them to take the road of brigandage.

The collective biography of the Bokkerijders, which I compiled from the surviving court records and a few contemporary publications, reveals that these robbers were not bandits—that is, "outlaws"—in the strict sense of the word. On the contrary, virtually all of them led ordinary lives in their home towns. Most of the Bokkerijders were married and had children and a fixed residence. In fact, many were born and bred in the same area in which they carried out their raids—the east bank of the Lower Meuse. Some of the robbers even lived in the same village as their victims, and a few of them were close neighbors of the victims. This familiarity with victims and targets may explain the various forms of disguise that the robbers adopted. As mentioned before, they operated by night (hence one of their nicknames, *nachtdieven*—literally, night thieves). We know that the women used to dress as men, while the men often wore military attire and, to further hide their identity, made use of military idiom. Others blackened their faces and put on visors, wigs, false beards, caps, and other outlandish headgear. It should not surprise us, then, that the robbers fled when seen or caught in the very act of stealing. As local people, they had good reason to fear recognition. Thus, the Bokkerijders were far from being outlaws, vagrants, roaming beggars, or disbanded soldiers, although several had belonged to some of these categories at one time or another. Yet their military disguise as well as their relationship with an itinerant or peripatetic way of life are of fundamental importance for understanding the history of these bands.

Looking at the occupational background of the Bokkerijders, which I could trace for two-thirds of them, one finds artisans and retail merchants (peddlers, carters) strongly represented. Together they made up about 60 percent of the participants in all three stages of band operations, while farmers and day laborers accounted for scarcely 20 percent. For a distinctly rural area, people of agrarian background were notably underrepresented in the bands (see Table 1.3). Among the artisans, the skinners especially loomed large, most notably in the first phase. In fact, the first robber bands coalesced around a widely extended network of skinners—people whose job it was to kill sick animals, to dispose of dead cattle, to flay horses, and to remove other offal and remains. Skinners also assisted the executioner; they did the dirty work, such as dragging dead bodies of convicts from the prison to the gallows, where they had to hang them in chains or bury their remains.

[37]

Table 1.3. Occupational Background of Bokkerijders

	1st Phase	2nd Phase	3rd Phase	Total
Artisans	61	14	135	210
Skinners	17	—	5	22
Ironworkers	17	4	18	39
Shoemakers	5	7	20	32
Saddlers	1	—	6	7
Spinners and weavers	14	2	44	60
Others	7	1	42	50
Commerce/transport	21	4	31	56
Agriculture	10	5	70	85
Day laborers	8	3	50	61
Farmers	2	2	20	24
Authorities	3	3	11	17
Miscellaneous	27	2	30	59
Innkeepers	5	—	10	15
Entertainers	6	—	3	9
Miners	6	—	2	8
Beggars	4	1	4	9
Soldiers*	6	1	5	12
Others	—	—	6	6
Total	122	28	277	427

Note: Occupational background is available for only two-thirds of the Bokkerijders.
*An additional dozen of the robbers for whom we know occupations also had military experience.

Together with some of their womenfolk, skinners from a dozen different villages and towns in the eastern Meuse valley (see Figure 1.1), were the main protagonists in the church robberies that were carried out in the early 1730s in at least twenty-five different locations. But the skinners also had an important part in the preparation and organization of the other raids in the first phase, while the division of the booty and sale of stolen goods (through Jewish receivers in the larger towns) was often in their hands.

The network of skinners was distinctly regional and endogamous. Like elsewhere, the endogamy of the skinners in the Lower Meuse resulted from the low value that the society put on their work (Wilbertz 1979; Blok 1981a, 1981b). Charged with the disposal of carrion and other refuse, their profession brought them into contact with dirt, with "matter out of place." Hence they were stigmatized and placed at the margin of established society, which explains their low chances of marrying outside their occupational group. Nor could they easily enter into other occupations or crafts. Having their business at the edge of the village or

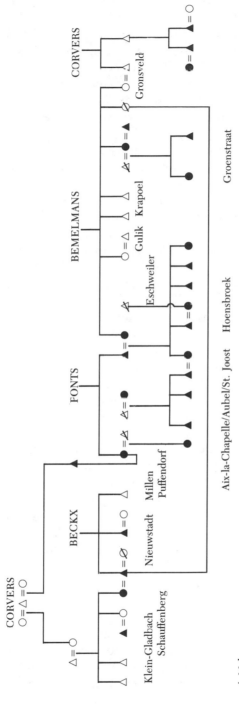

Figure 1.1. Endogamous Network of Skinners in the Lower Meuse, 1730–1743

Source: Archival records researched by the author.

△ Males
○ Females
▲● Members of bands
△○ Deceased persons

[39]

in small rural hamlets near the larger settlements, the skinners were also marginal in a more literal sense—they were geographically and physically separated from the community they served. Because one family of skinners could provide for an entire rural community, the isolated positions of these craftsmen generated a far-flung, interlocal network of kin relations covering a large part of the eastern Meuse valley (see Figure 1.1 and Map 1).

The skinners shared their low social status, peripheral location, and tactical mobility with other occupational groups that were strongly represented in the bands. We hear of peddlers, part-time beggars, musicians, jugglers, carters, innkeepers, and shoemakers. Although all these people had a fixed residence (and thus certainly did not belong to the *fahrende Leute*, or itinerant people), many of them moved a great deal between the villages and towns, while some formed main junctions of social networks. It is among these linkmen, especially the skinners, innkeepers, and shoemakers, that we find the most important leaders of the bands.

Apart from these more or less itinerant folk (to whom also belonged the mostly poor spinners and weavers, who became more prominent in the later stages of the Bokkerijders' exploits), the skinners maintained relations with people involved in leatherwork, such as the saddlers, shoemakers, and cobblers, whose number rose sharply during the last phase of the bands. The robber bands were thus tied together by occupational links, ties of sociability, linkages of kinship and marriage (certainly not restricted to the group of the skinners), and local bonds. Quite often these various types of relations were intertwined, adding to the social cohesion of the Bokkerijders, who were settled along the frontiers of this politically fragmented area. They lived in the smaller neighborhoods near larger places, or on the outskirts of villages and towns.

Thus, the Bokkerijders were "ordinary" citizens and at best part-time robbers. They had a permanent residence, which in itself gave them civil rights denied to all *fahrende Leute*. One should therefore distinguish them from outlaws and vagrants, who could be arrested and tried straightaway simply because they lacked a domicile. One bailiff stated his predicament in the summer of 1743: "Although apparently free and respectable citizens, these robbers are even worse and more dangerous than the foreign vagabonds, vagrants, and thieves, against whom the placards and edicts have provided sanctions." Indeed, the accumulation of evidence required for the arrests slowed court proceedings to a considerable extent, which enabled many suspects to leave the area. As already noted, well over one hundred of the robbers were tried in absentia.

Many Bokkerijders occupied marginal positions and were highly mobile. Both tactical mobility and peripheral location made them less subject to tight forms of social control. These conditions held particularly true for the skinners, who could therefore organize themselves over considerable distances. Together with representatives from other marginal and mobile occupations, the skinners were more effective than the judicial authorities, who were bound to small districts, so in a way the regional, endogamous network of the skinners provided the infrastructure of these bands, while, as we shall see, the skinners also set the tone for the ideological orientation of the robbers.

No less important for understanding the composition and organization of the robber bands were other implications of the skinning trade. Their visits to farms at unusual times enabled them to acquire an intimate knowledge of the area in which they worked. Their sense of place must have been formidable, for they could find their way in a large area in the middle of the night, going to the rendezvous and target and returning before dawn, every step of which required coordinated timing. Even more than the peddlers, carters, entertainers, and other itinerant folk, skinners had an excuse to hang around at unlikely times and places. As emergency butchers, their presence at an uncommon location at an unusual time did not raise suspicion, and neither did their carrying of heavy packs and bundles. Moreover, the skinning trade required considerable physical strength and adroitness with knives. The skinners did not hesitate to use the same tortures on their victims that hangman's assistants used, such as burning people with hot sulfur or boiling oil and threatening to cut them up.

Other occupations prevalent among the robbers had similar implications for their means of organization and orientation. For example, the shops and workplaces of shoemakers and cobblers must have become meeting places similar to inns and taverns (Hobsbawm and Scott 1980). In fact, we know that at least four shoemakers and six innkeepers were prominent as leaders in all three phases of the Bokkerijder movement. Together with the skinners who assumed positions of leadership in the bands, these shoemakers and innkeepers also had an important part in both the recruitment and the organization of the bands. It seems that spinners and weavers too moved around a lot, and hence were much like some of the peddlers and carters, going back and forth between town and countryside. Similar patterns of mobility could be ascertained for

[41]

the cobblers, who often had to visit scattered farms and hamlets to carry out their craft.

Yet the social and spatial organization of the skinners and their allies cannot explain why these people organized themselves into robber bands and attacked and broke into churches and farms, maiming and sometimes killing the inhabitants. The organizational aspects tell us only how the robbers operated and suggest their power chances vis-à-vis other localized groups, such as the farmers and especially the authorities, who were tied to jurisdictions of limited size in an area characterized by extreme political fragmentation. The implications of the crafts and trades prominent in the bands certainly did not determine the operations of the robbers. On the other hand, we cannot understand the actions of the Bokkerijders without taking into consideration certain aspects of their occupational background.

Social Protest

The established rural population of farmers (from whom the local authorities were largely recruited) excluded from their ranks the skinners and other marginal people, such as the entertainers and peddlers, as well as most of the spinners and weavers, many of the cobblers and saddlers, and other impoverished artisans—in short, what Turner (1974) described as "the structurally weak." It should therefore not surprise us that the Bokkerijders directed their operations against the principle symbols of this rural social order—namely, Roman Catholic churches, chapels, rectories, and tenant farms. The churches were not only plundered, but also often ritually attacked and subjected to various forms of ritual desecration. Here we move into the realm of the so-called "countertheater of the poor," which involves forms of popular protest that attack symbols of authority by means of parody, inversion, mockery, and other subversive comments (see Thompson 1974). Yet if the exclusion and stigmatization to which the skinners and many of their associates were subjected provided them with a cause, this leaves us with the question of why the bands took shape around 1730 and not before.

It is very likely that the skinners in this part of western Europe enjoyed a certain measure of prosperity in the decades around 1700. Both the military operations that afflicted the area until the early eighteenth century, and the cattle plagues that struck various regions of the Continent during the second decade of that century, may have favored the skinning trade as much as they must have taken a toll from the farmers. After these scourges came to a temporary halt around 1720, the skinners must have entered a difficult period. There are indeed several indications for a notable decrease in employment for skinners in the 1720s and 1730s. We know that some of them had to insist on their local monopoly, others were continually in search of work, and still others had to move their business to other locations. Being skinners, they had few chances of finding employment outside their trade, so there were various appeals to their kinsmen. The wanderings of some of these skinners tell us something about the size of their regional network of kinsmen and affines. They also reveal that several of these artisans had lost their moorings and began to assume the characteristics of people living a vagrant life (Wilbertz 1979:154–159; Küther 1983:53–55). Contraction of employment, a recurrent phenomenon in postwar periods (see Beattie 1974), may also have forced some of the ironworkers to join the bands. Although impoverished, these craftsmen retained their sense of cohesion (predicated on their guildlike organization) as well as their mobility and their expertise with locks and keys.

One suspects that social resentment and class tensions, as well as poverty and unemployment, did much to inspire the operations of the Bokkerijders; most of the bands' outings involved a distinct element of hostility toward the established rural population, notably priests and wealthy tenant farmers. Especially during the first episodes, when the skinners and other artisans held in low esteem were prominent in the bands, victims were often severely beaten, regardless of their age and sex. Some were killed, or died soon after the attacks. As far as the plunderings of churches are concerned, the Bokkerijders did not restrict themselves to the theft of money and Mass vestments, chalices, and other cult attributes. During the 1730s, when churches seem to have become favorite targets, there were further desecrations in the form of parodies of the Mass. Following one successful looting of a church, a skinner distributed the holy Host on more than one occasion.

Elements of this popular countertheater were also conspicuous in the initiation ceremonies that accompanied incorporation into the bands. Apart from the robberies, which remained "family affairs" of sorts, larger operations in which more than a hundred people participated were carried out. With the expansion of the bands, recruitment and incorporation became formalized. New members had to swear an oath of allegiance and submit themselves to an initiation ritual in wayside chapels, the open air, and other liminal locations, or simply at the home of a

[43]

local leader. In a sense, these ceremonies formed a continuation of the more spontaneous parodies of the Mass enacted by the skinners and took the form of inverted Roman Catholic liturgy. For instance, novices had to crawl on all fours into a chapel, sometimes going in and out backward. There were improvised altars with burning candles, holy statuettes, and images of the saints. The novitiates had to spit on a crucifix and throw it on the floor and step on it, while swearing off God and the Holy Mother and dedicating themselves to the devil.

It must have been these kinds of rituals of *Teufelsbundner* (confederates of the devil), as well as the remarkable mobility of the bands, that earned the robbers the name *Bokkerijders* (literally, billy goat riders). One does not find this denotation in the court records, although the judges acknowledged the existence of a sworn confederacy. The name was bestowed on the robbers by the local populace and had its roots in an ancient and widespread folk belief that associates the billy goat with the devil and his work, and with the notion of magical flight. As one of the local priests put it in 1779, when the history of these bands had come to an end:

> In many places, this band was given the name of *Bokkeryers*, that is to say, they rode on billy goats when they went out at night to steal. These billy goats would not have been natural billy goats, but the devil in the form of one or more billy goats. This devil would have carried them through the air in a short time to the place where they wanted to be, so that they were transported in a single night ten, sixteen, twenty hours away, to steal and to have their meeting; and they returned on the back of this billy goat. Some of the band have started to confess this and tried to make a hotchpotch of it. (Sleinada 1779:61–62)

Such meetings must have enhanced the cohesion of the robbers' network, ensured the secrecy of their conspiracy, reinforced their daring, and instilled in them a sense of belonging to a countersociety. These ceremonies appeared at a time when the bands started to grow rapidly and could not be tied together only by links of kinship, marriage, friendship, occupation, and locality, though such bonds continued to play an important role.

In the course of the 1750s and 1760s, the organization of the attacks was increasingly fashioned after military models. Although the number of ex-soldiers and people with military experience among the robbers was remarkably small (less than two dozen) and their share in leadership was equally limited, already from the beginning the operations of the bands bore a strong resemblance to the outings of looting soldiers (Gutmann 1980). From the mid-1750s on, when a local physician who had served as a recruitment officer in the Austrian army assumed leadership, the bands were organized on the model of a militia, with various divisions and subdivisions. At this stage, women had virtually disappeared from the bands. Thus an armylike organization was superimposed on a preexisting regional network of robbers that on the face of it was welded together for attacks on churches and farms. Actually, the large-scale operations seem to have served other goals.

Several clues suggest that the Bokkerijder bands had, in the third and final phase, developed into an abortive protest movement of sorts. This orientation of the bands is attested by several unsolicited statements of convicted band members. Some of them referred to what they called a "Brotherhood of Happiness." Others spoke of the impending foundation of a "New Kingdom" in which all property would be shared and "all of us have to be equal." Still others emphasized that once the bands had reached full strength they would steal, murder, and rob, killing all those who refused to join them. Moreover, several large-scale operations against farms, which took place shortly before the demise of the bands, were apparently highly unusual robberies. There were well over 200 participants, even though a dozen or so might have sufficed. Besides, the booty was often ridiculously small, and the victims were conspicuously spared. For all these reasons, one cannot but regard these outings as maneuvers of an incipient militia, aimed chiefly if not only at mobilizing large numbers of people from many different villages and towns in the Dutch and Austrian territories of the Lower Meuse. For most of the rank and file, these outings were disguised as ordinary attacks and robberies, for which they were modestly paid afterward. It is significant that the local leaders in this phase of the history of the Bokkerijder bands were primarily involved in recruiting new members for the bands, and we know that several of the candidates received handsel when they enlisted to join in a hitherto undisclosed expedition. As one convicted robber put it, "eventually taking everything from the Rich, and that everyone should do his utmost to recruit new members for the Band." Considering the available evidence, it looks as if the operations were there for the robbers, not the robbers for the operations. However this may be, the bands never made it into a real militia, let alone into a full-fledged political movement.

Paradoxically, the extreme fragmentation of political domains in the Lower Meuse did not prevent the authorities from coming to terms with the robber bands and eventually stamping them out altogether. Organized across the boundaries of various territories and jurisdictions, the bands could deceive and elude the bailiffs and their assistants for years. What triggered the series of trials against the Bokkerijders were not large-scale, regionally coordinated searches or hunts (which occasionally occurred with respect to roaming beggars and vagrants), but simply individual arrests of band members who had committed thefts on their own. Hard-pressed by the courts, these people began to talk, revealing the names of their accomplices, many of whom were consequently arrested and interrogated. In this way, court proceedings snowballed. It would be wrong to assume that the fragmentation of power domains inhibited cooperation between the authorities of different jurisdictions. Once the first arrests were made, courts began to exchange information about convicts, fugitives, and the whereabouts of other suspects. In addition, Bokkerijders who had fled were arrested in neighboring territories and, on request, extradited, as happened with some robbers who had tried to enlist in the regiments of the garrison towns of Düsseldorf, Maestricht, and Namur.

We now return to the actual theme of this chapter, the idiom of public executions in the Lower Meuse and a consideration of some aspects of the growing resistance against theatrical punishments at the end of the eighteenth century.

The Theater of Punishments and Its Decline

The sentences passed on the Bokkerijders in the early 1740s still showed all the characteristics of theatrical punishments with which people in most parts of early modern Europe had become familiar (see Foucault 1977; Schild 1980; Dülmen 1984; Blok 1984; Spierenburg 1984). The executions were not only public, carried out in or near the home towns of the convicts, but also true spectacles, intended for an audience that included kinsmen, friends, neighbors, and other fellow townsmen of the condemned. The crowd knew the person who was being put to death, and, as we shall see, the actual punishment often conveyed the nature of the crime.

Invariably situated at the limits of the jurisdictions, the place of execution was a clearly demarcated location, usually an elevation or hill (hence the denotations *galgeheuvel* and *galgeberg* [gallows hill], which still survive as toponyms). Thus the condemned had to be escorted all the way from the place of detention to the liminal location. Such processions were very much a part of the theater of punishments. The condemned were on exhibition, which reinforced their humiliation and infamy even more. A local man who had witnessed public hangings even into the late eighteenth century recalled during an interview in 1848:

> The place of execution of our territories was usually located on the border of the commune. The gallows of the village of Oirsbeek, for example, were situated at the other side of Amstenrade, at Treebeek, on the border of the commune of Heerlen. Those who were condemned to be whipped, branded, or broken on the wheel were put on a cart and transported to this location. The constable led the way. As a sign that a sentence had been passed, he carried the red-painted rod of justice: a prickled stick of about 90 centimeters long with golden acorns as garlands. After him in the parade came the bailiff with the alderman. The militiamen from the parish of the condemned surrounded the cart. They were armed with rifles and had cockfeathers on their hats. The banner and drum were covered with mourning crepe, and the drummer beat a funeral march. As the procession arrived at the place of execution, the militia gathered around the gallows to keep the crowd at a distance. Then the bailiff read out the sentence, whereupon the condemned mounted the ladder. When the bailiff took the rod of justice and let it sink, the hangman's rope fell. (Habets 1889:25)

For many Bokkerijders condemned in the early 1740s, such processions constituted only the preliminaries of their ordeals. While out of a total of well over one hundred convicts about fifty were hanged in chains, "until their remains fell off," more than forty robbers were subjected to further tribulations before they expired or were finally put to death (see Table 1.2). Each of these afflictions conveyed something about the crimes they had committed. Foucault rightly observed that the body of the condemned man formed an essential element in the ceremonial of public executions: "It was the task of the guilty man to bear openly his condemnation and the truth of the crime that he had committed. His body—displayed, exhibited in procession, tortured—served as the public support of a procedure that had hitherto remained in the shade; in him, on him, the sentence had to be legible for all" (1977:43). The main elements of this code included three forms of punishments: the gallows, the wheel, and fire. Ordinary thieves were whipped and banished; those who had committed qualified thefts were hanged; murderers and bandit leaders were broken on the wheel; and arson and sacrilege (e.g., church robberies) were punished by various forms of burning. Because the

[47]

Bokkerijders had indulged in all these felonies, and because the local courts of the villages and towns in the eastern Meuse valley seemed to have seriously tried to reenact these crimes, at least initially, the sentences passed on the robbers provide us with several examples of the "theatrical reproduction" of delicts in executions.

The symbolic vocabulary included the case of one man who, before he was hanged, had his face blackened and two fingers of his right hand cut off. A German pamphlet published in 1744 reported:

Dabey auch (wie Viel im Leben)	Thereby also (as many had been when alive)
Wurd geschwärzt ihr Angesicht,	Were blackened their faces,
Um das auch an Tag zu geben,	To make this also known,
Eh' sie wurden hingericht.	Before they were executed.
Man thät die zwei Finger brennen	One burned the two fingers
Dessen der geschworen hat,	Of those who had sworn,
Nur den Teufel zu erkennen,	To recognize only the devil,
Wurd gestraft auch zu Neustadt.	They were punished also in Nieuwstadt.

Because many robbers had also broken into churches and committed various profanities, their execution included several combinations of capital punishments as well as various forms of burning at the stake. No less than twenty Bokkerijders were garroted and then burned. At least one robber was executed the same way, after having his right hand first smeared with sulfur, then burned, and finally chopped off. Several others, who had held leading positions in the bands, were broken on the wheel and decapitated, after having the right hand burned and chopped off; their bodies, together with the severed limbs, were displayed on the wheel, and their heads were put on iron pins.

Some of these executions assumed the character of true *spiegelstraffen* (literally, mirror punishments)—that is, the executions, or certain stages of them, were meant to reflect exactly the nature of the crimes the condemned had committed. This was the case, for example, with the robbers who had blackened their faces while breaking into houses and farms. Similar literal reenactments of the delicts were included in the execution of two skinners. One of them had, among other things, murdered a traveler with his stick and killed an innkeeper with his knife. Before he was broken on the wheel and burned, he received a stab with a knife in his side and four blows with the stick on his head. His brother, who had misled the judges, had his tongue sliced off before he was burned at the stake. Another robber had his right hand burned and cut

[48]

off; their bodies, together with the severed limbs, were displayed on the fur on the limbs of one of his victims and set fire to it in order to make her disclose the location of her money and other valuables. But this specific punishment was also applied to those who had broken into churches.

A theatrical element—again emphasizing the infamy of the condemned and his family—was not lacking in some of the additional punishments. We know of some cases in which the house of the convict had to be demolished with the stipulation that no building was to be erected on the site for the next hundred years. Theatrical dimensions were also obvious in the punishments of virtually all forty-six people who had died in detention. Like elsewhere, convicts who had died in prison were also tried, or rather a sentence was passed on their remains. In only four cases were the bodies, upon request, returned to kinsmen and then buried in the churchyard or elsewhere, "in unconsecrated earth." Usually, however, the local skinner took charge of the bodies, dragging them on a sledge all the way to the gallows at the border of the jurisdiction, where he either buried or hanged them in chains, depending on the degree of decomposition. The bodies of those who had committed suicide were usually hanged from the gallows by one leg. Two of the suicides had their faces blackened for the same reason as their associates mentioned above. But why were suicides hanged by one leg? Perhaps it was an attempt to express, by a symbolic inversion in a mirror punishment, the unusual and criminal character of suicide committed by someone who was already exceptional and criminal. Leach observed on the logic of such reversals:

> In days when the monarchy was a locus of greater power than is now the case, those who had caused the King offence were punished first by being incarcerated in dungeons below ground and then by being hung on gibbets with their bodies suspended above the heads of passers-by. The inner logic of such customs includes such reversals as the following: if living Kings are "above" normal commoners, they are still more above criminals. But if dead Kings are buried below us in the ground, then dead criminals should be suspended above us in the air. Such arguments do not explain *why* offenders were alternately imprisoned below ground in dungeons and then suspended above ground on gibbets, but they do show that such apparently contrasted customs are mutually consistent. (1972:336)

What also underscores the importance of the theatrical element in the punishments under the ancien régime was the fate of those who were flogged and banished. Some of them were put on the scaffold with the hangman's rope around their neck, indicating that their next offense would be punished by death. Thus exhibited, they were whipped, receiving a fixed number of blows with a fixed number of birches, whereupon they were banished from the district. The element of spectacle could be as strong in some of the sentences passed on those who were tried in absentia. Although most of them seemed to have simply been banished, we know of at least eleven Bokkerijders who were hanged in effigy. Also in these cases, the "executions" took place on the usual location in the home towns of the condemned.

As specified in the sentences pronounced by the local courts, the main function of these public executions was "to inspire fear and to set an example." Although the recruiting areas of the robbers shifted somewhat over the years, one cannot say that the mass executions did much to discourage brigandage in these territories of the Lower Meuse, let alone stamp it out altogether. The bands reemerged on two occasions in more or less the same districts, with increasing enthusiasm and growing numbers. First, in 1749—after a brief interval during which the movement of troops in the last phase of the Austrian War of Succession precluded any brigandage in the area—Bokkerijder activity assumed the form of a short "entr'act" in which one encounters familiar faces next to new ones. Later, in the 1750s and 1760s, the bands operated on a larger scale and became much larger, including several hundred participants, many of them from Dutch territories. More than once the robbers carried out attacks in places not far from where the trials and executions of their confederates were in full swing. Yet a third reemergence did not take off, probably because of the radical political changes taking place at the end of the eighteenth century, when the French occupied the Low Countries and the Rhineland and introduced a more centralized system of administration. On the other hand, organized brigandage may also have exhausted itself in the Lower Meuse before political integration took place.

Considering all the sentences pronounced and carried out during the second and third phases of trials—that is, during the early 1750s and throughout the 1770s—and comparing them with the baroque punishments of the early 1740s, one cannot fail to notice an overall attenuation of the *supplices* (torture). First, the element of fire was conspicuously absent from the theater of punishment, and the combination of elements of various capital punishments in one and the same execution did not occur either. Second, most of the death sentences passed in the 1750s and 1770s involved simply hanging; of 262 convicts, 254 were sent to the gallows, while hanging occurred in only about half the death sentences carried out in the early 1740s (see Table 1.2). Distinctly theatrical elements were present in relatively few cases: in the execution of six band leaders who were broken on the wheel; in nine cases of convicts who were flogged and banished; in ten cases of robbers who were tried in absentia and hanged in effigy; and in thirty cases of convicts who had died in prison and whose bodies were dragged to the gallows by the local skinner. Finally, at least sixty Bokkerijders were tried in absentia and simply banished from these territories. Thus, compared with the sentences pronounced in the 1740s, the symbolic vocabulary of these late eighteenth-century punishments had lost much of its eloquence. It is perhaps revealing that the long series of verdicts passed in the 1770s started with two cases of garroting, a sentence never to be repeated. The last sentences pronounced in this phase included three cases of confinement, a number of banishments, and several cases of suspects released from detention.

The attenuation of corporal punishments in the Lower Meuse fitted a more general European pattern. It was part of the gradual, long-term transition from corporal punishment to confinement (Foucault 1977; Langbein 1977; Spierenburg 1984). This is also attested by the views and proposals of a government official in one of the Dutch territories in the eastern Meuse valley, Louis Adriaan Pélerin, who was appointed *luite-nant-voogd* (vice-governor) of Valkenburg at the end of 1775 when the trials against the Bokkerijders were already drawing to a close. Pélerin showed specific concern with the way the local courts proceeded against the robbers. In his letters to the Estates General in The Hague, he argued compassionately and persuasively for moderation of the penalties to be imposed on the still surviving members of the bands, especially the rank and file. Shocked by the mass executions as well as by the use of torture to obtain confessions, which he described as "horrible," "barbarous," and "in conflict with humanity," Pélerin pointed out that torture had already been abolished in several neighboring countries and that executions on such a large scale risked missing the point of corporal punishment in public—that is, to inspire fear and to set an example. He mentioned that indeed the massive executions in the 1770s had caused serious trouble among the local population and that the authorities had to call on the garrison in Maestricht to prevent the outbreak of disorder during the executions.

Rather than punishing people for crimes already committed, Pélerin, like other enlightened jurists in late eighteenth-century Europe, advocated putting the emphasis on prevention of crime. His plea for the

[51]

establishment of workhouses and the abolition of kermesses and other popular festivals (of which there were many in the area), and his suggestion to restrict the distribution of alcohol and the number of inns and taverns, was based on the assumption that one could prevent crime by controlling the populace. His proposal to improve police regulations and to introduce a *marechaussée* (constabulary) of sorts served the same goal. The Estates General reacted favorably to these proposals, most of which were consequently carried out (Habets 1887).

The concerns involved in these reforms were not only humanitarian. In the emphasis on restraints and confinement, one can discern a growing preoccupation of the enlightened elite with the *classes dangereuses*, whose ranks had started to grow dramatically from the mid-eighteenth century on (see Chevalier 1978). Moral and pragmatic considerations were indeed closely intertwined. We are dealing, on the one hand, with a growing sensitivity regarding the use of violence and all kinds of "disorder"—including various manifestations of popular culture, such as dissolute behavior at kermesses and in taverns—and, on the other hand, with the recognition that both judicial torture and theatrical punishments had run their course and were becoming counterproductive. The authorities realized that one could control crime in both a more "civilized" and more effective way by improving and extending controls over the population. In fact, with the political integration of various territories and the formation of modern bureaucratic states, central control over larger populations became more stable and effective. And it was precisely in such states as Prussia and Austria that judicial torture was first abolished and that death sentences were often substituted by extraordinary punishments involving various forms of confinement (Langbein 1977). Apart from a growing sensitivity, this may help explain why the reforms proposed by Pélerin were favorably received by his superiors in The Hague. It may also explain why the Bokkerijder bands did not reemerge in the Lower Meuse for a third time.

REFERENCES

Beattie, J. M. 1974. "The Pattern of Crime in England, 1660–1800." *Past and Present* 62:47–95.

Blok, Anton. 1979. "Wie waren de Bokkerijders?" *Tijdschrift voor Sociale Geschiedenis* 5(2):168–200.

———. 1981a. "De rol van vilders in de Bokkerijdersbenden." *Volkskundig Bulletin* 7(2):121–142.

———. 1981b. "Infame beroepen." *Symposion* 3(1–2):104–128.

————. 1984. "Openbare strafvoltrekkingen als *rites de passage*." *Tijdschrift voor Geschiedenis* 97(3):470–481.

Chevalier, Louis. 1978. *Classes laborieuses et classes dangereuses à Paris, pendant la première moitié du 19e siècle*. 2d ed. Paris.

Dülmen, Richard van. 1984. "Das Schauspiel des Todes." In Richard van Dülmen and Norbert Schindler, eds., *Volkskultur. Zur Wiederentdeckung des vergessenen Alltag (16.–20. Jahrhundert)*, pp. 203–245. Frankfurt am Main.

Foucault, Michel. 1977. *Discipline and Punish: The Birth of the Prison*. Trans. Alan Sheridan. Harmondsworth, Eng.

Gierlichs, W. 1972. *De geschiedenis der Bokkerijders in 't voormalig land van 's-Hertogenrode*. 2d ed. Maastricht.

Gutmann, Myron P. 1980. *War and Rural Life in the Early Modern Low Countries*. Assen.

Haas, J. A. K. 1978. *De verdeling van de Landen van Overmaas, 1644–1662. Territoriale desintegratie in een betwist grensgebied*. Assen.

Habets, J., ed. 1887. "Ambtelijke brieven en andere bescheiden over de Bokkerijders in het Staatsch Land van Overmaas, 1775–1782." *Publications* 24:1–113.

————. 1889. "Een Valkenburgsch dorp in 1789." *Publications* 26:3–28.

Hobsbawm, E. J., and Joan Wallach Scott. 1980. "Political Shoemakers." *Past and Present* 89:86–114.

Küther, Carsten. 1983. *Menschen auf der Strasse. Vagierende Unterschichten in Bayern, Franken und Schwaben in der zweiten Halfte des 18. Jahrhunderts*. Göttingen.

Langbein, John H. 1977. *Torture and the Law of Proof: Europe and England in the Ancien Regime*. Chicago.

Leach, Edmund. 1972. "The Influence of Cultural Context on Non-verbal Communication in Man." In R. A. Hinde, ed., *Non-verbal Communication*, pp. 315–347. Cambridge.

Philips, J. F. R. 1975. "Enige aanduidingen omtrent de bevolkingsontwikkeling van de 17e tot het einde van de 18e eeuw in het gebied van de huidige provincie Nederlands Limburg." *Jaarboek van het Sociaal-Historisch Centrum voor Limburg* 20:1–47.

Roebroeck, E. 1967. *Het Land van Montfort. Een agrarische samenleving in een grensgebied, 1647–1820*. Assen.

Schild, Wolfgang. 1980. *Alte Gerichtsbarkeit. Vom Gottesurteil bis zum Beginn der modernen Rechtsprechung*. Munich.

Schrijnemakers, M. J. H. A. 1984. *Rode. De oudste nederzettingsgeschiedenis van het Land van Rode*. Maastricht.

Sleinada, S. J. P. 1779. *Oorsprong, oorzaeke, bewys en ondekkinge van een godlooze bezwoorne bende nagtdieven en knevelaers binnen de Landen van Overmaeze en aenpaelende landtstreeken ontdekt, etc.* Reprinted in Maastricht in 1972.

Slicher van Bath, B. H. 1963. *The Agrarian History of Western Europe, A.D. 500–1850*. Trans. Olive Ordish. London.

Spierenburg, Pieter. 1984. *The Spectacle of Suffering: Executions and the Evolution of Repression: From a Preindustrial Metropolis to the European Experience*. Cambridge.

Thompson, E. P. 1974. "Patrician Society, Plebeian Culture." *Journal of Science History* 7(4):382–405.

Thurlings, T. L. M., and A. A. P. van Drunen. 1960. "Sociaal-economische geschiedenis." *Limburgs Verleden* 1:191–247.

Turner, Victor. 1974. *Dramas, Fields, and Metaphors: Symbolic Action in Human Society.* London.

Wilbertz, Gisela. 1979. *Scharfrichter und Abdecker im Hochstift Osnabrück. Untersuchungen zur sozialgeschichte zweier "unehrlicher" Berufe im nordwestdeutschen Raum von 16. bis zum 19. Jahrhundert.* Osnabrück.

Wouters, H. H. E. 1970. *Grensland en bruggehoofd. Historische studies met betrekking tot het Limburgse Maasdal en, meer in het bijzonder, de stad Maastricht.* Assen.

[2]

Law and Social Change in Nineteenth-Century Norway

Vilhelm Aubert

The most cursory inspection of the legal situation in Norway at the beginning of the nineteenth century—and of any modern nation at that time—compared with the situation today reveals great changes. How are we to make sense of these changes? Can they reasonably be termed development or evolution? Do we on closer inspection find amid the changes in specifics also the preservation of some stable traits, a possible nucleus of "the legal"? We are looking for *patterns* of change, for some order in the myriad changes in details. There are a number of schemes of interpretation and selection of criteria in the more or less "classical" literature on social and/or legal change: from status to contract (Sir Henry Maine), from Gemeinschaft to Gesellschaft (Ferdinand Tönnies), from public law to private law to public law (Karl Renner), from repressive law to restitutive law (Emile Durkheim), and not least, Max Weber's idea of rationalization as a historical trend that also encompasses law.

The scope of this chapter, which is primarily to describe changes rather than explain them, does not permit a thorough exploration of Karl Marx's thesis that law is a superstructure caused by a base of the relationships involved in production. However, the way the law deals with the major cleavages and contradictions in the Norwegian society is a main concern here. In order to see whether it is meaningful to speak about a humanitarian trend—a *Zug nach Milde*, as often claimed with respect to criminal law—the varieties of means of coercion and governance, which play a minor role in the theories mentioned above are the focus here. Because the presentation is limited to the nineteenth century, the origin and development of the welfare state and its interesting legal adjuncts are also outside the scope of this chapter. The period covered is one of preparation for industrialization, a period of intensive nation-building in which Norwegian lawyers took a more prominent part than did lawyers of other European countries.

The "Two Nations"

From our viewpoint, the two most salient and partly contradictory aspects of the nineteenth century are that Norwegian society was composed of "two nations" but that it was nevertheless conceived of as a "law state" (*Rechtsstaat*) proclaiming equality before the law. How was this combination possible, how were the inherent tensions dealt with, and what kinds of changes did they trigger? The concept of the "two nations" has been used to emphasize the depth and significance of the gap between social classes, especially with reference to British society in the last century. In Norway it was usual to distinguish between "the common people" (*almuen*) and "the cultured people" (*de kondisjonerte*). This conceptualization refers to an agrarian society with a large subsistence sector, and one where the civil servants played a more dominant role than in other European countries at the time. The civil servants (*die Beamten*) were to a large extent descendants of foreigners, immigrants from Denmark, Germany, Great Britain, France, and other European countries. So although the "two nations" bore considerable resemblance to the division between an upper class and a proletariat, the cultural dimension may have been more prominent than in some other European class societies.

The duality of the Norwegian population was expressed in legal terms in the Constitution of 1814. The constitution was influenced by the American (1776) and the French (1789) declarations of human rights. Although it was based on the theory of the sovereignty of the people, the franchise was limited by a criterion of ownership and education. Because a great number of former tenant farmers had become freeholders during the period preceding 1814, between one-third and one-half of all adult males above the age of twenty-five were eligible to vote in parliamentary elections. They were termed the "active" or "real" citizens, and they were more numerous in Norway than in any other European country at the time (J. Seip 1974:42). The allodial rights of inheritance preserved this property structure in agriculture, once gained, but the majority of the rural population constituted tenant farmers, cotters, servants, and laborers. The duality between the "common" people and the "cultured" people was crossed by another—that between men and women. We shall return to this duality.

In spite of what has been stated regarding a basic cleavage in the population, some historians have characterized the nineteenth century as the period of the "law state." The rule of law had been consolidated in the Constitution of 1814, which offered protection against arbitrary government interference in the private spheres of the citizens: no person should be punished or deprived of his property without due process of law. The judiciary was a pivotal institution within this legal ideology. Predictability of, and if necessary defense against, government interference, guaranteed by independent courts, was the main content of the rule of law. The justification for characterizing this society as a "law state" is more formal than real. Most people had few rights to be defended against arbitrary exertion of power, but the few they had were important. Although the penal law was harsh, the common people had a defense against arbitrary arrest. The small freeholders could seek protection of their property rights in fairly incorrupt courts. Even the cotters had some defense against arbitrary evictions, and the servants against untimely dismissal.

The scope of this chapter prevents me from giving a comprehensive picture of the legal development in nineteenth-century Norway. Instead, I choose to analyze the regulation of labor relations and related topics because of the interdependence between the law in this field and the more pervasive aspects of the social structure. In this area the legal rules may appear to be primarily adaptations to changing economic and social conditions, and not so much factors contributing to social change. In certain areas of private and administrative law, the promotional function of legal reforms would have been more prominent.

Criminal law is emphasized because it must be assumed that its function is closely linked to the nature of the state as a means of governance. Changes in the administration of criminal justice must be viewed in the light of changes in the scope and mode of operation in the state apparatus. Again, law as an instrument of social change recedes into the background. Procedural law is chosen because changes in this area might be used to test certain widely accepted assumptions about a trend toward higher levels of rationality. Max Weber is the main proponent of this view. Judicial organization and recruitment of personnel, as well as the access to justice, constitute the preconditions for the realization of the rule of the law. It is of interest to study the relationship between this ideal and the actual institutional arrangements.

The Poverty of the State

In retrospect, poverty is a crucial aspect of the nineteenth century, especially the early nineteenth century. From our point of view it is particularly important to note a consequence of this—the poverty of the state. Early in the nineteenth century, the state budget amounted to no more than a few percent of the gross national product. The national product in its turn amounted to no more than one percent of the gross national product in 1985.[1] The state budget in 1985 constituted nearly one-half of the gross national product. This change in the scope of state activities, mirrored in the budget, is certainly one of the most momentous political changes to have taken place in modern times. It is a change with obvious implications for the functions of law.

The poverty of the state must have been one reason why the leading jurists of the time so strongly rejected the possibility of using rewards as a means of governance. This theme runs through legal theories in the nineteenth century, not only in Norway but more generally in Europe, even though the poverty of the state was more glaring in Norway than in such countries as England and France. One is bound to ask how the old apparatus could possibly govern? One aspect of the answer is that the state did not to any large extent govern. A subsistence type of social control prevailed. Another answer has to do with sources of legitimacy of a religious, ideological, and national nature. The symbolism of the newly won freedom from the Danish suzerainty, as well as the constitution, were sources of national pride. However, inspection of the allocation of state resources may contribute to an understanding of the mechanisms of governance.

In the period 1821–24, some 40 percent of the annual public revenues were spent on the army and the navy (37 percent) and on the administration of justice and the police (3 percent). In the period 1851–54, 41

[1]A quantitative comparison of an industrialized nation and a predominantly agrarian nation can provide only a rough estimate of the scope of the change.

percent of the state budget was allocated to military expenditures, and 9 percent to the administration of justice and to the police. By the end of the century, military expenditures still accounted for approximately 30 percent of the state budget. We see how the definition of the state as an organization with a monopoly on the legitimate use of force within a given territory is mirrored in the allocation of state resources. This is further emphasized by the source of the state revenues—predominantly customs duties.

Historians have paid little attention to the impact of the military as an institution and a force in Norwegian society, these budget figures notwithstanding. From the point of view of social control, we may assume that conscription and military service had some influence on the recruits, mostly rural youth. It contributed to a sense of national identity, loyalty to the (Norwegian) state and the (Swedish) king. Although most of the youth had some elementary schooling and were literate, the army may have served an educational function, albeit on a minimal level. Military fortresses played an important part in the administration of criminal justice. They were used as prisons for convicts sentenced to "slavery" for more serious crimes. We do not know whether the very presence of the military in the countryside, symbolized by the officers sitting on their farms, had deterrent effects, but we can probably assume that such was the case, even though the military was not (with an exception in 1827) actually used to curb popular unrest.

Although the resources of the state were heavily concentrated on means of coercion, control, and conflict resolution, its power was severely limited. For this reason we find a plethora of what might be termed subsistence social controls and subsistence means of conflict resolution. I am not concerned with the purely informal social pressures and encouragements that exist as all-pervasive elements in any type of social interaction. I am referring to those institutions of control and conflict resolution that are reflected in legislation and that therefore have some kind of public stamp, an authorization by legal rules.

Religion and church as a means of control will not be discussed, although the threat of supernatural sanctions, as well as the promise of eternal bliss, seem to have been universally important mechanisms of social control in all societies that are deficient in means of secular control. It should be mentioned, however, that public confession in church was still in use as a form of chastisement at the beginning of the nineteenth century, authorized by the great codification (Norwegian Law [NL]) of 1687.

The subsistence type of social control is linked to the concept of the

[59]

"two nations" as well as to a patriarchal system of law enforcement. There were those citizens whose behavior and relationships were directly regulated by formal law, and there were those who belonged to a more or less extended household and who were as such supervised and sanctioned by the master.

The Regulation of Labor Relations

The rule of law demands, in principle, that all penalties inflicted on the citizens be authorized by law: *Nulla poena sine lege.* However, just as some of the power to tax citizens was farmed out to civil servants, some of the power to punish was delegated to private citizens. According to an old Servants and Vagrants Act, which remained on the books until 1891, the master had the right to chastise his children and servants "with stick or whip, but not with weapons." There could not be any guarantee of equality before this kind of law, which also evidenced the prevalent mixture of family and occupational roles.

In early nineteenth-century Norway the servants constituted the largest single category of the farm population. In 1835 there were 124,600 servants, 103,000 freehold farmers, and 100,000 cotters. In 1825 the proportion of servants was even higher (Steen 1957:59). The relations between the farmer and the cotter, and similarly the conditions of the servant, were based on a contract. Two decrees of 1750 and 1752 stipulated that if the cotter himself had cleared the plot allocated to him, he was entitled to a lifelong contract and the right of his widow to remain. These decrees can be viewed as an early type of labor-protection legislation; they offered some predictability and defense against arbitrary eviction, but no reliable protection against poverty and starvation. The law did not offer a similar kind of protection to cotters who had not themselves cleared the land, although local customs may have done so. The contracts varied between the districts with respect to the amount of obligatory work demanded of the cotter. In some cases it was essentially a labor contract, in other cases it was primarily a tenancy agreement, providing a house for a family, all depending on local ecological and demographic conditions.

The legislation on master and servant relations in force during the nineteenth century did provide servants with some rights. For example, a servant could be served notice only at specified times during the yearly cycle, and it would have to be done twelve weeks in advance of the day they were to move, the so-called "days of moving" (*faredagene*). However, they could be fired at any time for a whole range of more or less diffuse reasons, some of which referred to "immoral" or "indecent" behavior not only within the household but also outside it. In the cities the servants, as members of the master's household, were with few exceptions unable to marry. The legal construction of the servant was academically defined in the Law of Persons, and William Blackstone offered: "The three great relations in private life are 1) That of *masters and servants. . . .* 2) That of *husband and wife. . . .* 3) That of *parent and child*" (Blackstone 1809:422). The definition of the servant as a member of the household appears very clearly in the words of a commission appointed by the Department of Justice to prepare a new code around the turn of the century:

> It follows from the subordinate position of the servant that it must be at the disposal for the master at any time and has no claim on leisure time during the day, or on holidays, unless this has been explicitly agreed on. Thus, it is not allowed to leave the house without permission, or to overstep the free time permitted. Likewise, the beginning and the termination of the working day is settled by the master, albeit without arbitrarily neglecting local customs. . . . From the position of the servant, it follows, furthermore, that it owes the master obedience—even though the master cannot obtain obedience through the application of force—and is obliged to behave decently and peacefully, as well as comply with the order of the house as determined by the master. (*Tyenderetten* 1900:11)

Until the middle of the nineteenth century it was against the law for the common rural people to be without employment. To be unemployed was defined as vagrancy and sanctioned by penalties. Similar ordinances existed for some cities, but toward the middle of the nineteenth century these enactments had more or less ceased to function. Still, they are interesting as symptoms of a whole ideology of labor relations and a certain view of class relations.

The Constitution of 1814 was influenced by the American and the French declarations of human rights, according to which all people are born equal. But if there is ever any reason to add George Orwell's supplement—"But some are more equal than others"—it must be in this context, for it is apparent that the laws concerning servants do not deal with them as a category of people who have chosen a particular kind of occupation, but rather as people born into a lower estate, carrying

[61]

with them social characteristics that are almost ethnic in nature. Until 1898 this was also reflected in the franchise that excluded those who "as servants belonged to somebody else's household." Female domestic servants were denied the right to vote until 1913. The rationale for this prolonged exclusion from the electorate was the dependency, the lack of freedom, and the obligations to the master. However, the causes were even more profound; they were based on the idea that the nation consisted of two groups, the "active citizens" and the common people.

The restrictive conception of citizenship is also reflected in the relations between the sexes. Only those who were born male could be equal. Section 50 of the constitution reserved the right to vote for Norwegian citizens alone, without making any exception for women. The same was the case with section 92, concerning the right to hold public office. In 1818 a proposal was presented to Parliament to add to the above clauses "citizens of the male sex," but this was rejected on the grounds that the term "Norwegian citizen," in this particular context, could not conceivably be interpreted as implying women too. Admittance of women to public office again became an issue in 1896. On the basis of the opinion of the Faculty of Law at the University of Oslo, the Justice Department declared that the term "Norwegian citizen" could not be interpreted as comprising women.

To get a more complete picture of class relations in Norway in the early nineteenth century, we must also pay attention to the kind of merchant capitalism that was an important aspect of the economy, although of minor scope. Even though a great deal of mercantilistic regulation had been abolished before 1814, some privileges remained. Merchants in the cities had a monopoly on most kinds of trade—for example, the export of fish and lumber. This legal, and also de facto, monopoly created a dependency relationship between the merchants and clientele of freeholders and independent fishermen. Much exploitation took place, causing considerable unrest and resistance. Gradually, as a concomitant of the new ideology of economic liberalism, the remaining regulations were eliminated.

When these legal monopolies in the fisheries disappeared, the new freedom of trade paved the way for the emergence of local merchants, the so-called "peninsular kings," especially in northern Norway. The relationship of these merchants to their clientele was unregulated by public law, but they frequently had an actual monopoly on all transactions, with the fishermen falling under their sway. In principle, transactions were executed under the general private law of property and contract. Although the fishermen were freehold farmers or tenant farmers most of the year, they were dependent on and often heavily indebted to the "peninsular king," who provided them with equipment and food for the seasonal fisheries as well as with necessities of life that the family was unable to produce. In return, the merchant received the catches. The debts might result in the merchant's taking the freehold as collateral while the fisherman-farmer and his family stayed on as tenants. Eviction was rare. The remnants of this "quasi-feudal" relationship could be found up to World War II.

The above descriptions of the servants, cotters, and de facto dependent fishermen-farmers do not exhaust the range of labor relationships in the nineteenth century. Blue-collar and black-coated workers lived in the cities and around some mining centers and large sawmills. Compared with the servants, these workers constituted for the major part of the nineteenth century only a small minority of the working population. Most of the labor relations with such employees were unregulated by public law, with the exception that the situation of the employees of some state-owned mines and works was dealt with in special ordinances—for example, that for Röros Copper Works of September 12, 1818, which left very little to the choice of the contracting parties.

Toward the end of the nineteenth century, the industrialized sector of the economy had expanded in terms of manpower as well as in terms of its contribution to the national product. In 1890 it was still lagging behind agriculture, including forestry and fishing, as a contributor to the gross national product, 24.3 percent as opposed to 31.6 percent. In 1910 the relationship was reversed to 26.2 percent from industry and 23.7 percent from agriculture. In 1890, as well as in 1910, shipping contributed with between 11 percent and 12 percent to the national product. In 1875 the contribution of shipping had been even greater—13.6 percent.

Aboard ships, paternalistic relations between the skipper and his crew prevailed. In part these relations were sanctified by law, going back to the very detailed regulations contained in the codification (Norwegian Law) of 1687. The ecological and technological conditions of seafaring formed the ship into a total institution that implied that occupational and household roles were mixed, but because the ship's crew was an all-male society, the mix was not the same as in the case of the servants. The very detailed new laws of seafaring of 1860, as well as the revised law of 1893, testify to the importance the legislators attributed to this sector of the economy. A belief in economic liberalism and in the freedom of contract does not seem to have presented any obstacle to regulations of labor relations when such regulation seemed to serve national (export) or other strong interests.

During the last decades of the nineteenth century, Norwegian shipping rose to third in world ranking in terms of tonnage. The law of 1860 contained a number of criminal clauses dealing with disobedience and deviance on the part of the crew. In principle, it also offered crew members protection against a variety of calamities, including brutality and offensive behavior on the part of the skipper. As it were, Norwegian ships at that time offered the crew only half the pay received by British sailors. The low cost of labor, as well as the neglect of safety measures, were important aspects of the formidable financial success of the Norwegian merchant marine.

In industry, however, the legislators were reluctant to interfere. The first piece of legislation, limiting the freedom of contract, referring to factory work, can be dated to an act of 1892 regulating child labor, ninety years after the first British law regarding child labor. In 1915 a law that limited the daily work hours to ten (albeit with many exceptions) was adopted (A. Seip, 1984:120). In principle, freedom of contract was given a much wider scope in industry than in labor relations in agriculture, although all labor relations were based on an agreement between the parties.

In practice, the laborers of both categories were often given no choice but had to take what they got. The contract gave the employer the right to command the worker (Renner 1949:106ff.). In some of the developing industrial regions, paternalism prevailed in the sense that the employer felt a responsibility for the workers and their families, reciprocated by loyalty on the part of the workers. In other regions, such traditions were lacking, and the coercive aspect was so blatant that no belief in the freedom of contract could conceal it. Private law of property and contracts provided a de facto, almost public authority to govern and discipline a work force (although not by violence).

Contracts and Rationality

Max Weber made a distinction between status contracts and purposive contracts. A status contract is an agreement by which the parties become something in relation to each other that they previously were not. An enduring relationship is created. The parties enter into reciprocal roles for a specified or open-ended period of time. Purposive contracts do not create roles, but leave the parties as they were, except for the creation of specific rights and obligations. The bonds created by purposive contracts can be ephemeral, as between buyer and seller in a supermarket, but they can also form a long-lasting bond, as between a bank and its customers. An important criterion of distinction is whether the contract implies membership in an organization or group, including the dyad of the married couple. As Weber pointed out, the status contract is normatively derived from household relations and establishes functioning social units. It does more than facilitate exchange, which is the function of the purposive contract.

In nineteenth-century Norwegian society, the contracts between masters and servants, as well as between farmer and cotter, corresponded in important respects to the ideal type of the status contract. In the case of the servant, this was reflected in formal law and in how lawyers interpreted the statutes. The cotter's rights and duties were less specific in the old statutes, and the contracts showed great variations between different districts and regions, as already mentioned. However, the working cotter often found himself in a lasting unequal partnership with the landlord. We must assume that the specific norms regulating this relationship depended on local custom. Whether these should be viewed as customary law or simply as prevailing norms may be a moot point.

The shift from status contracts to contracts closer to the purposive ideal type has been a concomitant to the process of change in Norwegian society from a predominantly agrarian society to an industrialized society. In Weber's terms, the purposive contract represents a higher level of rationality and a later stage in legal development than the status contract does. There is, however, a discrepancy in our material, between the formal aspect of the nineteenth-century legal system and the actual nature of labor relations. Because of the natural, ecological, demographic, and economic conditions, these relationships were to some extent modeled on household relations and on the kind of authority prevailing within the household. The law itself, and the personnel responsible for its enforcement, was quite advanced, however. It is difficult to determine whether, or in what sense, the present-day legal system represents a higher level of rationality.

At this stage it is necessary to distinguish between two kinds of rationality. One, the utilitarian and pragmatic, corresponds closely to Weber's concept of *Zweckrationalität*—purposive rationality. Within this kind of logic, the task consists of selecting the proper means to

[65]

further a specific goal. The basis for establishing means-ends relationships could be science, technology, economics, or medicine, or it could
be common sense, based on personal or group experiences. The other
type of rationality has a less certain affiliation with Weber's concept of
Wertrationalität—value rationality. Whether or not this concept corresponds to Weber's, the second type of rationality can be characterized
by the application of a deductive logic. Choices are made by applying
norms to a factual situation and deducing the consequences. This is the
logic of the law and "the morality of obligation" in Lon Fuller's interpretation (Fuller 1964:5ff.). The judge finds that a defendant has actually
committed an act that corresponds to the description of larceny in the
criminal law. He should therefore be punished as stipulated by the same
law. This is the kind of reasoning at the heart of decision-making in
compliance with law, and it is also the cornerstone of the rule of law.

Although legal reasoning does not in practice exist in pure form, but is
interspersed with pragmatic considerations of various types, it is the
orientation toward this model that has made the law so useful for conflict
resolution and that has also bestowed on it an appearance of certainty
and precision. Unlike means-ends reasoning, it does not deal in proba-
bilities, and it seems capable of providing an either/or answer to most
questions, regardless of their difficulty. Legal reasoning is thrown as a
web, a scheme of interpretation in the hands of lawyers, over a real
world of clashing interests and attempts to solve problems in a pragmatic
fashion. The predictability offered by the law has to do with the probable
reactions in the event a dispute is presented to the courts or subjected to
some other legal test. The law sets the constituent rules of the game in
the market and establishes the minimum requirements expected of a
legitimate participant as creditor, debtor, buyer, seller, employer, employee. But it does not provide certainty with respect to how the market
will develop, or for that matter how a marriage will turn out, even if duly
contracted according to legal form.

We have no way of knowing whether the status contracts established
in nineteenth-century Norway were rational in the sense that they
furthered the goals of the parties, or of any one of the parties in an
optimal way. They undoubtedly aimed at achieving the goals of survival
or wealth and were considered to further these goals in the given
circumstances. The natural and social conditions at the time gave scant
opportunity for establishing labor relations with, for example, a clear
division between household and occupational roles. Although the Ser-

vants Act did reflect this diffuse situation, it nevertheless specified the obligations of the servant as an employee, and not just as any member of the household.

Written law had already in the beginning of the nineteenth century achieved a high level of formal rationality in terms of codification and the precision of statutes. A corps of well-educated lawyers who played a dominant role in the governance of society had been established. During the eighteenth century, there had been marked progress in legal education and an increase in the requirements for access to the bench and higher positions in the civil service. The judiciary occupied a prestigious role in Norwegian society. In some respects, however, the bureaucracy had not reached the level of rationalization envisioned in Weber's ideal type. Not until the end of the nineteenth century were the last vestiges of the old fee system, which implied some confusion of public and private funds, abolished.

To achieve formal rationality in written law is one thing, to achieve rationality in real social life is another. It is even difficult to find criteria of rationality in social action, one reason being the possible discrepancy between what is good for the actor and what is good for the community. But there are also other sources of this difficulty. If we are to use the concept of rationality, whether in the pragmatic means-ends sense or in the normative deductive sense, it must be conceived of as a procedural concept. It refers to a mode of thinking and decision-making, irrespective of whether it actually leads to truth, justice, or the satisfaction of needs. In spite of the difficulties mentioned, it makes sense to ask questions about the relative and changing preponderance of these two types of approaches to social problems and to planning.

Let us return for a moment to the distinction between status contracts and purposive contracts. It is in the field of consumption that we observe most clearly the increasing predominance of purposive contracts, simply as one aspect of the growing money economy. A subsistence economy does not mean that the individual produces for his or her own individual needs. The basis of subsistence is the farm—often with the additional access to fishing, hunting, woodcutting, and the like. The produce of the farm also supported the servants, sometimes a pauper, and the parents of the farmer would be given what they needed for their livelihood—a house, food, firewood, and so on. This subsistence type of pension right was a burden on the farm itself; it could not be bought or sold. Barter between neighbors on the basis of reciprocity served as a means of

[67]

exchange without any monetary intermediary. In the subsistence economy, consumption rights depend partly on ascribed kinship status and partly on the status contracts of marriage and of service.

I have emphasized the legal ordering of the relations between social classes in the nineteenth century. In the references to the Servants Act, the relationship to vagrancy was mentioned. Possibly because of the scarcity of state resources, the emphasis on coercion was predominant in the upper-class view of the common people. In what follows, we shall look at the development of the criminal law.

Criminal Law

The main legal basis for administration of criminal justice at the beginning of the nineteenth century was the Norwegian Law of 1687, and a royal decree of 1789 on theft. On the one hand, the 1687 law reflects the poverty of the state in the sense that the sanctions prescribed are to a large extent corporal punishments—whipping, mutilations, branding, and pillorying, as well as the death penalty. These are inexpensive sanctions. So also were the public degradation ceremonies, such as confession and chastisement in church. Fines and the loss of property were prescribed punishments for a number of delinquencies. Insofar as such punishments as deportation to the fishing outposts in the north, workhouse assignment, or slavery in military fortresses were implemented, it was done with a view to production.

A subsistence type of legal control is also made apparent in the extent to which the policing, prosecution, and executive powers were left to the master of the household or to the victim of the offense. "Private penalties" was a common term. Fines should be paid to the victim or the master, either as restitution or as a fee for the contribution to maintenance of law and order. The class aspect is glaringly apparent. One estate was authorized by law to discipline another.

The development from private penalties as prescribed by the Law of 1687, to the system of exclusively public penalties that emerged in the nineteenth century, appears to contradict Durkheim's thesis concerning progression from repressive to restitutionary law (on this point, see Lukes and Scull 1983:14). Durkheim seems to have ignored the significance of the increasing wealth of the state for the forms of legal control. It should also be noted that while the legal text delegated punitive power to private citizens, in Norway the provincial governor himself had to do much of the prosecutorial work. The law was modeled on conditions in

Denmark, where a manorial system was widespread. Manors existed in only five districts in Norway, where the landlord was equipped with judicial power, the *birkerett*. In most parts of the country, however, there were no lords of the manor to carry out prosecutorial and judicial power.

The penal system was cruel. Theft and infanticide were in most cases met with a death sentence. However, a characteristic trait of the system around the turn of the eighteenth century was the frequency of royal pardon. Mercy, as well as privileges, were important aspects of governance by the grace of the monarch. This aspect of the system can be contrasted with Weber's concept of formal legal rationality. It was a symptom of the prevalence of traditional authority mixed with the charisma of the king. It was fuel to the popular conception in Norway that the Danish king, and later to some extent the Swedish king, was a good father, certainly better than his unpopular underlings—the bailiffs and tax collectors.

During the period 1815–40 the number of prisoners increased by a factor of between 2 and 3 relative to the size of the population. The majority of these, sentenced as recidivists or for grave crimes, were kept in chains, in "slavery," in military fortresses. Women and other delinquents were kept in penitentiaries or workhouses. Women constituted about one-fifth of the prison population, a larger proportion than today. The great increase in the prison population reflected some increase in the crime rate, but probably even more the substitution of imprisonment for corporal punishment and the death penalty. An act of 1815 abolished most corporal penalties other than whipping.

There was a growing awareness in leading circles that the prisons were in abominable condition and that the situation of the inmates was unacceptable. There had been no construction of new prisons to accommodate the quadrupling of inmates. After a prolonged period of preparation, a new criminal code was issued in 1842. This was another step in the direction of milder penalties, although convicts sentenced for the gravest crimes were regularly kept in chains until 1872 (Sandvik 1980: 93ff.). Up to the time of the new criminal code, imprisonment had been viewed either as a special kind of corporal punishment or as forced labor. With the revision of the criminal law, the main emphasis was on correction. A new central penitentiary was constructed on the model of the Philadelphia system, a main feature of which was that the inmates spend time in isolation and have ample opportunity to ponder and repent their misdeeds.

[69]

The criminal code of 1842 was harsh but extremely systematic, thus corresponding to the procedural ideal of the rule of law. Its discrimination against the poor is apparent in clauses 12 and 13, on theft in the forest: "Unauthorized removal of leaves or evergreen branches from trees in the forest, or of pieces of trees that have been felled by wind or that have dried, and which have not already been visibly brought together by somebody else, should be punished by a fine of from 60 shillings to 20 dollars." If the pieces of wood appeared in a heap, the offense might still be subsumed under this mild clause if it was a question of firewood (Schweigaard 1883, Vol. 2:439). In other cases, removal of the wood was considered theft and met with more severe penalties. One is struck by the similarity between this clause in the Norwegian penal code and the corresponding clause in the German law, so scathingly attacked in Marx's famous article of 1842, "Debatten über das Holzdiebstahlgesetz" (Marx and Engels 1970:109ff.).

From the 1840s to the end of the century, there was a steady decline in the number of prisoners, but one does not find a corresponding decrease in the relative number of individuals convicted of delinquencies (Christie 1975:242–246). The increasing use of suspended sentences and fines may account for some of the discrepancy, which has not, however, been fully explained in the criminology literature.

A revision of the criminal code in 1874 reduced the penalties for a number of crimes and increased the options available to the court with respect to the kind of sanction inflicted. The "Act on the Limitation of the Infliction of Corporal Chastisement" of 1891 should also be mentioned in this context. It reflects an amelioration of the patriarchal system, inside and outside the family, embedded in the Norwegian Law of 1687, even though the practical consequences may have been modest. The act deprived the master of the household—as well as the superintendents of some public institutions, and skippers and craftsmen—of some, but not all, of their power to ensure discipline by physical means. The act represented a further step in the state's appropriation of the monopoly on the lawful use of force.

Penalties or Welfare?

The last decades of the nineteenth century were characterized by new concepts of crime and punishment that were strongly influenced by continental, especially German, criminological theories. The reformist zeal must also be viewed in the light of considerable turbulence in the economic, demographic, and political fields. Ministerial responsibility to Parliament was introduced in 1884, after an unusually divisive political contest. At the same time, the first regular political parties were established—the Labour Party in 1887. The first strikes occurred. Emigration to the United States took on great proportions, as did migration from the countryside to the cities. Shipping became a major industry. Industrialization was on its way. The union with Sweden approached dissolution, which finally occurred in 1905. A rapid extension of the franchise took place.

One might condense all these changes into the words "rapid modernization." Modern attitudes toward the treatment of deviance were expressed in a new emphasis on social policy and treatment. I shall mention only two examples of this. The new criminal code of 1902, still the major source of criminal law, will not be dealt with here. However, two years earlier, in 1900, Parliament passed the Act on Vagrancy, Begging, and Drunkenness. There was no longer any question of dealing with servants and vagrants in the same statute. A process of legal differentiation had taken place, corresponding to a shift in the nature of labor relations and a reduction in the social gap between employers and employees.

The Vagrancy Act authorized the courts to sentence drunkards to long and often indefinite terms of forced labor in prisonlike workhouses for repeated but minor misdemeanors. The Poor Law had for a long time contained a clause authorizing police to place vagrants in workhouses for periods of up to six months without due process of law. From the point of view of the rule of law in a purely formal sense, the Act of 1900 represented an advance. In other respects, it represented a step backward, especially because of the pronounced and unjust asymmetry between the offense—appearing repeatedly drunk in public places—and the very long terms of forced labor in an unpleasant environment. The law was not revised until 1970 (see Christie 1960).

The prominent jurists who fathered the Vagrancy Act of 1900 justified the new law in the most modern and humanitarian language as establishing a system of treatment and correction. Drunkenness was construed as a condition analogous to illness, in need of cure rather than punishment. A cure should last until the illness disappears, which in the case of many alcoholics may be a very long time. This new ideological construction of the drunkard reduced legal justice and equality before the law to secondary considerations. Proponents of the Vagrancy Act did not argue

[71]

that extended deprivation of the freedom of alcoholics might protect their wives and children from brutality and abuse, and critics of the vagrancy law have not paid attention to this aspect of the law. It is interesting to note that this argument would have gained considerable support in recent years, even if it could not have saved the Act of 1900.

The second example taken from the reform period in the last decades of the nineteenth century is the "Act on Treatment of Neglected Children," drafted in 1900 (Dahl 1985:94ff.). This act established child welfare boards charged with a number of tasks and authorized to use various measures vis-à-vis children who presented serious problems, ranging from juvenile delinquency to neglect or abuse on the part of their parents. One measure available to the child welfare boards was placement in a "school house" or reformatory school. Such placement, even when caused by delinquency, was not intended to be a form of punishment. Reports from the twentieth century emphasize the penal nature of these "schools." Just as in the case of vagrancy and drunkenness, a socially felt need to remove individuals from their previous social environment was combined with a benevolent and humanitarian ideology. The foreign influences derived from the same sources and were mediated by some of the same national key figures. The justification for sidestepping courts and implementing involuntary institutionalization as a means of correction was the necessity to raise and educate minors. The houses of correction were construed as schools or even homes. The stringencies of the rule of law were apparently not applicable, because it was a question of providing the children with new resources, not of depriving them of anything. From now on child-saving should be a government responsibility, not left to private philanthrophy.

There is an inherent tension between the rule of law and legal reasoning, on the one hand, and the optimal pursuit of goals with the most effective means, on the other. The theory that provided legitimation for the new correctional measures has been termed "positivism." The new criminology was undoubtedly influenced by the success of the natural sciences as the fundament of industrialization. A belief in social engineering arose, founded on the adoption of a purposive rationality that tended to reduce the significance of the deductive and normative rationality of the law.

Theories seldom leave lasting results, unless they can be used to further the interests of concerned groups with some power to influence events. In this case, the ideological trend was grasped by two professional groups that were dissatisfied with conditions in the fields of their immediate concern. Many criminal lawyers, particularly those associated with the prison system, disliked the practice of putting wayward children in prison. They were troubled by the plight of these children and were concerned about the kind of influences they were exposed to in prison. They wanted children removed from prisons and responsibility for them transferred to other agencies.

The leading teachers and educators had a different problem. They were about to reform the elementary school system through a unification that would bring all pupils, regardless of social-class background, into the same classroom. The new Elementary School Act of 1889 went a long way in this direction. To make the new unified school system generally palatable to the bourgeoisie in the cities, it seemed appropriate to assure those in need of assurance that their "good" children would not be contaminated by the presence of "bad" working-class pupils. Ideologically, the reformatory schools administered by the child welfare boards in the best interests of the children themselves served as a guarantee that the regular school system would not be burdened with the presence of wayward or neglected children. The common interest of criminal lawyers and educators became an important force behind the establishment of reformatory schools. It must, of course, be viewed not only in the light of the general "positivist" trends of the day, but also with the urbanization and concomitant uprootedness of certain sections of the large cities in mind. Quite generally, registered criminality, then as now, was predominantly an urban phenomenon.

The great reforms in criminal law toward the end of the last century pose interesting problems concerning the relationship between law and ideology, and the changing social and economic structure. First, legal change cannot be fully understood by reading the arguments in the preparatory reports preceding the passing of a new enactment. The reasons given and the theories on which they rest must often be seen as legitimation for the achievement of other goals and for the furtherance of interests that are not clearly expressed. The second result, related to the first, is that there will often be a discrepancy between the law on the books and the law in action. This does not mean that such laws, although they may fail in relation to their stated goals, are inconsequential. The legal reforms around the turn of the century set the stage for the more profound reforms initiated, although not finally solved, by the emergence of the welfare state.

[73]

Procedural Law

An inspection of changes in legal procedures might be a suitable testing ground for theories assuming a progressive rationalization of law over time. We will consider criminal law and civil procedural law separately. As mentioned previously, some of the criminal procedure in the eighteenth century was left in the hands of private citizens, but in Norway the provincial governor (*amtmann*) was left with most of the prosecutorial tasks. He had at the time a wide variety of administrative functions as the local representative of the royal power (Holme 1985), which meant that there was no specialized prosecutorial branch of the government. It also implied that the Ministry of Justice could instruct in matters pertaining to prosecution. From the point of view of the rule of law, it meant that the potential defendant's protection against state power was weaker than it later became.

Another weakness is expressed in a law passed in 1827. Before that year, defendants had the right to defense counsel paid out of public funds. The Act of 1827 introduced an officer of the court called a "reporter," who was charged with detailed preparation of the trial and served as a mixture of prosecutor and defense counsel. The law assumed that the reporter's function would be carried out primarily by bailiffs and sheriffs. The defendant could still hire legal counsel at his own expense, which in practice severely limited this custom. The judge himself also had considerable responsibility for preparing the indictment.

The procedure was inquisitorial. In terms of the rule of law, this is clearly a flaw, but as measured against criteria of rationality, the matter is more complicated and the answer not so certain. As a means of bureaucratic processing, the inquisitorial procedure may be more efficient than leaving the matter to an adversary process, where each of the two contending parties present their own and misleading version of facts and rules. On the other hand, it could be claimed that a sharp division of prosecution, judgment, and defense corresponds to an ideal of specialization of tasks. We gain more understanding by looking on the later change from an inquisitorial to an adversary type of process as a shift in the distribution of power instead of as a change in the degree of rationality.

Political circles soon came to realize that the criminal procedure corresponded poorly to the ideal of the rule of law as expressed in the Constitution of 1814. It did not compare favorably with the judicial systems in countries functioning as models for Norwegian lawyers either. An interest in the jury system arose, as did interest in the adversary process and the specialization and independence of the prosecutorial office. However, the period of gestation for a new general procedural code was extremely long. The new principles of trial by jury as well as a separation of prosecutorial tasks from the general administrative office of the provincial government were not introduced until 1887. Already in 1866 the office of the "reporter" had been divided into two—a prosecutor and a defense counsel. The Act of 1866 had also made it obligatory to specify the indictment in detail.

The changes prescribed by the Act of 1887 are ambiguous in terms of rationality. The establishment of a separate prosecutorial branch of the government that could receive instructions only from the cabinet, not the Ministry of Justice, could well be viewed as an element in the general move toward a higher degree of functional specificity in public administration. But the jury system represents a departure from the move toward a more specialized bureaucratic organization based on experts. Whatever the consequences were, and they were certainly not revolutionary, introduction of the jury was regarded as a political victory for the democratic forces. It was assumed that the jury system deprived the leading strata of civil servants and lawyers of some of their power by transferring it to the people. From the point of view of societal integration, it may well be that the jury represented some kind of rationality, but not the kind one usually has in mind when discussing the running of organizations, firms, and bureaucracies.

The principle of lay judges had a long historical tradition, broken by the Norwegian Law of 1687. In civil and criminal cases, the court was reduced to the single professional judge appointed by the absolute monarch. There were exceptions to this general rule, insofar as eight lay jurors participated in litigation over allodial or property rights, as well as in cases concerning life or honor. The establishment of the jury system and lay judges in the district courts in the Act of 1887 had a more immediate predecessor in the 1860 Act of Seafaring. The latter act established maritime courts composed of the district judge and two laymen with experience in seafaring and shipping. This served as a model for the later introduction into the court system of experts on a variety of issues.

The extremely prolonged preparation of the Criminal Procedure Act of 1887 invites a few remarks on time and the law. While the waiting period may have been unusually extensive, it is a fairly common feature for legislative projects that raise matters of principle. This often results

[75]

in proposals being discarded after they have received considerable public attention, and it constitutes an important ingredient in the symbolic function of law. While the old and unpopular law is still in force, those who dislike it are to some extent pacified by the promise of better times. In principle, it is admitted that there may be due cause for their grievances and that it is only a matter of time before the situation will be corrected. However, as the popular saying goes, "While the grass grows, the cow dies."

Up to the end of the eighteenth century there had been a continuous professionalization of the judiciary. By then the judges had become well-educated jurists, but they were still only partly on a regular salary. For the remainder, they had to extract their income from fees paid for their offices by the population. Some districts were fat, others were lean. Because the regular salary was derived from a tax on the farms in the form of the tithe, this too varied with the wealth of the district. There was no clear separation of private funds and public funds—and in Weber's terms this was a flaw in relation to the ideal typical model of a bureaucratic office. One might also view this situation as an example of a subsistence type of social control. According to the Act on Remuneration of 1872, judges and bailiffs were to receive fixed salaries from the state. From then on, public funds were separated from private funds.

Around the turn of the eighteenth century a new element was introduced in civil litigation. From then on, the board of conciliation served as obligatory first instance in civil suits. An act of 1824 confirms and specifies in great detail the procedural rules pertaining to this new institution, which has survived to the present day. Conciliation boards were composed of two lay counselors, whose task was to mediate between the contending parties and to seek a solution by consent. Until 1866 these boards had no authority to pass a verdict. The establishment of the boards of conciliation can be viewed as another symptom of the poverty of the state in a country with an extremely dispersed settlement of the population. The judges would have been unable to reach the clientele, and vice versa, without incurring exorbitant costs to be paid by the clientele.

The institution seems to have been very popular, and it taught a large number of board members a great deal about the law. There is, however, an interesting contrast between the detailed formality of the code itself and, as we must assume, the informality of the proceedings. From one point of view, the detailed code notwithstanding, the establishment and extensive use of conciliation boards appears to contradict a trend in legal development toward ever higher levels of rationality. It introduces

[76]

a new lay element at a crucial stage in the administration of justice. Although the 1824 code contains eighty-six sections, it leaves great discretionary powers to the boards in their administration of the proceedings. It should also be noted that the conciliation boards served as miniature legal academies and thus served to spread at least some rudiments of legal thinking among broad strata of the population.

The boards of conciliation were established by royal decrees of 1795 and 1797 according to French models, with the intention of reducing litigation. Statistics show an increase in cases dealt with by these boards, from 12,759 in 1814 to 64,685 in 1827. From 1827 to 1849 there were ups and downs, with a peak of 86,376 in 1838. In around 60 percent of the cases, an agreement between the parties was reached or the case was terminated because the plaintiff was absent. As it turned out, only one in ten cases was appealed to the courts. Thus, the intention of reducing litigation was fulfilled, although some of the complaints brought before the boards of conciliation might not have led to a suit even if the boards had not existed (Röer 1978).

In 1866 an amendment to the Law of 1824 authorized the boards of conciliation to pass judgment in minor debt cases, numerically a very bulky part of the caseload. Today the boards function largely as small-claims courts. In 1972, some 52 percent of all cases before them were terminated with a verdict in the absence of the defendant, usually concerning a debt. Only 7 percent of the parties were reconciled in front of the board. In family matters, appearance before the board is usually no more than an empty formality, a necessary condition for bringing a lawsuit for separation or divorce (Aubert 1976:195).

Concluding Remarks

I began by referring to some well-known theoretical approaches to legal change. It turns out, however, to be difficult to present a historical narrative based on a certain respect for factual "details" and couched in theoretical language. The theories serve a useful function by suggesting what one should look for, but they can also function as blindfolds if the historical material is treated solely as a testing-ground for theoretical assumptions. There is such a thing as letting the data speak for themselves, even if their presentation throws doubt on the relevance of concepts and classifications respectfully adopted from the theoretical literature.

The preceding presentation puts great emphasis on the nature of the state, not just on the legal system as such. The impulse to consider the wealth or poverty of the state as a particularly significant aspect of governance is derived from work with the legal system of the postwar welfare state. The welfare state exerts most of its control through its distribution of material resources—above all, money. This raises the question of whether large sections of modern welfare and related legislation establish a legal system based on rewards rather than on "commands backed by force."

In the material presented, one can perceive an ideological move away from the very harsh and very comprehensive penal system, a system that to some extent delegated punitive powers to private citizens. It was from the beginning an inexpensive system, gradually to be supplanted by a system demanding more resources from the state. The only great scholar who dealt at some length with the problems of sanctions and who included rewards was Jeremy Bentham (1962:192–265). His views on rewards in relation to law are somewhat contradictory, or at least enigmatic, and they are also largely unknown. It must remain for another occasion to investigate the relevance of his analysis to the task of describing and explaining legal development.

The historical material reflects relatively clearly the salient features of the basic cleavages in the Norwegian society of the nineteenth century, as well as some changes in the economy and the class structure. These changes would be more pronounced, of course, were we to follow the trend into the twentieth century and up to the present day. The description of legal change is fragmentary. If space had permitted, it would have been highly appropriate to deal here with changes in social legislation— the development of what has been termed the "social assistance state" (Seip 1984) and to follow the development to the welfare state.

The legal changes described in this chapter must be viewed as responses to changing social and economic conditions, but that does not mean they are linked to structural changes by strict causality. The legislators' interpretation of the social conditions is also influenced by other factors, not least by more general European ideological currents. It is therefore often a moot point whether the legal development is optimally adapted to the demands of the economy or to the interests of the groups that hold the power to issue laws. The initial poverty of the state, as well as the gradual increase of the wealth of the state, have been decisive economic factors.

Another significant question is whether the legal texts and efforts described above have, in their turn, influenced the course of events. Because the notion of planning through law had fallen out of favor during the dismantling of the old legal privileges, and because the state remained relatively poor throughout the nineteenth century, it is difficult to find concrete traces of such influences. We might have seen more of it had we studied, for example, the changes in company law or patent law. However, we are led to assume that the very existence of a fairly well developed legal system, a corps of relatively uncorrupt civil servants, and a growing legal profession contributed to the kind of trust that is conducive to economic growth. It is to be expected that a comparison of the legal developments of the nineteenth and twentieth centuries would reveal a change. The ideology of economic and welfare planning, supported by the new power of the labor movement, especially in the period after 1945, presents the problem of law as a driving social force in a new light.

What does the historical material show about rationality and development? Above all, it illustrates the difficulties involved in the very use of rationality as a yardstick for legal systems. In terms of form, the legal texts do not exhibit clear-cut changes. Modes of conflict resolution may have varied, but not according to a unilinear trend toward ever higher levels of formal legal rationality. Toward the end of the century, the courts were given more discretion in the choice of penalties. This could be seen as a reduction in the kind of rationality that rests on deductive logic while at the same time representing an increase in terms of purposive rationality. The same trend might be found in the legislative debates and reports, with the greater emphasis on pragmatic considerations. How should one select means—based on what was assumed to be scientifically established—to further the goals of education, treatment, and deterrence? The spirit of future-oriented planning was entering the legal arena with renewed strength.

Acknowledgments

I thank Susan Powers, of the Institute of Sociology, University of Oslo, for her assistance in improving my English.

REFERENCES

Aubert, Vilhelm. 1976. *Rettens sosiale funksjon.* Oslo.
Bentham, Jeremy. 1962. "The Rationale of Reward." In *The Works of Jeremy Bentham,* vol. 2, New York. Reproduced from the John Bowring edition of 1838–43.

Blackstone, William. 1809. *Commentaries on the Laws of England*, vol. 1, chap. 14. 15th ed. London. First edition 1765.

Christie, Nils. 1960. *Tvangsarbeid og alkoholbruk*. Oslo.

———. 1975. *Hvor tett et samfunn*. Oslo.

Dahl, Tove Stang. 1985. *Child Welfare and Social Defence*. Oslo.

Fuller, Lon. 1964. *The Morality of Law*. New Haven.

Holme, Jörn. 1985. *Fra amtmann til statsadvokat*. Oslo.

Lukes, Steven, and Andrew Skull, eds. 1983. *Durkheim and the Law*. Oxford.

Marx, Karl, and Friedrich Engels. 1970. *Werke*, vol. 1. Berlin.

Renner, Karl. 1949. *The Institutions of Private Law and Their Social Functions*. London.

Röer, Inge-Lise. 1978. "En reform med varig virkning? Forlikskommisjonene i deres første tid." Mimeographed term paper on file with the Institute of Private Law, Faculty of Law, University of Oslo.

Sandvik, Gudmund. 1980. "Lov, dom og straff." In *Norges kulturhistorie 5*. Oslo.

Schweigaard, Anton Martin. 1883. *Commentar over Den norske Criminallov*, vol. 2. Kristiania.

Seip, Anne Lise. 1984. *Sosialhjelpstaten blir til*. Oslo.

Seip, Jens Arup. 1974. *Utsikt over Norges historie*, vol. 1. Oslo.

Steen, Sverre. 1957. *Det gamle samfunn*. Oslo.

Tyenderetten efter norsk og fremmed lovgivning [The law of servants according to Norwegian and foreign law]. 1900. Kristiania.

[3]

A Redistributive Model for Analyzing Government Mediation and Law in Family, Community, and Industry in a New England Industrial City

June Nash

The ideology of a free market attributes the economic decline of American industry to government intervention. Yet most of the restrictions on business enterprise have evolved within corporate capitalist structures, both with the help of government acting in their behalf and independently within oligopolistic structures. Government interventions promoted by corporations are so entangled with those designed to rectify the imbalance endemic in capitalist society that any attack on government regulation is necessarily very selective. Redistributive mechanisms operate in all the major institutions concerned with production, exchange, and consumption. These may be customary or backed by law; some may be considered "natural," and hence justifiable in a free-enterprise economy, while others are tagged as special-interest provisions.

An analysis of the redistribution that occurs in several arenas—at the site of production in the firm, at the site of reproduction in the household, and at the level of the state in public agencies—will clarify the political aspects of what are often treated as simple economic transactions. The study of exchange relations by Polanyi, Arensberg, and Pearson (1957:253ff.) points to redistributive mechanisms as occurring in the evolution from simple exchange to market practices, with redistribution a means of legitimizing and strengthening the political position of the patriarchal households of Hebrew, Greek, and Roman times. Their linkage of redistribution with the legitimization of authority is an ongoing process that persists in the modern welfare state, where it coexists uneasily with market mechanisms of exchange as government agencies at national, state, and local levels try to overcome the inequities incumbent on capital accumulation. So important are these counterweights to centralization of economic power and polarization of wealth that the current attack on regulations that have evolved in trade union and political struggles might threaten the corporate hegemony central to the modern state.

A redistributive model of the evolution of custom and law must consider the coordinates of time, place, and role relationships operating in each institutional context. Redistribution involves people in a chain of interactions relating to corporate group structures that persist beyond the life of any individual and may be independent of the dyadic ties existing between any members. The time horizon often involves several generations in the case of families, and spans a century in the case of corporations (Gluckman 1968). Yet government agencies that intervene in these structures operate on annual budgets within the four-year presidential terms, where priorities are set in response to a changing political ideology. The difficulty in coordinating these differently timed institutions can defeat long-term goals, usually in a way that is not favorable to the weaker member.

Differential degrees of commitment to space also create problems of coordination for a work force, a community, and a corporation. Automated technology and integrated production have increased the mobility of firms, enabling them to set up production sites in remote places and dismantle them with less cost and disruption of corporation schedules than formerly. Tax laws favoring investment in new sites and in new technology exacerbate this tendency toward mobility. Workers tied by family, mortgages, and cultural preferences to specific areas and communities are the victims of the new mobility. The threat by corporations to move is a powerful means of reducing claims for returns to workers in the form of wages and to communities in the form of taxes, thus upsetting the redistributive mechanisms won over decades.

The disparity in time and space commitments of corporations, communities, and families makes coordination of social planning ever more difficult. Added to this are differentiated goals of segments of the population. The allocation of roles in production is locked into a segmented market, with stereotypes related to gender, age, and ethnicity channel-

[82]

ing people into differentially compensated jobs that vary in a status hierarchy. While the mystique of job specialization sets criteria guiding the allocation of these roles, empirical studies indicate that education and skill are not attuned to rewards.[1] The labor market is shaped by class, ethnic, and gender dominance hierarchies in the wider society. These segmented markets control entry through corporate group structures in trade unions and professional societies with disparate and often conflicting goals.[2]

The evolution of custom and law regarding distributive mechanisms often fails to address the disparities in time, place, and role commitments. Indeed, the regulations often exacerbate the differences. For example, laws enacted in the nineteenth century restricting exploitation of women and children through limiting the hours of work effectively curbed the competitive position of women in the labor market. Pollution restrictions and Occupational Safety and Health Administration (OSHA) controls ensuring safety in the workplace accelerated capital flight and added to the loss of employment opportunities. Benefits negotiated by trade unions promoted the hiring of temporary and part-time workers. The piecemeal fashion with which social legislation is approached ignores the context in which a solution for one problem becomes the source of even greater problems. In the dismantling of the welfare reforms during the Reagan administration, there has been an even greater tendency to remove programs that effectively reduced disparities in income. The Omnibus Reconciliation Act of 1981 eliminated benefits that enabled many women to work, and the resulting impact was to increase the welfare roles (U.S. Dept. of Housing and Urban Development 1984).

The different and often contradictory impacts of these regulations can be seen more clearly when we observe the process in the interactions within a community. Pittsfield is an industrial city in western Massachusetts that has experienced the rise and decline of textile and electrical machinery manufacturing.[3] The city has undergone all the major

[1]See, e.g., Bibb and Form 1977; U.S. Department of Labor 1982a, 1982b. The need for family-organized statistics is becoming more recognized. Sylvia Lazos Terry (U.S. Department of Labor 1982b:39) points out: "Unemployment affects the economic well-being of the family unit as well as that of the individual." However, the impact of the family is often cushioned by the presence of other earners or other sources of income.

[2]Gordon, Reich, and Edwards (1982) discuss the political consequences of a gender and racially segmented work force, but they disregard the impact of redistribution of returns from those segregated jobs in the domestic arena (see Nash 1983).

[3]See Boltwood 1916, Smith 1876, and Willison 1957 for local histories of Pittsfield.

changes affecting corporate capitalism since the turn of the century, when General Electric Company bought the William Stanley Company, which produced the first alternating-current power transformer. General Electric became the principal employer in a city that grew with the expansion of electrical machinery production during World War I and the 1920s. It experienced the rise of industrial trade unions in the late 1930s, participated in the post–World War II strikes, and suffered the loss of many production jobs that went to the plants opened up by General Electric in the South during the 1950s. Smaller competitive capitalist firms have been swallowed up by conglomerates, and many more production jobs employing female workers were lost as they transferred such operations to other sites. In the recession of the 1970s, many more layoffs occurred in the power-transformer division, and only half those workers found jobs in the expanding defense activities with contracts for the Polaris missile and the automatic gearshift for the Bradley V fighting tank. A major shift in population came about as over 8,000 people, more than one-tenth the population, left town between 1970 and 1985.

This high outward migration, the growing incidence of alcoholism, and divorce and unemployment rates hovering around 8 percent in the United States are measurable signs of the personal and social costs involved in these crises. The holistic view offered here may enable us to evaluate the relative effectiveness of measures that affect the redistribution of the "social fund," defined here as the proceeds from economic activity made socially available through wages and taxes. We shall first look at the special arenas in which this occurs: the workplace, or site of production; the household and family, or site of social and biological reproduction; and the public and private agencies that intervene to strike a balance. This artificial separation for analytical purposes will be followed by an integrative view of the interactions occurring daily among all those who participate in them.

Redistribution at the Site of Production

The fiction contained in marginal productivity theory that wages are direct payments for each individual worker's contribution to production conceals the political process of redistribution.[4] Manager-owners pool

[4]The concept of productivity-bargaining was introduced during World War II in discussions with the War Labor Board. Edelman and Fleming 1965 and Goldberg et al. 1975 include articles in their anthologies that discuss the impact of the rhetoric of productivity

returns from production and disburse them to a wide variety of person-nel; only a small portion goes to direct producers. Trade unions and state agencies intervene in those decisions to set the amounts of wages and benefits and their allocation to different segments of the labor force. The accepted purpose of trade unions, in John Kenneth Galbraith's phrasing of mainstream economic theory, is "to replace the determination of wages by the market with a process of negotiation which protects the individual union member from the market" (Galbraith and McCracken 1983:31). The state, in turn, serves "to temper market with price sup-ports, minimum wage legislation, unemployment compensation, and old age pensions" (ibid.).

The issue I raise is whether market forces ever did operate freely to set prices prior to the introduction of trade union and government regula-tion. Was there ever a time when the supply of and demand for labor determined the actual amount given as wages? How did the different scales of payments for men and women that always existed in large industrial establishments become fixed? Are market forces anything more than ad hoc explanations for what takes place in a political struggle over redistribution?

David Ricardo's thesis that the relative quantity of labor establishes the value of a commodity in exchange casts the issue of what determines the price of labor in the realm of nature. Thus the "natural price of labour," Ricardo (1930:75) states, depends on "the price of the food, necessaries, and conveniences required for the support of the labourer and his family." That which is considered essential is derived from "habit which that money [received as wages] will purchase." But whereas Ricardo posited the exchange value as equivalent to the costs of re-producing labor inhering in the wage, Karl Marx distinguished the surplus value created over and above the wage as the basis for the extraction of profit. How this surplus value is created, expropriated, and distributed is a political relationship between labor and capital (Marx 1973:662–664). Competition among enterprises, just as that among workers, may set a price that fluctuates in the short run with the supply and demand for the product or the labor power, but this does not explain the "laws" governing the relationship. Marx states, "Competition gener-ally, this essential locomotive force of the bourgeois economy, does not

on bargaining. Union negotiations based on a "needs approach" are less effective than productivity-bargaining during an inflationary economy, when wages have already been set above survival needs, but the difficulty with productivity-bargaining is that the political stance of collective solidarity is broken and discrepancies arise.

establish its laws, but is rather their executor. Unlimited competition is therefore not the presupposition for the truth of the economic laws, but rather the consequence—the form of appearance in which their necessity realizes itself" (ibid., p. 552).

Both capitalists and workers have worked unceasingly to protect their interests from the untrammeled operation of the market. Both sides have appealed to government and other institutions, including religious, kinship-based, and community networks. Both trade unions and corporate managers have tried to manipulate the supply of labor—the former by limiting access to jobs, the latter by encouraging immigration at an earlier time in history, restricting entry of large employers in communities that have established plants or, currently, moving production abroad. These actions are largely confined to the monopoly sector of capitalist enterprise, where larger profit margins and longer time horizons enable unions to extend the range of their control, and corporations to influence state and local governments.

The fact that competitive marginal capitalist firms persist and employ a less favored "secondary" work force changes the nature of this struggle. Alliances are made between representatives of management and workers to protect the vested interests of each. Thus redistribution in the form of wages, salaries, and profits differs according to the type of enterprise as well as the category of work. The strength of the claims made by each segment of the work force is related to the cultural and social characteristics of the members within it, as much as it is to the specific contribution in production. Symbiotic ties relate workers and managers in competitive capitalist firms with those in the monopoly sector in ways that affect their engagement in the political struggle for redistributive gains.

In Pittsfield, the evolution of redistributive mechanisms that went into wage and profit determinations was shaped by features that are distinctive to the electrical machinery industry as well as those characterizing the labor movement. Growth in the electrical machinery industry depended on a large and growing market. The U.S. economy met these qualifications in the late nineteenth century. The relative homogeneity of the market for public utilities for the transmission of electrical current, trolley transportation, and industrial dynamos and generators enabled the engineer-entrepreneurs who promoted the industry to plan the production facilities that could produce such gigantic units (Passer 1953:1–4; Walton and Cleveland 1964:16). This all required an unsurpassed level of capital expenditure, which in itself limited the number of competitors.

[86]

Production for such a market required a more dynamic view of supply-and-demand functions than classical or even neoclassical economic analysis permitted. An increase in the supply of electrical current expanded the potential use of electrical products. This consumption in turn stimulated the generation of power, expanding the market for turbine generators and transmission equipment. Ralph Cordiner, president of General Electric in the 1950s, summed up the market outlook that motivated production: "Each new use of electricity accelerates the turn of the circle—creating a bigger potential market for GE products, not only in end-use equipment, but in equipment to produce, transmit, and distribute electric power" (cited in Greenwood 1974:15).

These characteristics of the market for major electrical machinery tied to the consumption of consumer durable goods dependent on the expansion of electricity promoted two strategies in the industry: The first was oligopolistic control of the market shared by the two giants, General Electric and Westinghouse, necessitated by the advanced time horizon and huge capital expenditures required in the production of major electrical machinery. The second was the development of consumer markets through worker insurance, unemployment insurance, and credit unions to ensure installment purchases of durable electrical equipment (Greenwood 1974:15; Passer 1953:4). The first strategy was achieved by 1905, when the first electrical trade association was organized "in the interest of stabilizing market shares and furthering the interests of manufacturers" (Walton and Cleveland 1964:204). The second strategy was targeted in the 1920s, when under Gerard Swope's leadership General Electric set out to promote the consumer utilities market by advancing workers' insurance, pensions, and credit that enabled workers to buy the products they made. Today the credit association and employees' pension fund is an important source for the accumulation of capital that is used for investment, often in overseas branches that compete with national development.

"Welfare capitalism" (Montgomery 1979) operated within a context of repression of independent trade unions with communication channeled through company-controlled councils until 1939.[5] As a result, wages remained at the same level or lower than during World War I, despite

[5]Despite the paternalism of workers' councils within the corporation prior to the development of industrial trade-unionism, wage increases were minimal. When the councils voted for a ten-cent increase during the formation of the United Electric (UE) shop, management suppressed the results of the vote. According to Matles, this belied the company's claims that unions were not needed, and the UE gained favor in its drive for membership (Matles and Higgins 1974:67ff.).

the high market demand throughout the 1920s. Although the workers' councils in each plant put forth wage demands, the company did not heed them (Matles and Higgins 1974). The benefits in pensions and sick leave were minimal, and most were whittled away during the depression. There never were any maternity benefits prior to the organization of the industrial union, and a woman usually lost her job merely for getting married. While the rising demand for labor during the 1920s had little effect on improving wages or hours, the depression had a profound effect on the position of labor. The job became a gift, and supervisors or foremen in hiring positions were courted by desperate job hunters.

The notion of a job being a gift to the worker developed throughout the depression, as management took back some of the gains in security and pensions made in the preceding decade. Thus managerial control extended from determination of the wage share of earnings from sales to the control over redistribution of jobs. A company policy of retaining family heads discriminated against older workers who had grown children and were nearing retirement age. It also discriminated against women, who were never categorized as heads of families even when they were supporting their husbands and children. All married women were fired, whether their husbands were working or not. The Mafia was the only affirmative-action business in town; its agents made sure that the children of widows were given the first chance to distribute bootleg liquor. Since wages had never been allowed to rise very high in response to the increasing demand for labor in the 1920s, there was not a great proportional decrease during the depression. But because there were many layoffs and few worked a full week, all a working family's labor resources were needed to maintain income at subsistence levels. Those who were employed by General Electric were assessed one percent of their earnings to pay people on layoff.

For these reasons, I question Galbraith's claims that trade unions owe their existence to their function of replacing "the determination of wages by the market with a process of negotiation which protects the individual union member *from* the market" (emphasis added). In fact, trade unions raised wages beyond the subsistence level so that workers could hold out for a market price. Industrial unions altered the basis for negotiating workers' demands at the production site, moving the basis of their claim from subsistence needs to their contribution to production.

Legalization of trade unions with the Wagner Act of 1933, and the establishment of the National Labor Relations Board to enforce the act in

1935, restructured the field of labor-management relations, not by undermining the market but by legalizing unions and thus strengthening the position of labor within the market. The Fair Labor Standards Act of 1938 confirmed this position by establishing a floor below which the wage payments could not fall with the minimum-wage policy. The rhetoric and strategy of collective-bargaining negotiations are premised on competitive market conditions. This contributed to the bureaucratization of trade unions as they became committed to preserving the legal basis for collective bargaining.

At the same time that these broad hegemonic controls were exerted on the trade unions, such corporations as General Electric limited entry of other large employers into the city. Labor union leaders of the 1950s told me about how General Electric officials discouraged the sale of public property to Sikorsky Aircraft, which wanted to construct a testing base for helicopters being made for the Korean War. Union Carbide was given the cold shoulder when it showed interest in moving corporate headquarters to Pittsfield, and others say that the move by General Motors to open a parts manufacturing plant was discouraged too. Whether these moves were actually opposed by the corporation and the town officials, I do not know, but clearly the terms were not attractive enough to bring them in. That policy changed after the 1969 General Electric strike, when GE workers throughout the nation stayed out for 101 days.[6] The economic devastation to the local and regional economies effected by this strike was so great that the mayors and national congressmen banded together and tried to get the corporation to accept a federal mediator, a step the union supported.

Following the strike, the corporation changed its policies. Instead of restricting entry into the labor market area by other firms, the managers, many of whom occupied positions on the city's policy-making boards, urged the promotion of new enterprises in the community. It was time to stop being "the big guy on the block"[7] and to take a back seat. Expansion of the firm's middle-size and small power transformer production was transferred to Shreveport, Louisiana, and Rome, Georgia, plants.

Capital flight, not only to other sites in the United States but also overseas, became a threat and a reality in subsequent labor problems.

[6]I have analyzed the changing structure of labor-management relations in a series of strikes occurring between 1916 and 1969 at Pittsfield's General Electric (see Nash 1984).

[7]Quotation from interview with a former head of community relations at Pittsfield General Electric.

These policies were promoted by tax laws that favored investment in new facilities in the 1970s and 1980s.

Despite the growing freedom from market, community, or even stockholder constraints, corporations have sought further deregulation through their representatives in President Reagan's term of office (see Heldman, Bennett, and Johnson 1981; Freeman 1981). A frontal attack on the minimum wage, the hours ceiling, and OSHA regulations are part of a programmed attempt to reduce labor's position from that of a freely bargaining unit in the market to a repressed, barely surviving member of an internally competitive work force. The politics of redistribution with a growing favorable balance of power and financial resources in the hands of the corporation has in fact destroyed the market processes in the name of which they operate in the monopoly sector.

Deregulation resonates favorably with primary work-force members because of the identification with property-holding, taxpaying interest groups concerned with government spending on welfare. Labor leaders are careful to separate the victories of labor—the National Labor Relations Act, Social Security, Medicare, the Fair Labor Standards Act, and OSHA—from Aid to Families with Dependent Children (AFDC), food stamps, and Medicaid. Having accepted the boundaries to their constituency imposed by the anticommunist cold war tactics of the McCarthy era, the trade union movement has failed to address the broader issues that involve all workers.

The trade union commitment to a market ideology viewing the wage as an isolated economic factor negates the political issues involved in redistribution. While unions accept takebacks in contract negotiations on the basis of competition from abroad and declining productivity, there is as yet no demand for redistribution of profits when gains are made. Even more damaging to their morale is the fact that, when the corporation urged them to improve productivity to save jobs in the power transformer division and they responded by cutting work time and improving quality, they just received further layoffs. When the corporation finally announced in November 1986 that it intended to shut down production of power transformers in the plant and open a facility with the competitor, Westinghouse, in Canada, the workers were outraged. Yet their indignation was not directed at the power of the corporation to direct investment decisions so much as at its failure to adhere to principles of market competition. A delegate to the International Union of Electrical Radio and Machine Workers (IUE) congress at which this decision was announced expostulated, "They are climbing into bed with the competitor and leaving us bare-assed out in the cold!"

[90]

Redistribution at the site of production concerns not only the relative shares of employees and corporate owners and managers. It also bears on the relative shares received by the various parts of a segmented labor market. In a large corporation organized by an industrial union that includes the bulk of the production work force, female workers benefit from contract gains along with men, but their proportionate earnings are lower because of a segregated labor policy. Few women rise above the rank order of 14 in a job hierarchy that ranges from 8 to 24, while most men enter at that level as stock boys, and after a few years of service most men are distributed in the range of 18 to 20. Men's jobs were considered more skilled, or heavy, dirty, and requiring a great deal of climbing, lifting, and other active work, while women's jobs were generally seden- tary assembly or clerical work. The Equal Opportunity Act of 1972 caused some shake-up of the work force as women in relatively small numbers sought the better-paying though more strenuous male jobs. Equal opportunity requirements are more effective in the large corpora- tion because military contracts are contingent on their fulfillment. The corporation avoids the union contract by hiring temporary "Kelly girls" for much of the clerical work.

Firms in the competitive sector use other strategies for avoiding high wages for females required by union contracts or government regula tions. The managers of a small braid factory gave preference to women who were married to General Electric workers because they would not strive for independent retirement benefits for health or retirement through unionization. A plastics company that was bought out by Ethyl Corporation ignored the complementarity inherent in this employment policy, and when it cut off the medical benefits for female workers, the women turned to union organization. When they won a contract, the company cut out the production unit that employed the women on injection mold machines, keeping the skilled, mostly male mold-makers unit.

The complementarity of male/primary, female/secondary employee relationship was beginning to break down as increasing numbers of female-headed families meant that women working in the smaller firms recognized that they could not make their wages cover the costs of raising a family. As a result, female workers were becoming more de- manding, and the longest strike in Pittsfield's history was carried out by female workers in a garment factory. When they won a National Labor Relations Board settlement approving a contract with the International Ladies Garment Workers Union, the company went underground and assumed another name until it was finally forced out of business. The

[91]

nurses in the Berkshire Medical Center also proved to be the most militant strikers during our research, and their demands for wage increases and improved shifts won the support of large sectors of the public.

Redistribution in the Family

The pooling and redistribution of income in the family overcome some of the burdens that the secondary labor force members experience in a segmented job market. Women, who are the largest proportion of low-paid service workers in the community precisely because of their greater share of domestic responsibility, may exercise some power over the allocation of income of other family members. When married women take on part-time work, their pay covers "extras"—meals in restaurants, entertainment, new furniture purchases. When the job is a full-time commitment, they allocate it to education for the children, clothing for themselves and the children, and a major share in the purchase of food. Children who work full-time and remain at home are expected to pay for their board, but few families charge rent.

This is the "American system." In the early decades of the twentieth century, when immigrants settled in Pittsfield, children turned over their entire paycheck to the family and were given an allowance of fifty cents or a dollar. Parents were expected to save some for their children's marriages and assistance in forming an independent household. Now none of the older generation is alive, and the American system prevails.

Women's commitment to work varies with the number and ages of their children as well as the stability of the husband's job and the kind of work they themselves perform. In our interviews with one hundred General Electric workers, both employed and those on layoff, we found that more than half had spouses who were fully employed. Of those who were married and for whom information on spouses' work was acquired, forty-three (63 percent) worked, and for all but three of them it was a full-time job. Three women went into full-time work when their husbands were laid off. Nine worked at General Electric along with their spouses. Sixteen were engaged in service jobs—for example, hairdressers, nurses, salespeople, waitresses—service work that comprised 43 percent of the employment. Five (13 percent) were schoolteachers. Of the five female workers in the survey only two were married, and both their husbands worked for General Electric.

[92]

Hartman (1981) summarized studies on housework responsibilities when both spouses work performed in the 1960s and 1970s. She concluded that only minimal and insignificant changes had come and that the major difference was that fewer hours were spent doing housework because of more efficient organization of time and better technology. I found considerable differences among generations who began work in the 1930s, 1960s, and 1980s, with continually more progressive attitudes as well as activities related to sharing responsibilities on the part of both spouses. There was a great deal of flexibility in the household division of labor among couples where both worked. All the working women continued to do the shopping, a preference on their part. The outside/inside work division that characterized families with non-wage-working wives persisted with some modifications. The major contrasts are between members of pre–World War II generations and those beginning work after the war. Vicky, whose working career began in 1921 when she was sixteen years old, continued to do all the housework even though she was the main support for her family, which included one child. She describes her routine when she was forced by a layoff at the General Electric plant to seek employment in New York State, where she stayed during the week, returning on weekends: "I liked my job there very much, but I had the upkeep on the house. My husband was here and all the expenses were the same or even more. I used to work six days and come home for three days, then go back to work six more days, then have three more days off. I came home on my three days and cooked up a storm so he'd have food here. That was in 1953." Although she never expressed resentment about this uneven division of labor in the several interviews I had with her, she laughed somewhat scornfully when I asked if her husband minded her working, and when we were raking leaves that fall she swore she would cut down a tree her husband had planted.

Theresa began work as a clerk in General Electric's traffic control office in 1937 when she was seventeen years old. Because of the union she did not lose her job, as Vicky did, when she got married in 1952, and because her husband, who was an alcoholic, never kept a steady job, she was forced to keep on working after having three children. She had the full responsibility for house care and getting the children to day care and schools. Added to this was the burden of caring for the man himself and worrying about his whereabouts when he was not home. She turned to her own family for help, and was proud that she never had to go on welfare.

[93]

Men and women of the younger generation who entered the work force in the 1960s and later have a much more flexible division of labor. When women work outside the house, they arrange their shifts so that one parent will be at home when the children return from school. Tight schedules involve complex routines in the delivering of working spouses and children when there is one car and two jobs. A change in shift for one spouse involves readjustments for the other. Women like working in hospitals, which have full twenty-four-hour work schedules that offer a range of part-time and full-time shifts that they can work in with their husbands' shift. Another preferred employer is the Berkshire Life Insurance Company, which offers excellent day care for employees' children. Fast-food restaurants offer flexible schedules for part-time employees as an alternative to raising wages to attract workers. These schedules are advertised on the menus and billboards along with the day's specials. Because of their double responsibilities, women find forced changes in the hours of work even more stressful than men do, because the home work of cooking cannot be adjusted readily, particularly when there are young children.

Young men in their thirties are becoming involved in more than superficial ways with their children. Three men who were laid off have undertaken full responsibility for getting the children ready for school and preparing their lunches. We have observed men during interviews who managed the children very successfully and apparently without resentment, responding to the little crises of cuts and fights in an experienced manner. Working women all preferred to continue doing the shopping, an indication of greater managerial responsibility in food preparation, but men take charge of meals that they prepare for themselves and the children while their wives are working, and both share cleaning and laundry chores.

This redistribution of labor within the family does not involve extended family ties; it takes place within the nuclear family, where it is not ordinarily observed. All our respondents in the random sample of one hundred, except four unmarried youths, lived in their own home, and in only one case did a family in which the wife ordinarily worked have the assistance of the wife's mother living with her to help care for the children. Another woman's mother tried to take care of her daughter's children, but they both agreed it did not work out well, and a sitter was hired.

These changes are taking place so rapidly that data included in Hartman's summary from the late 1960s and 1970s no longer characterize the

[94]

solutions being worked out in the 1980s. These findings seem to be corroborated by a study by Maret and Finley (1984) in two periods— 1974 and 1976—showing consistent trends toward greater sharing of domestic tasks in that short span of years within the same households.

I had expected that there would be a significant difference between production workers and engineers in the amount of shared household responsibility. Although I have too few cases of the latter from which to generalize, I found that the job pressures on engineers to upgrade their knowledge by taking courses in the nearby colleges and in-job training meant that they were away from home much longer than the normal eight-hour working day. This left their wives even more in charge of the home, whether they worked or not.

The balanced reciprocity that occurs between spouses in the household may break down under stressful conditions. One man's first marriage could not survive the 101-day strike of 1969, when his wife went to work full-time and berated him for failing to support the family. Women who went on strike in the garment shop also describe the intolerance of husbands when they were involved in organizing meetings. They also seemed less willing to tolerate demands on their time and energy by their husbands when they became politicized by the union drive. Three women I interviewed separated from their husbands in the course of a four-month strike. A woman who took a "man's job" when the government required defense contractors to open up some of the segregated job opportunities in the plant made more money than her husband, who was working in the same shop she entered, because she received an "adder" (an amount added to regular wages when piecework was abolished). Although she denies that her marital breakup resulted from this threat to her husband's position, their twenty-year marriage, during which five children were born, did end shortly after.

What seems to happen is that personal transformations brought about by the structural changes occurring in the wider society raise questions about a given set of accommodations and precipitate new decisions. It is not simply an accumulation of grievances experienced over many years around the same set of expectations, but rather a break in the expectations, that precipitates a crisis of consciousness. The division between family and the industrial marketplace is a fragile eggshell, subject to shattering internal obligations that no longer conform to external demands. The sense of exploitation that women may have had was tempered by an awareness of the greater danger and hardship men experienced in jobs classified as male jobs. Older women resisted the

[95]

breakdown in gender segregation in the plant because of this factor. With the implementation of the Equal Opportunity Act, when a woman was bumped from her job she was presented with both "male" and "female" jobs to be bumped to. Older women did not want the strenuous, dirty, and dangerous jobs, yet they could not turn down more than two such jobs without being permanently laid off. Equal opportunity, in this sense, plays into managerial control of the work force to an even greater degree than the sex-segregated jobs that gave women the option to refuse a whole category of those jobs.

The household as an arena of redistribution is indeed an important stage that conditions the wider social struggles. The quiet revolution taking place as men become familiar with domestic chores may become a paradigm for change in other arenas. Pronounced differences in the degree of responsibility men take on in the home is correlated with age, and the trend is toward increasing participation in household tasks measured in time and commitment. These changes were not legislated, as they were in Cuba (where the law makes it possible for a woman to bring her husband to court for failure to perform household chores), but rather changes in customs. Customary attitudes used to dictate full-time responsibility for domestic tasks whether a woman worked outside the home or not, but new rules and expectations are bringing about changes in personalities and roles related to gender. Vicky would not have considered it possible to neglect her husband's meals, even while Joan would not tolerate her husband's demands after she moved into a man's job at General Electric. But some younger women expect to find a hot meal already prepared when they come home from work.

Redistribution and Government Mediation

Government mediation through welfare provides an arena that, in Peattie and Rein's terms (1983:30ff.), serves to arbitrate and reconcile the claims of various groups and interests based on political and legal grounds. Peattie and Rein argue that because these claims for Aid to Families with Dependent Children (AFDC) or Medicaid do not stem from the beneficiaries' contribution to production, as in the case of wages, or contribution to reproduction, as a housewife in the family, they are outside the realm of "natural" claims. The ideological justification for these "artificial" claims comes either from input (as in Social Security, Medicare, and in a more remote sense, veterans' benefits) or from need (as in AFDC, food stamps, and Medicaid).

[96]

Because government funds are derived from sectors of the population that may or may not benefit from such programs directly, the political interpretation of government redistribution does not follow from class relations in production. In Pittsfield, unionized production workers have a hierarchy of values related to government programs that categorize the programs funded by input as "victories of the labor movement" and those with a means test as "bureaucratic government spending." They try to avoid falling into this second category at all costs. I have known women who worked full-time even with small children at home and at minimum-wage rates lower than what they would receive from AFDC, and I have been told about elderly people eating cat food rather than ask for food stamps. Retired workers would prefer to negotiate their claims for higher pensions with their employer rather than with the state. "We built General Electric," say retired workers who organized a retirees' club related to the local, "and they owe us a pension that permits us to live in dignity." Dignity means without the help of children or welfare payments. Each year these retirees picket the plant, asking for donations from workers and making their claims on the corporation known.

The evolution of legislation concerning the human resources and welfare needs of the nation responded to structural changes in the population, to economic cycles, and to reevaluations of what the reciprocal rights and obligations of workers, citizens, and family members were. Only some of these emanated from production, where they were defined in terms of contribution to production. Others originated in the family and community and were related to problems of people who were not part of the work force. The recognition that—in addition to the deserving poor who were the target for charity and some public welfare at the turn of the century—the very nature of capitalist production required intervention to sustain those who suffered layoffs in industrial cycles and to provide for those who suffered from industrial accidents or disease came gradually. Added to these were the elderly who could no longer work, and youth entering the work force. The special concerns of women who were the sole support of children first came in the form of aid to widows in 1919, and only later were professional welfare services instituted for the divorced or never married mothers. The aged are a growing constituency who unite the problems of retired workers with those who never were in the work force.

Each increment of welfare involved a concomitant admission that the social institutions that involved the claimant were inadequate. At the same time, it required on the part of recipients a self-definition that made their needs explicit. The slow progress reflected both the resistance by the conventional institutions of work and family and community to admitting their inadequacy, and the clients' resistance to admitting their needs. The ideology of the free market pervades both donor classes and recipient classes in the United States and may be the reason the nation is lagging behind most other industrialized nations in social welfare (Wilensky 1975).

In order to overcome these obstacles to redistribution in the public arena, it is essential to develop a concept of a "social fund"—public revenues made available to social agencies working with the population that is to be served. First, to convince legislators, it is necessary to identify and enumerate the constituency that is in need. Second, the target population must be mobilized in their own defense. This requires a cognitive reorientation overcoming socialization practices that stress independence, individual solutions, and suffering in silence. Finally, it is necessary to reeducate people about the validity of these centralized funding agencies, which the public often identifies with graft and Tammany Hall practices. I shall discuss this process with regard to three groups whose needs are beginning to be addressed by public and private agencies: the youthful unemployed, female heads of families, and the retired in relation to their place in the changing composition of the population. The evolution of custom and law shows the interplay of ideology and behavioral norms in response to sectoral disparities in income and level of living that promote the redistribution of the social fund.

In none of these cases was the pooling and redistribution of funds an automatic response. Public recognition of a need was often a belated response to the increasing numbers of the cohort in the population. When retired workers began to live longer in the decade of the 1960s, they became a political force to reckon with; as the youthful unemployed increased in numbers, they found an advocacy group; and as divorced and unmarried female heads of households increased, programs related to their needs sprang up. What is needed with each group is a critical mass that will attract the attention of congressmen and senators. Tables 3.1 and 3.2 show trends in Pittsfield compared with national trends in the decade 1970–80.

Change in Pittsfield is in the same direction as national averages, toward an older population but at a greater rate. The percentage of people over age sixty-five is 14, up two points from 1970, while national averages are up 1.6 percent. While there are fewer in the youthful

Table 3.1. Population Trends by Age-Group in Pittsfield, 1970–1980 (percent)

Age-Group	United States		Pittsfield	
	1970	1980	1970	1980
Under 5	8.4	7.4	8.0	6.0
5–14	20.0	15.0	20.3	14.9
15–24	17.5	18.4	15.3	17.2
25–34	12.2	17.0	10.3	14.6
35–44	11.4	11.6	11.1	10.1
45–54	11.5	9.6	12.7	10.9
55–64	9.1	9.6	10.2	12.2
65+	9.8	11.4	12.0	14.0
Total	99.9	100.0	99.9	99.9

Source: "Unemployment Survey," *Current Business*, July 10, 1983, p. 3.

dependent category, ages up to twenty-four (38.1 percent, compared with 43.6 percent), national averages are slightly less—decreasing from 45.9 percent to 40.8 percent. The city has the same percentage in the earning years from age twenty-five to age sixty-five—47.8 in Pittsfield, compared with 47.8 nationally.

The changes at the lower and upper ends of the population pyramid will have cumulative effects on the distribution of the social product. Predictably, there will be more recipients of pensions and fewer donors to such funds as Social Security. Youth unemployment will further limit the contributions to the wage fund that is the major source of redistribution, particularly because corporate taxes have been increasingly cut. In

Table 3.2. Unemployment by Age-Group in Pittsfield, 1981–1982 (percent)

Age-Group	1981	1982
All civilian	7.6	9.7
Men 20+	6.3	8.8
Women 20+	6.8	8.3
Both sexes 16–19	19.6	23.2
White	6.7	8.6
Black	14.2	17.3
Married men	6.0	7.4
Women who head household	10.4	11.7

Source: "Unemployment Survey," *Current Business*, July 10, 1983, p. 3.

the period 1970–82, female-headed families doubled, comprising 28 percent of families in the central cities and 17 percent in the suburbs. Among black families, those that are headed by females are the norm, with 52 percent falling into this category. These structural changes in household composition are correlated with increases in the number of women in the labor force and with increases in recipients of AFDC. While in 1982 the percentage of female-headed households in Pittsfield seems low when compared with national figures (11.7 percent in Table 3.2), it is rising. Women are fast becoming a critical political force by virtue of these changes that shift them from the status of dependent wife to independent wage-earner or dependent welfare recipient. The political change has been noted in the "gender gap" in voting behavior.[8] The most marked change is in the proportions of the elderly—from a life expectancy age of forty-two in 1850, the life expectancy in the United States rose to age seventy-three in 1979.[9]

Demographic swings reach a critical mass when behavior is visibly affected by the numbers clustering in a given category. Although we do not have a calculus for determining when this happens, it is clear that such a mass has been reached in the political behavior of women and the elderly, who have become their own advocates for redistribution of the social product. Youth are less likely to make claims for themselves, but many groups rise in their defense, either out of concern for delinquent behavior of the untrained and unemployed or out of a commitment to salvaging a human resource. Action for government intervention is analyzed in relation to each of the age-groups below.

Youth Programs

Youth programs have moved from private, religious charities to public and private secularized agencies. At the turn of the century, the goals of the programs were in terms of moral improvement, but today the programs are cast in the idiom of sportsmanship and competition. The Young Men's Christian Association (YMCA), the Boys' Club, the Girls' Club, the Catholic Youth, and the Jewish Youth address the interests and problems of the young. The YMCA in Pittsfield was organized in 1888, the Boys' Club around the turn of the century, and the Girls' Club

[8]Erie, Rein, and Wiget 1982 provide a particularly insightful analysis of the gap in gender political perception.

[9]Uhlenberg 1977 provides many insights into the changes in policies regarding age cohorts and the demographic shifts as each age comes to maturity.

not until 1924. This reveals the greater concern with boys running wild if they did not have parental supervision. The YMCA's 3,500 members include many families drawn from middle income groups. The 5,100 members of the Boys' Club include many children who have single parents, and they are generally considered to be from lower-middle-class income groups. All the clubs express a concern with developing a complete person, morally, physically, and mentally. Yet they differ not only in target populations but in aims. "The Boys' Club shoots with a shotgun at their clientele," the YMCA director told us. "We have a more rifle approach. We're after a concern, a task, and we aim for that group and we deal with it."

Movement from childhood into adulthood assumes movement from play to work roles. During the 1960s, recognition that prosperity did not automatically integrate all Americans in the rising economy led to some innovative programs designed to circumvent the welfare system while attending to the problems of the disadvantaged. Vista, the Job Corps, and community action programs recognized the disparities in education, job opportunity, and socialization processes. Initially the Job Corps was conceived for boys, because, according to Sundquist (1969:43), "it was typically young men rather than young women who were dropping out of school and the labor market." Later, the programs of the Comprehensive Employment and Training Act (CETA) involved the whole population, extending to the training and retraining of workers of both sexes and all ages. Job creation was included, along with job training in private industry. This meant that the service sector in other agencies was expanded by employing trainees in park work, hospitals, museums, and school lunch programs.

When CETA was transformed into the Job Training Participation Act in 1983, the immediate impact was a cut in the budget. In Pittsfield the budget went from $7.5 million in 1978 to $1 million in 1985, and none of those separately funded efforts was secured for more than a few months. Job creation was removed, causing hardships in other agencies that had relied on the help provided by the trainees. The failure of any given participant in a program meant that the agency was given reduced allocations. In effect, this meant that all the financial risks of working with lower-class populations was shifted from public sources to these human-service agencies themselves. The emphasis on numbers of participants recruited and moved through the programs as the chief criterion in judging the programs further discouraged any creative activities.

Despite these setbacks, a dedicated staff of thirty to thirty-five, some of whom were recruited during the 1960s and 1970s, when expectations about overcoming inequality were high, try to respond to the many unmet needs that a staff of one hundred used to do. They try to assess what is needed in the labor market and adjust their training to that. They now have a sales and marketing program with North Adams College and a word-processing course at the Berkshire Community College, as well as many on-the-job training positions in about 200 different businesses for machinists, secretaries, dental assistants, plastics mold-makers, medical technicians, and nurses' aides, for instance. The programs tend to be aimed at an existing set of low-level entry occupations. This, combined with their dependent, step-by-step funding, discouraged any attempt to develop more creative careers. Employers benefit from the free employment services provided by the state, as well as from the wage subsidy during the training period and for a short time following full-time employment. The further provision of tax credits to employers who employ trainees encourages such employment.

Head Start, one of the Great Society programs that has operated in Pittsfield for twenty years, began with classes for sixty-five students in 1965 and has increased to 242 classes in nine centers in Berkshire County. The program continues to take the holistic approach to health, nutrition, and social services—in addition to education, which marked its origins. The program enjoys strong support in the community, and its twentieth anniversary was noted with awards presented by the district's U.S. congressman. The program has served 3,900 children, whose progress was duly noted on the occasion of the anniversary.

Female Heads of Families

Women are taking the brunt of changing family norms, both in increasing poverty levels and as victims of abuse by husbands and estranged mates. Nine-tenths of families headed by a single adult in the United States are headed by females, and the numbers of female-headed families have doubled for blacks and increased by 75 percent for whites (Weiss 1984; HUD 1984). President Reagan took pride in his administration's cuts of $2 billion in AFDC benefits and $2.3 million in food stamps, but these cuts have removed the incentive for women receiving benefits to take on full-time (and often less secure) jobs because they would lose their benefits under the new regulations. According to a HUD report (1984:283), the "harsh rule that prohibits an AFDC recipient from disregarding any earnings after four months" makes AFDC recipients reluctant to "plunk into uncertain jobs," with the resulting problems of child care and complicated travel arrangements.

The Pittsfield office of the AFDC program has a staff of fifty-five, including thirty social workers, three administrators, and fourteen clerical workers. The caseload has dropped from an average of 1,789 clients a month in 1982 to 1,383 in 1985. The drop can be attributed to the inability to do the outreach necessary for those who cannot work their way through the bureaucratic maze, not to a drop in need. The caseload has also declined despite rising need because of the way eligibility is figured since the Omnibus Reconciliation Act was passed.

The greatest need is that of those who cannot move through the bureaucratic maze, such as deinstitutionalized mental patients, alcoholics, and older people who reject welfare. Some cases that fall through the net are cared for by the Salvation Army and the Christian Center, which provide emergency rations and shelters. When welfare and food stamps are used up, or during the three weeks after application for welfare, there are seven emergency food pantries that serve about 375 families a month. The clients appearing in these emergency centers are increasingly families—not individuals, as was the case formerly.

My informant added, "Welfare is, for some, 'addictive.'" The subsidized rental, heating supplementaries, food stamps, and basic income of from $315 for a family of two to $445 for a family of four are extremely attractive in a fluctuating economy with layoffs continually threatening a wage-earner, and rising prices cutting into income. According to the welfare spokesperson, it is "very traumatic to leave Mother Welfare. It is a very warm and secure, though sometimes a demanding and demeaning institution." By minimizing the opportunity to combine income-earning opportunities with welfare, the Reagan cuts have eliminated exits from full dependency on welfare.

Rising numbers of people below the poverty line—34.4 million in 1982—indicate that more and more people are falling out of the safety net. There are estimates that 2 million are in need and not receiving help. The major initiative in the face of these declines is Reagan's "enterprise zones" for inner cities, which would remove taxes and regulatory "inhibitions"—minimum wage, union recognition, and other laws that were the fruit of fifty years of labor struggles to encourage employers to give the gift of a job to people (HUD 1984).

In response to specific needs of women and children, several groups have developed. The Women's Center in Pittsfield began as a volunteer group in 1975 and grew to a $175,000 operation in 1982. Its first activities were in intervention in times of crisis, usually precipitated by wife abuse. The center provided legal advocacy for divorce proceedings, a hiring hall, and job counseling. When a hotline for receiving calls was established, the number of calls increased from 295 in 1980 to 412 in 1981. The latest program, begun in 1983 and called "Displaced Homemakers," is funded by Bay State Skills with $171,000 in 1983. Displaced Homemakers is directed at women whose lives are predicated on their roles as wives and mothers and who have suddenly lost claims to wage redistribution or Social Security benefits because of divorce or death of the spouse. The social worker who worked with these women compared them with veterans, who, she said, are also committed to carrying out "society's goals of protection of the nation and our home and our values," but whereas the veteran will receive educational benefits and be given preferred status in training for jobs, widows and displaced homemakers are the last to be hired and the first to be fired, because they lack seniority in the work force.

The dilemma women face in politicizing their claims is that they lose the rights that are defined in relation to dependent roles in the household when they seek autonomy as wage-earners or as claimants for public assistance. The failure of the Equal Rights Amendment to pass in state legislatures and become national law indicates the fear women have of losing their claims as dependents in a society which has thus far assumed that they will gain a share of the socially available surpluses by virtue of their status as wives and mothers. In this period of transition, any move to equalize their position in the labor market becomes a threat to that status. The legislation that came out of the New Deal "confirmed the dependency relationships of women and the deserving poor" (Erie, Rein, and Wiget 1982:2). By drawing in the minorities and the poor, the Great Society programs made the working majority feel threatened. Their sacrifices to advance their own mobility and that of their children seem negated by such help to the improvident.

Despite these contradictions, women have become the most vocal sector of the population in their attempts to redress the losses they experience as they move from the dependent status of wives and mothers, protected by a patriarchal family, to independent but subordinate members of the secondary work force. Along with the demands for rights in the workplace, they are looking for support among women to protest the increasing violence against women and children. In Pittsfield during the fifth annual "Take Back the Night" march in 1984, women spoke out for the right to walk without fear after dark without requiring a protector. AWARE—the All Women's Advocacy, Relief, and Empowerment project in Pittsfield—works with the Battered Women's Task Force and the Women's Services Center to ensure legal support for women who have experienced assault.

Retirees and the Aging Population

The most significant legislation regarding redistribution to the older population is Social Security. The Social Security Act was the keystone for the construction of the welfare state when it was passed in 1935, and along with the Fair Labor Standards Act of 1938 it established the minimum wage and instituted the eight-hour day. In addition to regulating the labor market, it moved retired workers from the ranks of welfare recipients to pensioners and transformed disabled workers from beggars to independent status. Only later were wives and widows added. The system had grown from a limited insurance plan to a "gigantic tax system aimed at redistribution of current income from workers to retirees and other beneficiaries" (Mait 1978:35). The passage of the bill in 1935 was clearly related to the growing awareness of "the mounting human problems of dependent old age in an industrial urban economy," when "people could not go back to the security of the farm life, nor could they rely on the income from the recently laid off son. The loss of savings through bank failures and depreciated investments had reduced many self-reliant people to dependence on relief" (ibid., p. 43).

The increasing number currently covered by Social Security upsets the balance between the amounts contributed by employed workers and the benefits received by retirees. In 1940 there were 145.8 workers for each beneficiary, and by 1972 there were only 2.9 workers per beneficiary—an increase from 3 million recipients to 30 million. Since then the number of people receiving benefits directly and as beneficiaries has risen to 34 million, representing one-seventh of the total population of the United States and about one-third of the working population.

Declining employment rates attributable to deindustrialization and automation are in part responsible for the imbalance between workers and beneficiaries. In contrast to corporate managers, who have shown no concern with this problem at the local or national level, retirees from General Electric in Pittsfield have started a campaign for taxing robots to pay for Social Security. In June 1982, retired workers of the IUE Locals 254 and 255 went out on a picket line at the main gate of Pittsfield's GE plant. The messages on their signs should teach a historic lesson to plant

[105]

managers, government representatives, and the public in general. One read: "MUST WE BEG FOR THE GOOD THINGS?" Another said: "A DECENT MEDICAL PLAN IS NOT A LUXURY." But the statement that went beyond what we see in the media or business journals was Guy Pelegrinelli's sign: "ROBOTS SHOULD PAY SOCIAL SECURITY."

The wording of the signs shows that workers have a more profound sense of the implications of technological change and its link with the redistributive system essential for maintaining the social system intact than do the hired economists of business or government. While management specialists in the burgeoning field of automation worry about the competitive market in gearing up plants for robots, workers in industry and those who are retired are concerned with the fundamental problems that threaten our society—first and foremost, unemployment. Without wages and income, who can consume the flow of products that robots are capable of producing? But no less important are the taxes needed to pay for the basic social services won over the years by organized labor—pensions, Social Security, medical insurance, education for children, and retraining workers displaced by automation. Some method of redistributing the gains from production must be reinvented at the same time that robots are being substituted for human labor. The call of General Electric retirees for a tax on robots is an innovative solution to a problem that professional economists have not addressed.

Retirees have more immediate goals regarding their pension from General Electric. The pension fund has an annual interest return of $800 million, only $400 million of which is disbursed to living workers who are retired. Leo Rodgers, president of the retirees' club, stated the case for increasing pensions at a meeting of the IUE conference board during national negotiations. He pointed out that those who retired prior to 1970 averaged about $100 a month from their GE pensions. This, added to $230 a month from Social Security, did not cover normal expenditures in the year 1979. The pensions received by these retirees had been adjusted upward by 40 percent to account for inflation; yet in the same period, GE workers had received cost-of-living increases amounting to 115 percent. "The working people who produced goods for the world market," Rodgers pointed out, "enabled the existence and the flow of profits" of their employers. Retirees' past contributions to their industry should receive recognition in the form of increased pensions and an improved medical insurance plan.

In another area of redistribution, funds from state and private sources are pooled to provide for the needs of the elderly at home or in centers.

[106]

The Berkshire Home Care service enables older people to remain in their own homes when they become unable to care for themselves completely by providing strategic services with a staff of paid and volunteer workers. Since 1974, when the service was begun, they have had a 90 percent increase in their casework, operating with a budget of $48,000 initially and now with $2.5 million. The homemaker volunteers help the elderly with light cooking and housework. They also provide bus service and health services, as well as nutritional centers, where advice on diet and instruction in food preparation are given.

Many of the general welfare aids in the county, such as assistance in paying energy and housing bills, are aimed directly or indirectly at senior citizens. More than 1,200 volunteers put in many hours working for the elderly throughout the county, in hospitals, as drivers providing rides for the elderly and the handicapped, and providing "meals-on-wheels." Mental health counseling and a program called "Good Grief" help the elderly deal with death and dying. A hotline telephone service enables the sick to summon aid immediately. Legal services, occupational therapy, and free recreational trips enable the elderly to live active lives. An intergenerational child-care service promotes the extended ties that have been lost in so much of American life.

This extraordinary level of activity shows a remarkably successful fusion of community concerns typical of a small town, combined with the know-how and practiced administration of a bigger city. According to the director, the subtle balance of private and public funding and the mix of volunteer and professional help will go down the drain if federal funding is reduced, because stable input is necessary to build programs. Formerly, CETA workers mixed with the volunteers, "helping like one of the family." Reaganomics has destroyed this, and crippled the rest of the program as well. The specious call for turning such public activities back to private charities does not take into account that although well over 50 percent of these programs are already financed by funds from United Way and volunteer work, the core payments from regular federal government sources sustain the whole structure.

The complex network of service organizations with board members drawn from industry and labor is a complementary part of an anarchic mode of production in which workers and their families bear the brunt of shifts in the business cycle. These quasi-public agencies contrast with state welfare agencies, which categorize their clients as far removed from the hard-working, sports-loving, privatized family mode of living that characterizes other citizens. Even now, with many forced to go on welfare, some people would rather eat cat food than check out a grocery cart using food stamps. As these numbers increase, the onus for relief will shift from the recipients to the system for failing to provide employment. This time is fast approaching, as notable increases in emergency centers show. The nights of lodging provided by the Pittsfield Salvation Army totaled 6,750 from June 1984 to January 1985, and in December the local press (*Berkshire Eagle*, January 25, 1985) estimated that there were ten to twenty street people. The emergency meal centers provide about 375 families with food each month, and the state Department of Public Health found malnutrition affecting 2 to 4 percent of the children in the state (*Berkshire Eagle*, March 26, 1984).

Conclusions

Redistribution is a process of circulating resources and rewards within a social system in a way that reinforces a given structure of social relations. Claims for disbursements are based either on contributions to the common source of funding or on need. While this distinction seems clear-cut, the size of the distribution often bears little relationship to the contribution. Wages and salaries are never directly calibrated to the contribution of the individual even at the site of production, and far less in the area of sales, services, and transportation. Cultural variables modified and transformed by a power structure enter into the remuneration of everyone from the doorman to the highly skilled technician. A redistribution model enables us to perceive the political economy involved in all such transactions.

When we integrate the perspectives gained from an analysis of the redistribution in each domain, we can understand what structures the corporate hegemony. The redistribution of wage incomes that occurs in the home reinforces hegemonic power relations in the wider society when women remain married to wage-earners in the preferred sector of the labor force. Even when they are working at jobs with low incomes and no benefits, they can then rely on medical insurance as dependents, and support for children from the male wage-earner. But single heads of family recognize the exploitation that drives their wages below the costs of social reproduction, and it is they who go out on the picket lines protesting the low wages in the competitive firms or service jobs in which they work. Their double disadvantage as women and as workers in segregated, low-paying jobs is compounded by women's disadvantaged position as single heads of families with no backup help at home.

[108]

Thus women are the principal clients of state agencies that have intervened to modify discrimination on the job or that disburse income maintenance funds. The rising number of women in the labor force—up to 37 million in 1979, compared with 20 million in 1960—is matched by rising levels of welfare costs, which have gone from $25 billion to $264 billion in 1979 (Erie, Rein, and Wiget 1982:1). Reversals cutting $35.2 billion from social outlays since 1982 have been especially traumatic for women and children. These major upheavals threaten the basis for security, and even the survival, of this population. As yet, the "gender gap" that surfaced in the congressional elections of 1982 has not extended to the presidential elections, nor has the surface discontent been translated into a deeper consciousness of what the issues are in political economic terms. Welfare dependency may have undermined some of the political responses to changes in the 1970s, but the removal of most subsidies may counteract such trends.

As we compare the claims stemming from the arenas of production, reproduction, and governance, we can see the ideological bases for validation of shares in production. Sometimes the claims from two arenas are convergent, as when retirees seek to reinforce the process of redistribution with a tax on robots, thus limiting the firm's tendency to replace wage-workers with machines, and at the same time replacing taxes lost on wages; or when displaced homemakers demand status akin to the veterans who have served their country, in seeking reentry into the labor force in a privileged position. These kinds of convergences will strengthen the political basis for realizing their claims. More often, the claims from different arenas are taken as contradictory, as when widows of Social Security recipients try to continue work and lose most of those benefits. Wage-workers in the primary sector tend to view all the welfare interests as a threat to their take-home pay, instead of seeing the advantage they may have when welfare disbursements overcome the desperation of job-seekers who might otherwise drive down the wage rate. According to Piven and Cloward (1982), Great Society programs strengthen the political position of the work force as well as of those who can stay out of it because of subsidies, and the current attack on welfare is in recognition of its effect on the accumulation of capital.

The evolution of legislation in the 1930s set a floor for impoverishment in the United States. That floor became a staging area for the Great Society programs that brought about a redistribution of wealth in the 1960s. A study by the U.S. Bureau of the Census (*New York Times*, April 17, 1985) demonstrated that these programs, including Social Security and AFDC, reached 45 percent of all households, or 39.1

million of the nation's 83.6 million households. Of this total, 37 percent received entitlements that did not require a needs assessment, and 19 percent received aid from programs geared to the needy. The 1985 budget submitted to Congress made deep slashes in these programs, with cuts of $18.7 billion over the next three years to Medicare, $5 billion to Medicaid, and reductions in rental assistance, public housing, congregate meals, and meals-on-wheels, as well as low-income energy assistance and legal services. The total amount cut from all domestic spending for the fiscal year 1986 was $30.4 billion, an amount that just about equaled the sum that was added to the budget for military spending. The guns-or-butter choice, wrote Seymour Melman (*New York Times*, April 22, 1985), can no longer be ignored: either we continue escalating the arms race and destroy programs that would ensure the productive potential of our nation or we "couple a joint process of agreed arms reduction with conversion from a military to a civilian economy."

As the wage basis for claims on the system is narrowed through automation and robotization, the need to strengthen claims on other grounds becomes increasingly important. Peattie and Rein (1983) highlight this in their equation of earning "not as an isolated economic factor but as institutionally determined as claims on consumption arising out of kinship relations or through the welfare system." The diminishing share of wages in the gross national product and the failure to tax rising corporate profits by the Reagan administration threaten the basis for social welfare legislation. We need to restore the basis for claiming a larger share of production by underwriting the legitimate claims of families and communities with continuous funding of programs with an institutional basis that takes them out of a political feuding arena.

REFERENCES

Bibb, Robert, and William H. Form. 1977. "The Effects of Industrial, Occupational, and Sex Stratification on Wages in Blue-Collar Markets." *Social Forces* 55(4):974–996.
Boltwood, E. 1916. *The History of Pittsfield, Massachusetts from the Year 1876 to the Year 1916*. Pittsfield, Mass.
Brenner, M. Harvey. 1973. *Mental Illness and the Economy*. Cambridge, Mass.
Chinoy, Eli. 1955. *Automobile Workers and the American Dream*. Garden City, N.Y.
Edelman, Murray, and R. W. Fleming, eds. 1965. *The Politics of Wage Price Decisions: A Four Country Analysis*. Urbana, Ill.

Erie, Steven P., Martin Rein, and Barbara Wiget. 1982. "Women and the Reagan Revolution: Thermidor for the Social Welfare Economy." Paper presented at 1982 Annual Meeting of the Western Political Science Association, San Diego, California.

Freeman, Roger A. 1981. *A Preview and Summary of the Wayward Welfare State.* Stanford, Calif.

Galbraith, John Kenneth, and Paul W. McCracken. 1983. *Reagonomics: Meaning, Means, and Ends.* New York.

Gluckman, Max. 1968. "The Utility of the Equilibrium Model in the Study of Social Change." *American Anthropologist* 70(2):219–237.

Goldberg, Joseph, et al. 1975. *Collective Bargaining and Productivity.* Champaign, Ill.

Gordon, D., M. Reich, and R. C. Edwards. 1982. *Segmented Work, Divided Workers: The Historical Transformation of Labor in the United States.* Cambridge, Eng.

Greenwood, R. G. 1974. *Managerial Decentralization.* Lexington, Mass.

Hartman, Heidi. 1981. "The Family as Locus of Gender, Class, and Political Struggle: The Example of Housework." *Signs* 6(3):366–394.

Heldman, Dan C., James T. Bennett, and Manuel H. Johnson. 1981. *Reregulating Labor Relations.* Dallas.

Magdoff, Harry, and Paul Sweezy. 1981. *The Deepening Crisis of United States Capitalism.* New York.

Mait, Stephen H. 1978. "Social Security: A Program to Prevent Poverty." In Herman Berliner, ed., *Programs to Prevent or Alleviate Poverty* (Hofstra University Yearbook of Business Series) 12(2):32–113.

Maret, Elizabeth, and Barbara Finlay. 1984. "The Distribution of Household Labor among Women in Dual-Earner Families." *Journal of Marriage and the Family* 46:357–364.

Marx, Karl. 1973. *The Grundrisse.* Middlesex, Eng.

Matles, James J., and James Higgins. 1974. *Them and Us: Struggles of a Rank-and-File Union.* Boston.

Montgomery, David. 1979. *Workers' Control in America: Studies in the History of Work, Technology, and Labor Struggles.* New York.

Nash, June. 1983. "Segmentation of the Work Process in the International Division of Labor." In Steve Sanderson, ed., *The Americas in the New International Division of Labor,* pp. 253–272. New York.

———. 1984. "Impact of the Restructuring of the World Capitalist System on the New England Industrial Community." In C. Bergquist, ed., *Labor Systems and Labor Movements in the World Capitalist Economy,* pp. 243–266. Los Angeles.

Oakley, A. 1974. *The Sociology of Housework.* New York.

Passer, Harold C. 1953. *The Electrical Manufacturers, 1875–1900: A Study in Competition, Entrepreneurship, Technical Change, and Economic Growth.* Cambridge, Mass.

Peattie, Lisa, and M. Rein. 1983. *Women's Claims.* Cambridge, Mass.

Piven, F. Fox, and Richard A. Cloward. 1982. *The New Class War.* New York.

Polanyi, Karl, Conrad M. Arensberg, and Harry W. Pearson. 1957. *Trade and Market in the Early Empires*. New York.

Ricardo, David. 1930 (1821). "Principles of Political Economy and Taxation." Reprinted in Joseph Freeman, Joshua Kunitz, and Louis Lozowick, eds., *Voices of the Industrial Revolution*. New York.

Smith, E. A. 1876. *The History of Pittsfield, Berkshire County, Mass., from the Year 1800 to the Year 1876*. Springfield, Mass.

Sundquist, James L., ed. 1969. *On Fighting Poverty: Perspectives from Experience*. New York.

Sweet, Morris L. 1981. *Industrial Location Policy for Economic Revitalization*. New York.

Uhlenberg, P. 1977. "Changing Structure of the Older Population of the U.S.A. during the Twentieth Century." *Gerontologist* 17:197–202 (June).

U.S. Department of Housing and Urban Development (HUD). 1984. *Community Planning and Development: Urban Conditions and Trends*. The President's National Urban Policy Report. Washington, D.C.

U.S. Department of Labor, Bureau of Labor Statistics. 1982a. *Labor Force Statistics Derived from the Current Population Survey: A Databook*, Bulletin 2096. Washington, D.C.

————. 1982b. *Unemployment and Its Effect on Family Income*. Bulletin 2148. Washington, D.C.

Walton, Clarence C., and Frederich W. Cleveland. 1964. *Corporations on Trial: The Electric Cases*. Belmont, Calif.

Weiss, Robert S. 1984. "The Impact of Marital Dissolution on Income and Consumption in Single Parent Households." *Journal of Marriage and the Family* 46:115–27.

Wilensky, Harold. 1975. *The Welfare State and Equality: Structural and Ideological Roots of Public Expenditures*. Berkeley and Los Angeles.

Willison, G. E. 1957. *The History of Pittsfield, Mass., 1916–1955*. Pittsfield, Mass.

Zaretsky, E. 1976. "Capitalism, the Family, and Personal Life." *Socialist Revolution*, nos. 13–14.

[4]

Constitution-Making in Islamic Iran: The Impact of Theocracy on the Legal Order of a Nation-State

Said Amir Arjomand

Max Weber noted that the rationalization of sacred laws is substantive in character because there is no interest in separating law and ethics. Therefore, the theocratic influence produces legal systems that are combinations of legal rules and ethical demands. The result is a specifically nonformal type of legal system (Weber 1978:810–811). Islamic law (*shari'a*) is a good example. Furthermore, the ideal character of Islamic law predominated over its practical aspect from the very inception of its development in the eighth century. In this period, when "religious people were pushed into the background by the rulers, they, like the Jewish rabbis under Roman rule, occupied themselves with research into the law, which had no validity for the real circumstances of life but represented for themselves the law of their ideal society" (Goldziher 1971, 2:41–42). Despite gigantic strides in subsequent centuries to embrace various areas of social and economic practice, the ideal character of Islamic law remained pronounced, and many pious jurists would question the propriety of using the sacred law for the purpose of reconstructing social and political practice.

After a notable attempt by Ibn al-Muqaffa' to incorporate Islamic law into the state failed in the mid-eighth century (see Goitein 1968), the sacred law became largely theoretical and the state developed a secular jurisdiction of its own. Consequently, the sacred law of Islam became a "jurists' law" instead of a "judges' law" (see Weber 1978:820 and Schacht 1950:95,102). In practice, "public law" remained the province of the ruler and his tribunals. The jurists thus tacitly ceded administrative, fiscal, and criminal law to the state. However, the theoretical supremacy of the *shari'a* as God's command was never questioned. This theoretical supremacy introduced the possibility of invidious contrasts between custom and secular law, on the one hand, and the sacred law, on the other.

Being a "jurists' law" reinforced the infusion of Islamic law with ethical considerations and the relative indifference of Islamic law to the administration of justice. The medieval legal literature abounds with expressions of distaste on the part of the jurists for the office of judge (Coulson 1969:58–60). The moralistic antipathy of the pious jurists to the administration of justice militated against any *procedural* rationalization of Islamic law (Schacht 1935:222), and the result was the informality Weber singled out and used for the designation of his category of "*qadi*-justice." The administration of Islamic law—*qadi*-justice—was marked by the absence of procedural formalism. A perceptive French observer of seventeenth-century Iran was struck by the informality of the procedure at the *qadi*'s home, the lack of coordination between judges, and the absence of hierarchical rationality in the judiciary organization (Arjomand 1984:209).

The procedural informality of *qadi*-justice went hand in hand with the dubious status of written documents. The decisive factor in establishing evidence in Islamic law is the oral testimony of a witness. "The existence of a document constitutes, at best, only corroborative evidence" (Udovitch 1985:460). Its value as evidence derives from the moral probity of the individual who testifies to its authenticity. Citing Wakin (1972) and Rosen (1980–81), Geertz (1983:190–191) singles out this concern with "normative witnessing" as the most striking characteristic of the Islamic judiciary procedure, thus emphasizing the *personal* character of the Islamic administration of justice.

Historically, Shi'ite law has shared all the above characteristics— moral idealism in jurisprudence, and informality and personalism in the administration of justice—with Sunni Islamic law. Furthermore, its exclusion from the domains of public law and criminal justice was more pronounced than was the case with Sunni Islam generally (Arjomand 1984). The revolutionary break with this past came in 1979, when the Shi'ite hierocracy (the *'ulama*) inherited the political and judiciary organization of the Iranian nation-state as formally rationalized by seven decades of Western-inspired modernization. The declared aim of the Ayatollah Khomeini had been to transform the Pahlavi state into a theocracy and to Islamize its judiciary system. I suspect that, before embarking on this project, Khomeini and his clerical followers did not realize that attainment of these goals would entail a legal revolution in Shi'ism. But embark on their project they did, and the legal revolution they thus initiated is in full swing.

As is well known, Weber saw the modern state as the typical societal organization of rational-legal domination. The true Islamicization of the modern state into a Shi'ite theocracy required a drastic transformation of the Shi'ite sacred law. From being a "jurists' law" it was to be transformed into the law of the state. Law-finding, the typical activity of the Islamic jurists, was to be replaced by legislation and codification. Shi'ite law was to be extended to cover public law fully. It was also to cover criminal justice. Its penal provisions, never enforced in a millennium, were to become fully operative. Procedurally, Shi'ite law was to be enforced through the modified mechanism of the inherited formally rationalized and hierarchical judiciary organization modeled on the West European civil law systems. All this meant that the moral idealism of Shi'ite law had to give way, at least partly, to practical realism, that its procedural informality had to yield to a formally rationalized bureaucratic court system, and that its often unpractical personalism had to succumb to more impersonal and efficient procedures involving much greater reliance on written documents and impersonal forms of evidence. With firm determination, the clerical rulers of Iran have embarked on a historically unprecedented comprehensive program of codification of Shi'ite law in all spheres, including criminal law. They have operated the bureaucratic judiciary system, bringing it under gradually increasing control as trained Islamic jurists become available for its offices, and they have sought to facilitate the use of documents and impersonal evidence by shifting the emphasis from "normative witnessing" to the knowledge (*'ilm*) of the judge as the crucial factor in establishing the facts pertinent to a case (see Arjomand 1988:184–188).

It is impossible to cover all aspects of this thorough legal revolution in a single chapter. I therefore propose to cover the first and perhaps the fundamental step in this legal revolution. This fundamental step was taken when Khomeini and his followers decided, partly through the force of circumstances, that their Shi'ite theocracy was at the same time to be a constitutional state. The principles of theocracy, with their full implications within the framework of the rational-legal order of the

[115]

modern nation-state, were to be worked out and embodied in the Constitution of the Islamic Republic of Iran.

The Iranian Constitution of 1979 in the Legal History of the Modern Middle East

The history of constitutionalism in the Middle East and in North Africa begins in the 1860s with the Tunisian Constitution of January 1861 and the establishment of a parliament (Majlis Shura al-Nuwwab) and promulgation of a fundamental law (*la'iha asasiyya*) by Khedive Isma'il of Egypt in October 1866 (Khadduri 1966:24ff.). The first Ottoman constitution was promulgated by Sultan 'Abd al-Hamid in December 1876, only to be suspended in February 1878 (Lewis 1966:14). The second wave of constitutionalism was ushered in by Iran in 1906. In August 1906 a National Consultative Assembly was set up by a royal decree. It drew up and passed a "Fundamental Law," ratified by the monarch on December 30, 1906, and a "Supplementary Fundamental Law," ratified on October 7, 1907.

The ideas and terminology of constitutionalism traveled from western Europe to Iran through the Ottoman Empire. The term for "constitution" in the Ottoman Empire and Iran, *qanun-e asasi* (*esasi* in Turkish), is indicative of its mode of accommodation in the Muslim legal universe. The word *qanun* entered into Arabic in the early Middle Ages. It retained its original Greek fiscal connotations as regulation of land taxes, but also acquired the more general sense of a code of regulations and state law. From very early in the Islamic period, the penal system and the maintenance of order became subject to "regulations" (*qawanin*) of the rulers (Linant de Bellefonds 1978, 4:556). Somewhat later, in financial and public administration, *qanun* came to mean regulations laid down by the ruler independently of the Sacred Law. This development came about partly because with the emergence of the science of jurisprudence (*usul al-fiqh*) in the ninth century the boundaries of jurisprudence were so narrowly drawn that administrative regulations were not included. In any event, new administrative regulations became the exclusive province of the ruler's law or state law. After the Mongol invasion, the notion of independent state law was greatly strengthened. This development culminated in the promulgation of the great *qanuns* of the late fifteenth and early sixteenth centuries, notably that of Uzun Hasan in Iran and those of the Sultans, Mehmed the Conqueror, Bayezid,

[116]

Selim, and Süleyman the Lawgiver (Qanuni) in the Ottoman Empire (Inalcik 1978, 4:558–559,566). In the latter part of the sixteenth century and early in the seventeenth, regulations promulgated by the Sultans became increasingly coached in *shar'i* terms and incorporated rulings of the foremost religious dignitary of the empire, the *shaykhül-Islam* (Inalcik 1969:136; 1978, 4:560,566). This last trend did not have a counterpart in Iran, where Shi'ism had been established as the state religion in 1501.

Against this background, *qanun*, as state law, constituted the precedent for the adoption of European legal codes in the modern Middle East. *Qanun* came to refer to the codes inspired by European legislation and introduced by the state, and the constitution, as the foundation of public law, was naturally regarded as "the fundamental *qanun*." Nevertheless, owing to the alliance between the constitutionalists and some of the Shi'ite religious leaders, the "rule of law" had also been equated with Islam in the Iranian constitutionalist ideology. The Sacred Law was conceived as an unalterable fundamental law within the framework of which parliamentary legislation ought to take place. Therefore, though heavily influenced by Belgian and French models, the Iranian Constitution of 1906–7 was by no means un-Islamic. The preamble to the Fundamental Law states that the purpose of the Parliament was "to promote the progress and happiness of our kingdom and people, strengthen the foundations of our government, and give effect to the enactment of the Sacred Law of His Holiness the Prophet." Article 1 of the Supplementary Fundamental Law states that the official religion of Iran is Shi'ite Islam, and article 2 declares: "At no time must any legal enactment of the sacred National Consultative Assembly . . . be at variance with the sacred principles of Islam, or the laws established by His Holiness the Best of Mankind." Furthermore, a committee of no less than five authoritative jurists (*mujtahids*) was to be set up with veto power over parliamentary legislation to "reject and repudiate, wholly or in part, any proposal which is at variance with the sacred laws of Islam, so that it shall not obtain the title of legality. In such matters the decision of this committee of *'ulama* shall be followed and obeyed, and this article shall continue unchanged until the appearance of His Holiness the Proof of the Age [i.e., the Hidden Imam]." Finally, as in the Ottoman Constitution of 1876 (Lewis 1966:12), the duality of the traditional legal system was recognized and endorsed by article 27 of the Supplementary Fundamental Law, which stated that the judicial power "belongs to the *shar'i* courts in matters pertaining to the Sacred Law (*shar'iyyat*) and to civil courts in matters pertaining to customary law *('urfiyyat)"* (Lambton 1966:43–44).

The Shi'ite *'ulama* did participate in the legislation of the early parliaments, and their influence was reflected in some of the laws enacted in this period. For instance, the first civil code, promulgated in 1911, not only acknowledges the traditional dual judiciary system but also made the *shar'i* courts superior to the civil courts in many ways:

> *Article 146.* When there is a dispute over whether a case falls under the *shari'a* or the *'urf*, it may not be referred to a state court of law without the agreement of a competent *mujtahid.*
>
> *Article 149.* The state courts may not hear appeals from the verdicts of the *shar'i* courts. Such appeals must be referred to the assembly of *mujtahids.*
>
> (Banani 1961:77–78)

However, far from continuing unchanged until the reappearance of the Hidden Imam at the End of Time, article 2 of the Supplementary Fundamental Law soon became a dead letter, and the judiciary reforms of the 1920s and 1930s step-by-step reduced the competence of the *shar'i* courts until the civil and penal codes of 1939 and 1940 finally omitted all reference to the Sacred Law and to *shar'i* courts (Banani 1961:78–79; Greenfield 1934).

Drafting the Constitution

Khomeini's ideas on theocracy were set forth in a series of lectures published as a book in 1971. It is significant that in the book, *Islamic Government*, there is no mention of an Islamic *republic*. There is reason to believe that Khomeini considered the Islamic republic to be the appropriate form of government only for the period of transition to the truly Islamic government. In that final stage, sovereignty would belong to the hierocracy on behalf of God and there would be no room for sovereignty of the people or for the supremacy of the state as the presumed embodiment of the national will. Khomeini's project required a drastic withering of the state to an appropriate size. The judiciary system was to be desecularized and brought under the control of the hierocracy, and the jurisdiction of the state was to be restricted to matters "which are beneath the dignity of Islam to concern itself with," such as traffic regulations and the running of the economy (Personal interview with Khomeini, January 1979). The legislative branch would pass laws regarding these matters and these matters only, and the executive branch would implement them and manage the day-to-day affairs of the country. Beyond this, Khomeini had given little thought to the exact nature of a modern theocratic state.

The political and "publicistic" activities of the militant Shi'ite clerics in the 1960s and 1970s impressed on its leading elements, such as the late Ayatollahs Motahhari and Beheshti, the need for a distinct Islamic ideology. In this enterprise they were decisively aided by such Islamic "modernists" as Bazargan, Shari'ati (d. 1977), and Bani-Sadr. These modernist laymen were their masters in the art of formulating and elaborating a coherent ideology. Nevertheless, deep down the Shi'ite hierocracy was suspicious of the modernist lay ideologies and considered them somewhat contaminated by the secular ideologies of liberalism, nationalism, and socialism. This is especially true of Khomeini himself, who wanted his movement to remain purely Islamic in orientation and membership. In 1972, in a typical statement that demonstrates his resolve on the creation of a theocracy, Khomeini warned that the problems of Iran would not be solved so long as "the nation of Islam" remained attached to "these colonial schools of thought [i.e., political philosophies] and compared them to divine laws [of Islam]." The differences between the militant Shi'ite clerics and the Islamic "modernists," who variously accepted elements of nationalism, liberalism, and socialism, did not take long to surface during the revolution. The militant clerics attacked the liberal nationalists first, and then the Islamic modernists.

Already in 1978, Ayatollah Motahhari had stressed the need for vigilance lest the nationalist and liberal intellectuals attract the clerical elite as they had done during the Constitutional Revolution. In May 1979, less than five months after the revolution, the Ayatollah Beheshti considered the time ripe for openly fighting nationalism and liberal democracy in the person of Hasan Nazih, president of the Bar Association. In a speech demanding the trial of Nazih for treason, Beheshti referred to the years 1962–63, and especially June 1963, as the turning point in Iranian history at which the direction of "the pure Islamic revolution" was determined in clear contradistinction to nationalism and liberal democracy. A few months later, Beheshti incorporated this view of the militant hierocracy into the preamble to the Constitution of the Islamic Republic:

Although the Islamic way of thinking and militant clerical leadership played a major and fundamental role in [the constitutional and the

nationalist/anti-imperialist] movements, these movements rapidly dis-
integrated because they became increasingly distant from the true Islamic position.

At this point, the alert conscience of the nation, led by . . . the Grand
Ayatollah Imam Khomeini, realized the necessity of adhering to the true
ideological and Islamic path of struggle.

The plan for an Islamic Government based on the concept of the
"Governance of the Jurist" (*velayat-e faqih*), which was introduced by
Imam Khomeini . . . gave a fresh, strong incentive to the Muslim people and opened the way for a genuine ideological Islamic struggle. This
plan consolidated the efforts of those dedicated Muslims who were
fighting both at home and abroad.

As one of the most articulate representatives of the militant Shi'ite
hierocracy, Beheshti attacked "modernist" attempts to reconcile nationalism, liberal democracy, and socialism with Islam as "syncretic
thought" (*elteqati*) and presented the theory of "Governance (or Man-
date) of the Jurist," said to be the result of research by the militant
hierocracy on the issue of Islamic government since the 1960s, as the
purely Islamic alternative. There can be no doubt that Khomeini and his
followers did not have clear plans for Islamic government in the 1960s.
The only concrete proposal put forward by Khomeini in 1963 was that
the government hand over the responsibility for national education and
the pious endowments to the hierocracy and allow them a few hours on
the national radio (Bakhash 1984:32). Although Khomeini did put forward the idea of *velayat-e faqih* around 1970, as indicated in his interview with the author, he had not worked out the institutional and
constitutional implications of the idea by January 1979. It is amply clear
that he wanted the state to be subordinate to the hierocracy and that he
was firm and careful in this regard. However, he attached little significance to constitution-making and was prepared to accept in draft a
constitution approved by the cabinet and the Revolutionary Council in
June 1979 with only minor changes. In fact, he proposed to bypass the
promised constituent assembly and submit the draft directly to a referendum. It is highly significant that Bazargan and Bani-Sadr insisted on
the election of a constituent assembly while Hojjatol-Islam Hashemi-
Rafsanjani asked the latter, "Who do you think will be elected to a
constituent assembly? A fistful of ignorant and fanatic fundamentalists
who will do such damage that you will regret ever having convened
them" (ibid., pp. 74–75).

It was decided to hold elections of an Assembly of Experts on August 3, and the draft constitution instantly became the subject of debate by various secular parties and organizations. These debates alarmed Khomeini. At the end of June, he told the Shi'ite clerics that revision of the draft had to be undertaken from an Islamic perspective and was their exclusive prerogative:

> This right belongs to you. It is those knowledgeable in Islam who may express an opinion on the law of Islam. The constitution of the Islamic Republic means the constitution of Islam. Don't sit back while foreignized intellectuals, who have no faith in Islam, give their views and write the things they write. Pick up your pens and in the mosques, from the altars, in the streets and bazaars, speak of the things that in your view should be included in the constitution. (Ibid., p. 78)

And they did. At this point, a process largely independent of the personal inclination of the participating Ayatollahs was set in motion—that of working out the full logical and institutional implications of Khomeini's theocratic idea in the framework of the modern nation-state. This impersonal process, a novel rationalization of the political order (Arjomand 1985), unfolded in the form of the constitution-making of the clerically dominated Assembly of Experts, which concluded its deliberations in mid-October 1979. Their proposed draft was ratified by the referendum of December 2–3, 1979.

Theocratic Government in the Constitution of 1979

The Constitution of the Islamic Republic of Iran is an astounding document, perhaps without parallel since the writings of thirteenth-century canonistic advocates of papal monarchy and Pope Boniface VIII's bull of November 1302, *Unam Sanctam*. It places the judiciary system under the exclusive control of the hierocracy, with provision for extensive revision of the legal codes to render them Islamic. The constitution is also remarkable in being related to Qur'anic verses and to Traditions as sources of the Shi'ite sacred law in an appendix. Furthermore, putting a doctrinally new emphasis on the continuous quality of Imamate (*imamat-e mostamarr*), it endows the jurist, as the representative of the Hidden Imam, with supreme power over men and responsibility only to God. Finally, it sets up a clerically controlled Council of the Guardians (Articles 91–99) with inordinately extensive powers to represent the Shi'ite religious institution and to ensure that the legisla-

[121]

tive and executive branches of the state remain within the straitjacket tailored for it.

Fully aware of their historic mission, and considering their enterprise of global significance and importance (*Ettela'at*, 20, 22, and 29 Shahrivar 1363), the clerical members of the Assembly of Experts aired a wide variety of ideas on precisely how the *velayat-e faqih* should be implemented. The version that carried the day was the one put forward by the president of the assembly, Ayatollah Montazeri, in July 1979. Montazeri argued that, according to the Shi'ite beliefs, government and the law pertain to the "just jurists" on behalf of the Hidden Imam, of the Prophet, and of God and that therefore "the enactment of general and detailed laws" is the prerogative of the Shi'ite jurists. Furthermore, "the executive power should also be under their supervision and command, and in reality the Executive are their [the religious jurists'] representatives and not independent. Judging is also the right of the jurist or whoever is appointed by him. Therefore, the three powers—the legislative, the executive, and the judiciary—are interlinked and are not separated, and all three lead to the just jurist" (Izadi 1980:275–276).

Montazeri's ideas on the implementation of theocracy shaped the constitution drawn up by the clerically dominated Assembly of Experts. Its central idea was enunciated in the preamble as "governance of the Just *Faqih*":

> In keeping with the principle of governance (*velayat-e amr*) and the continuous (*mostamarr*) Imamate, the Constitution provides for the establishment of leadership by a *faqih* possessing the necessary qualifications and recognized as leader of the people. This is in accordance with the Tradition "The conduct of affairs is to be in the hands of those who are learned concerning God and are trustworthy guardians of that which he has permitted and that which he has forbidden." Such leadership will prevent any deviation by the various organs of government from their essential Islamic duties.

The idea was translated into law as follows:

> *Article 5.* During the Occultation of the Lord of the Age (may God hasten his renewed manifestation!), the governance (*velayat-e amr*) and leadership (*imamat*) of the community of believers devolve upon the just and pious *faqih* who is acquainted with the circumstances of his age; courageous, resourceful, and possessed of administrative ability; and recognized and accepted as leader by the majority of the people. In the event that no *faqih* should be so recognized by the majority, the leader,

or the Leadership Council, composed of *fuqaha* possessing the afore-
mentioned qualifications, will assume these responsibilities in accordance with Article 107.

Article 107. Whenever one of the *fuqaha* possessing the qualifications
specified in Article 5 of the Constitution is recognized and accepted as
marjaʿ and leader by a decisive majority of the people—as has been the
case with the exalted *marjaʿ-i taqlid* (source of emulation) and leader of
the revolution, the Grand Ayatollah Imam Khomeini—he is to exercise
governance and all the responsibilities arising therefrom. If such should
not be the case, experts elected by the people will review and consult
among themselves concerning all persons qualified to act as *marjaʿ* and
leader. If they discern outstanding capacity for leadership in a certain
marjaʿ, they will present him to the people as their leader; if not, they
will appoint either three or five *marjaʿ*s possessing the necessary qualifications for leadership and present them as members of the Leadership
Council.

Article 110. The leadership is to be assigned the following duties and
powers:
a. appointment of the *fuqaha* on the Council of Guardians;
b. appointment of the supreme judicial authority of the country;
c. supreme command of the armed forces, exercised in the following
    manner:
    (i)   appointment and dismissal of the chief of the general staff;
    (ii) appointment and dismissal of the commander-in-chief of the
          Corps of Guards of the Islamic Revolution;
    (iii) the formation of a Supreme National Defense Council, com-
          posed of the following seven members:
          the President
          the Prime Minister
          the minister of defense
          the chief of the general staff
          the commander-in-chief of the Corps of Guards of the Islamic
          Revolution
          two advisers appointed by the leader
    (iv) appointment of the supreme commanders of the three branches
          of the armed forces, based upon the recommendation of the
          Supreme National Defense Council;
    (v)   the declaration of war and peace, and the mobilization of the
          armed forces, based on the recommendation of the Supreme
          National Defense Council;
d. signing the decree [formalizing the election] of the President of the
    Republic after his election by the people. The suitability of candi-
    dates for the presidency of the Republic, with respect to the qualifica-
    tions specified in the Constitution, must be confirmed before elec-

tions take place by the Council of Guardians, and, in the case of the first term, by the leadership.

e. dismissal of the President of the Republic, with due regard for the interests of the country, after the issue of a judgment by the Supreme Court convicting him of failure to fulfill his legal duties, or a vote of the National Consultative Assembly testifying to his political incompetence;

f. pardoning or reducing the sentences of convicts, within the bounds of Islamic criteria, after receiving a recommendation [to that effect] from the Supreme Court.

On the issue of legislation, Montazeri and the clerics were prepared to compromise over their alleged right to enact "general and detailed laws" with the democratic principle of popular sovereignty. The legislature was to consist of a popularly elected parliament, the Majlis. Its legislation, however, was conditional upon the approval of the Council of Guardians and, materially, of the clerics in that Council:

Article 91. In order to protect the ordinances of Islam and the Constitution by assuring that legislation passed by the National Consultative Assembly does not conflict with them, a council to be known as the Council of Guardians is to be established with the following composition:

a. six just *fuqaha*, conscious of current needs and the issues of the day, to be selected by the leader or the Leadership Council; and

b. six jurists, specializing in different areas of law, to be elected by the National Consultative Assembly from among the Muslim jurists presented to it by the Supreme Judicial Council.

Article 96. The determination of whether legislation passed by the National Consultative Assembly is compatible with the ordinances of Islam depends on a majority vote by the *fuqaha* on the Council of Guardians; and the determination that it is compatible with the Constitution requires a majority vote by all members of the Council of Guardians.

Article 98. The interpretation of the Constitution is the responsibility of the Council of Guardians, and depends on the approval of three-fourths of its members.

It is interesting to note that there is no mention of the principle of consultation (*shura*) or democracy as a defining characteristic of the Islamic Republic. The principle of *shura* makes its appearance only in Article 7. The commentator Madani explains the subsidiary role of consultation (*Sorush*, no. 175, January 1, 1983, p. 41). The principle of consultation is accepted, but as a subsidiary to the principle of Imamate. "Islamic consultation is possible only when Imamate is dominant. In other words, consultation is at the service of Imamate." The Qur'anic verse III:153 (*wa shawirhum fi'l-amr* etc.) is said to imply that the actual decision-maker is the Prophet, who was also the Imam. The commentator adds that the advocates of the *shura* during the drafting of the constitution either did not firmly believe in Islam or were contaminated by "syncretic" thinking and were trying "to link the *shura* to the principle of national sovereignty."

Conclusion

As we have seen, the clerical constitution-makers of 1979 not only claimed the judiciary prerogatives and supervisory power over legislation reserved for them in the constitution of 1906–7 with a vengeance, but also added to it their novel clericalist claim: the right to rule on behalf of God. It is this last claim, embodied under the rubric of "Governance of the Jurist" into the articles on leadership (articles 5 and 107–112), which makes the theocratic Constitution of the Islamic Republic of Iran unique in the constitutional history of the Middle East. To appreciate this uniqueness fully, it is instructive to compare Iran's Constitution of 1979 with the 1956 and 1962 constitutions of the Islamic state of Pakistan. The Pakistani constitutions contained the famous "Repugnancy Clause," which stated that no law should be enacted "which is repugnant to the Holy *Qur'an* and the *Sunnah* [Tradition of the Prophet]." The provisions made to enforce this article in the 1956 constitution were vague, and the Constitution of 1962 set up an Advisory Council of Islamic Ideology appointed by the president. In January 1953, while the draft constitution was being intensely debated, the *'ulama* of Pakistan demanded that the religious jurists determine the issue of "repugnancy to Islam." They proposed that "there should be appointed five *'ulama* in the Supreme Court who, along with some judge to be nominated for the purpose by the Head of the State in consideration of his *tadayyun* and *taqwa* (religiosity and God-fearing piety) and his knowledge of Islamic law and learning, should decide whether or not the law in dispute is in conformity with the Qur'an and the Sunnah" (Mawdudi 1960:371). It is interesting to note that even this demand would have made the Pakistani constitution comparable only to the Iranian Constitution of 1907, but in no way could it match the theocratic Constitution of 1979.

This is hardly surprising. The prolonged process of constitution-making in Pakistan was dominated not by the *'ulama* but by the secular political elite. In his comments on the draft constitution of 1956, the leader of the *Jama 'at-e Islami*, Mawlana Abu'l-A'la Mawdudi, even took a step back from the *'ulama's* position in 1953. Mawdudi's position was remarkably secular in retrospective comparison with the Iranian Constitution of 1979. The recommendation of the conference of *'ulama* in January 1953, he maintained, was still the best solution to the issue of repugnancy of laws to Islam, which "should be decided by the Supreme Court, and for the first 10 or 15 years five *'ulama* should be appointed to help the Supreme Court in deciding such disputes. Anyhow, if the members of the Constituent Assembly are not at all prepared to accept this proposal then *the only acceptable solution is to leave it to the decision of the majority of the total number of Muslim members of the Legislature*" (ibid., p. 401; emphasis in the original).

The clerical rulers of Iran interpret the uniqueness of the theocratic Constitution of 1979 to mean that it is the first and so far the only true Islamic constitution designed to implement the rule of God on earth within the framework of modern nation-states. They are silent over its roots in the distinctive clericalism of Shi'ism, which is not shared by Sunni Islam, and present it as a universal blueprint for Islamic government throughout the world. Whether the Islamic militants of other countries accept this claim and are likely to incorporate it into the goals of their Islamic revolutions is for the future to determine.

REFERENCES

Algar, H., Trans. 1980. *Constitution of the Islamic Republic of Iran.* Berkeley, Calif.
Arjomand, S. A. 1984. *The Shadow of God and the Hidden Imam.* Chicago.
———. 1985. "Religion, Political Order, and Societal Change: With Special Reference to Shiite Islam." *Current Perspectives in Social Theory* 4:1–15.
———. 1988. *The Turban for the Crown: The Islamic Revolution in Iran.* New York and Oxford.
Bakhash, S. 1984. *The Reign of the Ayatollahs.* New York.
Banani, A. 1961. *The Modernization of Iran, 1921–1941.* Stanford, Calif.
Coulson, N. J. 1969. *Conflict and Tension in Islamic Jurisprudence.* Chicago.
Encyclopedia of Islam. 1954 to present. 2d ed. 6 vols. to date. Leiden.
Geertz, C. 1983. *Local Knowledge: Further Essays in Interpretative Anthropology.* New York.
Goitein, S. D. 1968. "A Turning-Point in the History of the Muslim State." In S. D. Goitein, *Studies in Islamic History and Institutions.* Leiden.
Goldziher, I. 1971. *Muslim Studies.* 2 vols. London.

Greenfield, J. 1934. "Die geistlichen Schariegerichte in Persia und die moderne Gesetzgebung." *Zeitschrift für Vergleichende Rechtswissenschaft* 48:157–167.

Inalcik, H. 1978. "KANUN; Financial and Public Administration." In *Encyclopedia of Islam*, 2d ed., vol. 4:558–562. Leiden, 1954 to present.

———. 1978. "KANUNNAME." In *Encyclopedia of Islam*, 2d ed., vol. 4:562–566. Leiden, 1954 to present.

———. 1969. "Suleiman the Lawgiver and Ottoman Law." *Archivum Ottomanicum* 1:105–138.

Izadi, M. 1980. *Gozari bar Zendegi va Andiseh-ha-ye Ayatollah Montazeri*. Tehran.

Khadduri, M. 1966. "Egypt." In *DUSTUR: A Survey of the Constitutions of the Arab and Muslim States*. Reprinted with additional material from *Encyclopedia of Islam*, 2d ed. (Leiden, 1965).

Khomeini, R. 1971. *Hukumat-e Islami*. Najaf and Tehran.

Lambton, A. K. S. 1966. "Iran." In *DUSTUR: A Survey of the Constitutions of the Arab and Muslim States*. Reprinted with additional material from *Encyclopedia of Islam*, 2d ed. (Leiden, 1965).

Lewis, B. 1966. "Turkey." In *DUSTUR: A Survey of the Constitutions of the Arab and Muslim States*. Reprinted with additional material from *Encyclopedia of Islam*, 2d ed. (Leiden, 1965).

Linant De Bellefonds, Y. 1978. "KANUN; Law." *Encyclopedia of Islam*. 2d ed. Vol. 4:556–557. Leiden, 1954 to present.

Mawdudi, A. 1960. *Islamic Law and Constitution*. 2d ed. Trans. and ed. Khurshid Ahmad. Karachi and Lahore, Pakistan.

Rosen, L. 1980–81. "Equity and Discretion in the Modern Islamic Legal System." *Law and Society Review* 14:217–245.

Schacht, J. 1935. "Zur soziologischen Betrachtung des Islamischen Rechts." *Der Islam* 22:207–238.

———. 1950. *The Origins of Muhammadan Jurisprudence*. Oxford.

Udovitch, A. 1985. "Islamic Law and the Social Context of Exchange in the Medieval Middle East." *History and Anthropology* 1:445–465.

Wakin, J. 1972. *Function of Documents in Islamic Law*. Albany, N.Y.

Weber, M. 1978. *Economy and Society*, ed. G. Roth and C. Wittich. Berkeley and Los Angeles.

PART II

Exporting and Extending Legal Orders

[5]

Law and the Colonial State in India

Bernard S. Cohn

In the second half of the eighteenth century, the East India Company had to create a state through which it could administer the rapidly expanding territories acquired by conquest or accession. The invention of such a state was without precedent in British constitutional history. The British colonies in North America and the Caribbean had from their inception forms of governance that were largely an extension of the basic political and legal institutions of Great Britain. The colonizing populations, even when drawn from dissident political and religious groups in Great Britain, still were thought of as English or British. The laws of these colonies were the laws of Great Britain.

The indigenous populations encountered in North America were quickly subjugated, relocated, or decimated, and even though there continued to be, from the colonial perspective, a "native" problem, it was a military and political one, requiring little in the way of legal or administrative innovation. In the Caribbean colonies, the indigenous population had all but been destroyed before British sovereignty was established, and the basic form of production through the plantations worked with enslaved labor was largely responsible for the maintenance of law and order. For the whites, the system of governance was much like that of the North American colonies. Only in Ireland, and to a lesser extent in Wales and Scotland, did the British face a colonial problem that required innovation. The solution in Ireland was the establishment of a Protestant landholding elite, with the virtual creation of plantations that a depressed Catholic peasantry provided with labor and rents.

Creating Instrumentalities of Rule in Colonial India

In all the British overseas Colonies, at least until 1776, there was little debate concerning the role of the Crown and Parliament and about the basic jural and legal institutions of rule. Debates in Great Britain and raised overseas by white colonists shared a common discourse, were based on assumptions about the nature of the state and society, and could be encompassed within the existing institutions of rule. The constitutional and legal issues presented by the emergence of the East India Company, a major territorial power in India after the Battle of Plassey in 1757, could not simply be analogized to existing colonial experience. A whole new set of issues, for which there was no precedent, presented themselves. The issues included questions about the nature of sovereignty in India. Generally speaking, most of the British who were concerned with India agreed that India had a state system—which by the middle of the eighteenth century was in decline and disarray but which had recognizable institutions and functions of a state. They also agreed that the peoples of India, unlike the Indians and slaves of the New World, had an ancient civilization and forms of local self-governance that were stable and deeply entrenched. The sheer size of the eastern territories and the huge numbers of people becoming subjects of the East India Company were seen as signs that some of the existing state forms should be adopted. The key resources of India were the products of labor, not natural ones, and they involved a well-developed market system. In Bengal and parts of South India, the East India Company had succeeded in acquiring control of the financial resources of the state in the form of taxes, through which they could acquire commodities for export and support the buildup of military power to defend their territories from Indian and French adversaries. The East India Company had over time acquired many of the attributes of a state, in European terms. It could wage war, make peace, raise taxes, and administer justice to its own employees and to increasing numbers of Indians who inhabited the territories in which the company was acting as the sovereign.

Debate centered on the question of whether a private company that was exercising state functions could do so on the basis of royal grants and charters. What responsibilities did such a private company have for the well-being and prosperity of its subjects? These and many subsidiary issues were to be argued and to become central political issues from 1760 to 1790. By 1785, a dual principle of sovereignty had been established. The East India Company could administer its territories in its own name for the profit of its stockholders—but under regulations passed by Parliament, which would periodically review the adequacy of the company's system of governance in India. Although employees of the company owed allegiance to the British Crown, the natives of India—be they peasant or territorial rulers allied to the East India Company—did not. The company claimed its legitimacy in India from grants received or extracted from Indian rulers—for example, the grant *Dewani* of Bengal in 1765, which made the company the responsible agent for assessment and collection of the revenues of Bengal. Concerns with constitutional questions, at home and in India, and with the construction of legitimacy that would enable the company to act as the state, were complex and difficult, but it was the pragmatics of building its administrative instrumentalities of rulership that were to engage those in India who were most directly concerned with the management of the company's territories.

In 1765 Clive wrote to his employers, the Court of Directors of the East India Company, informing them of the Mughal's grant of the *Dewani* of Bengal and claiming that the company "now became the Sovereigns of a rich and potent kingdom" and that they were not only the "collectors but the proprietors of the nawab's revenues." The directors' response to this news was less than enthusiastic, because they believed that Englishmen were "unfit to conduct the collection of revenues and to follow the subtle native through all his arts, to conceal the real value of his country, to perplex and elude the payments" (Srinivasachari 1962:184). Instead, the Directors envisioned their British servants supervising the collection and spending the revenues. There was a contradiction in what they were recommending, since the assessment and collection of land revenue was a complex and difficult job and in the hands of Indian specialists. If the British could not master the details of the revenue system, they would be dependent on those "subtle natives," who could "perplex" them at every turn. When in 1772 the British attempted to control their Indian subordinates by going into the "field," it was, as a modern historian has written, "a journey into the unknown. . . . At every step they came up against quasi feudal rights

[133]

and obligations which defied any interpretation in familiar Western terms. The hieroglyphics of Persian estate accounts baffled them. . . . they could not easily master the language in which ancient and medieval texts relating to the laws of property were written; for tradition recorded only in memory and customs embedded in a variety of local usages wielded an authority equal to that of any written code" (Guha 1963:13).

In the British cultural system, the capacity to assess taxes was inextricably linked with law. The courts established and protected property rights and were the instrument for enforcing payment of the "King's share of the revenue." The British in India initially tried to find who "owned" the land, so that person could be made responsible for payment of revenue. In theory this seemed simple, but in practice, as Guha suggests, it was fraught with difficulties. Forms of knowledge that would enable the foreign rulers to frame regulations that would guarantee their obtaining what they thought was the just share of the surplus of agricultural production had to be acquired or created. After 1765, the British so badly managed the task of assessing and collecting land revenue that within five years they found that their actions had caused a horrendous famine, in which they estimated that a third of the population of Bengal had died. The famine left in its wake large tracts of land that were uncultivated and rapidly turning into wasteland. Hence they added to their perplexing efforts to create information a theoretical set of questions about how best to revive agricultural production in Bengal. Both the famine and the revenue policies of the British also led to a breakdown in law and order; roving gangs (*dacoits*) began to prey on a helpless peasantry and to disrupt trade.

Hastings and the Redefinition of Traditional Forms of Authority and Rule

Warren Hastings, who had a successful career in India as a commercial and diplomatic agent for the East India Company, was appointed in 1772, under a new parliamentary act, to the newly created position of governor-general and was instructed by the Court of Directors to place the governance of the Bengal territories on a stable footing. Hastings had to contend both with Indian complexities and British venality. Since 1757, appointments to the East India Company's service in Bengal were viewed as means of quickly attaining a fortune and, on return to England, the life of a successful country gentleman. He was also constrained by a cumbersome form of government by a council of five, of which Hastings was in effect only first among equals.

The crucial actor in Hastings' plan for the better administration of Bengal was to be a British officer designated a "collector." The collector would have mixed executive and judicial powers in a defined area, a "district," whose boundaries followed preexisting Mughal revenue units termed *circars*, which were the constitutent units of the subas (provinces). Hastings had invented the emblematic figure of British imperialism who was to appear in Africa, Southeast Asia, and the Southwest Pacific, the man on the spot who knew "the natives," who was to represent the forces of "law and order."

The premise of Hastings' plan was the idea that during the seventeenth century the Mughals had an effective administrative structure, clearly not based on European principles, but nonetheless consonant with Indian theory and practice. He was also aware that during the previous fifty years in Bengal this system had all but crumbled under almost constant warfare, maladministration, the growth of local chieftains who had usurped imperial powers, and the privatization of public offices.

Having been a scholar at Westminster, Hastings brought to his task a good "classical" European education. Perhaps more important for the first fifteen years of his career, even though concerned with the East India Company's trading activities, he was stationed up-country near the court of the last of the effective nawabs of Bengal. There he acquired first-hand knowledge of how an Indian state functioned and could not totally share the prevalent British ideas that Indian rulers were despotic, corrupt, and extortionate. He believed that Indian knowledge and experience as embodied in the varied textual traditions of the Hindus and Muslims were revelant for developing British administrative institutions.

One of the first Persian works to be translated into English was the *Ain-i-Akbari,* by Abul Fazal, an "account of the mode of governing" under the most illustrious of the Mughal emperors, Akbar. The account is part prescriptive and part descriptive. It contains the rules and regulations by which the Mughal court governed, but it also offered detailed discussions of the properties of a good ruler, vivid accounts of the varieties of animals kept by the king, of how to lay out a camp, and of how jewels and other valuable items were classified. Also included were what the British thought of as more practical matters—the regulations of the judicial and executive departments, a survey of the lands, and a "rent

[135]

roll" of the Mughal empire (Davies 1935:65–72; Feiling 1966:92–107; Marshall 1973; Blochmann 1965 (1873):v–ix).

Hastings encouraged a group of younger servants of the East India Company to study the "classical" languages of India—Sanskrit, Persian, and Arabic—as part of a scholarly and pragmatic project aimed at creating a body of knowledge that could be utilized in the effective control of Indian society. He was trying to help the British define what was "Indian" and to create a system of rule that would be congruent with what were thought to be indigenous institutions. Yet this system of rule was to be run by Englishmen and had to take into account British ideas of justice and the proper discipline, forms of deference, and demeanor that should mark the relations between rulers and ruled. According to one of his biographers, Hastings "had to modify and adapt the old to fit English ideas and standards. He had to produce a piece of machinery that English officials could operate and English opinion tolerate . . . to graft Western notions and methods on to the main stem of Eastern Institutions" (Davies 1935:71).

However these tasks were to be accomplished, they had to pass the basic test applied by the owners of the East India Company—that the administration should produce a fixed and regular return in the form of revenue, which was to pay all the expenses of the colonial state as well as provide a profit for the investors. Throughout the history of the company and its successor, the Imperial Government of India, the best indicator of efficiency of the administration was its capacity to collect 100 percent of the assessed revenues. The British logic of administration rested on the capacity to classify actions into prefixed domains. If payment were made in cash or in kind by an agriculturalist to a superior, who appeared to have "rights" to the land, these payments were "rent," the receiver was a "landlord," and the payer was a "tenant." If the receiver of payments appeared to have a political function, maintained an army, provided protection, supported religious institutions, and displayed emblems of sovereignty, then the payments were taxes and the relationship constituted that of ruler and subject.

Hastings's "collector," in addition to his executive functions as a tax collector, was to preside over two courts. One, which dealt with revenue and civil litigation and followed Hastings's understandings of Mughal practice, was called the court of *Dewani;* the other, which dealt with internal order and criminal law, was called the *Faujdari* court. The substantive law to be administered in the *Dewani* court was Hindu law for Hindus and Muslim law for Muslims. In the *Faujdari* courts the law to administer was "Muslim" criminal law; in the *Dewani* courts the collector was to preside along with his Indian assistant, the *Dewan*. Sitting as a judge, the collector, was to establish the "facts" in the case based on testimony, usually in the form of depositions from witnesses, and the documentary evidence was placed before the court. The *Dewan* and a Hindu law officer (*pandit*) were to find the "law" that was applicable to the case. If the dispute to be adjudicated involved Muslims, the law that applied was to be determined by a Muslim law officer (*maulavi*). It was assumed that in both traditions there were legal texts that were in effect "codes," which were known and could be interpreted by legal specialists (usually referred to by the British as "law professors") who could provide authoritative decisions on the particular sections of the codes that applied. In stressing the importance of using "Indian law," as it could be objectified out of textual traditions, Hastings was rejecting the prevalent European theory that the Indian state was despotic.

India as Lawless: The Despotic Model

The word "despot" is derived from a Greek word applied to the head of a household, and from this point of view, to govern despotically was to rule "as a master over a slave." By extension, to the Greeks, despotism meant arbitrary rule, and Aristotle "made this extended meaning apply specifically to certain governments, in which legitimate royal power was intrinsically the same as master over slave" (Koebner 1951:276).

Alexander Dow, an East India Company servant, prefaced his translation of Ferishta's *History of Hindostan,* a history of the Muslim conquerors of India published in 1770–72 by writing:

> The history now given to the public, presents us with a striking picture of the deplorable condition of a people subjected to arbitrary sway; and of the instability of empire itself, when it is founded neither on law, nor upon the opinions and attachments of mankind. . . . In a government like that of India, public spirit is never seen, and loyalty a thing unknown. The people permit themselves to be transferred from one tyrant to another, without murmuring; and individuals look with unconcern upon the miseries of others, if they are capable to screen themselves from the general misfortune. This, however, is a picture of Hindostan in bad times, and under the worst Kings. As arbitrary government can inflict the most sudden miseries, so, when in the hand of good men, it can administer the most expeditious relief to the subject. We accord-

[137]

ingly find in this history, that the misfortunes of half an age of tyranny, are removed in a few years, under the mild administration of a virtuous prince. (Dow 1772, 1:xi)

Dow, and other English historians as well, stressed that the arbitrariness of the political order caused the salient characteristic of despotism to become the insecurity of property. The British believed that the Mughal emperor "owned" all the land of Hindustan and could distribute in the form of grants and *jagirs* to support the military nobility (*Omrah* or *Amirs*) throughout their lifetime or during his lifetime. They also believed that at the death of the emperor or a noble the land escheated to the Throne (but Dow recognized that in many cases such grants were renewed and given to a son of the holder). They understood that some of the Hindu kingdoms, such as those ruled by the Rajputs in western India, were in effect held in perpetuity by ruling families as subjects of the Mughals and was confirmed by payment of an annual tribute.

As with property, so also with honors. The Mughal emperor was thought to be the sole source of all honors in the state. These honors were not hereditary, as they usually were in England. They lasted only for the lifetime of the person to whom they were granted. The British believed that this prevented development of a status group in the polity that could check the arbitrary power of the emperor, as in European states. In the model of the Mughal empire created by the British, there were no primogeniture for inheriting the throne (*masnad*), and each succession of a Mughal was accompanied by a bloody war. "The power of disposing of the succession naturally belongs to a despot. During his life, his pleasure is the law. When he dies his authority ceases" (ibid., 2:xxxiii). The Mughal might nominate one of his sons, not necessarily the oldest, but the son must still fight for the throne. A "prince must die by clemency, or wade through the blood of his family to safety and Empire" (ibid., 3:xxxv).

Although it was recognized that there was "law" in India, that "law" was believed to be different from the European kind. Because the government was seen as based on "no other principle than the will of one [the Mughal]," the law was based upon his will, and hence, argued Orme (1805), there could not be "any absolute laws in its constitution; for these would often interfere with that will." Orme believed that in 1752 there were "no digests or codes of laws existing in Indostan: The Tartars who conquered this country could scarcely read or write; and when they found it impossible to convert them to Mohammedanism left

[138]

the Hindus at liberty to follow their own religion. To both these peoples (the lords and slaves of this empire), custom and religion have given all the regulations at this time observed in Indostan. . . . Every province has fifty sects of Hindus; and every sect adheres to different observances" (ibid., p. 437). The British realized that there were a large number of judicial officials in India, and a regular system of courts, with the Mughal's *darbar* (court) at the top, and that redress was always open to the subjects of the emperor by going to his court to seek justice. But the courts found in the country were thought to be "extremely venal." Orme described the process of the administration of justice thus:

> The plaintiff discovers himself by crying aloud, Justice! Justice! until attention is given to his importunate clamours. He is then ordered to be silent, and to advance before his judge; to whom, after having prostrated himself, and made his offering of a piece of money, he tells his story in the plainest manner, with great humility of voice and gesture, and without any of those oratorical embellishments which compose an art in freer nations.
>
> The wealth, the consequence, the interest, or the address of the party, become now the only considerations. . . . The friends who can influence, intercede; and, excepting where the case is so manifestly proved as to brand the failure of redress with glaring infamy (a restraint which human nature is born to reverence) the value of the bribe ascertains the justice of the cause.
>
> Still the forms of justice subsist; witnesses are heard; but brow-beaten and removed: proofs of writing produced; but deemed forgeries and rejected, until the way is cleared for a decision, which becomes totally or partially favourable, in proportion to the methods which have been used to render it such. . . .
>
> The quickness of decisions which prevails in Indostan, as well as in all other despotic governments, ought no longer to be admired. As soon as the judge is ready, everything that is necessary is ready: there are no tedious briefs or cases, no various interpretations of an infinity of laws, no methodized forms, and no harangues to keep the parties longer in suspense.
>
> Providence has, at particular seasons, blessed the miseries of these people with the presence of a righteous judge. The vast reverence and reputation which such have acquired, are but too melancholy a proof of the infrequency of such a character. (Ibid., pp. 443–446)

In summary, the model of the Mughal-Indian political system was absolute and arbitrary power, unchecked by any institution, social or political and resting in the person of the emperor, with property and honors

[139]

derived solely from the will of the despotic ruler. There were no fixed rules of inheritance and, above all, no primogeniture; succession to the throne was based on an inevitable struggle among the sons of the emperor. Justice was dependent not on the rule of law but on the rule of men, who could be influenced by money, status, and connection in the exercise of their office of judge.

The idea that India had been ruled by "despots" was revalorized in the nineteenth and twentieth centuries as one of several ruling paradigms that formed the ideological infrastructure of British rule in India. In its cleaned-up version it was expressed thus: Indians are best ruled by a "strong hand," who could administer justice in a rough-and-ready fashion unfettered by rules and regulations. The courts, their procedures, their regulations, and the propensity of Indians to perjury and to the suborning of witnesses only served to delay justice and made the simple peasant folk of India the prey of the urban-based lawyers, merchants, and agitators. This would lead to the alienation of the "natural" loyalty the masses always felt for the strong, benevolent despot. As benevolent despots, the British were to appear in several forms—as "platonic guardians," as patriarchs habitually addressed by the simple folk as *"ma-bap"* (mother and father), as authoritarian rationalist utilitarians, and in times of crisis as the not-so-benevolent Old Testament avengers (Iyer 1960; Wurgaft 1983:17–53; Hutchins 1967:17–153).

India as a Theocracy: Classical Models of the Indian State

Simultaneously with the development of the despotic model, Hastings and some of his associates in Calcutta were elaborating a countermodel of India as a theocratic state. This model included established and highly detailed codes of conduct that had the power of law and had already been worked out in the ancient era (as far as Hindus were concerned) and since the time of the Prophet in the Sacred Law (for Muslims). For both Hindu and Muslim law there were extensive bodies of texts and commentaries and sophisticated legal specialists who were the maintainers, expositors, and interpreters of these legal traditions.

In 1772 and 1773 a parliamentary committee was investigating the affairs of the East India Company and trying to decide what institutions of governance were most appropriate for restoring law, order, and prosperity to the company's territories. In this context, influenced by the

"India as despotic" theory, it was argued that because *there was no law* in India, British law and institutions should be introduced into the vacuum. On hearing these reports, Hastings lobbied influential members of the Court of Directors and Parliament to prevent this, arguing that British law was too technical, too complicated, and totally inappropriate for conditions in India. He declared that the "ancient constitution" of Bengal was very much intact (Gleig 1841, 1:273,401). Writing to the Lord Chief Justice in 1774, Hastings denied the validity of the idea that India was ruled by nothing more than "arbitrary wills, or uninstructed judgements, or their temporary rulers" and the notion that "written laws are totally unknown to the Hindoos, or original inhabitants of Hindostan" (ibid., p. 400). The Hindus, Hastings averred, "had been in possession of laws which continued unchanged, from remotest antiquity." These laws were known to the Brahmins ("professors of law," found all over India) and supported by "public endowments and benefactions." These professors received a "degree of personal respect amounting almost to idolatry" (ibid.). This attitude of reverence for the Brahmin specialists in law was so entrenched that it was left unmolested even by Muslim governments.

The logic of Hastings's model of Hindu law read as "an ancient constitution" required that it be made accessible to the British who now were sitting as judges in the civil courts and would have to pass judgment on disputes "concerning property, whether real or personal, all cases of inheritance, marriage and caste; all claims of debt, disputed accounts, contracts, partnerships and demands of rent" (Great Britain, House of Commons 1772–73, 4:348). Some way to authoritatively establish the content of Hindu law to be administered in the East India Company's district courts had to be found. To this end, Hastings persuaded "eleven of the most respectable pandits in Bengal" to compile from the Shastric literature on Hindu law a code that could be translated into English for the newly appointed judges to use. Because at the time there was no European in Calcutta who knew Sanskrit, the compilation by the pandits was translated first into Persian and then from Persian into English. As if this chain of translations is not tortuous enough, the Persian translation was done by a Bengali Muslim, who would discuss in Bengali with one of the pandits the passages being translated and then gloss them into Persian. The English translation from the Persian was by a young civil servant, H. B. Halhed, and published in London in 1776 as *A Code of Gentoo Laws or Ordinations of the Pundits* (R. Rocher 1983:51). In his preface, Halhed described how the work had been produced:

[141]

The professors of the ordinances here collected still speak the original language in which they were composed, and which is entirely unknown to the bulk of the people, who have settled upon those professors several great endowments and benefactions in all parts of Hindostan, and pay them besides a degree of personal respect little short of idolatry, in return for the advantages supposed to be derived from their studies. A set of the most experienced of these lawyers was selected from every part of Bengal for the purpose of compiling the present work, which they picked out sentence by sentence from various originals in the Sanscript [*sic*] language, neither adding to, nor diminishing any part of the ancient text. The articles thus collected were next translated literally into Persian, under the inspection of one of their own body; and from that translation were rendered into English with an equal attention to the closeness and fidelity of the version. (Halhed 1776:x)

The original compilation in Sanskrit was termed *vivadarnavasetu*, "bridge across the sea of litigation," and was circulated in Persian, Sanskrit, and English version and used in the East India Company's courts until the early nineteenth century (Derrett 1968:240–241). The two leading scholars of the code disagree about its relationship to the legal traditions of eighteenth-century Bengal. Derrett (ibid., p. 240) argues that the topics covered—"Debt, Inheritance, Civil Procedure, Deposits, Sales of Strangers' Property, Partnership, Gift, Slavery, Master and Servant, Rent and Hire, Sale, Boundaries, Shares in Cultivation of Lands, Cities, and Towns and Fines for Damaging Crops, Defamation, Assault, Theft, Violence, Adultery, Duties of Women"—were topics Hastings believed would be useful in the district courts. He also asserts that the order in which the sections appear "does not correspond with anything known to the usual Shastric texts" (ibid., p. 241), that the pundits were working on a list of topics supplied by Hastings (ibid., p. 241).

In a recently published detailed study of Halhed's career, Rosane Rocher (1983:51) argues that the Sanskrit version of the code was a "traditional compilation of the *Nibandha* type, i.e. excerpts from a variety of authoritative sources, and extensive commentary." She attributes the difference between her interpretation and Derrett's to the fact that his was based on the English version of the code, which does not accurately reflect the Sanskrit original (ibid., p. 65, n. 20). The enduring significance of Halhed's translation has much less to do with the further development of the East India Company's legal system than with its role in establishing Indological Studies in Europe, where the work was read in English and in translation in French and German, for information about the "mysterious" Hindus.

In his preface to the translation of the Gentoo Code, Halhed makes it clear that his interests were not primarily legal, but concerned more with explicating Hindu thought, religion, and customs in relation to establishing a policy of toleration, on the part of the British toward the conquered Indians. Halhed held up the model of the Romans, "who not only allowed to their foreign subjects the free exercise of their own religion and the administration of their own civil jurisdiction, but sometimes, by a policy still more flattering, even naturalized parts of the mythology of the conquered, as were in any respect compatible with their own system" (Halhed 1776:ix). Halhed's reference to Roman imperial policy adumbrates the next phase of British efforts to find a basis for their legal system with respect to Hindu personal law in the work of Sir William Jones.

Sir William Jones (1746–1794), a classical scholar who studied Persian and Arabic at Oxford and qualified as a barrister, had by the time of his appointment to the Crown Court in Calcutta, in 1783, published a number of translations of Arabic and Persian works and written one of the first modern Persian grammars. In addition, he had an active political career and was a major intellectual figure of the time (Mukherjee 1968; Cannon 1964). Jones had long lobbied his political friends for an appointment as a judge in India, which he hoped would provide him with financial security and the opportunity to further his orientalist studies. He originally did not think he would learn Sanskrit because he was too old, but as he began his judicial career in India he found that Halhed's code was badly marred—"rather more curious than useful" (see Cannon 1970, 2:797). There were Persian translations of some Sanskrit legal texts, but Jones believed these were defective too. He was therefore at the mercy of "native" lawyers, as were the other British judges, and he determined to learn the rudiments of that "venerable and interesting language," Sanskrit, in order that the "stream of Hindu law remain pure" (ibid., pp. 666–680). By 1786, Jones felt his Sanskrit was good enough that he could decide between differing opinions of his pandits by reading the "original tracts" and pronouncing whose interpretation of the law was correct (ibid., p. 718).

Shortly after his arrival in India, Jones sent Edmund Burke, the leading critic of the administration of the East India Company in Bengal, his ideas for the "Best Practicable System of Judicature" (ibid., pp. 643–644, n. 1). British law, Jones wrote to Burke, could not become the law

[143]

of India because that would be counter to the very nature of an established legal system. There was no doubt in Jones's mind that British law was superior to the law existing in India, but even "a system of *liberty*, forced upon a people invincibly attached to opposite *habits*, would in truth be a system of tyranny." The system of judicature "affecting the natives of Bengal" had to be based on the "Old Mogul constitution." The basis of the law to be administered in the company's court should be digests of "Hindu and Mahomedan laws" compiled by "*Conogos* [keepers of land records] and *Maulavis* and *Pandits*," whom Jones (and most of the British at the time) considered to be a combination of legal scholars and practicing lawyers. There should be attached to the East India Company's court "native interpreters of the respective laws," but the honesty and competence of these interpreters had to be guaranteed by careful selection and by pay adequate to place them above temptation. The British judges, however, had to be in a position to be able to "check upon the native interpreters." This was to be accomplished through the "learning and vigilance" of the British judges. "The laws of the natives must be preserved inviolate," and the decrees of the courts must be conformable to Hindu or Mahomedan law" (ibid., pp. 643–644).

If the system Jones hoped to see implemented was to succeed, it would require that several forms of knowledge become codified and public. The British judges and other officials would require access to what Jones and others believed at the time was "*the Hindu* and *the Mahomedan* law," locked up in the texts and the heads of pandits and maulavis. A fixed body of knowledge that could be objectified into Hindu and Muslim law had to be found. This body of knowledge could be specified, set into hierarchies of knowledge linearly ordered from the most "sacred" or compelling to the less powerful.

Jones and others believed there was historically in India a fixed body of laws, codes, that had been set down or established by "law givers" and that over time had become corrupted by accretions, interpretations, and commentaries. They also believed that this jungle of accretions and corruptions of the earlier pure codes was controlled in the present by the Indians the British thought of as the Indian lawyers. An Ur-text that would simultaneously establish *the* Hindu and Muslim law and free the British from depending on fallible and seemingly overly susceptible pundits and maulavis for interpretations and knowledge had to be found or reconstituted. The task also had to be accomplished somehow by using the knowledge that their Indian guides, the mistrusted pandits and maulavis, seemed to monopolize. Even before arriving in India, Jones seemed to distrust Indian scholars' interpretations of their own legal traditions, a distrust that grew in India. He wrote to the Governor-General Cornwallis in 1788 that he could not with "an easy conscience concur in a decision, merely on the written opinion of native lawyers, in any case, in which they could have the remotest interest in misleading the court" (ibid., p. 795). Jones wanted to provide the British courts in India, the Crown, and the East India Company with a sure basis on which to render decisions consonant with a true or pure version of Hindu law. Then the pandits, the Brahmins, and the Indian "lawyers" henceforth could not "deal out Hindoo law as they please, and make it at reasonable rates, when they cannot find it ready made" (ibid., p. 684).

What began as a kind of personal effort to correct what he saw as the villainy or venality of some of the law officers of the court was to grow within a few years of Jones's arrival in India into a much more ambitious project to compile a "complete digest of Hindu and Mussulman law" (ibid., p. 699). In proposing this to the Acting Governor General, Jones worried that if his plan were known to the officials in London he would be accused of "proposing to be made the Justinian of India" (ibid.). By 1787, Jones had formulated a plan for the administration of justice in India that he believed would be in accord with the Indians' own principles of jurisprudence. The goal was to develop "a complete check on the native interpreters of the several codes" (Jones to Rouse, in ibid., p. 720). Jones wanted a "complete digest of Hindu and Musliman Laws, on the great subjects of Contracts and Inheritances" (ibid., p. 721). He wanted to employ two pandits and two maulavis at 200 rupees a month, and two writers (one for Sanskrit and one for Arabic) at 100 rupees a month. The modus operandi would be that of Tribonian, compiler of the Justinian Code, and the digest would consist of only "original texts arranged in a scientific method" (ibid.). Jones then went on to describe the texts he wanted to abstract and translate:

> I would begin with giving them a plan divided into Books, Chapters, and Sections; and would order them to collect the most approved texts under each head, with the names of the Authors, and their Works, and with the chapters and verses of them. When this compilation was fairly, and accurately transcribed, I would write the Translation on the opposite pages, and after all inspect the formation of a perfect index. The materials would be these; Six or Seven Law Books believed to be divine with a Commentary on each of nearly equal authority; these are analogous to our Littleton, and Coke. (Ibid., pp. 721–722)

In March 1788, Jones formally wrote to Cornwallis to request government support for this plan. He reiterated the argument that the compilation and its translation into English would establish a "standard of

Justice" and that the English judges would have accessible to them the "principles" and "rules of law applicable to the cases before them" (ibid., 795). Thus Cornwallis hoped to become "the Justinian of India," and Jones by implication would become the Tribonian. The British government would give to the natives of India "security for the due administration of justice among them, similar to that which Justinian gave to his Greek and Roman subjects," Jones wrote to Cornwallis (ibid., p. 798). Cornwallis was quick to agree to support Jones's efforts to assemble the pandits, maulavis, and munshis to carry out his ambitious plans (ibid., pp. 801–806); Sinha (1972:626,660–661). From 1788 until his death in Calcutta in 1794, Jones continued to devote as much time as he could spare from his regular judicial duties to supervising the assembling and collating of the materials that were to become the *Digest*. At his death in 1794, the compilation in Sanskrit and Arabic texts was complete, and he had begun translating them into English (Tripathi 1978:349). By 1797 the English translation was completed by H. T. Colebrooke and published as *The Digest of Hindu Law on Contracts and Successions* in Calcutta in 1798.

The Court of Directors of the East India Company expressed their respect for Jones's achievements in India by commissioning a monument placed in St. Paul's Cathedral by the sculptor John Bacon (the Younger). Jones in the statue is depicted wearing a toga, with pen in hand and leaning on two volumes that "are understood to mean the Institutes of Menu" (Smyth 1826, 2:631).

Jones, and especially his successor, Colebrooke, established a European conception of the nature of Hindu law that was to influence the whole course of British and Indo-British thought and institutions dealing with the administration of justice down to the present. There was an inversion and contradiction in Jones's efforts to fix and translate what he believed to be the crucial aspects of Hindu law. Jones was trained in English common law, which although it embodied principles, legislation, ideas of natural law, and the concept of equity and justice was essentially seen as case law. Case law was a historically derived law based on the finding of precedent. It was flexible and above all subject to multiple interpretations by judges and lawyers. Jones and other jurisprudes of his time saw the English common law as responsive to historical change. Because the manners of a nation of people—or today we might say their culture—could change, legislation would be ineffective "unless it was congenial to the disposition, the habits, the religious prejudices, and approved immemorial usages of the people for whom it was enacted" (Jones 1798:75). But it appears that Jones believed that even though manners, habits, dispositions, and prejudices were not fixed or immutable, the Hindus of India had usages that were fixed from time immemorial. Unlike the British with their case law, in which a lawyer could trace changes both in manners and in customs as well as in the law, the Hindus therefore lived a timeless existence, which in turn meant that differences in interpretations offered by Pundits must have arisen from ignorance or venality.

Jones and the British believed that the original or earliest legal text was assumed to have the most authority. Jones's conception of Hindu law was that its authority was seen by Hindus to derive from its "sacredness" and its antiquity. The authoritativeness of Hindu law was compounded by the texts being written in Sanskrit, which as a language was unchanging, ancient in origin, and sacred. Colebrooke (1873, 2:465), translator of the *Digest*, believed that "the body of Indian law comprises a system of duties religious and civil." This being the case, the portions of the texts dealing with what the British thought of as ethical and religious matters—instructions for rituals, incantations, speculative philosophy, and even rules of evidence—all had to be excised to produce what the British thought of as the rules determining "contracts" and "succession." The object was to find and fix a Hindu civil law concerned with the topics that Jones, a Whig in political and legal philosophy, was centrally concerned with—those rights, public and private, that affected the ownership and transmission of property.

Jones, like Hastings, rejected the idea that India's civic constitution was despotic. He believed that in antiquity in India there had been "legislators" and "law givers," of whom Manu was "not the oldest only, but the holiest" (Jones 1798:76). What Manu and subsequent commentators had therefore created was "a spirit of sublime devotion, of benevolence to mankind, and of amiable tenderness to all sentient creatures . . . [that] pervades the whole work; the style of it has a certain austere majesty that sounds like the language of legislation and extorts a respectful awe" (ibid., pp. 88–89). Jones wanted to restore to India its laws, which pre-dated the Islamic invasions. To be content and productive under British rule, the 30 million black subjects of the East India Company, "whose well directed industry would add largely to the wealth of Britain" needed no more "than protection for their persons, and places of abode, justice in their temporal concerns, indulgence to their prejudices of their own religion, and the benefit of those laws, which they have been taught to believe sacred" (ibid., pp. 89–90).

[147]

Colebrooke and the Discourse on
the Nature of Hindu Law

Colebrooke, who completed the translation of Jones's *Digest* after his death in 1794, had been appointed to the East India Company service in 1782. His father was a banker who had an active role in the management of the company. Educated at home, Colebrooke had a good knowledge of classical languages and a special interest in mathematics. The latter interest led him in India to study Sanskrit, as he wanted to acquire knowledge of the "ancient algebra of the Hindus" (Colebrooke 1873, 1:53). In 1795 he was posted as a judge in Mirzapur, where he had access to the Hindu College in Banaras recently founded by the East India Company "to preserve and disseminate a knowledge of Hindoo law" and to "collect treatises on the Hindoo religion, laws, arts and sciences" (Narain 1959:171).

With access to this collection and to pandits in Banaras, Colebrook's interest shifted from mathematics to Hindu thought, culture, and law. He was a much better Sanskritist than Jones, and he developed a quite different conception of the nature and function of Hindu law. He also had a much firmer grasp on the nature of Shastric texts and their history. More than any Englishman, Colebrooke fixed an interpretation of variation in the legal texts that was to become standard in the British courts. "The *Dharma-sastra* or sacred code of law . . . is called *smriti*," Colebrooke wrote, "what was remembered, in contra distinction to *sruti*, what was heard." The *Smriti* or *Dharma shastra*, he wrote in a memorandum to Sir Thomas Strange, Chief Justice of Madras, is a form of knowledge concerned with "inculcating duty or the means of moral merit" (Colebrooke 1873, 1:666; Strange 1825). Colebrooke argued that *Dharma satra* had less to do with what Europeans thought of as substantive law, legal norms, and more to do with what was forensic law, which was concerned with the nature of pleadings in court or evaluation of evidence and the logic of legal argument.

Law, to Jones, was a set of prescriptive norms, the breach of which would be the cause for judicial redress. Such norms could best be sought, Colebrooke pointed out, in collections called *Sanhitas*, which Hindus attributed to holy sages or sacred personages. These collections were extensive in number. Colebrooke went on to explain that these ancient sages produced treatises on which subsequent Hindu lawyers or pandits commented; the whole, the original treatises and the numerous commentaries on them, formed the body of legal texts. In addition, a vast number of texts "were subject to the same rules of interpretation and collected in *Mimamasa*"—disquisitions on the proof and authority of precepts, which Indians "considered as a branch of philosophy, and is properly the logic of the law" (Colebrooke 1873, 1:95). *Mimamasa* was and is the method used to reconcile conflicting texts of equal authority by applying various rules for the interpretation of words, phrases, and sentences; it was also a style of argumentation (Derrett 1973:51–52).

While English jurisprudence of Jones's time sought certainty in the law, through either "rationality" or an ultimate appeal to ideas of natural law, Hindu jurisprudence sought flexibility through fixed means to interpret what had been revealed to man in terms of principles of right action and proper duties. A British lawyer schooled in case law was skilled in finding precedent in the case record and by analogy relating this precedent to a particular case. The Hindu lawyer, a logician and dialectician, sought reconciliation of conflicting interpretations through analysis of meanings and intentions. It must be remembered that Colebrooke, unlike Jones, was not trained in English law and did not have the knowledge of Roman law—aspects that marked Jones's intellectual approach to Hindu law. Colebrooke's solution to the problem of conflicting interpretations was to suggest that there were regional variations or differences that led to the "construing of the same text variously" (Colebrooke 1873, 1:95). Ultimately, Colebrooke attributed the variations to historical and cultural differences in India, "for the whole Hindu people comprise diverse tongues; and the manners and opinions prevalent among them differ no less than their language" (ibid., p. 96).

Colebrooke organized the differences conceptually, in what he termed "schools" of Hindu law. Ludo Rocher (1972:168) has argued that the invention of the concept of schools of Hindu law "engrafted upon Hindu law an element which was foreign to it." The source of Colebrooke's conceptions, Rocher argues, was based on several misconstructions. Colebrooke viewed the commentaries on Hindu legal texts as the work of "lawyers, juriscouncils and lawgivers" reflecting "the actual law of the land" (ibid., p. 170). This was analogous to early modern English jurisprudes who sought English law in the varied customs of different parts of Great Britain. The second misunderstanding was the analogy made between Hindu law and Muslim law. The British were familiar with Muslim law, with its relatively clear distinctions between Sunni and Shia, with the Sunni having four variations: Hanafi, Shafai, Maliki,

and Hanbali. Colebrooke seems to have analogized this to Hindu law,
yielding a symmetrical set for Hindu law to match what were thought of
as the schools of Muslim law:

Colebrooke believed that the text, compiled by Jagannatha under
Jones's direction was defective because it did not order the "discordant
opinions maintained by the lawyers of the several schools" of Hindu law
(Colebrooke 1873, 2:479). In Colebrooke's view each school had fixed
"doctrines," and English judges therefore needed access to "those authentic works in which the entire doctrine of each school, with the
reasons and arguments by which it is supported, may be seen at one view
and in a connected shape" (ibid., p. 978).

If those Indian scholars who were cooperating with the British could
not compile the texts that demonstrated the stability and completeness
required for the administration of Hindu law in British courts, European
methods must be used to achieve these ends. Colebrooke's solution was
to supply a chronology to establish the authenticity the texts seemed to
lack. The search for the oldest text was supposed to yield the most
authoritative and authentic statement. If one could establish a chronological sequence of texts and trace them to a single original source, the
tremendous variation added by subsequent commentators could also be
controlled. Indian texts did have authors. Frequently one author cited
another, and some texts appeared to contain bare facts about the relative
chronological ordering of authors and commentators, but information on
the history and age of authors was "very imperfect, as must ever be the
case in regard to the biography of Hindu authors" (ibid., 2:487). An
agreed-on authoritative, fixed chronology was not established. Gradually over the next forty years, after Jones announced his intention to
provide Hindus with their own laws through the mediation of English
judges assisted by court-appointed Pandits, a peculiar kind of case law
came into being. At base there might be reference to a text of a particular
author who was thought to represent the norm of a particular regional
school, but it is the chain of interpretations of precedents by the English
judges that became enshrined as Hindu law in such collections as
Thomas Strange's *Elements of Hindu Law*.

After the reform of the judicial system in 1864, which abolished the Hindu and Muslim law officers of the various courts of India, and after the establishment of provincial High Courts, publication of authoritative decisions in English had completely transformed "Hindu law" into a form of English case law. Today when one picks up a book on Hindu law, one is confronted with a forest of citations referring to previous judges' decisions—as in all Anglo-Saxon–derived legal systems—and it is left to the skills of the judges and lawyers, based on their time-honored abilities to find precedent, to make the law. What had started with Warren Hastings and Sir William Jones as a search for the "Ancient Indian Constitution" ended up with what they had so much wanted to avoid— with English law as the law of India.

REFERENCES

Blochmann, H. 1965. *The Aini Akbari* [Translation]. New Delhi. First published in Calcutta, 1865.

Cannon, Garland. 1964. *Oriental Jones*. Bombay.

———. 1970. *The Letters of Sir William Jones*. 2 vols. Oxford.

Colebrooke, H. T. 1873. *Miscellaneous Essays by H. T. Colebrooke*. 3 vols. London.

Davies, A. M. 1935. *Strange Destiny: A Biography of Warren Hastings*. New York.

Derrett, J. D. M. 1968. *Religion, Law, and the State*. New York.

———. 1973. *Dharmashastra and Juridical Literature.* Wiesbaden.

Dow, Alexander. 1772. *The History of Hindustan*. 3 vols. London.

Feiling, Keith. 1966. *Warren Hastings*. London.

Gleig, G. R. 1841. *Memoirs of the Life of Warren Hastings, First Governor-General of Bengal*. 3 vols. London.

Great Britain, House of Commons. 1772–73. *Reports from Committee on East Indies to Great Britain's House of Commons*. Vol. 4. London. Reprinted 1804.

Guha, Ranajit. 1963. *A Rule of Property for Bengal*. Paris.

Halhed, H. B. 1776. *A Code of Gentoo Laws; or, Ordinations of the Pundits*. London.

Hutchins, Francis G. 1967. *The Illusion of Permanence*. Princeton.

Iyer, Raghaven. 1960. "Utilitarianism and All That." In Ragahavan Iyer, ed., *South Asian Affairs* 1, St. Anthony's Papers 8. London.

Jones, Sir William. 1798. "Preface." *The Digest of Hindu Law on Contracts and Successions*. Calcutta.

Koebner, R. 1951. "Despots and Despotism: Vicissitudes of a Political Term." *Journal of the Warburg and Courtald Institutes* 14:276.

Marshall, Peter. 1973. "Warren Hastings as Scholar and Patron." In Ann Whiterman et al., eds., *Statesmen, Scholars, and Merchants*, pp. 242–262. Oxford.

Mukherjee, S. N. 1968. *Sir William Jones: A Study in Eighteenth-Century British Attitudes to India*. Cambridge, Eng.

[151]

Narain, V. A. 1959. *Jonathan Duncan and Varanasi*. Calcutta.

Orme, Robert. 1805 (1792). "General Idea of the Government and People of Indostan." In *Historical Fragments of the Mogul Empire*. London.

Rocher, Ludo. 1972. "Schools of Hindu Law." In J. Ensink and P. Gaeffke, *India Maior: Congratulatory Volume Presented to J. Gonda*, pp. 167–176. Leiden.

Rocher, Rosane. 1983. *Orientalism, Poetry, and the Millennium*. Delhi.

Sinha, Raghuber, ed. 1972. *Fort William–India House Correspondence*, vol. 10. Delhi.

Smyth, George L. 1839. *The Monuments and Gennii of St. Paul's Cathedral and of Westminster Abbey*. London.

Srinivasachari, C. S., ed. 1962. *Fort William–India House Correspondence*, vol. 4. Delhi.

Strange, Thomas. 1825. *Elements of Hindu Law*, vol. 1. Madras.

Tripathi, Amales, ed. 1978. *Fort William–India–India House Correspondence*. Delhi.

Wurgaft, Lewis D. 1983. *The Imperial Imagination*. Middletown, Conn.

[6]

Contours of Change: Agrarian Law in Colonial Uganda, 1895–1962

Joan Vincent

Unless we are acquainted with the circumstances which have recommended any set of regulations, we cannot form a just notion of their utility.
—John Millar, *Observations Concerning the Distinction of Ranks in Society* (1771)

The connections between the introduction and passage of law in colonial Uganda and the development of the country's natural and economic resources are often overlooked. A look at the various powerful interests in the colony and metropole engaged in the making of statutory law in early modern Uganda provide us with background for looking at the actual legislation introduced and its heavily agrarian component. The three successively introduced bodies of law—transplanted imperial law, native feudal law, and so-called "customary law"—correspond to phases in the transformation of colonial agriculture and serve to routinize agricultural practice. There also appears to be a relationship between the coexisting but unrecognized folk law of the colonized people and the hegemonic imperial law that created both a new command structure and a new social order in Uganda, but that relationship is not explored here. [1]

[1]Field and archival research for this chapter was conducted in Teso District, Kampala, and Entebbe, Uganda, between 1966 and 1970. Further archival research was carried out in England and at the Colonial Record Office between 1976 and 1986. Research was funded by a grant from the Ministry of Overseas Development of the United Kingdom

Joan Vincent

Legal Blueprints: British Imperial Law in the Making

In 1874, it is said, the principal legal officer in the Gold Coast colony asked the Colonial Office in London to send him some textbooks and other legal materials to enable him to draft a statute defining the laws for the courts to apply. The Colonial Office sent him the Gold Coast Reception Statute, so-called because it legitimated the colony's "receipt" of English common law and provided that its courts should apply the common law of England, the doctrine of equity, and with reservations, statutes of general application (Seidman 1969). Out of such legends of "muddling through" was Great Britain's reluctant imperialism made.

The Gold Coast Reception Statute became the prototype for the reception statutes of most of the British African dependencies, including the protectorate of Uganda—but not for all. The Colonial Office mind discerned common or similar circumstances among some dependencies but not among others, and for some aspects of their identities but not for others. The common and statute law of England was indeed received by Uganda, Nyasaland, Northern Rhodesia, and most West African colonies, but in Kenya codified law from British India was introduced, supplemented only by English common-law legislation. In southern Africa, Roman-Dutch law and provincial law (from one South African province only) was put into effect (Allott 1980). What was being expressed, in part, in the application of these various blueprints was a vision of the way different imperial possessions would be encouraged to develop, given the objectives and historical circumstances of their consolidation within the empire.

A certain need for flexibility within each territory was recognized, and "received law" was supplemented or modified by rules allowing local laws to be passed. This was done through the Africa Order in Council (1889), which was replaced by the Uganda Order in Council in 1902. These initially took the form of "orders" or "regulations" and placed considerable power in the hands of the colonial governor, the man on the spot. As the colony began to take shape, its body of law came to include

---

and by faculty grants from Barnard College of Columbia University. I would like to thank Karla Chaucer for preparing the final version of this chapter, and June Starr, the members of the Bellagio conference, and an anonymous reader for their suggestions. The chapter was revised while I was on a fellowship from the National Endowment for the Humanities at the National Humanities Center, 1986–87.

gazetted by-laws, codified "native law and custom," administrative directives, and eventually, as regional representation developed, district council resolutions.

Although all these varieties of law gave off an aura of local initiative, many of them owed their existence and form to a central bank—or clearing house—of imperial legislation. What was "borrowed," sometimes by the secretariat in Uganda and sometimes by the legal draftsmen at the Colonial Office, were *sections* of enactments from other colonial dependencies. The minuting on the reports and dispatches that accompanied the transfer of such legislation set out the Colonial Office view of constitutional and social differences between the Uganda protectorate and other colonial territories and the implications these had (in the official mind) for Uganda's future economic development. For example, in January 1909 a dispatch from the governor of Uganda to the secretary of state for the colonies (C.O. 536/25) enclosed a memorandum drafted by the colony's land officer. It began "Uganda is a planter's and not a settler's colony" and went on to argue that freehold grants and grants of land on a large scale were needed "if capital is to be attracted." The draft reply from the Colonial Office began courteously enough: "I am naturally reluctant to disturb a system of dealing with land which you and your Land Officer believe to be reasonable and well suited to the conditions under which the development of the Protectorate must proceed. Nor do I lose sight of the fact that . . . [etc.]." It then went on to compare the Uganda situation with that of Kenya and northern Nigeria. Five copies of a Northern Nigerian Lands Committee Report were then sent to the governor for his own information and that of his land officer and legal department. Thus, it was made clear—in fact, determined—gently but with all the power of the centralized imperial government, that Uganda was to be developed not along the same lines as Kenya, the neighboring settler colony, but similar to the Northern Nigerian emirates with their cash-crop peasantries.

An integumental body of colonial legislation underpinned Great Britain's expanding imperialism within a global economy. Uganda was simply one "undeveloped colonial estate" among many. Law, governors, administrative officers, technological innovations, agrarian experts, and, above all, armies were allocated and transferred from one dependency to another as the need and advantage arose. Law in colonial Uganda, as it developed, reflected a historical conjuncture of sometimes conflicting local and imperial visions and interests.

[155]

Joan Vincent

The Lawmaking Process in Colonial
Uganda, 1905–1934

"To look at law and records in legal activity is to look at the tracks left by combatants and their allies" (Kidder 1979:300). Imposed law in the colonial territories reflected the articulated interests of the ruling class, but it was at the same time an outcome of fractional struggle within that class. While lawmaking in the hands of members of the ruling class serves their interests, the particular form that the law takes and the impetus that projects it into the societal arena derive from events in the course of their struggles against one another and the compromises finally reached.

General laws, as we have seen, were initiated in London. Further enactments were then initiated within the protectorate itself. Their origin varied according to the interests affected. The general tenor of enactments effecting agrarian change emanated from a branch of government itself, from the governor, from an administrative department such as the Department of Agriculture or the Veterinary or Forestry services, or from district or provincial administrations. The Legal Department of the colony then prepared drafts and routed them through the chief secretary and the governor to the secretary of state for the colonies in London.

This was the formal process, but scope for passage through the back door existed in both the colony and the metropole. A governor might be particularly susceptible to missionary pressure, and international concerns might be expressed or commercial pressures asserted. In the early days, when Colonial Office management was not fully formalized, governors were frequently required to give an account of how proposed enactments had been arrived at. The colonial lawmaking process is thus accessible from the dispatches, minutes, appointment books, and correspondence that ensued.[2] The way policy was translated into an ordinance reflected the real politics of the colonial situation.

For example, it was generally understood by the Colonial Office and the governor that a successful colonial administration took into account the interests not only of natives but also of immigrants. In Uganda the immigrants were mainly "European" (mostly British and South African) and "Asian" (from the Indian subcontinent). Four distinct pressure

---

[2]As far as Colonial Office documents are concerned, a fifty-year rule is in operation at the Public Record Office, London.

groups operated within the small expatriate community—traders and merchants, planters, cotton-ginners, and cotton-buying middlemen. At first, mutual interests outweighed nationality and race and all belonged to the Uganda Chamber of Commerce (UCC) formed in May 1905 to represent to the government the general interests of the commercial sector. The Uganda Chamber of Congress devoted a major part of its activity to inhibiting the administration from placing too many restrictions on commercial transactions; in fact, a UCC legislative subcommittee was set up expressly for this purpose.

A measure of success was achieved. Between 1902 and 1906, fifty-seven pieces of separate legislation (not counting amendments) had been enacted, controlling goods in transit, customs, road and wharfage dues, ivory, townships, breach of contract, registration of documents, registration of vessels, customs consolidation, poll tax, port regulations, public ferries, Uganda companies, land transfer, and the like. Reaching out to construct a new command structure, Uganda's legal officer, like his colleague earlier in the Gold Coast, had "borrowed" from the imperial repertoire in anticipation of the new colonial society in the making. The UCC felt that he had overreached himself, and their interjection into the legal process was effective—only six new pieces of legislation were introduced in 1907. At the 1907 annual general meeting of the UCC, its president emphasized that they had been "freed from a whole number of new laws and ordinances, creating legal trouble and hampering trade, such as [previously] filtered regularly out of the Secretariat long before they were required" (quoted in Engholm 1968:36).

Engholm (ibid., p. 11) argues that the immigrant lobbies were successful not only in modifying policies put forward by the government but also in preventing such policies from becoming law: "policies have been too often attributed to the Protectorate Government alone which were, in fact, the outcome of concessions to immigrant pressure." The African voice was completely silent during these years. Officers of the colonial administration were considered to be protectors of African interests, and indeed they often were, challenging and thwarting expatriate commercial enterprise (Vincent 1982, 1987).

By 1911 the Uganda Chamber of Commerce no longer served the needs of the European population adequately. Its numbers had been swelled by an influx of new planters, the economy had diversified, and commercial competition took on ethnic dimensions—for example, the Europeans formed the Uganda Planters Association, and the Asians formed the Indian Association. When the export of cotton began to

[157]

dominate the economy after World War I, the Uganda Cotton Growers Association (UCGA) came into existence to operate independently of both the UCC and the ethnic associations. It proved to be a most effective lobby on the colonial government, not least because of its metropolitan connections with the Manchester Chamber of Commerce.

The year 1920, when investment in Uganda amounted to between $650,000 and $1 million, was the critical juncture in the struggle between administrative and commercial forces—that is, between colonialism and capitalism. By this time the commercial sector, dominated by the cotton growers association, was substantially influencing the colonial government and affecting legislation. It was not alone, however. Other lobbies, particularly those of the Church Missionary Society and the various interests underlying the International Labour Organization, lobbied in Great Britain for legislation to check the excessive exploitation of African cotton producers in the colonies. Their operations were directed at governors on leave, the secretary of state for the colonies, Colonial Office officials, members of the House of Commons, and that amorphous but sometimes effectively aroused entity, British public opinion.

A focus solely on formal associations oversimplifies the processes involved in the making of colonial legislation. Besides the formal visits and representations made by lobbyists and private interests, a great deal was achieved through what might be called "overlapping directorates." Members of the Colonial Office staff punctiliously reported at least some of the visits made to them by individuals articulating personal networks (e.g., those who belonged to the same clubs, who had graduated from the same schools and universities, or who were related by kinship and marriage). In matters colonial, as in all else, this was the way gentlemanly business was done in Edwardian England (Hyam 1979; Vincent 1987).

The Routinization of Agrarian Transformation

Between 1895 and 1902, fifty "Regulations" were enacted under the Africa Order in Council of 1889. Most arose out of the need to establish law and order, but legislation intended to develop the colony's agricultural potential was introduced almost immediately. Land, game, forests, and labor were the subject of eleven of the fifty regulations. Then, in 1902, "ordinances" were introduced under the Uganda Order in Council. Between 1902 and Uganda's independence in 1962, there were

1,575 more pieces of legislation. Of these, 807 were amendments and repeals, suggesting the flexibility of the legislative process within the rapidly developing colonial state and its function in routinizing change.

During the sixty-seven years of its existence, colonial Uganda moved through three phases in the development of its agrarian policy. Each reflected sequential response to the way agrarian capitalism was developing. In its formative phase (1895–1922) the colonial state had to transform its noncapitalist African subjects into landowners and wage-earners. Then, as it embarked on a phase of consolidation and retrenchment (1923–46), the nascent class differences that were emerging had to be taken into account, and a payoff found for those who had gained from cooperation with the government and private interests. Finally, as postwar Britain contemplated dismantling its empire (1946–62) and colonial Uganda moved toward the devolution of authority, the social and political unrest beginning to reflect the uneven capitalist development of Uganda's regions had to be appeased and controlled, in a third phase. Legislation reflected and brought about the fulfillment of each policy in turn.

Locally enacted legislation, in particular, reflected the moments of agrarian crisis that marked the shift from one phase to another. The problems created by the use of forced labor led to the introduction of the Masters and Servants Ordinance (No. 19) of 1913, but it was not until 1922 that "feudal" forms of labor extraction were taken off the statute books. Missionary reporting of local abuses to the Colonial Office, questions in the House of Commons, a labor "scandal" in neighboring Kenya, an influx of settlers to Uganda, and the formation of the International Labor Organization after the war all contributed to the legislative change.

Emergent class differences among the rural population in the second phase, and the shift toward "betting on the strong," were marked legislatively by a Registration of Titles Ordinance (No. 22) in 1922. A Post Office Savings Bank Ordinance was introduced in 1926, the Uganda Credit and Savings Bank Ordinance in 1930. The ultimate recognition of wealth differentiation—a graduated tax—was contested and introduced only after independence. In the second phase the most significant indicator of an emergent entrepreneurial class was the passage of the Cooperative Societies Ordinance (No. 5) in 1946. Until that time, African agricultural entrepreneurs had been obliged to operate under the Registration of Business Names Ordinance (No. 11) of 1918. In 1932, East Africa's governors had debated whether governments might themselves establish cooperatives among Africans, partly to mute the political success of their indigenous forms of agrarian organization. Draft bills to establish government cooperatives were drawn up in 1935 and 1937, but on both occasions they had to be dropped at the insistence of the Uganda Chamber of Commerce and the Indian Association. The nature of the government's own commitment is open to question, since the chief secretary confidentially reassured those bodies that "the introduction of this legislation is not indicative of any intention on the part of Government of fostering or promoting the development of co-operative societies, but only of controlling them" (Secretariat Record of the Proceedings of the Legislative Council 1937:7, quoted in Engholm 1968:240; see also Vincent 1987:7).

The resettlement crisis of the third phase is less clearly evident from the statutory ordinances but is well reflected in locally drafted law. The ethos of the era is captured in the Town and Country enactments of 1951 and 1954, possibly in the Specified Tribes (Restrictions of Residence and Removal) Ordinance (No. 25) of 1955 and surely in the changes in Crown lands legislation. The critical legislation, however, is No. 1 of 1955, District Administration (District Councils), along with No. 2 of 1955, African Authority (Amendment), which gave local governments the task of codifying "customary law" and establishing resettlement projects in congested regions.

Legislation did more than provide a political mechanism for overcoming the crises of agrarian capitalism in Uganda. It also provided for the reproduction of agrarian development. Law itself, in its procedures, tends to promote a concentration on the dramatic, but as Malinowski (1935) observed, the subtlety and true effectiveness of law lies in its "invisible realities." It is difficult to convey the extent to which colonial agrarian law shaped the day-by-day enterprises and routinized the tasks of Ugandan peasants. A distinguished African courts adviser in Uganda, H. F. Morris, quotes Sir Winston Churchill advocating in 1908 that the resources of the country should be developed by the government itself, even if it involved assuming many new functions. Morris continues, "It is, however, hard to believe that Churchill could have foreseen the degree to which control by the state over the activities of the individual in almost all aspects of economic and social development would be carried out during the next half century. The influence of the state was, however, evident not so much in its actual undertaking of economic and commercial ventures . . . as in the *detailed control exercised through a monumental body of legislation* over the citizens of the country particularly insofar as the exploitation of the country's natural resources is concerned" (Morris and Read 1966:375; emphasis added).

The Incorporation of African Customary Law

In the first and last phases of its transformation of agrarian society in Uganda, the colonial state reached out toward indigenous African law. The development of capitalist agriculture required a degree of control over people, and specifically over labor, that English common law did not provide for but that was found in the kingdom of Buganda. Convenient "contract" laws were borrowed from Buganda's vast repertoire of landlord-*bakopi* (peasant) relations. In Buganda the "compulsory contract" (the *Rechtszwant zum Kontrahieren* of Weber) took the form of *kasanvu* and *luwalo*. Kasanvu required that every able-bodied man work on public projects unpaid for one month a year. Luwalo called for one month's unpaid labor from the same men, but in this case they were required to work for the local chief at any tasks the chief directed them to do. The workers themselves had no control over the timing of their call-up, and it could be (and usually was) peremptory as well as mandatory. Of all the grievances against chiefs recounted to me in Uganda, and there were many, such corvée labor and the beatings that accompanied it were the most strongly felt.

In districts outside the kingdom of Buganda, the retention of the Luganda terms *kasanvu* and *luwalo* hid the degree to which these were colonial innovations. This feudal contract controlling labor reflected the uneven exploitation of African farmers.[3] As Michael Burawoy (1978:31–32) put it in his study of the organization of consent: "The dilemma of the capitalist mode of production is to obscure the existence of surplus and at

---

[3]"Feudal law" is not a concept currently in use among sociologists and anthropologists of law, but as law becomes treated less as a universal category and more as a historical product (as the editors urge in the introduction to this volume), it seems likely that the concept will become useful. I use the term "feudal" strictly to convey an "exploitative relationship between landowners and subordinate peasants, in which the surplus beyond subsistence of the latter, whether in direct labour or in rent in kind or in money, is transformed under coercive sanctions to the former" (Hilton 1973:30). Colonial administrators in Teso viewed the Buganda kingdom, whence *kasanvu* and *luwalo* were borrowed, as a feudal state. A striking instance occurred during a training course on local government given to Teso chiefs in 1952. Comparisons were also made with the role of sheriffs and magistrates in English local government. (See Teso District Archives, Miscellaneous, 1952, p. 45.)

the same time guarantee its appearance." The Buganda modes, along with the use made of Baganda agents as the enforcers of coercive measures, furthered the camouflage.

If the introduction of coercive feudal law initiated the process of capitalist penetration in the colonial state, the incorporation of "customary law" marked its closing phases. A recognition that "native laws and customs" existed had been there from the start, built into the common law by the Uganda Order in Council of 1902. Received English law was subject to three qualifications (Morris and Read 1966):

1. The law was to be in force "only so far as the circumstances of the country and its inhabitants permitted."
2. In the making of ordinances, the governor was to respect existing native laws and customs unless these conflicted with justice and morality.
3. Courts in all cases in which natives were parties were to be guided by native law and custom where this was (a) applicable, (b) not repugnant to justice and morality, and (c) not inconsistent with general law.

These qualifications clearly recognized potential conflict in operation between English laws and "customary law." The provisos made it certain that the former would win out in the high court of the land.

The Struggle over Codification

The recognition of "customary law" in Uganda brought about not simply legislative conflict but also expression of different interests among the two sectors of its population most involved. First, administrative officers differed among themselves over the desirability of codifying "native law and customs." Second, and more important, Africans disputed among themselves the content and legitimacy of the "customary law" they were required to formulate. The outcome of their confrontations had a lasting effect on the "distinction of ranks" in rural society. It also had considerable potential for agrarian change because it dealt with such crucial underpinnings of capitalist development as land tenure, marriage, and the inheritance of property.

All "tribes" were thought to have bodies of customary law, and in a "one-tribe district" like Teso, for example, customary law was applied

[162]

universally throughout the district. However, its center of manufacture was Teso's three southern counties, where economic development was most advanced. One can name the localities, dates, and people involved. Codified by the administration with the help of chiefs and gatherings of "big men," the aphorism that what is "traditional" or "customary" are things from the past that it is fruitful to recall in the present seems particularly apt in the Teso case. Under the colonial regime, chiefs and "big men" had been well placed to accumulate capital. The voices of the cotton producers—the peasants—were muted in the power-laden grass-roots context in which the administration conducted its inquiry. Only the rural capitalists had the ear of those empowered to codify the "tradition" they had invented. Legislation, it is said, affords "an arena for class struggle, within which alternative notions of law [are] fought out" (Thompson 1975:288). In the Teso arena, the district officers held the ropes, selected the combatants, and then legitimated the outcome of their struggle. "Customary law," then, was the codification of elements of indigenous law by district officers and their native advisers (see also Chapter 11, by Sally Falk Moore, in this volume). As Read has suggested, the prominence that colonial governments gave to customary law should be viewed not as a matter of altruism—that is, of giving the Africans the form of justice they appreciated and understood—but as recognition that "customary law" was *increasingly more convenient as administrative authority developed;* in particular, the imprecision and adaptability of rules of customary law made them useful instruments for preserving administrative control and buttressing recognized African authorities" (Read 1972:167–170; emphasis added). Again, Read's view is well supported by the political contest in Teso between the colonial administrators and their appointed chiefs. In changes in the legal sphere, we may recognize the outcome as representing the administrators' victory in the combat; the peasantry would appear to have lost on all sides.

The first published codification of "Iteso Customary Law" appeared in 1957. It attempted to collate and tabulate the body of law administered by the native courts of the district,[4] and it recorded "native law and custom," ancient and modern, district council resolutions, and gazetted bylaws, as well as administrative directions issued by the district com-

---

[4]In the discussion after this material was presented at the Bellagio conference, Elizabeth Colson noted that the training of chiefs and court clerks in colonial Africa emphasized procedure and standardization rather than substance. This in effect contributed to the reproduction of those aspects of customary law that maintained the status quo.

missioner as supervising magistrate of the native courts (Lawrance 1957). The considerable divergences of opinion on the law were attributed to "the process of change [being] at different stages throughout the district" (ibid., p. 244).

"Customary law," as the term is used here, refers to codification of elements of African law by a colonial power. It is, unwittingly or wittingly, a selective matter, and it represents a compromise between those recognized as leading elements in indigenous societies and the colonial administrators who co-opted them. The processes involved, and their implications, were clearly described by Sir Henry Maine when he observed that the recording and codification of customs "at once altered their character." "They are generally collected from the testimony of the village elders; but when these elders are once called upon to give their evidence, they necessarily lose their position. . . . That which they have affirmed to be custom is henceforward to be sought from the decision of the Courts of Justice, or from official documents which those courts received as evidence. . . . Usage, once recorded upon evidence given, immediately becomes written and fixed law" (Maine 1961:72). The flexibility of unwritten African law has constantly caused comment among anthropologists and jurists, and upon occasion has even become a political issue. In Uganda the codification of customary law was encouraged less than elsewhere in East Africa—perhaps an indication that the country perceived its role as that of a peasant sector in a regional capitalist economy (Vincent 1982).

The first steps toward codification were in response to outside pressure following the 1933 Bushe Report (*Report of the Commission of Inquiry into the Administration of Justice in Kenya, Uganda, and Tanganyika Territory in Criminal Matters*). In 1934, Jack Driberg, a former district officer in Uganda, became a lecturer in anthropology at Cambridge. He proposed that a traveling commissioner be appointed to East Africa for three years to collate district materials on "native law and custom." The governors of the three territories were unanimous in denying unofficial persons access to the district records. The timing of this series of events is yet to be explored (C.O. 874/3/24213), but it must certainly be viewed in the context of concern expressed in Great Britain by the Howard League for Penal Reform. Agitation was rife over the apparent conflict between European and African justice in East Africa.

Questions of codification arose again in the mid-1950s. Those who argued for codification tended to do so on the grounds of the needs of senior courts. Thus, "one reason why the recording of customary law is so essential is to enable the courts to refer to a generally approved or an 'authorized version' of the law, sanctioned by chiefs and people. Without a written report there can be no certainty in the law, nor is it wise to bring about changes in the law (the necessity of which arises with increasing frequency) without that sure knowledge of it, and of its underlying principles, which only written law can give" (Moffett 1955: ix).

These two lines of argument, the *principle of the rule of law* and the *practical requirements of change*, were particularly timely in the 1950s. In Uganda, returning veterans and educated postwar teachers were beginning to stir their peasant compatriots to thoughts of national independence and self-sufficiency. The cooperative movement and the trade unions were beginning to get off the ground. The formation of nationwide political parties was in the offing. Social and economic discontent, along with political unrest, were forcing change on the protectorate government, even as more development funding flowed into the country as Great Britain sought to invest in the colonies in order to readjust its balance-of-trade payments with the United States. All these developments brought the localized farmer more fully into the political arena. The contradictions of customary law for the African, and common law for the European and Asian, became more marked. A postwar thrust to propel Africans into positions of entrepreneurial responsibility—controlled as it was—brought them to the brink of national consciousness, and over.

Those who argued for codification required that African law would stand up in court. The procedural requirements of cross-examination and the control of expert evidence were uppermost in their minds. There had long been debate over the relative merits of professional magistrates vis-à-vis administrative officers acting as justices of the peace, and the Bushe Commission had come down squarely in favor of the former. In the commissioners' view, familiarity with customary law was less important than formal authoritative textbooks, yet the Uganda government had not encouraged their publication, as had Tanganyika. What usually happened in the senior courts was that "assessors" sat with the judge or magistrate, helping him evaluate the "customary law" evidence presented.

By and large, in Uganda to a greater extent than in the other East African territories, the two systems of courts operated virtually independently of one another (Twining 1964). Yet it was generally agreed, both by those who favored the codification of customary law and those who

[165]

opposed it, that it was desirable to move toward one legal system for the entire population—African, European, and Asian alike. Those who argued against codification put the case that the strength of customary law lay in its flexibility, its sensitivity to rapid change in a still developing country. This, they suggested, could be attributed to the very fact that it *was* unwritten, an argument that was already part of a long English legal tradition that prided itself on the merit of its unwritten British constitution, compared with the unwieldy declarations of the United States and other European powers. Customary law could be assimilated into the general law of Uganda uncodified, they suggested—fervent in their fears of "premature crystallization" or "ossification" of the law. Whether more was at stake in Uganda in the 1950s than debate over the native law and custom requires further study. Clearly, however, those who argued against codification won the day.

Customary Law and Folk Law

The point has already been made that customary law, as recognized by the colonial government, was not the same as the legal system that might have been reconstructed among indigenous peoples by anthropologists. It is no use seeking in customary law a folk system that contested "the institutionalized procedures of the ruling class" (Thompson 1978:261) or a "jurisprudence of insurgency" (Tigar and Levy 1978:310–330). That folk law such as this existed in the form of a lived law in use at the local level as people managed the imposition of imperial, feudal, and customary law is beyond question, but it is also unfortunately beyond the scope of this chapter, which focuses on the imperial contouring of change. The value of the model of imperial law described here rests "on the extent to which it gives shape to our picture of the process corresponding to the contours which the historical landscape proves to have" (Dobb 1946:8). Recognition of lived folk law and, above all, being able to distinguish it from customary law, is the beginning of reading between the lines.

REFERENCES

Allott, Anthony. 1980. *The Limits of Law*. London.
Burawoy, Michael. 1979. *Manufacturing Consent: Changes in the Labor Process under Monopoly Capitalism*. Chicago.
Dobb, Maurice. 1946. *Studies in the Development of Capitalism*. Rev. ed. London.

Engholm, G. F. 1968. "Immigrant Influences upon the Development of Policy in the Protectorate of Uganda, 1900–1952, with Particular Reference to the Role of the Legislative Council." Ph.D.(Econ.) diss. University of London.

Hilton, Rodney. 1973. *Bond Man Made Free: Medieval Peasant Movements and the English Rising of 1381.* New York.

Hyam, Ronald. 1979. "The Colonial Office Mind, 1900–1914." *Journal of Imperial and Commonwealth History* 8 (October):30–55.

Kidder, Robert L. 1979. "Toward an Integrated Theory of Imposed Law." In S. E. Burman and B. Harrell-Bond, eds., *The Imposition of Law*, pp. 289–306. New York.

Lawrance, J. C. D. 1957. *The Iteso.* Oxford.

Maine, Sir Henry. 1861. *Ancient Law.* London.

Malinowski, Bronislaw. 1935. *Coral Gardens and Their Magic: A Study of the Methods of Tilling the Soil and of Agricultural Rites in the Trobriand Islands.* London.

Moffett, J. P. 1955. *Tanganyika: A Review of Its Resources and Their Development.* London.

Morris, H. F., and James S. Read. 1966. *Uganda: The Development of Its Laws and Constitution.* London.

Read, James. 1972. *Indirect Rule and the Search for Justice: Essays in East African Legal History.* Oxford.

Seidman, Robert B. 1969. "A Note on the Gold Coast Reception Statute." *Journal of African Law* 13:45–51.

Thompson, Edward P. 1975. *Whigs and Hunters.* London.

Tigar, Michael, and Madeleine Levy. 1978. *Law and the Rise of Capitalism.* New York.

Twining, William. 1964. *The Place of Customary Law in the National Legal Systems of East Africa.* Chicago.

Vincent, Joan. 1982. *Teso in Transformation: The Political Economy of Peasant and Class in Eastern Africa.* Berkeley and Los Angeles.

———. 1987. "Sovereignty, Legitimacy, and Power: Prolegomena to the Study of the Colonial State in Early Modern Uganda." In Ronald Cohen and Judith Drick Toland, eds., *State Formation and Political Legitimacy*, pp. 137–154. New Brunswick, N.J.

[7]

Thinking about "Interests": Legislative Process in the European Community

Francis G. Snyder

The Council shall, on a proposal from the Commission and after consulting the Assembly, acting unanimously during the first two stages and by a qualified majority thereafter, make regulations, issue directives, or take decisions, without prejudice to any recommendations it may also make.
—Rome Treaty, art. 43(2), par. 3

In August 1973, between 60,000 and 80,000 people protested against a French government plan to extend a military camp at Larzac that was reportedly one link in the chain of NATO bases in Mediterranean Europe. The demonstration was part of a continuing popular struggle by sheep farmers and others, waged against what they saw as an authoritarian central government. Described as the first major national event involving Paysans-Travailleurs, a radical young farmers and farm workers association (Lambert 1975:16), it also coincided with a partial breach in the decade-old hegemony of the Fédération Nationale des Syndicats d'Exploitants Agricoles (FNSEA) in French neocorporatist agricultural politics (Gervais 1972; Keeler 1981a, 1981b; Sokoloff 1980).

At the same time, changes in the world political economy altered some of the basic parameters within which multinational companies operated in the international meat trade. The 1973 oil crisis, on the one hand, led to an increase in the world price of crude oil. It resulted in a rise in incomes in the Middle East, thus stimulating a greater demand in the mainly Muslim countries for imported lamb and mutton. On the other hand, the relative profitability of beef and sheep production in the main exporting countries (Australia, New Zealand, and Argentina) shifted in favor of sheep. These factors converged to cause a sharp increase in world sheep production (Centre Français du Commerce Extérieur 1974, 1:154; Broders 1981:332–334; *Agra Europe* 1982:1, 52; Taylor 1982:1).

Concurrently, in 1973, the United Kingdom and Ireland joined the European Common Market (European Community, or EC). Both the United Kingdom and, to a lesser extent, Ireland were major sheepfarming countries, whereas France had previously been the EC's principal lamb producer. The enlargement of the European Community thus posed especially difficult political, economic, and legal issues, centering on the United Kingdom's continuing relationship, through the Commonwealth, with New Zealand. Great Britain's imports of New Zealand lamb represented approximately 85 to 90 percent of the total pre-1973 EC lamb imports (including intra-EC trade), amounting to between 90 percent and 95 percent of the European Community's total lamb imports from non-EC countries.

Then, following British and Irish accession, the Commission of the European Communities proposed a new agricultural commodity regime or common organization of the market, meant to regulate the market in lamb and mutton, known officially as sheepmeat. This regime was the first comprehensive regulatory scheme for an agricultural commodity since the heady 1960s. In the face of economic recession, nationalist protectionism, and centrifugal political trends, it was not only intended to promote intra-EC trade and to protect European producers, but also designed to use European Community law as a potentially potent symbol of Western Europe's continuing economic unity.

These apparently unconnected events formed part of a legislative process—the making of supranational economic regulatory legislation in the European Common Market. Elaboration of the EC sheepmeat regime, which began in the early 1970s, occupied almost a decade. With this process as the context (see also Snyder 1985b, 1987b), this chapter focuses primarily on the question of "interests." How do (might, should) we think about interests? That this question is important, not only for students of European Community law but also for legal anthropologists concerned with law and disputes, is a central thesis of the chapter. Conceptions of "interests" and "interest representation" underlie any study of law in society, even though they may be conceptualized in different ways, depending on the theoretical perspective. They serve as analytical tools for understanding legal ideas, institutions, and processes, and as such help to define the salient features of law's social context. Conceptions of "interest" are also crucial elements in explanatory theories. They underpin any analysis of law that is not solely doctrinal and that considers law to be integral to social and economic relations. Thus they are indispensable to any understanding of the causes and consequences of the creation, reproduction, or transformation of law.

This chapter illustrates one way of thinking about interests. The first main section proposes some ways of reconceptualizing interests. Turning to the example of the common organization of the market in sheepmeat, a second section sketches the principal structures involved in the making of the sheepmeat regime. A third section considers some of the ways in which these structures were related to interests.

Reconceptualizing "Interests"

It is useful to begin by sketching briefly the way the interests involved in European Community lawmaking have previously been conceived. We can then develop several propositions that will help us to reconceptualize "interests."

A Paradox

Lawmaking in the European Community presents a challenging paradox. The legislative process, compared with that of other international organizations, is often described as remarkably visible. "Negotiations in Brussels are played out amidst the glare of publicity; agreements when reached are set out in legal phrases and prescribe formal mechanisms for implementation" (H. Wallace 1983:75). Participants in making law on important issues include not only a broad range of European Community institutions, but also a wide variety of individuals, governments, groupings, and interest groups. The representation of some interest groups is highly institutionalized. In addition to numerous EC advisory committees (Economic and Social Committee 1980a), European-level interest groups represent employers, workers, and other interests, both formally and informally (Economic and Social Committee 1980b). The agricultural sector—the subject of the Common Agricultural Policy

(CAP), the major common policy of the EC—is especially well represented, both at the EC level in Brussels and within the (now twelve) Member States (Averyt 1975 1977; Economic and Social Committee 1984; Commission 1986).

Except in this formal sense, however, the nature and role of specific interests in European Community lawmaking remains generally opaque. Our conceptualization of these interests is still relatively ill-defined. This lack of transparency and of clear focus is sometimes ascribed partly to the types of issues or policies in question. A large proportion of Common Market legislation, especially with respect to the CAP, consists of economic regulation. Economic regulatory law is often viewed as concerning inherently technical matters and therefore deemed to require the cooperation, if not the consent, of the regulated groups and other political clients. Consequently, negotiations and compromises on important legislative details occur inevitably outside the public arena (W. Wallace 1983:412; see also Lowi 1972; Gerlich 1986). Thus, while the initial phases of European Community lawmaking may be public and extremely open, the final and critical stages are usually conducted in great secrecy (Butt Philip 1983b:21; see also Donat 1979).

The conflicts and compromises of interest that not only shape but actually constitute European Community legislation have been depicted in several valuable accounts (e.g., Lindberg 1963; Gerbet and Pepy 1969; Rosenthal 1975; Averyt 1977; Feld 1980; H. Wallace, W. Wallace, and Webb 1983). Such accounts, however, are still few in number (Butt Philip 1983a:17). More important, despite their merits they have made in many respects only a limited contribution to our understanding of interests, in either empirical or general theoretical terms. For example, more than fifteen years ago the Common Agricultural Policy was characterized as "an exclusive club, thoroughly defended by impenetrable technical complexities" (Lindberg and Scheingold 1970:160). Since then it has been the subject of more studies than perhaps any other European Community policy. Nevertheless, it was recently described in one of the best studies of EC policy-making as so well entrenched that the economic and political forces that underlie and sustain it remain largely invisible (Stevens and Webb 1983:321).

Furthermore, the development of a more adequate conception of interests in this context has been hindered by the particular orientation and implicit assumptions of policy studies. Since the formation of the Common Market, the study of policy, policy-making, and lawmaking in the European Community has been largely the province of specialists in policy studies. This field has been dominated successively by the neo-functionalist, intergovernmentalist, and interdependence approaches (see Webb 1983; George 1985:16–35). Despite substantial differences among them, all three approaches have been limited, as far as the study of interests is concerned, by several shared features. The first was a theoretical focus on European integration, "a process leading toward institutionalised regional unity" (Keohane and Nye 1975:394) and thus a strong teleological orientation. Second, even when (and by) emphasizing the rise of new political actors, they continued to employ a method of analyzing politics that was premised essentially on a rational-choice, utilitarian actor model (see Keohane 1982; Keohane and Nye 1975:391; Hindess 1984). Based on methodological individualism, this conception of politics tended to assume the pluralism of political and economic power. Consequently, it defined interests as policy preferences, utilitarian interests, the fulfillment of needs, or "real" interests based on hypothesized ex post facto choices (see Connolly 1972). This notion of interests was based ultimately on the choices of individual agents. Third, even when taking into account not only interest groups but also elites, policy studies have generally failed to relate the role of elites to the class structure, thus assuming an unproblematic relationship between politics and economics (see Holland 1980:90). Fourth, the interdependence approach took into account certain differences in relative power, as in the analysis of the differential vulnerability of actors to changes in rules (Keohane and Nye 1975:370). But as a consequence of its basic model of politics, it failed to consider unarticulated, objective interests. Fifth, these approaches, like other pluralist theories of politics, neglected not only the role of class interests but also the various faces of power (see esp. Lukes 1974). Sixth, in concentrating exclusively on individual actors or organizational structures, they usually failed to consider the level of the system as a whole (see Alford and Friedland 1985).

Some Propositions

In much of the policy studies literature it is often considered, if not simply assumed, that interests antedate structures, that in legislative processes, for example, interests interact within and around structures, and that interests and structures together produce outcomes. A similar view is expressed, from a very different standpoint, in the following: "The concept of political representation involves three elements: the content of what is represented (economic classes and their interests); the means of representation (political apparatuses and organisations); and the representation itself (the practices of those apparatuses and organisa-tions)" (Cutler et al. 1977:170). Interests are thus frequently used as merely another term, a form of shorthand, for political actors or agents. The state, in this view, is often seen as a neutral structure. A sharp distinction is drawn between form (or structure) and content. The main burden of analysis is on the content of policy, and the formal structures or methods of policy-making (or lawmaking) are not integral to, or determinants of, the content of policy and hence are not problematic (see also Offe 1975:135,140–141). The questions for the analyst, there-fore, are (1) What produces interests? (2) How are interests represented? and (3) How do interests interact within structures, and how are they influenced by structures, in producing the outcome?

If we are to develop a more satisfactory conception of the role of interests in making European Community law, we need a different way of thinking about interests. I suggest that, in studying legislative pro-cesses, it is more fruitful to consider that interests do not antedate structures and that in specific circumstances interests result largely from structures and processes.

We can illustrate, and perhaps go beyond, this partial reversal of the conventional argument by a simple play on words. The conventional argument may be summarized as follows: interests (pass through) struc-tures (resulting in) outcomes. In this formulation, both interests and structures are given, that is, they antedate the legislative process; and interests, structures, and outcomes are discrete. By manipulating the three terms of this summary statement, we can generate a range of six different and potentially more interesting propositions:

a. Interests structure outcomes.
b. Interests "outcome" structures: interests come out of, or at least derive partly from, structures.
c. Structures interest outcomes: structures have an interest in out-comes, either in the sense of partly determining outcomes or in the sense of having a stake in outcomes, so structures will affect, or try to affect, outcomes.
d. Structures "outcome" interests: structures come out of interests.
e. Outcomes structure interests.
f. Outcomes interest structures: structures have an interest in out-comes, in the sense that outcomes affect structures.

A brief reflection on this list will show that propositions (a) and (e) are reciprocals, (b) and (d) are reciprocals, and (c) and (f) are equivalent.

[173]

After performing the necessary operations (a ↔ e, b ↔ d, c ≅ f), we are left with three propositions:

1. interests ← [structure] → outcomes
2. interests ← [come out of] → structures
3. outcomes interest structures [structures have an interest in outcomes]

These admittedly crude propositions find wide, albeit eclectic, support in a diverse literature. For example, the first proposition may appear partly to express the classic pluralist conception of pressure-group politics. However, if read, with more attention to the middle term, "structure," as it should be, it indicates not that the clash of interests determines outcomes, but rather that the configuration of interests limits the range of possible outcomes. Thus, market structure, for instance, influences the degree and form of regulation. The same proposition, conversely, encapsulates Lowi's insight that "policies determine politics": "different ways of coercing provide a set of parameters, a context, within which politics takes place" (Lowi 1972:299; see also Daintith 1982:210–217).

The second proposition—if "interests" are defined actively as "agents"—may be seen as a shorthand expression of Giddens's theory of structuration, particularly the duality of structure: "The constitution of agents and structures are not two independently given sets of phenomena, a dualism, but represent a duality. . . . The structural properties of social systems are both the medium and the outcome of the practices they recursively organise" (Giddens 1984:25; see also Giddens 1979:693; Comaroff and Roberts 1981:230). More specifically, this proposition suggests a political definition of interests. Neither states nor corporatist arrangements, so-called "private interest governance"—such as the relationships between the FNSEA and the state in France, or the National Farmers Union (NFU) and the state in Great Britain—simply aggregate or express preexisting interests. Instead, they help to create, shape, and sustain interests (see Hawley 1983:248,250; Streeck and Schmitter 1984[?]:25; Keohane 1982:330).

The third proposition emphasizes the interrelationship of structures and outcomes. It may be read, first, as referring to Marx's dictum that people "do not make [history] just as they please . . . but under circumstances directly encountered given and transmitted from the past" (Marx 1968:97). Institutions, organizations, and other structures may determine, shape, or condition specific outcomes or, more frequently, the range of potential outcomes. Structures thus are neither neutral nor simply a framework. Both structures and form influence outcomes, such as policies and laws, but in addition, "fixed, defined interests . . . become embodied in institutions and ideologies in a post hoc manner in and through conflict" (Hawley 1983:250). Past struggles and compromises, as well as continuing conflicts, represent previous outcomes that impregnate and hence shape existing structures.

These three propositions need to be elaborated further, but nevertheless they may be useful in helping us circumvent two analytical difficulties that are frequently encountered in thinking about "interests." The first is the extent to which the term "interests" is commonly associated with pluralist theories of politics. "Interests" often evokes many of the basic assumptions of pluralism regarding the state, law, and society. In their synthesis of the major theoretical traditions in political sociology, Alford and Friedland (1985:30) remark: "Certain concepts have such a heavy historical weight of meaning—connotations, assumptions, hypothesis—buried in them that their use almost commits writer and reader to the implicit (and all the more powerful because of that implicitness) theory about the causes and consequences of the phenomena alluded to by the concept." They argue that the concept of "interest group" is theorized only within the pluralist perspective (ibid., p. 92). Nevertheless, "interest groups" and "interests" are not equivalent. Moreover, it is open to debate whether "interest" is a core concept of the pluralist perspective or whether it is what Gallie (1956) called an "essentially contested concept" (see also Williams 1983:171–173). The three propositions sketched above make room for a more complex, more subtle interpretation of the role of interests.

A second difficulty is the distinction often drawn between structure and agency. The dichotomous form of this distinction tends to grant the two terms a pregiven antinomic status (see O'Malley 1980). It also makes it difficult to imagine any logical relationships between them, except insofar as they are (1) separate and unconnected, (2) poles on a spectrum, or (3) dialectically related. In addition, this distinction, embodying only two terms, neglects any potential influence of outcomes—and hence processes—in creating and reproducing both structure and agency. One of our three propositions incorporates Giddens's significant attempt to transcend the dichotomy of structure and agency by a theory of structuration. Together with the other two propositions, it may help us to avoid what in this context would be an unproductive opposition of subject and object.

[175]

Structures

Structures, or structural constraints, are defined by Jessop (1982:252, 258) as "those elements in a situation that cannot be altered by agent(s) in a given time period." This definition, however, postulates too strong a distinction between structure and agency. Structure and agency form a duality. Structures represent outcomes of processes that have previously occurred; they are configurations of interests, congealed at least temporarily in the form of institutionalized sets of social relations. Only a fine line separates structures from processes. They are dialectically related, each being in a sense simply a transformation of the other. Any firm distinction between them depends ultimately on one's purpose and perspective (see also Nelken 1985). We can thus identify three types of structures in the making of the European Community's sheepmeat regime. They concern the economy, the state, and law.

The Marketing Chain

In discussing the structures involved in the making of the sheepmeat regime, it is convenient to begin with the sheepmeat marketing chain (filière). The expression "marketing chain" denotes an abstract representation of a portion of the economy. Its purpose is to isolate a certain field, thus facilitating an analysis of its organization and operation. The field is based on a specific product. It includes the units of production, enterprises, or parts of enterprises involved in the production or distribution of the product; services external to the enterprises that aim to regulate or influence the production, distribution, or consumption of the product in question; consumption; and all vertical and horizontal relations between enterprises in the particular field (Lauret 1983:723–733). This conception derives from Marxist political economy, classical economics, and systems theory. It bears a strong resemblance to Marx's (1973:99) notion of the relations of production, the unity of production, distribution, exchange, and consumption, but it is focused on a specific product. In addition, it contains both Marxist and non-Marxist elements, which, as we shall see, are incompatible in some respects.

Elsewhere I have used Marx's conception of the relations of production as an organizing framework within which to analyze relationships between economic and legal change (Snyder 1981). The conception of a marketing chain seems to be helpful, at least provisionally, in identifying and explicating the complex sets of economic relations involved in the

European Community legislative process. It has been widely used in studies of agribusiness, and its utility in the similar context of this chapter is suggested by the increasing internationalization and integration of the world food economy, especially since World War II (see Ghai, Luckham, and Snyder 1987). The "set of activities and relationships which interact to determine what, how much, by what method and for whom food is produced" (OECD 1981:10) is today largely international rather than national in scope. It embraces the provision of agricultural inputs, agricultural production, food processing, distribution and retailing, and household and extrahousehold consumption. The conception of a marketing chain helps us take into account the increasingly systematic nature of the food chain, the great integration of agriculture and industry, and the intimate connection between domestic and international processes. It should also facilitate detailed description and analysis of economic and legal relations in the European Community, which both distinguishes between and integrates different levels of analysis and different levels of abstraction (see Alford and Friedland 1985).

I have defined the sheepmeat marketing chain as a unique entity at the societal level of analysis. It thus is a commodity-specific kind of marketing chain (an institutional type) that is part of the food economy (a systemic entity). Viewed at the greatest level of abstraction, but still at the societal level of analysis, it comprises several segments. These segments are generic (though still commodity-specific) processes, such as production, processing, distribution, exchange, and consumption.

In order to understand how the sheepmeat marketing chain is related to interests, we must also examine it at the organizational and individual levels of analysis. At these levels, we can define the segments of the chain more specifically by distinguishing, within each segment, various elements or instances of different institutional types. Examples of these types include producers of inputs, livestock producers, exporters, importers, transporters, slaughterers, wholesalers, processors, retailers of different kinds, and various institutional and individual consumers. In fact, we must go even further and distinguish, for example, between different types of producers and different types of exporters, importers, and retailers. The former include hill farmers, upland farmers, and lowland farmers in the United Kingdom; peasants and more intensive farmers in France; and New Zealand sheep ranchers. They also include owner-occupiers, landlords, and tenants. The latter embrace multinational companies, large nationally based firms, and small businesses (see, e.g., Boutonnet n.d.; *Pâtre* 1984). These various distinctions may

[177]

be made either at the individual level of analysis or at the organizational level.

Any examination at a lower level of abstraction of the organizations and individuals in the sheepmeat marketing chain requires a discussion of unique entities. For instance, after 1860 the international trade in lamb was revolutionized by the development of freezing and shipping technology. Until recently, as already noted, it centered on the shipment of frozen meat from the southern hemisphere to the north, mainly from New Zealand to the United Kingdom (*Agra Europe* 1982:1). The trade was dominated by a handful of large companies (see Critchell and Raymond 1912; Perren 1978). Today the same firms by and large remain important, not only in the south-north trade but also in trade within the European Community. In 1972, for example, approximately 20 million lamb carcasses (300,000–320,000 metric tons) were imported into the United Kingdom from New Zealand. Nine companies accounted for about 85 percent of this trade. Between 55 percent and 60 percent was due to four companies: Thomas Borthwick and Sons Ltd., W. Weddel and Co. Ltd., Towers and Co. Ltd., and C.W.S. Ltd. (Centre Français du Commerce Extérieur 1974, 2:106). Borthwick was the largest British (and European) importer of lamb, which accounted for approximately 40 percent of its £164 million meat business. It had subsidiaries and branches in a dozen countries, including New Zealand, Australia, Great Britain, the United States, Canada, Japan, and France (ibid., pp. 129–131). Weddel was the largest importer of meat into the United Kingdom; lamb made up about 30 to 33 percent of its turnover (ibid., p. 133).

Among the slaughterhouses licensed by the British government to export lamb and mutton to France in the mid-1970s were those of the British Beef Company Ltd. and W. Devis and Sons. Both were owned by the Union International Company Ltd., which was controlled by the Western United Investment Company (UK), the holding company of the Vestey family. The Vesteys, like Sir Thomas Borthwick, were pioneers in the use of refrigerated ships and cold-storage depots. They have been described as "the world's largest retailers of meat, the owners of Britain's biggest meat importing business, Weddel's, and biggest meat retailing chain, Dewhurst" (Knightley 1980a:13), with 1,600 retail butcher shops (Commission 1977:95). Through Western United they own or control a wide range of diverse and relatively independent companies, including meat suppliers, importers and exporters, slaughterhouses, cold stores, wholesalers, transporters, and retailers in numerous countries within and outside the European Community, including New Zealand, Great Britain, and France (*Who Owns Whom* 1976: 688–689, 695–696; Knightley 1980b:63; Knightley 1981; Cranney and Rio 1974:7, 341–342, 345–352; Centre Français du Commerce Extérieur 1974, 2:133–134.

States

A second set of structures, in addition to the marketing chain, was involved in the making of the sheepmeat regime. It consisted of states. Two forms of state structures played a role in this legislative process: the "supranational state," or European Community, on the one hand, and the nation-states, which are the European Community's Member States, on the other hand. For reasons of space, I treat them here much more briefly and more formally than the marketing chain.

The European Community consists of three legally distinct entities: the European Economic Community (EEC), the European Coal and Steel Community (ECSC), and the European Atomic Energy Community (Euratom). These Communities share four institutions: a Commission, the supranational bureaucracy, which in fact employs fewer people than the British Ministry of Agriculture; a Council, composed of ministers representing the Member States; an Assembly (now called the European Parliament), which has mainly consultative powers; and a Court of Justice, modeled on the Conseil d'Etat, France's highest administrative court. Only these four institutions are given legal status as European Community institutions by the Community's founding treaty. A number of other institutions, however, also played an important role in the making of the sheepmeat regime. Of particular significance was the Special Committee on Agriculture (SCA), a subcommittee of the Council concerned with agricultural matters.

Established by the Treaty of Rome in 1957, the European (Economic) Community initially included France, Germany, Italy and the Benelux countries. The United Kingdom, Ireland, and Denmark became members in 1973. Greece joined in 1979, and Spain and Portugal acceded to membership in 1986. The original Community of Six thus was enlarged to embrace twelve Member States. During most of the sheepmeat regime negotiations, however, the European Community comprised nine Member States.

State structures in capitalist societies are an integral part not only of policy-making but also of the economy. In turn, they depend fundamentally on the accumulation of capital (see Offe 1975:126–127). Each of these states performed certain functions in the organization of the sheep-meat marketing chain. The French state, for example, allocated financial aid to lamb producers, financed a wide range of agricultural and marketing measures, and exempted from taxation certain revenues earned in cereals production, and then facilitated the investment of these funds in the sheepmeat marketing chain. France's national infrastructural plan for abattoirs, beginning in 1960, was designed partly to shorten the marketing chain and to encourage concentration. By means of classification and marketing schemes and health regulations, it controlled the quality of the product. It also regulated prices, in part through negotiations at the European Community level, and in accordance with European Community law and following the pre-1957 French pattern, it established intervention agencies that purchased surplus products or took other action in order to stabilize the market. Through licensing and deposit schemes, it regulated the flow of imports and exports. Some of these activities were allocative, some were productive (see ibid., pp. 128–129, 132, 136). Most, if not all, took place, at least nominally, within a normative framework provided by European Community law.

Law

Law also formed a structural element in the negotiations leading to the sheepmeat regime. Omitting national law, I consider three aspects of European Community law to be of special importance. The first was the Treaty of Rome, particularly its agricultural provisions and the way in which those provisions have been interpreted by the European Court of Justice. The Rome Treaty, the European Community's constitution, provides for adoption of a common agricultural policy (see, generally, Snyder 1985a). Together with the "four freedoms" concerning the free movement of goods, services, and capital and the projected common transport policy, agriculture is, from the legal standpoint, one of the "Foundations of the Community" (Treaty of Rome, part 2). The objectives of the common agricultural policy are defined in the Rome Treaty (art. 39(1)):

(a) to increase agricultural productivity by promoting technological progress and by ensuring the rational development of agricultural production and the optimum utilisation of the factors of production, in particular labour;

(b) thus to ensure a fair standard of living for the agricultural commu-

[180]

nity, in particular by increasing the individual earnings of persons engaged in agriculture;

(c) to stabilise markets;
(d) to assure the availability of supplies;
(e) to ensure that supplies reach consumers at reasonable prices.

These objectives are complex and to a great extent contradictory. They have been interpreted by the European Court of Justice so as to give priority to the maintenance of producers' incomes over increasing agricultural productivity or maintaining a given level of consumer prices. The link between farm income support and structural change has been given little official recognition.

The second structural aspect of law includes the legal principles, the major policy decisions, and the legal and institutional core of the Common Agricultural Policy. The basic principles of the CAP are the inclusion of agriculture in the European Community scheme, the exceptional status of agriculture with regard to general Rome Treaty rules, the adoption of a common policy for agriculture, unity of the market, and financial solidarity (see Snyder 1985a:15–16, 23–39). The major policy decisions concerning the CAP were made during the 1960s. Of central importance were the basic tenet that agricultural incomes were to be supported through market and price policy; agreement on a relatively high common price for the key commodity, cereals; and adoption of a European-wide market organization as the only form of common organization of the market, even though two other forms were legally possible under article 40(2) of the Rome Treaty.

The common organization of agricultural markets, together with the price system and related financial mechanisms, form the core of the CAP (see ibid., pp. 71–121). A market organization has been defined by the European Court of Justice as "a combination of legal institutions and measures on the basis of which appropriate authorities seek to control and regulate the market" (Joined Cases 90 and 91/63, *Commission v. Luxembourg and Belgium* [1964] ECR 625 at 634). Each market organization (often called a "regime") is constituted by a single Council regulation, supplemented as necessary by Council and Commission regulations specific to each product. In addition, "horizontal" regulations applying to all products have been adopted by the Commission with regard to common questions, such as licenses and export levies. These legal elements formed an important part of the *acquis communautaire*. Together with the principle that any difficulties would be resolved by transitional measures, they were taken for granted in the negotiations between the Six and later applicants for membership, including the United Kingdom and Ireland.

A third aspect was the ideology of CAP law. European Community law concerning the Common Agricultural Policy embodies a sharp distinction, common to many legal systems, between industry and agriculture. Agriculture is treated as a specific economic subsector, to some extent with its own rules, regulatory procedures, and processes of change. This conception of the distinctive nature of agriculture, and its discreteness in relation to the rest of the economy, is the basis of the Common Agricultural Policy. Yet CAP law itself is deeply contradictory. On the one hand, the legal distinction between agriculture and industry does not correspond to the technical economists' distinction or to popular stereotypes. On the other hand, the basic conceptual framework of the CAP is continually being undermined, partly by the very legal measures that are adopted under the aegis and in the name of this framework. The conceptual distinction between agriculture and industry, as expressed in European Community law, is thus the skeleton of a general ideological framework, which organizes and legitimates political discourse, European Community and national laws, and other social practices. It forms a kind of flexible grid, the movable structure of a powerful ideology, one that legitimates and partly masks the mechanisms—and sometimes the direction—of change (see Snyder 1987a).

Interests

So far we have been looking at various structures and it has been suggested that past conflicts of interests and previous outcomes are congealed, at least temporarily, in structures. Including but not limited to organizations, structures thus represent the mobilization of bias (Schattschneider 1960:71). We now turn to the converse—namely, some of the ways structures create, shape, and otherwise influence interests.

Objective Interests

Structures define, delimit, and shape objective interests—that is, interests that are not necessarily reducible to or dependent on individual consciousness (Balbus 1971:152–154; Jessop 1982:256; Dahrendorf

[182]

1959: 174, 178). Class interests deriving from the relations of production are one kind of objective interest, but not the only kind. Here, however, I refer primarily to this kind of objective interest, partly because of its complex interconnection with the marketing chain and partly because of its basic significance in capitalist societies.

The concept of objective interest is important in a study of the making of European Community law. First, the principal socioeconomic process in capitalist societies, viewed at the systemic level, is the accumulation of capital. At the systemic level, this process generates two general classes, which are the referents of a concept of an objective interest. The notion of objective interest thus reminds us of a particular level of abstraction, the systemic level (see also Snyder 1987b). This level of abstraction has often been neglected in studies of European Community law, especially those carried out within the framework of policy studies. The latter, as already noted, have been based mainly on pluralist theories of politics. Pluralists have concentrated primarily on the exercise of power rather than on its sources (Bachrach and Baratz 1962:948). They have therefore often failed to recognize even the existence of objective interests.

Second, the notion of objective interest points to ways in which the systemic process of the accumulation of capital, and the related systemic distinction between different classes, are manifested, and can be identified, at more specific levels of abstraction and at different levels of analysis. These other levels of abstraction refer to institutional types and specific entities; the levels of analysis include the societal, organizational, and individual levels (see Alford and Friedland 1985:16–21). Consider three examples. (1) The state is an institutional type at the societal level of analysis:

> Its power relationships, its very decision-making power, depends . . .
> upon the purpose and continuity of the accumulation process. . . . The
> criterion of the stability of accumulation is thus incorporated in the
> pursuit of interests and policies that, considered by themselves, may
> have little or nothing to do with accumulation. Accumulation, in other
> words, acts as the most powerful constraint criterion, but not necessarily
> as the determinant of content, of the policy-making process. (Offe 1975:
> 126)

Though referring primarily to the state in the sense of the European Community's Member States, this general point, as recent events have demonstrated, applies with equal force to the European Community. (2)

[183]

In the European Community and its major trading partners, "organisations representing labour and capital are not simply groups like any others. They are both less variable in their identification of interests and more powerful in relation to other groups" (Berger 1981:13; see also Offe 1981). (3) Research on state intervention in agriculture usually concentrates on the determination of farm prices and their effects on farmers. Yet a study of French agriculture recently concluded that what was really at stake was the distribution of the added value created by different segments of the marketing chain (Pivot 1985:86). In the light of our analysis, however, we must push this point further. It is necessary to distinguish not only between various segments, but also between the position of different class interests.

Third, the notion of objective interest identifies interests that are often not expressed or articulated but that are nonetheless crucial determinants of or influences on the legislative process and the content of legislation. My research on the sheepmeat regime tends to support many of the criticisms that have been made of studies of dispute-processing (see Cain and Kulcsar 1981–82; Kidder 1980–81; Starr and Yngvesson 1975). The key actors are not individuals; indeed, the use of the pluralist perspective to analyze such processes is often misplaced. Actors, however they may be defined, are not equal in socioeconomic strength, political power, or legal resources. This is apparent even from my brief sketch of the sheepmeat marketing chain. Instead, the most useful insights come from focusing on the organizational and societal levels of analysis—that is, on firms and states. Insights also result from moving to more general levels of abstraction—in other words, by considering not only specific entities or, what is more common, institutional types, but also systemic entities or generic processes, such as classes, class conflict, and class formation. This is particularly important when, as is common, disputes are not discrete.

In fact, once one moves away from the notion that intra-EC disputes are mainly between Member States, it is not easy even to identify the participants precisely. Our understanding is obscured in part by individualist, behavioralist, and intentionalist assumptions and connotations, which, as Lukes (1974:39) has pointed out, often seem to be built into the expressions we use when speaking about power. Although policy-making in the European Community is often described as remarkably open, it is sometimes difficult to find out very much about even the subjective interests involved. Consequently, it is essential to consider the possibility that the most important interests in the legislative process are not represented, directly or publicly.

[184]

In order to develop some of these points, let us consider two hypotheses. First, the interest of large firms, despite occasional, issue-specific lobbying through trade associations or individually, remain largely invisible but are nonetheless important. Except on rare occasions, such firms do not need to mobilize or express their interests publicly. This is the case particularly in highly concentrated sectors or segments of the marketing chain. In such contexts, some firms are so powerful that it is virtually unthinkable that, except in the very short run, legislation would go directly counter to their objective interests or subjective demands in any real sense. This, as Crenson (1971) found in a study of U.S. Steel, is power without participation or publicity. It derives, in part, from the ways in which the interests, claims, and expectations of such firms are already built into the history, structures, processes, and ideologies of the European Community and the CAP (see also Hawley 1983:250). The latter are implicitly oriented in favor of such interests. Products (or outcomes) of interests, these histories, structures, processes, and ideologies in turn reinforce these interests, thus contributing to the reproduction of the hierarchy of power relations.

These interests in effect exercise a determining influence on the agenda and content of policy-making and lawmaking. They do so in three distinct ways. The first, by far the least important, is through political participation by individuals, groupings, and groups in the making of decisions on key issues. The second is by non-decision-making: "the practice of limiting the scope of actual decision making to 'safe' issues by manipulating the dominant community values, myths, and political institutions and procedures" (Bachrach and Baratz 1963:632; see also Bachrach and Baratz 1962; Wolfinger 1971a, 1971b; Frey 1971). The third does not require the existence of grievances or disputes, nor does it necessarily occur through decisions. It is by institutional control over the political and legal agenda (see Lukes 1974).

A second hypothesis is that the structures described earlier in this chapter give rise to particular objective interests. For example, Murray's functionalist thesis distinguishes between six public functions that it is in the interest of capital to have performed, whether by a home state, a grouping of national governments, or an international organization (Murray 1971). These functions include the guarantee of property rights, economic liberalization, economic orchestration, provision of inputs, intervention for social consensus, and the management of external relations. Capital is not, however, homogenous. The objective interests of a capital in the types of public functions to be performed and the bodies to perform them will differ, in Murray's view, according to the

[185]

particular capital's degree of productive centralization, the state of overseas company development, the forms of international flows, the degree of dependence on state partiality, and the strength of foreign competition (see ibid.).

Such differences in objective interest may be refracted, at the organizational level of analysis, in different degrees of support for or opposition to European Community policies and laws. Holland argues: "the specific interests of sections within the main classes [of capital and labor] are related to different functions served for them by national state power, supranational institutions and international integration" (Holland 1980: 104). He distinguishes between multinational and national capital and between large and small enterprises. In his view, large-scale multinational capital has an objective interest in supporting negative integration, such as the removal of tariff barriers. Large-scale national capital, by contrast, has an objective interest in maintaining its home state's capacity to provide positive integration in its favor and to prevent or obstruct harmful negative integration. Similarly, small capital relies on its home state, not on the European Community, to protect it against the effects of increased liberalization and competition (see ibid., pp. 98–99, 104, 109, 112–113).

We can transpose these differences into a legal framework by distinguishing between standard rules and special rules. In the European Community, the standard rules are those enshrined in the Treaty of Rome, mainly in the provisions regarding what Holland calls negative integration. Those provisions concern the free movement of goods, services, labor, and capital. Special rules, in contrast, establish exceptions to or exemptions from the standard rules, or supplement them. Large multinational companies have an interest in securing compliance with standard rules. Agricultural producers, especially small farmers, have an objective interest in obtaining special rules; note that, as already outlined, agriculture as a whole is treated in the Treaty of Rome as a special sector. States, depending on the particular circumstances, may variously have an interest in enforcement of the standard rules, in special rules, or in some combination of the two. States that are not part of the European Community, such as New Zealand, have an objective interest in obtaining special rules, but such special rules differ from special rules within the European Community context. They constitute exceptions to the protectionist rules that usually apply to countries not in the European Community, but at the same time they embody the basic assumptions of the free movement of goods that are expressed in the Treaty's standard rules. We can thus understand why, in the words of a *Guardian* headline (October 31, 1979; p. 14; see also Wendling 1985:282), Great Britain's strong suit during the 1978–80 "lamb war" was jurisprudence while France's was the art of the possible.

Subjective Interests

But objective interests do not develop automatically into subjective, consciously expressed interests, such that, for example, in Marxist terms, a "class-in-itself" must necessarily become a "class-for-itself." Location in the relations of production does not therefore necessarily entail any specific class position in political struggles. In other words, there is no universal, invariant correlation between objective and subjective interests (see also Przeworski 1977; Snyder and Hay 1987). Instead, objective and subjective interests are dialectically related. An analysis of European Community lawmaking with regard to class interests, for example, must therefore adopt two distinct but related notions of class forces: one referring to structural determination, the other referring to class position (see Jessop 1982:242–256).

Although the structures that define or delimit objective interests do not automatically determine subjective interests, they nevertheless influence and shape them. Structures may "involve differential patterns of association and interaction and impose definite limits on the success of particular class projects, strategies and tactics" (ibid., p. 242; see also Jessop 1983). For example, by the early 1970s the FNSEA in France and the NFU in Great Britain had long been engaged in agricultural policymaking and lawmaking in neocorporatist arrangements with their respective states (see, e.g., Wilson 1979; Grant 1983a; Keeler 1981a, 1985). These structural arrangements, or forms of "interest intermediation" (Schmitter 1979:36; see also Gilb 1981; Olsen 1981; Lane 1985), did more than simply allow for the expression of interests; they actually created interests, both objective and subjective. Of course, this kind of interest, due to neocorporatist arrangements, is sometimes less significant in politics than objective, structurally determined class or other interests.

This discussion suggests two hypotheses concerning the relationship between objective and subjective interests. First, the greater the integration of the marketing chain (for a particular commodity), the more likely it is that the segments will produce a coincidence of objective interests. This coincidence of interests may or may not override objective interests deriving from the structural determination of classes. Second, the stronger the neocorporatist arrangements for policy-making and lawmaking in a given economic sector, the more likely it is that the segments that participate in these arrangements will articulate a common subjective interest. Viewed against the wide range of objective or subjective interests that might be incorporated in such arrangements, this common interest is necessarily "partial, incomplete and highly contradictory" (Hawley 1983:249). The state's role in such arrangements is selective, however, not that of a neutral arbiter or broker of other interests.

National Interests

The coexistence of national and European Community structures produces what in the context of EC policy-making and lawmaking are often expressed as "national interests." Different and often contradictory and conflicting objective and subjective interests thus are represented as a single, apparently coherent subjective interest. Such an expression is conditioned partly by the structure of European Community institutions. The making of the sheepmeat regime involved the Commission, the Council, the Special Committee on Agriculture, the European Court of Justice, and later the Sheepmeat Management Committee. Within most, if not all, of these institutions, the types of interests defined as legitimate, both organizationally and ideologically, were "national" in character. All the interests that were expressed subjectively, even before the Commission and the European Court of Justice, were therefore expressed as "national interests."

The conception of "national interest" is, however, extremely problematic. In most of the approaches to European Community policy studies, it tends to dissolve. The interdependence approach, for example, has often viewed the state, considered as a unitary political actor, as much less significant than either nongovernmental actors or transgovernmental relations. According to this approach, even when the existence of various domestic interests is admitted, these interests are assumed to be subordinated in a hierarchy of "national interests," paramount among which is national security. Yet when national security is not in question, as in economic matters, the conception of a single, overriding "national interest" is difficult to sustain. The standard proposition that "states act in their self-interest" begs two basic questions: "What self?" and "Which interest?" (Keohane and Nye 1975:398). Accordingly, proponents of the interdependence approach often argue that governments are best considered as coalitions of bureaucracies, loosely organized in a hierarchical manner, with each bureaucracy having its own interests (see ibid., pp. 398–399). This bureaucratic politics approach, however, denies the totality of the state (Krasner 1984:224).

At least two authors have tried to go further in analyzing the meaning of the "national interests" created in European Community policy-making. For example, Helen Wallace believes that national interest refers to the amalgam of individual vested interests and potential gains woven into the fabric of European Community policies: "Herein lies the essence of national interest in the context of Community bargaining. Community politics, like national politics, consists of a framework and a process through which the participants seek to attain their separate objectives and to conserve the status and material gains that they regard as appropriate" (H. Wallace 1981:114). More specifically, with regard to the CAP, Harvey believes the most significant aspects of national interest to be farm income levels, improvement of farm incomes, the costs to consumers or users of agricultural support, and the cost to taxpayers of agricultural support. The relative weight of these components in each country are determined by the structure and well-being of agriculture, the general economic environment, and the political and social environment (see Harvey 1982; H. Wallace 1981:122). Within this general framework, Harvey identifies the principal goal of agricultural policy as that of "achieving the lowest level of agricultural prices that is politically acceptable and consistent with the major aim of such policies, namely maintenance or improvement of agricultural income levels" (Harvey 1982:179).

These two authors are concerned with different levels of analysis, but their views of the meaning of national interest have several features in common. They tend to support the conclusion that policy-making (and hence lawmaking) in the European Community involves "jointly produced individual interests" rather than "common interests" (Scharpf 1985:33). They presume a pluralist theory of politics. They employ a rational-actor model of decision-making. They focus almost exclusively on subjective interests. Finally, they assume the existence of a "national interest."

The meaning of national interest may be illuminated further by referring briefly to an analogous, if not equivalent, concept—that of "public interest." The meaning of public interest has been particularly controversial, and therefore continually debated, in the field of industrial

[189]

relations. Pluralist students of industrial relations, like pluralist theorists of politics, commonly make three assumptions (see Hyman 1978:20–21). First, economic (and therefore political) power is widely dispersed. Second, despite this lack of concentration, it makes sense to talk of a "public interest." Third, a relatively impartial guardian of the public interest is the state. Each of these assumptions has been hotly contested (see Rees 1982). Hyman, for example, analyzes the ways in which the expression "public interest" has historically been used in British political discourse. Appeals to a notion of "public interest" rest on an organic conception of society. In a capitalist society, however, concepts of public interest in the domain of labor law will in Hyman's view be synonymous with employer interests—that is, with the interests of capital (see Hyman 1982). Yet if one accepts the general framework of a capitalist economy, appeals to a public interest are perhaps not all merely rhetorical. At the very minimum, "within an individual nation state there is a general interest in the continued self-expansion of national capital" (Crouch 1982:107). This may be so even though certain groups benefit much more than others and even though the determinants and the specific meaning of the public interest vary through time (ibid.). In addition, the "national interest" may also reflect a particular historical and cultural reality vis-à-vis other nations; the state thus may act as a means of international redistribution (White 1984:99).

The discussion thus far suggests three conclusions concerning the meaning of "national interest." First, the identification of a national interest is inevitably political. Even within a single nation or state it involves controversial, value-laden, distributive issues. Second, in any particular situation it is extremely difficult to discern a clear national interest. This is especially likely to be the case in a complex, multitier system of lawmaking, such as the European Community. Third, if the conception of a national interest has any core meaning, it lies at the societal level of analysis. In capitalist societies this core meaning centers on the accumulation of capital. A similar conception of national interest is embodied in Hawley's notion of "state overview interests," "the policy result of the imperatives of accumulation and legitimation, as interpreted through the visions of a dominant ideology or ideologies of its leadership" (Hawley 1983:251). Fourth, and correlative, the aims or interests of specific individuals or organizations do not embody or represent the "public" or "national interest," which can be distinguished from and contrasted to putative "private" or "special interests" (compare Wilson 1979; Pearce 1983). Instead, at these levels of analysis, we must necessarily consider the particular relationships of different types of capital, viewed at different levels of abstraction, to the state.

Conclusion

This chapter represents an attempt to think about "interests." The purpose is twofold: to explore an aspect of the social matrix of European Community legislative processes, and to lay part of the groundwork for subsequently mapping the bargains (see Strange 1982) that made up the sheepmeat regime. I have concentrated especially on the relationship between structures and interests. Structures, in the sense in which I have used the word here, are simultaneously representations of previous outcomes as well as frameworks, influences, and sometimes determinants of continuing conflicts and compromises. They do not necessarily determine interests, and neither are they the only factors that shape or create interests. Moreover, in the European Community as elsewhere, patterns of lawmaking concerning different issues may vary substantially (see Keohane and Nye 1975:395–406; H. Wallace 1983:53). Nevertheless, this discussion suggests several conclusions concerning how we must approach the subject of "interests" in relation to the lawmaking process.

First, interests must be analyzed neither as antecedent to structures nor as entirely distinct in nature from outcomes. Instead, they need to be seen as created, reproduced, and transformed both by structures and by outcomes. These processes occur, for example, by means of various forms of "proceduralization" (Schaffer 1982), which include determination of the schedule, timing, or rhythm according to which issues are considered; determination of the agenda, defining which issues are to be discussed and thus within what range decisions can be made; and determination of the arena, audience, group, or institution that is to influence, transform, or actually make a decision.

Second, our thinking about interests must go beyond the frameworks imposed by concepts of pressure groups, neocorporatist arrangements, or simple class interests. The concept of a pressure group is itself an analytic notion, implicitly if not explicitly part of a pluralist theory of politics. Neocorporatist arrangements are actually designed, in part, to create interests. But neither is it sufficient to posit the existence of subjective class interests that derive directly and solely from objective relations of production. Instead, interests must be analyzed in a rela-

[191]

tional context, one that recognizes the dialectical connection between objective and subjective interests.

Third, thinking about "interests" is another way of thinking about power. In delimiting different types of interests, it is necessary always to bear in mind the three faces of power (Lukes 1974). These different faces of power embody different types of interests. In this context, interests are understood as a stake, a concern, an involvement, or a necessarily or potentially affected relation. Power is often considered as shaping interests, which simultaneously influence the exercise of power. But in addition, as I have tried to show, "power" is in some senses merely another word for "interest," while an interest often amounts to a form of power.

Finally, the interrelationship of structures, outcomes, and interests needs to be understood at different levels of analysis and at different levels of abstraction. For example, structures help to create interests at the individual, organizational, and societal levels. States, law, and the marketing chain thus established, modified, and shaped various interests in the making of the European Community's sheepmeat regime. Conversely, this lawmaking process and its legislative outcome were ways of producing, reproducing, and structuring interests.

Acknowledgments

The Nuffield Foundation and the University of Warwick Research and Innovations Fund kindly provided financial support for the research on which this chapter is based. Earlier versions of portions of the chapter were presented at the London School of Economics Seminar Series on New Approaches to the Study of Law and Disputes on June 28, 1985; the Wenner-Gren Foundation for Anthropological Research International Symposium on "Ethnohistorical Models for the Evolution of Law in Specific Societies," Bellagio, Italy, August 10–18, 1985; the Law and Society Association Annual Meeting, Chicago, Illinois, on May 29– June 2, 1986; and the Faculteit de Rechtsgeleersheid, Rijksuniversiteit Groningen, The Netherlands, on April 8, 1987. I am grateful to participants in these sessions for helpful comments. I also want to thank especially Richard Abel, Maurice Bloch, Jean-Pierre Boutonnet, Jane Collier, the Commission and the Council of the European Communities, Hélène Delorme, the Fédération Nationale Ovine, Peter Fitzpatrick, John Griffiths, Barbara Harriss, the Meat and Livestock Commission (UK), Siân Miles, Sally Falk Moore, Jeanette Neeson, Simon Roberts, Philippa Ross-White, Boaventura de Sousa Santos, June Starr, Iain Stewart, and an anonymous reader for Cornell University Press. I alone, of course, am responsible for the contents of the chapter, and all translations are my own.

REFERENCES

Agra Europe. 1982. *The International Trade in Lamb and Mutton.* Special Report 15. Tunbridge Wells, Kent, Eng.

Alford, R. R., and R. Friedland. 1985. *Powers of Theory: Capitalism, the State, and Democracy.* Cambridge, Eng.

Averyt, W. F., Jr. 1975. "Eurogroups, Clientela, and the European Community." *International Organisation* 29:949–971.

———. 1977. *Agropolitics in the European Community.* New York.

Bachrach, P., and M. S. Baratz. 1962. "The Two Faces of Power." *American Political Science Review* 56:947–952.

———. 1963. "Decisions and Nondecisions: An Analytical Framework." *American Political Science Review* 57:632–642.

Balbus, I. D. 1971. "The Concept of Interest in Pluralism and Marxian Analysis." *Politics and Society* 1(2):151–171.

Berger, S. D. 1981. "Introduction." In S. D. Berger, ed., *Organising Interests in Western Europe: Pluralism, Corporatism, and the Transformation of Politics.* Cambridge, Eng.

Boutonnet, J. P. [c.1975]. "Les Circuits des ovins de boucherie en France." Montpellier, France.

Broders, M. 1981. "La viande ovine: Situation dans la Communauté économique européenne et dans le monde; le règlement d'organisation de marché." *Revue du Marché Commun* 248:326–337 (June–July).

Butt Philip, A. 1983a. "Pressure Groups and Policy-making in the European Community." In J. Lodge, ed., *Institutions and Policies of the European Community,* pp. 20–26. London.

———. 1983b. "Pressure Groups and European Community Decision-making." In J. Lodge, ed., *The European Community: Bibliographical Excursions,* pp. 46–55. London.

Cain, M., and K. Kulcsar. 1981–82. "Thinking Disputes: An Essay on the Origins of the Dispute Industry." *Law and Society Review* 16(3):375–402.

Centre Français du Commerce Extérieur. 1974. *Structure comparée de la production et de la commercialisation des viandes ovines dans la CEE,* 2 vols. Paris.

Comaroff, J. L., and S. Roberts. 1981. *Rules and Processes: The Cultural Logic of Dispute in an African Context.* Chicago.

Commission of the European Communities. 1977. *A Study of the Evolution of Concentration in the Food Distribution Industry for the United Kingdom.* Brussels.

Francis G. Snyder

————. 1986. *Directory of Non-Governmental Agricultural Organisations set up at European Community Level.* Munich.

Connolly, W. E. 1972. "On 'Interests' in Politics." *Politics and Society* 2:459–477.

Cranney, J., and P. Rio. 1974. *Le Dossier de l'industrie de la viande: Monographie de firmes et de groupes.* Paris.

Crenson, M. A. 1971. *The Un-Politics of Air Pollution: A Study of Non-Decision-making in the Cities.* Baltimore.

Critchell, J. T., and J. Raymond. 1912. *The History of the Frozen Meat Trade.* London. Reprinted 1969.

Crouch, C. 1982. "Changing Perceptions of a Public Interest." In Lord Wedderburn of Charlton and W. T. Murphy, eds., *Labour Law and the Community: Perspectives for the 1970s,* pp. 107–116. London.

Cutler, A., B. Hindess, P. Hirst, and A. Hussein. 1977. *Marx's Capital and Capitalism Today,* vol. 1. London.

Dahrendorf, R. 1950. *Class and Class Conflict in Industrial Society.* London.

Daintith, T. C. 1982. "Legal Analysis of Economic Policy." *Journal of Law and Society* 9(2):191–224.

Donat, Marcel von. 1979. *Europe: Qui tire les ficelles?* Paris. Originally published as *Brusseler Machenschaften: Dem Euro-clan auf der Spur* (Baden-Baden).

Economic and Social Committee of the European Communities. 1980a. *Community Advisory Committees for the Representation of Socio-economic Interests.* Teakfield, Eng.

————. 1980b. *European Interest Groups and Their Relationships with the Economic and Social Committee.* Teakfield, Eng.

————. 1984. *Directory of European Agricultural Organisations.* London and Luxembourg.

Feld, W. J. 1980. "Two-Tier Policy Making in the EC: The Common Agricultural Policy." In L. Hurwitz, ed., *Contemporary Perspectives on European Integration: Attitudes, Nongovernmental Behaviour, and Collective Decision-making,* pp. 123–149. London.

Frey, F. W. 1971. "Comment. On Issues and Nonissues in the Study of Power." *American Political Review* 65:1081–1101.

Gallie, W. B. 1956. "Essentially Contested Concepts." *Aristotelian Society* 56:167–198.

George, S. 1985. *Politics and Policy in the European Community.* Oxford.

Gerbet, P., and D. Pepy, eds. 1969. *La décision dans les Communautés européennes.* Brussels.

Gerlich, P. 1986. "Cause and Consequences in Legislation: An Introduction." *European Journal of Political Research* 14:267–271.

Gervais, Michel. 1972. "L'Economie agricole française, 1955–1970." In Yves Tavernais, Michel Gervais, and Claude Servolin, eds., *L'Univers politique des paysans,* pp. 3–40. Paris.

Ghai, Y., R. Luckham, and F. Snyder. 1987. *The Political Economy of Law: A Third World Reader.* Oxford.

Giddens, A. 1979. *Central Problems in Social Theory: Action, Structure, and Contradiction in Social Analysis.* London.

[194]

————. 1984. *The Constitution of Society: Outline of a Theory of Structuration.* Cambridge, Eng.

Gilb, C. L. 1981. "Public or Private Governments." In Paul C. Nystrom and William H. Starbuck, eds., *Handbook of Organisational Design*, Vol. 2: *Remodelling Organisations and Their Environments*, pp. 464–491. Oxford.

Grant, W. P. 1983a. "The National Farmers Union: The Classic Case of Incorporation?" In D. Marsh, ed., *Pressure Politics: Interest Groups in Britain*, pp. 129–143. London.

Harvey, D. R. 1982. "National Interests and the CAP." *Food Policy*, August, 174–190.

Hawley, J. P. 1983. "National Interests, State Foreign Economic Policy, and the World-System: The Case of the U.S. Capital Control Programme, 1961–1974." In Pat McGowan and Charles W. Kegley, Jr., eds., *Foreign Policy and the Modern World-System*, pp. 223–254. Beverly Hills, Calif.

Hindess, B. 1982. "Power, Interests, and the Outcomes of Struggles." *Sociology* 16(4):498–511.

————. 1984. "Rational Choice Theory and the Analysis of Political Action." *Economy and Society* 7(4):343–410.

Holland, S. 1980. *UnCommon Market.* London.

Hyman, R. 1978. "Pluralism, Procedural Consensus, and Collective Bargaining." *British Journal of Industrial Relations* 16:16–40.

————. 1982. "The Concept of 'Public Interest' in Labour Relations." In Lord Wedderburn of Charlton and W. T. Murphy, eds., *Labour Law and the Community: Perspectives for the 1980s*, pp. 95–106. London.

Jessop, B. 1982. *The Capitalist State.* Oxford.

————. 1983. "The Capitalist State and the Rule of Capital: Problems in the Analysis of Business Associations." *West European Politics* 6(2):139–162.

Keeler, J. T. S. 1981a. "Corporatism and Official Union Hegemony: The Case of French Agricultural Syndicalism." In S. D. Berger, ed., *Organising Interests in Western Europe: Pluralism, Corporatism, and the Transformation of Politics*, pp. 185–208. Cambridge, Eng.

————. 1981b. "The Corporatist Dynamic of Agricultural Modernisation in the Fifth Republic." In W. G. Andrews and S. Hoffman, eds., *The Fifth Republic at Twenty*, pp. 271–291. Albany, N.Y.

————. 1985. "Situating France on the Pluralism-Corporatism Continuum: A Critique of and Alternative to the Wilson Perspective." *Comparative Politics*, January, pp. 229–247.

Keohane, R. O. 1982. "The Demand for International Regimes." *International Organisation* 36(2):325–355.

Keohane, R. O., and J. S. Nye, Jr. 1975. "International Dependence and Integration." *International Politics* (Handbook of Political Science) 8:363–414. Reading, Mass.

Kidder, R. L. 1980–81. "The End of the Road? Problems in the Analysis of Disputes." *Law and Society Review* 15(3–4):717–725.

Knightley, P. 1980a. "Vestey: The Gilded Tax-Dodgers." *Sunday Times*, October 5, pp. 13–14.

Francis G. Snyder

————. 1980b. "The Tax-Free Twenties." *Sunday Times*, October 19, pp. 62–63.
————. 1981. *The Vestey Affair*. London.
Krasner, S. D. 1984. "Approaches to the State: Alternative Conceptions and Historical Dynamics." *Comparative Politics* 16:223–246.
Lambert, J. 1975. "Larzac: Farmers against the Army." *Agenor* 52:1–28.
Lane, J. E. 1985. "Introduction: Public Policy or Markets? The Demarcation Problem." In Jan-Erik Lane, ed., *State and Market: The Politics of the Public and the Private*, pp. 3–52. London.
Lauret, F. 1983. "Sur les études de filières agroalimentaires." *Economies et Sociétés, Cahiers de l'ISMEA*, serie AG, May 16, pp. 721–740.
Lindberg, L. N. 1963. *The Political Dynamics of European Integration*. Stanford, Calif.
Lindberg, L. N., and S. A. Scheingold. 1970. *Europe's Would-Be Policy: Patterns of Change in the European Community*. Englewood Cliffs, N.J.
Lowi, T. J. 1972. "Four Systems of Policy, Politics, and Choice." *Public Administration Review*, July–August, pp. 298–310.
Lukes, S. 1974. *Power: A Radical View*. London.
Marx, K. 1968. "The Eighteenth Burmaire of Louis Boneparte." In Karl Marx and Frederick Engels, *Selected Works in One Volume*, pp. 96–179. London.
————. 1973. *Grundrisse: Foundations of the Critique of Political Economy*. Trans. M. Nicolaus. Harmondsworth, Eng.
Murray, R. 1971. "The Internationalisation of Capital and the Nation State." *New Left Review* 67:84–109.
Nelken, D. 1985. "Legislation and Its Constraints: A Case Study of the Rent Act." In Adam Podgorecki, Christopher J. Whelan, and Dinesh Khosla, eds., *Legal Systems and Social Systems*, pp. 70–86. London.
OECD. 1981. *Food Policy*. Paris.
Offe, C. 1975. "The Theory of the Capitalist State and the Problem of Policy Formation." In Leon N. Lindberg, Robert Alford, Colin Crouch, and Claus Offe, eds., *Stress and Contradiction in Modern Capitalism: Public Policy and the Theory of the State*, pp. 125–144. Lexington, Mass.
————. 1981. "The Attribution of Public Status to Interest Groups: Observations on the West German Case." In S. D. Berger, ed., *Organising Interests in Western Europe: Pluralism, Corporatism, and the Transformation of Politics*, pp. 123–158. Cambridge, Mass.
Olsen, J. P. 1981. "Integrated Organisational Participation in Government." In Paul C. Nystrom and William H. Starbuck, eds., *Handbook of Organisational Design*, vol. 2: *Remodelling Organisations and Their Environments*, pp. 492–516. Oxford.
O'Malley, P. 1980. "Accomplishing Law: Structure and Negotiation in the Legislative Process." *British Journal of Law and Society* 7:22–35.
Pâtre (La Revue de l'élevage ovin). 1984. *Numéro spécial: Filière viande ovine*, 319 (Décembre) [Institut Technique de Èlevage Ovin et Caprin (ITOVIC), Paris].
Pearce, J. 1983. "The Common Agricultural Policy: The Accumulation of Special Interests." In H. Wallace, W. Wallace, and C. Webb, *Policy-Making in the European Community*, 2d ed., pp. 143–175. Chichester, Eng.

Perren, R. 1978. *The Meat Trade in Britain, 1840–1914*. London.
Pivot, C. 1985. "Offices d'intervention et régulation contractuelle en Agriculture." *Revue d'Economie Politique* 1:66–86.
Przeworski, A. 1977. "Proletariat into a Class: The Process of Class Formation from Karl Kautsky's *The Class Struggle* to Recent Controversies." *Politics and Society* 7(4):343–401.
Raux, J., ed. 1984. *Politique agricole commune et construction communautaire*. Paris.
Rees, B. 1982. "Frames of Reference and the 'Public Interest.'" In Lord Wedderburn of Charlton and W. T. Murphy, eds., *Labour Law and the Community: Perspectives for the 1980s*, pp. 129–136. London.
Rosenthal, G. G. 1975. *The Men behind the Decisions: Cases in European Policy-Making*. Lexington, Mass.
Schaffer, B. B. 1982. "To Recapture Public Policy for Politics." *Politics, Administration, and Change* 7(1):1–22.
Scharpf, F. W. 1985. "The Joint-Decision Trap: Lessons from German Federalism and European Integration." Discussion paper, May 1. Wissenschaftszentrum, Berlin.
Schattschneider, E. E. 1960. *The Semi-Sovereign People: A Realist's View of Democracy in America*. New York.
Schmitter, P. C. 1979. "Modes of Interest Intermediation and Models of Societal Change in Western Europe." In Philippe C. Schmitter and Gerhard Lehmbruch, eds., *Trends Toward Corporatist Intermediation*, pp. 63–94. Beverly Hills, Calif.
Snyder, F. G. 1981. *Capitalism and Legal Change: An African Transformation*. New York.
———. 1985a. *Law of the Common Agricultural Policy*. London. Translated as *Le Droit de la politique agricole commune* (Paris, 1987).
———. 1985b. "Whose Common Market? The Making of the EEC Sheepmeat Regime." Paper presented at the Wenner-Gren Foundation for Anthropological Research, International Symposium on Ethnohistorical Models for the Evolution of Law in Specific Societies, August 10–18, Bellagio, Italy.
———. 1987a. "L'Agriculture et l'industrie dans le droit de la CEE." *Droit et Société* 5(1):23–52.
———. 1987b. "New Directions in European Community Law." *Journal of Law and Society* 14(1):167–182. Also published in Peter Fitzpatrick and Alan Hunt, eds., *Critical Legal Studies in the United Kingdom* (Oxford, 1987).
Snyder, F., and Hay, D. 1987. "Comparisons in the Social History of Law: Labour and Crime." In Francis Snyder and Douglas Hay, eds., *Labour, Law, and Crime in Historical Perspective*, pp. 1–41. London.
Sokoloff, S. 1980. "Rural Change and Farming Politics: A Terminal Peasantry." In P. G. Cerny and M. A. Schain, eds., *French Politics and Public Policy*, pp. 218–242. London.
Starr, J., and B. Yngvesson. 1975. "Scarcity and Disputing: Zeroing-in on Compromise Decisions." *American Ethnologist* 2:553–566.
Stevens, C., and C. Webb. 1983. "The Political Economy of Sugar: A Window on

the CAP." In H. Wallace, W. Wallace, and C. Webb, eds., *Policy-Making in the European Community*, 2d ed., pp. 321–347. Chichester, Eng.

Strange, S. 1982. "*Cave! hic dragones:* A Critique of Regime Analysis." *International Organisation* 36:479–496 (Spring).

Streeck, W., and P. C. Schmitter. [1984?]. "Community, Market, State—and Associations? The Prospective Contribution of Interest Governance to Social Order." Working Paper 94, European University Institute, Badia Fiesolana, Italy.

Taylor, N. W. 1982. "A World Overview." In P. W. J. Clough, ed., *EEC Sheep Industry Perspectives and Implications for New Zealand.* Palmerston North, New Zealand.

Wallace, H. 1981. "Regional Politics and Supranational Integration." In D. M. Cameron, ed., *Regionalism and Supranationalism: Challenges and Alternatives to the Nation-State in Canada and Europe*, pp. 111–126. Montreal and London.

———. 1983. "Negotiation, Conflict, and Compromise: The Elusive Pursuit of Common Policies." In H. Wallace, W. Wallace, and C. Webb, eds., *Policy-Making in the European Community*, 2d ed., pp. 43–80. Chichester, Eng.

Wallace, W. 1983. "Less Than a Federation, More Than a Regime: The Community as a Political System." In H. Wallace, W. Wallace, and C. Webb, eds., *Policy-Making in the European Community*, 2d ed., pp. 403–436. Chichester, Eng.

Wallace, H., W. Wallace, and C. Webb, eds. 1983. *Policy-Making in the European Community.* 2d ed. Chichester, Eng.

Webb, C. 1983. "Theoretical Perspectives and Problems." In H. Wallace, W. Wallace, and C. Webb, eds., *Policy-Making in the European Community*, 2d ed., pp. 1–41. Chichester, Eng.

Wendling, S. 1985. "France: le dossier viande ovine." In Giuseppe Ciavarini Azzi, ed., *L'Application du droit communautaire par les états membres*, pp. 279–287. Maastricht.

Who Owns Whom, United Kingdom, 1976/77. 1976. Vol. 1. London.

White, G. 1984. "Developmental States and Socialist Industrialisation in the Third World." *Journal of Developmental Studies* 21:97–120 (October 1).

Williams, R. 1983. *Keywords: A Vocabulary of Culture and Society.* 2d ed. London.

Wilson, G. K. 1979. *Special Interests and Policymaking: Agricultural Policies and Politics in Britain and the United States of America, 1956–1970.* London.

Wolfinger, R. E. 1971a. "Nondecisions and the Study of Local Politics." *American Political Science Review* 65:1063–1080.

———. 1971b. "Rejoinder to Frey's 'Comment.'" *American Political Science Review* 65:1102–1104.

PART III

Receiving and Rejecting National Legal Processes

[8]

The Impact of Second Republic Labor Reforms in Spain

George A. Collier

What is the relationship between legislation and legal change? And how does one best come to understand the experience of legal change for those whose lives legislation affects? When we examine such issues concerning how legal institutions and processes reach into, shape, and are shaped by daily affairs in the lives of communities and individuals, we must consider questions of power, of meaning, and above all of their historical interplay.

Power must be a consideration, because the forms that laws take and the impact of those laws at the local level are each shaped by political struggle that is not static but constantly in tension, in flux. Legislation will be the outcome of political struggle, and sometimes it will even result from contention for control of the state itself. But legislation can also shape the context and trajectory of political struggle, creating within the political order new space over which old parties may contend and within which new interests may emerge, as Francis Snyder has illustrated in his discussion of the European Economic Community. Local communities, asymmetrically embedded as they often are in larger fields of power relations, experience the consequences of the political flux that ensues from legislation, and sometimes contribute to it.

Meaning must be a consideration, because signification always exceeds intention, in the legal arena as in any other. What legislation means to individuals differs in relation to each person's goals and objective interests according to the contextually and culturally specific terms in which they interpret their experience. The meaning of legislation in local communities may diverge substantially from what the legislators intended, especially insofar as signification will reflect the situationally specific terms in which those in local places interpret the law. Implementing agrarian decrees of the Spanish Second Republic in terms that drew meaning from customary property and employment relations, the villagers I discuss in this chapter imparted to the legislation meanings of personhood and honor quite different from those the lawmakers in Madrid probably envisioned.

The outcome of legislation thus involves both power and meaning, and the interplay resulting from the various interpretations given to and taken from the law in the politics that ensue from it. This chapter explores such consequences of early Second Republic agrarian reforms in Spain in terms of how the Socialists implemented and experienced them in an Andalusian sierra town that I shall call Los Olivos. The Socialists were strong advocates of agrarian reform in the Second Republic. As ministers in the coalitional provisional government of April 1931, Socialist leaders decreed reforms in agrarian employment. But these decrees, and the intention of adding land reform to them, inflamed conflict, particularly in the agrarian south. That conflict welled up into politics at the national level, setting back the advocates of land reform and watering down the terms in which land reform was finally legislated.

The intention here is to illuminate the impact of the reforms legislated for agrarian employment by studying the political struggle through which rank-and-file Socialists effected the reforms. The implementation was hard fought in Los Olivos, as elsewhere in the south, where disappointment and frustration with the slow pace of land reform is thought by historians to have radicalized the Socialist rank and file and eventually party leaders. But in Los Olivos the labor reforms radicalized the Socialists in a different way—by instilling a sense of accomplishment in them.

The measure of the Los Olivos Socialists' achievements should be in the terms of goals *they* sought in the concrete lived experience of their circumstances. Scholars have placed a great deal of emphasis on Second Republic land reform, but this is not what the Socialists of Los Olivos were concerned with, nor was it the sole concern of militant agrarian workers elsewhere in Andalusia. In Los Olivos the relationship of proprietor to employee, to which ownership of the means of production gave rise, was much more immediate than land tenure per se. And it was over jobs and working conditions, not land, that agrarian workers battled proprietors, winning revolutionary changes in relations of employment.

The revolutionary character of their struggle becomes intelligible only when understood in terms of the cultural meanings of owning property and working for wages in Los Olivos. Property enabled a man to be *autónomo*—self-sufficient and independent of any other person's beck and call. Lack of property forced a man to bow his head to others in order to support his family, and it made him suppress his own will in any matter that might anger his employers. Villagers experienced autonomy with reference to the familiar Mediterranean idiom of honor—masculine honor and family honor. The self-sufficient could assert their own honor, and they could question it with respect to those who demonstrated their insufficiency by having to labor for wages. Customary usages had developed around wage labor, ameliorating but not eliminating the inherent humiliation of wage labor.

When the Socialists took power in Los Olivos in 1933, they revolutionized employment by seizing for labor the prerogative of determining what land should be cultivated, by whom, and when. Stripping proprietors of their autonomous power to decide such matters, the Socialists deprived landownership of its cultural meaning and inverted the relationship of employer to employee. Thus, although they acted on the basis of early Second Republic agrarian legislation, whose intent was reformist, they did so in ways that were revolutionary for the manner in which they lived and worked.

The Early Second Republic Agrarian Legislation

By allying with modern Republicans at the outset of the Spanish Second Republic, the Socialists won significant reforms for agrarian labor.[1] To analyze these reforms and their effects, we must situate them in the context of political struggle that shaped them and that they in turn engendered. The Socialist alliance with moderate Republicans was a tactic in ongoing competition among leftist groups for preeminence in working-class leadership. The agrarian reforms were an initial victory for the Socialists. Over the first two years of the Second Republic, however,

[1]Preston 1978 gives the most nuanced account of the role of the Socialists in the Second Republic. I have also drawn from Herr 1971 in this account.

the reforms themselves gave rise to a reaction that embattled Socialists and moderate Republicans from the right as well as from the left.

Socialist participation in the government of the Second Republic came at a time when the Socialists were consolidating gains in the organization of agrarian labor at the expense of other working-class groups, notably the rival anarchists. In contrast to anarchists, who opposed a centralized state in every form, the Socialists had a history of compromising with the employing classes in order to advance socialism through legislation and collaboration in government. In the 1922–30 dictatorship of Primo de Rivera, the Socialists had collaborated opportunistically with the government, at least initially, enabling their Unión General de Trabajadores (UGT) to expand while the government closed down rival leftist organizations or forced them underground. Although the Socialists distanced themselves from Primo de Rivera toward the end of his regime, they strengthened their position by participating in Primo's program of arbitration committees for setting wage levels and settling labor disputes. During Primo's regime, and after his downfall in early 1930, the Socialists, through their Landworkers Federation (FNTT), made considerable headway in organizing agrarian labor, rivaling the anarchists on their own turf in the south.

Thus it was that moderate Republicans embraced the Socialists as trustworthy spokesmen for labor in the early Second Republic. The Second Republic was formed in April 1931 with a provisional government coalition of right-wing Progressives, Radicals from the center, and on the left four urban middle-class parties. Of the working-class parties, only the Socialists were in the coalition. Socialists were given three posts in the Republican coalition—the minister of justice, minister of finance, and minister of labor, the latter held by Francisco Largo Caballero. The Socialists used their posts to press for reforms in favor of the agrarian workers then flocking into their Landworkers Federation and the UGT. At one of the first cabinet meetings, the Socialists agreed to postpone land reform in return for immediate action on a number of other measures to alleviate agrarian unemployment and to aid poor tenant farmers. The reforms took shape in a series of edicts during the first ten weeks of the Second Republic, later embodied in legislation after the Cortes (parliament) completed drafting the new constitution.

Certain of the edicts regulated leases benefiting small tenant farmers, prohibiting landowners from expelling them in fear of future expropriation of leased property. The edicts called for rent reductions when justified by declines in a property's level of income. They gave formally constituted workers' societies preference in obtaining new leases of large properties. Other edicts enacted reforms designed to better employment. They set an eight-hour day. They set up "mixed juries" representing labor, property owners, and local government to arbitrate local disputes and to enforce labor legislation. They mandated preferential hiring of laborers within the municipal boundaries of an employer's property, and they required that owners either work their lands or turn their production over to local laborers.

These were significant and controversial policies in that they gave both labor and the state a role in setting the conditions for contracts that employers had theretofore been able to set independently. As Malefakis (1970:170) has emphasized, and as proved to be the case in Los Olivos, "the agrarian decrees of the Provisional Government constituted a revolution without precedent in Spanish rural life. For the first time, the balance of legal rights swung away from the landowners to the rural proletariat." In addition, the state set about to alleviate a crisis of unemployment by using the budget at all levels of government to hire labor for the construction of public works. In this way, public funds for public works to employ laborers within the framework of the new legislation began to be distributed to towns through provincial councils.

Socialists thus delivered significant legislative reforms to their growing agrarian constituency, but implementing the reforms was another matter. Growing opposition from the right during 1931–33 blunted the progressive thrust of the Second Republic, and the government had to fend off pressures from the left for more militant and revolutionary changes.

Resistance from the right developed as monarchist sympathizers and defenders of the traditional order fought for their privilege and power. While some groups plotted the overthrow of the Republic, others attempted to thwart proposed reforms by legal means. As the Cortes began to draft a constitution, the right rallied to defend the church from provisions to cut off state support for clergy and religious orders and to limit church wealth. The church joined the right in belligerent propaganda to found a mass right-wing coalition of non-Republican forces, out of which emerged the Confederación Española de Derechas Autónomas (CEDA) in February 1933. CEDA grew rapidly in agrarian areas by whipping up fears among small landholders that their property would be expropriated, and by lobbying for higher prices for wheat—a tactic that would benefit landowners at the expense of workers. And CEDA lobbied against the existing labor legislation and attempted to stall or

[205]

reverse legislation on agrarian leases or on proposed land reform. The right encouraged landowners to thwart labor by refusing employment to union workers and by withholding land from production or turning it into pasture.

As part of the governing coalition, Socialists at the national level were in a dilemma because resistance from the right elicited ever greater militancy on the left. Anarchist agitation and the use of the strike were growing in response to rightest provocation, yet the Socialists, in the government, were committed to sustaining legal order even in the face of militancy from within their own ranks. Thus the Socialists' accomplishments on behalf of the agrarian worker were problematic at best during the first two years of the Second Republic.

Opposition to Reforms in Early
Second Republic Los Olivos

In local places as much at the national level, Second Republic agrarian reforms took on meaning in political struggle. Local opposition to progressive early Second Republic reforms was strong in Los Olivos. To begin, a propertied elite firmly entrenched in municipal governance used reactionary tactics to attempt to break the fledgling socialist Syndicate of Agrarian Workers, which in turn struggled for the right to represent labor within the framework of early Second Republic agrarian legislation. It took the intervention of the provincial government to secure the union's rights, but in a context that rightists continued to dominate.

The political history of this struggle became known to me through ethnohistoric method attuned to issues concerning class, and this is pertinent to the historical theme of this volume. The Second Republic was an era that few villagers discussed forthrightly with Jane Collier and me in the 1960s, and they did so only later, after Franco's death and the election of the current Socialist government. Even now we have been able to make sense of Second Republic events only through methods designed explicitly to explore issues of class in systematic terms. We learned a great deal through interviews about family history—but especially about working-class poor, many of whom were killed in 1936— because one basis for our interviewing was the systematic and exhaustive reconstruction of the town's poulation from vital registry and census data that included individuals of all classes, many of whom would otherwise have been overlooked, forgotten, or left unmentioned. Los Olivos' Second Republic town hall minutes brought to life the inner maneuvering of protagonists in their struggle over agrarian issues, but once again the struggle's class dimensions became clear only by linking events to the class position of the protagonists as reconstructed from tax records and occupational categories in censuses.

Let me introduce Los Olivos from the standpoint of the political-economic background of this struggle. Preindustrial, labor-intensive capitalist agriculture complemented peasant agriculture in Los Olivos in the 1920s. A community of less than 1,000 inhabitants, Los Olivos was one of several villages oriented to Aracena, the administrative and principal agrarian market center in the sierra of northern Huelva, the westernmost province of Andalusia. In the nineteenth century, agrarian entrepreneurs had absorbed church property and town commons into agrarian estates and had passed power as a landed oligarchy to their descendants in this century. Celestino López, Los Olivos's *cacique,* or political boss, was part of this oligarchy. His power inhered in the employment he could offer on lands that comprised one-fourth of the municipality, and in being able to deliver the vote to the political machinery of both the provincial and the national government. It was against López's control of agrarian employment that the Socialists struggled.

Lesser agrarian proprietors and merchants from a handful of interrelated families shared power with López. Most important among these were the Morenos, who were prominent in commerce linking Los Olivos through the market town of Aracena to suppliers in Seville and Huelva. Moreno family members had served as mayor and justice of the peace. Two had controlled the church and the school. Some of the Morenos were progressives who were to take part in the Socialist union leadership; others were staunch conservatives.

Below the López and Moreno families were peasant smallholders and a sizable stratum of landless and frequently unemployed poor who labored for wages in the production of olives, hogs, fruit, vegetables, cork, and grains. In the 1920s many of these poorer worker and smallholding families of Los Olivos had been at the mercy of López for seasonal employment. These laborers, and many smallholders who eventually joined them, made up the rank and file of the Socialist union that contested López's power.

López had used reactionary means to control the town council in the 1931 elections that ushered in the Second Republic. Resorting to the tactics by which rural *caciques* had perpetuated their control of public office, López prevented the putting up of an opposition slate and took office himself under the terms of Article 29 of the municipal code. This article held that a slate that had "no opposition" could dispense with an election. Taking office with López were his manager, Patricio López, and several other men of property.

Socialists in Los Olivos quickly engaged López in a struggle to control municipal public works, prefiguring future battles over control of agrarian employment. Unemployment was on the rise in Andalusia in 1931 because of drought. Everyone agreed that it was the role of the state to alleviate unemployment through local public works. What was at stake in Los Olivos was the prerogative to determine who the "needy workers" were and how jobs should be provided to them. The Socialists claimed that prerogative for their Syndicate of Agrarian Workers.

The syndicate drew most of its initial rank and file from poorer townsfolk, among them muleteers and men who farmed tiny properties and worked seasonally for wages. The union was led by progressive men, several of them agemates, from wealthier Los Olivos families closely related to the conservative, traditional power-holders. Thus Ceferino Santis, president of the syndicate, was brother to one of López's councilors and allies. And Pablo Moreno, the syndicate's young ideologue, was from a merchant family that had sent him to work in a Seville store where he had been radicalized.

The basis for conflict over the control of public works inhered not only in the contending claims of two institutional bodies, the syndicate and the town council, but also in the ambiguity of who the needy unemployed were and to which body were they allied. The syndicate sought to represent families that made most of their living through wage labor. Yet Celestino López's faction included laborers as well. It included families that the rich patronized with year-long employment on local estates. And it included masons, ostensibly laborers in that they worked for wages, who enjoyed continual employment in rebuilding houses of the wealthy; masons also supervised most public construction funded through the town council. Many women and youth depended on domestic work for the wealthy, and thus dared not oppose them. Finally, the class position of many smallholding farming families was ambiguous, as youthful members worked for wages but aspired to some degree of autonomy that inheritance of smallholdings would eventually give them.

It was in this context that conflict over public works developed in Los Olivos during the summer months of 1931 after employment in the wheat harvest ended. Celestino López secured funds to repave several village streets and began hiring favored workers, in the name of the town council, to undertake the work. The syndicate contested the legitimacy of this employment, claiming the prerogative to determine who were needy laborers and insisting that workers had to join the union to be eligible for wages paid from public funds earmarked to relieve the unemployment crisis. Celestino López threatened to put the paving up for public bidding, a tactic that would probably have awarded the work to independent masons. The syndicate responded by violently disrupting the town council session of September 23, 1931, causing Celestino López to appeal to the provincial governor to send an official representative to restore order in the town.

The governor's representative arrived from Huelva on September 24, empowered by the governor to take whatever steps he saw fit to settle Los Olivos' conflicts. After hearing the grievances against the town council, he removed López and his manager from the council, but in so doing he turned its presidency over to one of López's associates, effectively leaving the town government in control of the López faction. The tactic served as something of a compromise to stem the conflict. At the same time, however, he ordered the council to cooperate with the syndicate in forming a *junta de policía rural* to draw up the *Bases de Trabajo* to regulate employer-worker contracts, steps provided for by the decree and legislation of the Ministry of Labor that López's council had never undertaken. By this act the governor forced the town council to recognize key provisions of the Second Republic's agrarian decrees that they had ignored, legitimating a specific role for the syndicate in the local management of labor relations.

Several months of uneasy compromise between the council and the syndicate ensued. The bodies collaborated in ongoing public works for a time, and they revived an older plan to construct a new entrance road to the town, exacting promises of funding from the governor. Yet the compromise satisfied neither faction. As it broke down, the councilors repeatedly tendered their resignations, only to have the governor insist that they remain in office pending completion of Republican legislation reforming the norms of municipal government.

The councilors thus served under protest for the remainder of 1931 and throughout 1932, and it was probably not with enthusiasm that they implemented such Second Republic measures as the establishment of a local employment office in which employers were supposed to list all their job openings and workers their availability for hire. For its part, in the early spring months of 1932 the syndicate renewed its complaints to the governor about the council's abuse of its responsibilities.

Substantively, the battle over who should be deemed needy labor continued even as ambiguities of class position between the two factions began to be sorted out. The syndicate wanted to monopolize representation of all workers as against proprietors by gaining control of the town council itself. It thus advocated ousting the council, and free elections to replace it, as the remedy for a host of charges against the council submitted to the governor in early July:

> We as Agrarian Socialists, protest the comportment of the Town Council, constituted under Article 29, for the most part made up of men who held office under the Dictatorship, all of them Monarchists in opposition to this Republic of Workers.
>
> While thirty fathers lacked even bread to feed their children, this dignified council spent municipal funds to pay for music and religious sermons during the fiesta of San José. They obliged the priest to parade the patronal saint through the town under armed guard, attempting thereby to provoke public violence. But we Workers recognized this act as a provocation, as an attempt to get us to shed our blood in the streets and thus to break up our Union, something that will not happen even if the streets should be washed in our blood.
>
> This Town Council is wholly in the service of the great *Cacique*, who threatens workers who seek employment from him and has them jailed. The council spent all of the tax surcharges for public works in paving a street that only goes to the *Cacique's* front door. . . .
>
> Because we could add innumerable charges to this list, we petition you to remove from office the councilors and above all . . . to order the election of a Council by popular vote. We trust that Your Excellency will see justice done. May Your Excellency live many years in favor of the Republic.

The governor asked the council to respond to these charges point by point, but he seems to have taken no explicit formal action to sanction the council.

In the first two years of the Second Republic, Los Olivos thus experienced continuing oligarchical domination of municipal institutions. Local power-holders allowed only token innovations of the Second Republic—the secularization of the cemetery, the opening of public schools, the naming of streets in honor of Spanish intellectuals, artists, and statesmen. In this context the Socialist workers union won grudging recognition and state backing of its legitimacy, but it was not until 1933 that local Socialists came to power in their own right and brought the agrarian legislation passed two years earlier fully into effect.

Los Olivos Socialists in Power, 1933–1934

López had constituted the town council by circumventing elections under Article 29 of the municipal code at the outset of the Second Republic. Such abuse posed a widespread problem. The remedy finally decided on was to replace councils constituted that way with administrative bodies representing labor, property, and the state while preparing for municipal elections under a reformed code that would ensure popularly elected councils.

In Los Olivos the interim council took office in January 24, 1933. Niceto Ortega, the schoolteacher, headed it in his capacity as public employee. As interim mayor, Ortega set out to improve and broaden education. He also collaborated closely with the Socialists. He joined the syndicate leaders in a visit to the governor to persuade him to concede funds for public works to build a new entrance road to Los Olivos. He also allowed them to rent a building owned by the town for the Casa del Pueblo, the public salon for UGT members and affiliates with facilities for party assemblies and a reading room with newspapers and leftist literature. The Casa del Pueblo was where the syndicate conducted its business, drawing up lists of workers resident in the municipality who were eligible for local employment. Finally, Ortega oversaw Los Olivos' first open municipal elections of the decade, on April 23, which the Socialist slate won.

The Socialists did not come to power at the most auspicious moment. By April 1933, Azaña's coalitional government had been shaken by the growing outcry against the January massacre of anarchists at Casas Viejas, Cádiz, who had momentarily seized power from the Civil Guard in an abortive uprising (Mintz 1982). The Socialists, as collaborators in the Azaña government, suffered from this opprobrium. The more general reaction that set in would lead to a rightist electoral landslide in 1933 and to the undoing or stilling of many of the reforms favoring the rural proletariat. Los Olivos' Socialists shared the adversity of these setbacks throughout their incumbency from April 1933 to October 1934.

Yet the Socialists accomplished much by way of local governance that they could be proud of. For the first time they held a majority in the bodies managing local labor relations, and they immediately used their position to wrest advantages for labor from the town's employers. Their first step was to raise workers' daily wages from 4 pesetas to 4.50 pesetas. They also called property owners to a public meeting to demand that they hire more workers and that they pay an advance on their property taxes for the council to use in public works employment. There is no record of what transpired in the meeting, but it cannot have been successful, for a few days later Santis petitioned the governor to send a representative to intervene with employers on behalf of laborers.

The Socialists' proudest achievement was the public works construction of a new entrance road for Los Olivos. In July 1933 the provincial government finally awarded them the contract for the long-awaited project. The contract gave them a year in which to build the road, and the syndicate dedicated almost all its energies to organizing the construction. Only members of the syndicate could labor on the project, using dynamite, pickaxes, and shovels to blast and grade a roadbed out of a granite hillside.

Looking to the future, and probably responding to Ortega's role in paving the way to their incumbency, the Socialists began to plan a complex of school buildings in Los Olivos. Under the most recent legislation, the state could provide a nearly total subsidy for such construction in a town of Los Olivos' small size.

The Socialists thus seized the opportunities provided by incumbency with considerable boldness. Their seventeen-month reign was a relatively proud one. They refurbished the Casa del Pueblo. They set up a *bar de izquierdas*, a leftist bar that counterposed itself to the López Casino. To make the town more attractive, they ordered property owners to whitewash all the buildings facing the streets. The roadway itself was the most tangible symbol of the syndicate's accomplishments, and even now rightists of Los Olivos grudgingly credit the Socialists with this major achievement. But more important even than the road was the Socialists' revolutionizing of labor relations in Los Olivos.

Land, Autonomy, and Labor Relations

During their seventeen-month incumbency in the town hall, the Socialists advanced and consolidated their organization and control of employment on the basis of the initial agrarian decrees and related legislation. In doing so, they laid the groundwork for revolutionary challenges to relations of production in Los Olivos. Yet these challenges did not involve *reparto,* the redistribution of property sought elsewhere in Spain by agrarian revolutionaries and enabled in moderation through land-reform legislation in September 1932. In order to appreciate the accomplishments of the Los Olivos Socialists, we must understand why they eschewed land reform and in what sense their labor initiatives were revolutionary. That is to say, we must analyze the meaning that the labor initiatives assumed in the lived experience of those hiring workers and those who worked for others.

Although we cannot be absolutely sure that the Socialists did not press for land redistribution in Los Olivos, I am convinced that it was not an important goal. There is not one mention of land reform in the hundreds of pages of town council minutes, litigation, and other documentation I have examined, and Los Olivos is not mentioned in state bulletins that reported land-reform initiatives. While this is negative evidence, the recollections of villagers support it.

One possible reason that redistribution was not sought is that land was much more equitably distributed in Los Olivos than in other Sierra de Aracena municipalities. The totally landless were not as numerous in the populace of Los Olivos as elsewhere. Many day workers had small holdings.

More important, Los Olivos Socialists probably avoided advocating land reform to avoid alienating smallholders from their cause. Smallholders in Los Olivos were more amenable to the Socialist cause than were their counterparts in such areas in Castile. Unlike peasants in Castile, whose experience with day workers was with laborers brought in at harvesttime from other towns and cities (Pérez Díaz 1976:125), smallholders in Los Olivos were closely tied to day workers in their town. Many were related to one another, members of smallholding families often worked side by side with day laborers to supplement subsistence farming. Hence, a worker-peasant alliance was quite justifiable in Los Olivos, and when the Socialists offered employment in public works during their incumbency in the town council in 1933–34, many smallholders did join the syndicate to avail themselves of jobs.

The Socialists thus united laborers and peasants in work, setting aside land reform—if it was in fact ever a goal. Instead, the relationships of work, of employer to employee, prove to have been central to alliances and cleavages in Los Olivos, much more so than differences in ownership of property per se.

To explain why relationships of employment were so significant, I must say something about the cultural meaning of *autonomía.* Villagers

of Los Olivos held to the ideal of masculine autonomy that was characteristic of property relations in agrarian societies of the Mediterranean.
The property system brought together a couple's productive assets and
vested the care of those assets in the male head of household. A family
estate of sufficient size enabled a man to protect and develop his family
interests with autonomy. Such a man could do what he wanted, free
from others' control, including standing up to others to protect his
family's honor.

Inequalities of wealth made it impossible for all men to live up to the
ideal. Men who controlled insufficient property had to bow their heads
in subservience to employers. Such men sacrificed autonomy perforce,
and in doing so called into question their ability to defend family interests and honor. Conversely, the man wealthy enough to hire labor held
in addition to autonomy the power to subordinate others, arbitrarily if so
desired, and even in ways that might compromise the subordinate's
family honor.

The ideal of masculine autonomy thus charged employer-employee
relations with special tension. In having to accept someone else's orders,
the employee implicitly acknowledged his lack of full autonomy and his
vulnerability to potential dishonor. In giving orders, either directly or
through a representative, the employer implicitly asserted his own
invulnerability and power.

Many of the usages and attitudes that Juan Martínez-Alier (1971)
describes as characteristic of Andalusian employment guarded against
the direct threats to masculine autonomy that employment entailed.
The use of foremen shielded employers and employees from direct
confrontation. Through unión—emphasizing workers' solidarity and the
strict equality with which what applied to one applied to all—workers
not only protected their class interests but also defended against any
questioning of their individual autonomy. By having well-defined standards as to what amount and quality of work fulfilled a worker's obligation to his employer to cumplir, workers not only resisted exploitation
but also subtly protected themselves from appearing to have to take
orders.

Seen in this light, the Bases de Trabajo of the Second Republic
implicitly challenged the autonomy of the proprietor to manage his own
affairs. They did so by altering customary usages of employment and by
giving labor the upper hand over employers in determining relations of
employment. The extent to which they did so can be seen in the Bases
drawn up for the Sierra de Aracena region by the Mixed Jury for Rural

Labor of Aracena in June 1933, just after the Socialists assumed power in Los Olivos.

In general, the *Bases de Trabajo* set minimally acceptable terms under which employers had to hire workers. These terms included minimum wages, extra pay for the transporting of equipment, a place to tie up and graze a mule or horse, hygienic lodging if a worker was to live on site, and so forth. Only employment at least as favorable to the laborer as specified in the *Bases* was permissible.

The *Bases* formalized workers' maximum responsibility to employers, in many instances reducing what a laborer had to do in order to *cumplir*. Instead of the customary work *de sol a sol* (from dawn to dusk), the *Bases* set the workday at six hours in winter and seven hours in summer, with extra hours paid as overtime. They specified reduction in the workday to compensate for any travel to work over two kilometers from a worker's home. They codified the degrees of respect that employers and workers were to show to one another, to foremen, and to these parties' families.

Worker solidarity and *unión* were institutionalized by the *Bases* in the functioning of municipal employment entities in which organized labor had a voice and often control. Laborers were to be hired on a weekly or semimonthly basis in rotation and in the strict order with which they had signed up for employment in the municipal Office of Employment and Labor Exchange. Employers could not hire workers for jobs that had not been listed in these offices. These provisions prevented employers from favoring some laborers and blackballing others. They also affirmed the dignity of work by preventing laborers from having to kowtow to employers in order to get jobs.

The *Bases* considerably restricted employers' autonomy in managing their agricultural property. They prohibited the use of reaping or threshing machinery and of plows in vineyards. They mandated yearlong contracts for a specific number of laborers, depending on the acreage a farmer owned and how it was cultivated. They limited the grounds on which employers could dismiss employees.

The *Bases de Trabajo* for the Aracena region were by no means unique in so tipping the balance of employment relations in favor of workers. *Bases* issued in other areas of Andalusia during 1933 were equally far-reaching. In Jaén, for example, the *Bases* codified the customary harvest practice of *rebusca* in ways that were highly advantageous to the proletariat. This practice permitted foragers to follow harvest teams into the olive groves to scavenge the fruit that had been left behind. Usually the *rebusca* began after harvesting was completed.

The 1933 Jaén *Bases* authorized the *rebusca* to begin after one-fourth of the harvest was in, leading proprietors to charge angrily that they were being robbed of their harvest.

The outcry of proprietors against the *Bases de Trabajo* for Aracena was equally angry. "The propertied class of Aracena has its hands up while the *Boletín Oficial* of June 14 takes aim at them with the rifle of the *Bases* contained therein," railed the *Diario de Huelva* as it lambasted the provisions mandating hiring of workers on yearlong contracts for properties of a specified size. Indeed, the *Bases* were far-reaching, and in the hands of representatives of labor who also controlled municipal governance they posed the potentially revolutionary threat of completely undermining proprietors' autonomy to put property to whatever use they wanted in capitalist production.

The Agrarian Experience of Reaction, 1933–1935

Understood in cultural terms, then, the labor initiatives legislated as reforms assumed more radical significance as agrarian workers and politicians implemented them at the local level. These developments were not without their political reaction, however. In substantial measure stimulated by agrarian conflict in the south (Preston 1984), reaction surged on the right from the provincial level to the national level during 1933 and 1934, leading to increasing use of public force against the left in the name of law and order, and culminating in the overt repression of Socialists and leftists in the autumn of 1934. Spaniards refer to the period of reactionary Republican government that followed the November 1933 electoral victory of CEDA, the rightist front, as the *bienio negro*, a two-year period of repression and of legislative repeal of many earlier Republican reforms.

The reaction tipped the balance of the state's agrarian concerns away from labor and in favor of proprietors. Although adhering to corporatist rhetoric that heralded agrarian workers as part of the *gran familia campesina* whose collaboration in work was vital for the economy, state agrarian policy in 1934 clearly aimed at getting harvests in without disruption or destruction. The government had begun to ignore earlier prolabor agrarian legislation, evoking heightened labor militancy, particularly in Extremadura. The threat of a harvest strike had been proclaimed on May Day by the Socialists, who were no longer in the government and who joined with the anarchists in the Frente Campesino to secure land reform and agrarian workers' rights. In response, the minister of the interior was given a free hand to prevent the strike. He instigated the wholesale arrest of towns' Socialist leaders and closed down the Socialist newspaper, *El Obrero de la Tierra* (Malefakis 1970:336–337; Jackson 1965:134–135). In June, strikes and work stoppages affecting harvests were declared illegal. The wave of arrests extended even to Socialist deputies in the Cortes, despite their constitutional immunities (Jackson 1965:137), evoking comparisons to the fascist repressions of German Social Democrats in 1933 and the Vienna Socialists in February 1934.

It was in this context that Los Olivos Socialists began to experience reaction and repression. Having lost control of the town council, the rightist opposition took to the courts in 1933, primarily in civil suits harassing Socialist leaders. Many of them brought suits of eviction against their tenants—including several leading Socialists and their kin as defendants—under one or another pretext to rid themselves of the threat of indefinite leases on unfavorable terms.[2]

These and other suits proliferated within a broader context of reaction in which successive governors of Huelva undertook to contain labor unrest. Whenever a general strike was anticipated, the incumbent governor would declare a state of alarm under the Ley de Orden Público and deploy the Assault Guard or Civil Guard to put suspects under "preventive" arrest. Preventive arrest was a common experience for the town's leading Socialists, who suspected that police forces were trying to provoke them. Socialist Mayor Ceferino Santis was arrested at least a dozen times and held without charges being brought against him.

As the threat of harvest strikes swept the country in May 1934, the arrests quickened. On May 2, the day after the Socialists had proclaimed the Frente Campesino, the governor suspended Ceferino Santis from his position as mayor and had him jailed. In early June 1934, workers went on general strike in towns throughout the province, and the governor arrested strike leaders, including Los Olivos' Socialist acting mayor.

Then in October 1934, in the wake of the Asturias Revolution and a wave of agrarian strikes in Andalusia, the governor announced orders from Madrid to remove from office every individual whose inclinations might oppose those of the state. On October 22 a large number of

[2]Eviction suits were a new consequence of Republican legislation in 1933, which was repealed in 1935. In Los Olivos, as elsewhere, many older property owners leased land to tenant farmers to procure income during retirement. These property owners recognized the repealed legislation as a threat to their power and their prerogatives as landlords.

Huelva towns, including Los Olivos, received orders replacing leftists on their councils with rightists. The state of alarm suspending civil rights was extended through 1935. Hundreds of town councilors were suspended throughout Spain, and up to 40,000 union leaders and former councilors were held prisoner (Jackson 1965:161). In Los Olivos the entire council was suspended and replaced with a slate headed by Celestino López, the former *cacique*.

Needless to say, these developments brought Socialist agrarian employment practices to a halt. López and his co-councilors made a clean sweep of all personnel involved in town government. The syndicate having been dissolved by order of the governor, the councilors closed down the Casa del Pueblo, the Socialists' meeting place and labor exchange. They fired Socialists from jobs and allowed private employers to do the same. They hounded former Socialist council members with charges of fiscal malfeasance and persuaded the governor to instigate criminal proceedings against them.

The rightist council also collaborated with the repressive Civil Guard, which the governor used province-wide to maintain order in the face of threatened general strikes. The council enlarged and refurbished the local Civil Guard garrison, which belonged to Celestino López, who happily agreed to sell the building to the town for 9,000 pesetas. For their part, the Civil Guard made their presence felt with a vengeance. Judicial records show that citations by the officers increased thirtyfold in 1935. Almost all the citations were to poorer townsfolk allegedly caught trespassing or improperly herding in the countryside, primarily on properties of the largest landowners. It had become clear that the state had backed the conservative propertied class against agrarian workers in the Huelva countryside during the *bienio negro*, reversing gains made by labor on the basis of earlier agrarian legislation.

The Socialist Vindication, 1936

Despite the reversals of the *bienio negro*, the Socialists of Los Olivos were able to reinstate and even advance their radical transformation of agrarian employment after general elections—won by the Popular Front coalition of Socialists, Communists, and left Republicans—returned the left to power in February 1936.

There were various sources of the greater militancy with which vindicated Los Olivos Socialists now reasserted their authority. Several of them had been jailed in Huelva with militant anarchists and Communists during the repression. The fact that the Popular Front had brought the parties of the left together added to their militance. The Socialists subscribed to a variety of left newspapers, in addition to the party organs *El Socialista* and *El Obrero de la Tierra*, so they were abreast of the redirection of Socialist party policy to press workers and peasant organizers to take the initiative in the Spanish countryside rather than wait for the Popular Front government to act.

Theoretically, the state still exercised its legitimate dominion, but in fact the balance of power had shifted to the local level and to labor more than ever before. At the national level, Socialist leader Francisco Largo Caballero convinced the Socialists not to accept ministerial posts in the government, so that they would have a freer hand than in the first *bienio* to respond to the militant demands of their rank and file. The FNTT pressed peasants to undertake land invasions on their own and to protect themselves from the Civil Guard with local militias of their own (Malefakis 1970:365–366). While the Socialists in Los Olivos carried out state decrees and legislation—restoring fired workers to their jobs, reinstating *juntas de policía rural*, and reestablishing local commissions to administer public works. In fact, they assumed the more direct and militant control of labor relations urged by party leaders. As happened in many other towns, the Socialists formed a *guardia cívico*, a local vigilante group, to back themselves up.

The Socialists in Los Olivos engendered a sense of utopian expectations similar to those that prevailed elsewhere in Andalusia (Jackson 1965:222). Many people of the village believed that a time was coming in which all property would be shared. The more militant leftists went into the countryside to bring back cows and goats to slaughter. They distributed the meat free, even to families on the right.

Lacking control of the local court and of the state's coercive power, the Socialists could not suppress the right as effectively as the right had repressed them during the *bienio negro*. Instead, the Socialists organized labor much more militantly than ever before. They harassed independent artisans who were not union members, forcing them to do menial tasks for the council usually done by women, such as mopping the floors of the town hall after council meetings. More to the point, the Socialists pressed home their advantage over wealthy agrarian proprietors in matters of employment. They divided union members into groups and assigned the groups to work on larger estates whether the owners accepted them or not. If not, workers were to sit with their tools

[219]

at the landowner's doorstep and demand their wages on Saturday anyway. This forceful *repartimiento* of labor is what villagers remember most of the spring of 1936, for it once again struck deeply at the autonomy of the property owner. It was a widespread practice, used, for example, in Ronald Fraser's Mijas (1972:106,122), which had arisen from the legally sanctioned mixed commissions of laborers and employers for regulating employment. Thus with the Socialists back in power, labor once again gained the upper hand.

Just as in 1933, agrarian laborers played their hand without attempting to seize land (as did happen in other regions at the time) because the *repartimiento* of labor was in itself sufficient to alter the cultural meaning of land ownership. Proprietors on the right recognized the forced allocation of laborers as an abrogation of their claimed right to manage their property and thus as a step toward its dispossession. As one man put it, reminiscing to me about the period, "We were no longer owners of what we owned." What proprietors lost was their much-cherished autonomy, their claim to being independent and hence free of any other man's beck and call. By stripping proprietors of their prerogative to set conditions of work, the Socialists had transformed the cultural meaning of property without altering its distribution. Building on what they had accomplished in 1933, the Socialists were effecting a radical transformation in the relation of employee to employer, if not in the ownership of capital. They had begun a revolution similar to that which was to sweep areas of Republican control (Bolloten 1979) after the military insurgency led by Franco broke out in July 1936.

In Los Olivos, insurgent forces took over within weeks of the July insurgency, bloodily decimating the Socialists and restoring the landed oligarchy to power. But that is another story.

Conclusion

I argued at the outset that when we study the relationship between legislation and legal change we must investigate power and meaning—the central considerations in contemporary political-economic and interpretive analyses—for two reasons. The first is that the forms that laws take and their impact on the local level are each shaped by political struggle, which can be understood in terms of the historically located class relations. At the same time, legislation shapes the context and trajectory of such struggle. The second is that the significance of legislation is always greater than the meaning intended for it. Legislation never speaks for itself. Its meaning is a matter of interpretation and contention. It must be understood in the cultural terms with which individuals experience and interpret it in relation to their goals and objective interests.

In studying early Second Republic agrarian legislation, how it was implemented and how it was experienced, I have posed questions of power and meaning and explored their interplay. This required analysis of both legislation and implementation in terms of the political struggle surrounding them, drawing attention to the articulation of these state and local developments. Questions about the experience of implementation—about the meaning attributed to employment practices by workers and employers—have suggested fresh conclusions about the significance of the early Second Republic agrarian legislation.

Most important, I would argue that the Socialists accomplished considerably more in reforming and revolutionizing agrarian labor than historians have credited to them. The Socialists of Los Olivos devoted their full energies to the arena of employment, and they had reason to be proud of their accomplishments. Land reform, for which Socialist party leaders struggled in the Cortes and on which historians have placed so much emphasis, was of little interest to the agrarian workers of Los Olivos. At the same time, transformations in the arena of labor in 1933 took on much more radical meaning for men of Los Olivos than historians have recognized. Charged with potent local understandings of the relationship of male honor to employment relations, these labor reforms threatened to invert power relations and to undermine the meaning of property and of employment in revolutionary ways. Preston, Malefakis, and others demonstrated that pressures from rank-and-file membership radicalized the Socialists' party leadership during the Second Republic, but they attributed the pressures to discontent with the slow pace of land reform. The case of Los Olivos suggests instead that rank-and-file fervor arose as much from the experience of victories won in the radical transformation of relations of employment in local arenas.

Acknowledgments

This account of Second Republic Socialists in "Los Olivos" (a pseudonym) draws on research supported by Research Grant No. HD-17351 from the National Institute of Child Health and Human Development.

[221]

George A. Collier

Reconstruction of Second Republic events in Los Olivos draws heavily on the documentary record of the minutes of the town council, as supplemented by other local archival materials and oral history of the era recounted to Jane Collier and myself by villagers we interviewed. This account also draws in part on my study titled *Socialists of Rural Andalusia: Unacknowledged Revolutionaries of the Second Republic*, published in 1987 by Stanford University Press, to which I am grateful for permission to reproduce or paraphrase certain passages in this chapter.

REFERENCES

Bolloten, Burnett. 1979. *The Spanish Revolution: The Left and the Struggle for Power during the Civil War*. Chapel Hill, N.C.

Collier, George A. 1987. *Socialists of Rural Andalusia: Unacknowledged Revolutionaries of the Second Republic*. Stanford, Calif.

Fraser, Ronald. 1972. *In Hiding: The Life of Manuel Cortes*. London.

Herr, Richard. 1971. *An Historical Essay on Modern Spain*. Berkeley and Los Angeles.

Jackson, Gabriel. 1965. *The Spanish Republic and the Civil War, 1931–1939*. Princeton.

Malefakis, Edward E. 1970. *Agrarian Reform and Peasant Revolution in Spain: Origins of the Civil War*. New Haven.

Martínez-Alier, Juan. 1971. *Labourers and Landowners in Southern Spain*. Totowa, N.J.

Mintz, Jerome R. 1982. *The Anarchists of Casas Viejas*. Chicago.

Pérez Díaz, Victor. 1976. "Process of Change in Rural Castilian Communities." In Joseph B. Aceves and W. A. Douglas, eds., *The Changing Faces of Rural Spain*, pp. 123–142. Cambridge, Mass.

Preston, Paul. 1978. *The Coming of the Spanish Civil War: Reform, Reaction, and Revolution in the Second Republic, 1931–1936*. London.

———. 1984. "The Agrarian War in the South." In Paul Preston, ed., *Revolution and War in Spain, 1931–1939*, pp. 159–181. London.

[9]

Entrepreneurs and the Law: Self-employed Surinamese in Amsterdam

Jeremy Boissevain and Hanneke Grotenbreg

In the 1970s, immigrants streamed into the Netherlands from Mediterranean countries and former Caribbean colonies, and in particular from Surinam. Many of these immigrants established businesses to supply the specific needs of the newcomers for food, clothing, and entertainment, but because small business in the Netherlands is regulated by a dense network of laws, they encountered many problems. The same maze of regulations confronts Dutchmen who want to start up on their own, but because immigrant entrepreneurs are unfamiliar with the Dutch language and culture, they have an extra handicap.

We explore the extent to which these laws affect the activities of Surinamese entrepreneurs in Amsterdam. What specific government regulations do they have to deal with in the Netherlands? To what extent are they able to cope legally? How and to what degree do they operate in the informal sector? Do they, in time, change their mode of operation? Do their activities influence government regulations? As far as we can determine, our research is unique in that it examines the effect of law on the activities of immigrant businessmen from three different ethnic groups who arrived from the same country at about the same time—the Chinese, the Creoles, and the Hindustanis from Surinam.

But before reporting on our research in Amsterdam, a brief word about Surinam and the Surinamese, local enterprise, and the experience of entrepreneurs in Surinam with government regulations. This background is essential in order to trace the development of Surinamese entrepreneurship and to understand the extent to which their experience with the law in Surinam differed from that in the Netherlands.

Surinam: Chinese, Creoles, and Hindustanis

Surinam became a Dutch possession after it was captured from the British in 1667. European investors soon established many agricultural enterprises, which brought about an immigration of white officers and plantation managers. Besides capital, the new colonists required labor, but the original inhabitants, the Arawak Indians, proved unsuitable for plantation work, so labor had to be brought in from elsewhere. First came enslaved Africans, an estimated 350,000 of whom were brought to Surinam this way (Lier 1971). The abolition of slavery in 1863 created a new shortage of labor, and plantation workers were recruited on a contract basis from all over the world—first Chinese, then Portuguese from Madeira, and then Lebanese. They soon left the plantations, many becoming traders and shopkeepers. Subsequently an agreement with Great Britain enabled planters to recruit contract labor in India. Increasingly these "Hindustanis" replaced others as the chief plantation work force. In the 1890s, plantation owners also began to recruit Javanese.

The result of this colonial labor policy was that Surinam became a society composed of a rich mixture of race, culture, and religion. Creoles (the descendants of the African slaves), Indians, Hindustanis, Chinese and Javanese, Christians, Hindus, Muslims, and many others now live side by side in one country (Kruijer 1977:9ff.). In this chapter we focus on the Chinese, the Creoles, and the Hindustanis, the ethnic groups from which most of the Surinamese entrepreneurs in Amsterdam have emerged.

Surinamese and Enterprise

The Chinese conform most closely to the ideal type of middleman-minority described by Bonacich (1973). Many Chinese emigrated to Surinam or were recruited to work as self-employed (Heilbron 1982:232). As a trading minority, they dominated the distributive sector of the

Surinamese economy. Chinese associations were active in Surinam, not only in the leisure field. They played an important role in organizing rotating credit associations that gave members access to capital. On the national level, these associations acted as pressure groups, representing the interests of more powerful Chinese to government and influencing trading practices, including pricing. There were important patronage and kinship links between the small neighborhood grocers and the wealthy merchants (Vermeulen 1984:92–96). It is interesting that Chinese immigrants in Amsterdam have so far not become heavily involved in retail trade. They left Surinam relatively late, and upon arrival found their traditional economic niche in Amsterdam occupied by the Hindustanis, so they turned instead to the restaurant field, where Indonesian and Hong Kong Chinese were already active. Their activities are now expanding.

The relationship between the Hindustanis and self-employment is somewhat more complex. Hindustanis were originally imported to Surinam as contract laborers for the plantations. On termination of the contract, however, they were offered the choice of remaining and becoming landowning peasants, and many did just that. But the first Hindustanis to become active in trade were not descendants of contract laborers. Many British Indians came to Surinam as traders and there recruited other Hindustanis to assist them (Heilbron 1982:149ff.). The growth of the city of Paramaribo is paralleled by the movement of Hindustanis to the city and its environs. Increasingly they began to produce vegetables and fruit for the city's markets, and organized transportation between rural areas and the city. Tradesmen, transport owners, and small farmers are entrepreneurs par excellence. They are accustomed to independence, making decisions, coordinating the family enterprise, and above all, saving to protect themselves against unforeseen events. The activity of Hindustanis in Amsterdam in the fruit and greengrocery sector is simply an extension of their activities in Surinam.

The experience of Creoles was very different. After failing as peasant farmers following their manumission, Creoles became increasingly involved in wage labor and crafts. Though at first active as market traders, they were gradually replaced by Hindustanis, who had closer links with rural suppliers (Kruijer 1977:69). In Surinam there are far more Hindustani and Chinese shops than Creole shops. Creoles are more active in the civil service, as white-collar workers in the larger firms, and above all, as skilled and unskilled wage laborers with the large companies that were exploiting Surinam's bauxite and timber wealth. Many Creoles are

[225]

unemployed and are obliged to "hustle" in Paramaribo in order to survive (Gelder 1984). The male Creole custom of spending a good deal of time outside the home with friends played an important role in the Creoles' choosing to establish cafés and coffee shops in Amsterdam.

The Chinese and Hindustanis in Surinam attempted to achieve a better life for themselves and their children through being self-employed. By contrast, the Creoles generally followed another strategy. Not the successful entrepreneur, but the senior civil servant, the professional, the highly skilled industrial specialist, provided ideal role-models for Creoles. These were positions that could not be attained without considerable further education, so this helps explain the greater attention Creoles have given to education, something Lier noted forty years ago (1971:186–187). We found that the children of self-employed Creoles generally attained a higher level of education than the children of self-employed Hindustanis (66 percent of Creole children went to advanced secondary schools or to the university, as opposed to 47 percent of Hindustani children—even though many more Creole children came from working-class backgrounds. (The average age of the children may have played a role here too. Creole children were slightly older, around sixteen, whereas Hindustani children were about twelve years old.)

In short, the socioeconomic background of these immigrant entrepreneurs and their experience with Surinamese laws regulating small business influenced their behavior in the Netherlands.

Regulations in Surinam

The Surinamese regulations governing the establishment of craft enterprises, shops, restaurants, and cafés required registration in the Register of Commerce, a legal idea derived from Dutch laws, but Surinamese authorities took local conditions into account and adapted the rules accordingly. Since 1955, Surinam has had a high degree of independence in internal affairs, and its laws reflected this.

After 1910 all established businesses had to be recorded in the Register of Commerce, and from 1952 it has been mandatory for certain enterprises to be licensed. Shop licenses were granted by the district commissioners, who were also empowered to regulate the types of enterprises requiring licenses. In general, such "permission chits" were granted to hawkers without difficulty.

Aspiring entrepreneurs were checked on several grounds: level of education, knowledge of their field and/or experience, creditworthiness, and whether that area was already overcrowded. But the requirements were not stringent. It was not necessary to obtain a diploma to demonstrate administrative capability, and the required level of professional expertise was "minimal," according to the specialists consulted. Furthermore, ordinances regulating conditions of work and personnel did not apply to so-called "family enterprises"; in fact, workers in enterprises employing less than thirty people had very little protection (Gelder 1984:135ff.). Payroll deductions were only introduced in the 1970s, and income tax a few years before that.

Many businessmen did not obtain the required licenses because they refused to pay bribes. One remarked to us:

> You have to pay *"tjoekoes"* for licenses. I did not want to get involved in that, so I worked without a license. I registered my business in someone else's name. Everyone knew that. The reason I did not obtain a license had to do with the fact that a distant relative was a member of Parliament. He was one of the biggest butchers in Paramaribo who supplied institutions. He worked against me. He was afraid that we would outdo him. He was naturally worried that others would obtain supply contracts.

Not having a license had never hampered this businessman's activities, but other people were able to obtain the necessary diplomas on the basis of work experience and could thus legally establish themselves as self-employed.

To summarize, then, many economic activities that were not in conformity with the law took place in Surinam. The official registration system left much to be desired. Loopholes in the existing laws, and inadequate controls, were responsible for a good deal of the irregularity, and many successful entrepreneurs appeared to be totally ignorant of the relatively simple regulations.

The Surinamese of Amsterdam

Immigration of Surinamese to the Netherlands has a long history, but until the 1960s the numbers of Surinamese were limited. After that they increased slowly until 1968, and then more rapidly, reaching a peak in 1974 and 1975. After the independence of Surinam in 1975, migration declined sharply, to rise briefly toward the end of the 1970s.

[227]

During the 1950s and 1960s, Surinamese immigrated to the Netherlands to find work, to study, and to assure a better life for their children (Budike 1982:52). During this period, the migrants were relatively well-to-do Creoles, but in the 1970s the social composition and the motives of the migrants shifted. Growing tension between the political and ethnic groups as Surinam approached independence encouraged many lower-class Surinamese to migrate. Large numbers of Hindustanis, worried about the political future of their own ethnic group following independence, also left for Holland. Of the estimated 180,000 Surinamese in the Netherlands, 40,000 now live in Amsterdam. Of these, approximately 65 percent are Creole, and 28 percent are Hindustani. The balance is composed of those of Chinese and Javanese descent.

The entrepreneurial activity of Surinamese in Amsterdam reflects their migration history. The first *tropica* shops, which sold a variety of Surinamese fruit, vegetables, and groceries, were established in the 1960s. A Surinamese bookkeeper began to import fresh vegetables from Surinam in 1964, but before that there had been no importation of fresh tropical fruit and vegetables. The *tokos*, shops catering to Indonesian immigrants, had sold mainly dried vegetables. Indonesian migrants had become used to making do with various substitutes purchased on the Dutch market.

The market for fresh tropical vegetables and fruit expanded with the stream of Surinamese immigrants, and *tropica* shops multiplied rapidly. Another entrepreneur stimulated this expansion by buying up twenty-five shops, converting them to *tropica*s, and renting them out, obliging the new tenants to purchase from him the fresh fruit and vegetables they needed. During the 1970s, Surinamese entrepreneurial activity diversified. Travel agencies, small restaurants, barbershops, butchers, cafés, driving schools, record shops, and more recently video shops joined the *tropica*s. This development has been extremely rapid, especially during the last six years. In 1983 there were approximately 250 Surinamese enterprises in Amsterdam.[1] The average age of the owners was thirty-eight, and the businesses had been established for about five years. Entrepreneurial activity is concentrated in retailing, catering, and crafts, and most enterprises are located near the open-air markets in the

[1]Our research was limited to Amsterdam; to craft, retail trade, and catering; and to entrepreneurs who had separate premises. The entrepreneurs studied were self-employed and pursuing an economic activity independently on their own account and at their own risk. Most enterprises have less than ten employees.

Table 9.1. Surinamese Business Activity by Ethnic Group

Business	Creole	Hindustani	Chinese	Other	Total
Tropica	0	27	6	1	34
Record/video	6	7	1	—	14
Barber	10	1	—	—	11
Goldsmith	1	2	3	—	6
Butcher	—	4	—	—	4
Garage	—	2	—	—	2
Tailor	2	2	—	—	4
Coffeeshop	24	3	—	—	27
Café	17	—	2	—	19
Restaurant / snack bar	11	14	16	6	47
Travel agency	6	5	—	—	11
Miscellaneous*	15	19	1	—	35
Total	92	86	29	7	214

*Includes diverse shops and market stalls.

older section of the city, where real estate is relatively inexpensive. For this reason, many immigrants settled there too.

Ethnic background plays an important role. Hindustanis and Chinese are, relatively speaking, more active than Creoles. Although Hindustanis form only 28 percent of the Surinamese population in Amsterdam, they control 40 percent of the enterprises. The Chinese are even more active. Hindustanis are most strongly established in retail trade, while Creoles and Chinese are concentrated in catering, as are Javanese (see Table 9.1). The reasons for the uneven spread of entrepreneurial activities are explored elsewhere (Boissevain and Grotenbreg 1986).

So the experience they brought with them from Surinam, their compatriots' demand for specific goods and services, and the existing opportunities in the Netherlands shaped the activities of the immigrant entrepreneurs. The majority established their enterprises in the so-called "formal sector" without further reflection. There they came face-to-face with the rule of Dutch law.

Self-Employment and the Law in the Netherlands

In the Netherlands, small entrepreneurs are bound by a great variety of rules that regulate establishment of an enterprise. These include municipal licenses, ordinances, and laws governing payment of taxes and social contributions.

[229]

Rules Regulating Establishment

Rules regulating the establishment of an enterprise date from the economic crisis of the 1930s. In 1935, conditions for establishing an enterprise in Amsterdam were formulated for the first time. Entrepreneurs need to be creditworthy and technically competent, and they had to establish that there was a "need" among consumers for the new enterprise. The object of these regulations was to counter the "fatal" growth of small businesses, which were being set up in response to increasing unemployment (Riel 1961:17). In 1937 the Establishment of Small Business Act came into effect at the national level. Although the new law did not include the "need" element referred to above, entrepreneurs still had to demonstrate that they had the necessary trade expertise and knowledge. This new requirement was an attempt to raise the level of competence in the trade, but it was also a legal barrier to entry. The object of this act and the 1954 Business Establishment Act was to promote orderly entrepreneurial activity.

The 1954 Business Establishment Act, the 1964 Beverage, Hotel, and Catering Act, and the 1971 Retail Trade Establishment Act provided a dense network of rules regulating the establishment of new enterprises. Regulations applicable to entrepreneurs include the following:

1. Enterprises must register with the Chamber of Commerce and the Register of Commerce.
2. All entrepreneurs active in a branch falling under establishment regulations must comply with those regulations. Exemptions from the trade knowledge/expertise provisions can be applied for at the Chamber of Commerce. Exemptions are granted on the basis of similar foreign diplomas, pressing local consumer needs, and "special cases." An entrepreneur more than forty years old who has had many years of experience in the field in which he wants to establish himself may also be granted an exemption after passing a practical examination.
3. Although a license is normally granted only if an entrepreneur has the required diplomas, he can also comply with the law by employing someone possessing a license.

The various laws governing establishment affect the entrance to the market of both local and foreign entrepreneurs. In practice it is extremely difficult for a foreign-born entrepreneur who has the required diplomas to obtain a license. The "pressing needs" and "special cases" are rarely judged acute enough to warrant an exemption. One consequence of this web of regulations is that those already in the field are protected against new entrants (Menger 1980:6).

Municipal Licenses

Entrepreneurs are also required to obtain municipal licenses for a range of activities—for example, for being open on Sundays and public holidays, remaining open after 6 P.M., playing music and running a catering establishment that serves alcohol. Various building licenses are required too, and restaurants must obtain a license to use the sewers. Those who want to use the terrace or sidewalk in front of their premises must obtain a special terrace license. Moreover, under the terms of the Beverage, Hotel, and Catering Act the municipality not only regulates the furnishing and equipment of catering establishments but also controls the morality and age of the owners.[2]

Taxes and Social Security

Finally, entrepreneurs are responsible for payment of income tax, value-added tax, and social security payments, among other things. They must also withhold from their employees' salaries income tax and the various contributions for which they are responsible under no less than nine different Social Security laws.

A number of special rules apply to children who live and work with entrepreneurs but who do not fall under any employee-insurance regulations. Income tax, old-age pension, and unemployment contributions must be paid on the salaries of children over fifteen years of age. Children who are still required to go to school (usually up to the age of fifteen) may do no work at all. Children no longer obliged to attend school may work up to eight hours a day. Employers face a legal maze that is steadily becoming more complicated. Municipal inspectors told us that laws regulating the various social contributions are now so intricate that no entrepreneur can possibly comply with them without professional assistance.

Self-employed Surinamese who want to establish an enterprise in the

[2]For example, budding catering entrepreneurs are never licensed if they are legally responsible to a guardian and under the age of twenty-five.

Netherlands on the basis of their experience in Surinam are confronted with yet another problem. While Surinamese regulations controlling self-employment resembled Dutch regulations, they were loosely enforced. The Dutch regulations are more extensive, more formal, and more severely controlled. Consequently, many Surinamese fail to comply with all the requirements of the law. Others have taken a much easier way out and have established businesses that fall outside the various Business Establishment Acts. These include coffee shops, snack bars (which serve no alcohol), record and video shops (which must sell full video tapes), tailoring shops (except for those making men's clothing), wholesalers, and driving schools. At present, the Dutch government is proposing to restrict the establishment of small restaurants and snack bars by placing them under one of the Business Establishment Acts. This will severely limit entrance to a field that has been relatively free of the red tape of the Business Establishment Act and hence very popular among Surinamese entrepreneurs (Ministerie van Economische Zaken 1982).

Informal Entrepreneurs

Many Dutch hold stereotypical views on immigrant entrepreneurs. They believe that most Surinamese businessmen would rather stay informal than pay taxes. Most Dutch shopkeepers, and some highly placed government officials, are convinced that ethnic entrepreneurs establish their businesses without the necessary diplomas and licenses. Some researchers state that immigrants "prefer" to establish themselves in the so-called "informal economy," the nonformalized sector (Bovenkerk 1982; Ellemers 1984; Pompe 1984; Tap 1983). The informal economy has many dimensions (see Begeer and Tuinen 1984; Breman 1976; Dijk 1980; Gershuny and Pahl 1980; Godschalk 1985; Nicholls and Dyson 1983), but in this chapter we shall focus on certain of its legal and fiscal aspects.

Informal entrepreneurs are entrepreneurs who do not comply with the following regulations:

1. Registration with the Trade Register of the Chamber of Commerce
2. Possession of the necessary permission to establish a business
3. Payment of value-added and income tax and Social Security contributions
4. Registration of employees, payment of minimum wage to em-

ployees, deduction of income tax and Social Security contributions from wages and payment to government.

Our minimum criterion is registration of the enterprise with the Trade Register. If entrepreneurs had not even complied with this minimum criterion, we considered them *completely informal*. It will be seen that the four criteria establish a continuum. If entrepreneurs comply with the first two criteria, chances are they comply with the third and fourth as well. We used these criteria to examine the extent to which Surinamese entrepreneurs in Amsterdam were informal or formal.[3] We found the following:

1. *Trade Register*. Of the 252 firms we examined, 83 percent had registered with the Trade Register. Thus 17 percent were completely informal.
2. *Permission to establish a firm*. Almost two-thirds of the Surinamese entrepreneurs were established in businesses requiring an establishment license. Of these, only 40 percent had obtained the required license or exemption.
3. *Payment of tax*. Nine out of ten entrepreneurs told us they had paid their income and value-added taxes. Those who had not registered their firms with the Chamber of Commerce naturally paid no tax. We do not know whether those who said they paid tax paid sufficient tax.
4. *Registration of employees and minimum wage*. These regulations were followed less strictly. In just over 70 percent of the enterprises we found relatives working alongside the owner. This was usually in Hindustani-owned businesses. In Creole firms it was more usual to find nonrelatives employed. While 64 percent of nonrelatives were registered with the labor office, this was done for only 16 percent of the working relatives. Generally speaking, the longer an enterprise had been established, the more often nonrelatives were registered. Enterprises that were completely informal registered none of their employees.

Many of those who were called employees or who were working in the enterprises were friends and close relatives who passed time in the shop and lent a helping hand. One of the entrepreneurs told us: "I would

[3]Unfortunately, a comparison with their Dutch colleagues is not yet possible. To date, surveys and studies of Dutch small businesses have been limited to enterprises that comply with all the regulations (see Tillaart et al. 1981).

rather get help from my family. For example, if my children don't have anything else to do, they work with me. When they are finished they go back to their homework. They do this in the shop. This means that I can keep my wage costs low. It also means that my children always finish their homework, because I see to that." So we often found children, grandparents, and other relatives working in the kitchen or behind the counter. Most were quite unaware of the stringent laws prohibiting children under fifteen from working in any capacity. Small enterprises are family enterprises. Everyone pitches in when the need arises. The Dutch have made this difficult. Inspectors see to it that the laws are obeyed. Some even maintain that the help of the children is "dishonest competition," although the law does not mention this; it is concerned exclusively with the physical and psychological well-being of the children.

Our informants were reluctant to discuss the salaries they paid employees. It was clear that they found the minimum wage and the Social Security contributions excessively high and had difficulty complying with them. In this they differed little from other ethnic and Dutch self-employed (Broeksma, Hennes, and Jansen 1981; Bovenkerk et al. 1983:147). In a period of rising unemployment, which can especially affect migrants who cannot obtain residence permission unless they are employed, many are willing to work for less than the minimum wage.

So while many Surinamese self-employed are formally "established," a substantial number operate informally. There are several cutural and structural reasons that they cannot or do not comply with the rules, many of which are related to practices brought from Surinam. Some assumed that the Dutch regulations were the same as those in Surinam. Others, especially Chinese and older Hindustanis, have a language problem. There is also a shortfall in the information about the intricate self-employment regulations. Religion and the operation of the exemption procedure also form obstacles. We shall return to these later.

Informal Entrepreneurship: A Technique for Survival

Informal entrepreneurs can be divided in two categories: those who are completely informal and those who are semiformal—that is, those who have registered with the Chamber of Commerce but have not yet complied with all the formal regulations. The level of education the completely informal entrepreneurs have attained is relatively high.

Many have had a secondary school or technical education. In spite of this, none was attempting to acquire the required business training or technical certificates. A number of the semiformal self-employed were studying for a certificate. Furthermore, all the completely informal operators had been employed before they established their enterprises, mostly by small entrepreneurs. This was in marked contrast to the semiformal entrepreneurs, 50 percent of whom had been self-employed in Surinam before they started up in Amsterdam.

The personal networks of entrepreneurs are an important resource, for they can provide access to capital and cheap, loyal labor. Completely informal operators had fewer relatives in the Netherlands than those who operated semiformally. Consistent with this, the former financed their enterprises exclusively with their own capital, while the latter were able to secure loans from friends, and even from banks.

At the same time, the completely informal operators seemed to be more interested in financial gain and more optimistic than their semiformal colleagues, and they were less cautious. They chose a business activity to fill what they saw as a need in the market. A number had first started at home, often in the evening, alongside their daytime employment. Gradually they had increased their clients, eventually renting specialized premises. It is difficult to predict how many completely informal operators will become formal by registering with the Chamber of Commerce and acquiring the necessary diplomas and certificates. It was quite clear that, before we interviewed them, many had been unaware of the mass of regulations with which they were obliged to comply. We can only speculate about their future.

We can predict with greater certainty that a number of the semiformal self-employed will formalize their status. The various controllers who check up on them will make them aware of the regulations and laws. Lack of familiarity with the law sometimes has disastrous consequences, as illustrated by the grim experience of Ling.

> Ling is fifty-eight years old. When he was twenty-two he went to work in his father's shop. After nine years he wanted to begin for himself. His father gave him 5,000 Surinamese guilders. "You know how it goes. You work at home for your father, so you don't earn anything. You only get some food and you work." Finally, when he was forty-seven, Ling emigrated to the Netherlands. On the advice of his children he bought a large Chinese restaurant in the seaside resort of Scheveningen. The family tried to run the restaurant together. They did not succeed. After two years Ling was bankrupt. The chief

reason was poor accounting and tax debts. He explained, "The restaurant was profitable only during the summer, but I had to pay tax for a whole year on the basis of the profit margin I had during the few summer months." He could not pay his tax debts. To meet some of these, he sold his house in Surinam. He now lives in a small flat with his wife. He can find no work. Everything is gone.

When they began, most immigrant entrepreneurs paid little attention to formal laws. Their primary concern was the market and establishing and maintaining good personal relations with clients and suppliers. The longer they were in business, the more aware they became of the formal regulations, for the controllers left them no peace. A female shopkeeper told us that she had been "frightened half to death" when she had been told to close her business because she had not been complying with the regulations. She speedily studied for and passed the required examinations. The controllers are not the only source of information about the rules and regulations. Several Hindustanis had contacted lawyers to learn about regulations, but the Chinese relied mostly on already established businessmen for their information. Many café owners were successfully piloted through the tangle of red tape by their breweries.

The most important source of information, however, was not government officials or the Chamber of Commerce or established businesses, but networks of personal acquaintances. Two-thirds of our informants learned about the need to register with the Chamber of Commerce from relatives and acquaintances. The length of time an enterprise has been established and the time its owner has spent in the Netherlands are factors that influence the formalization process. Formalization is also related to ethnic descent.

Formal businessmen can be divided in two categories: those who require an establishment license and those who do not. Of the category requiring a license, 43 percent of the Creoles had complied, while only 29 percent respectively of the Hindustanis and Chinese had done so. Of the enterprises not requiring establishment licenses, 61 percent were Creole, 22 percent were Hindustani and 17 percent were Chinese-owned. In terms of overall figures, it appears that three out of four Creole businessmen were *completely formal*, while this was true for only one out of three Hindustani businessmen. Of the *semi-formal* entrepreneurs, 15 percent were Creole and 75 percent were Hindustani. The Hindustanis thus seem to be more casual about meeting the requirements of the law than the Creoles.

A partial explanation for the difference in the formalization of Hindustani and Creole enterprises is that, generally speaking, the Creoles have had a much longer and more intense contact with the Netherlands than Hindustanis. All classes among Creoles consider the European type of education and lifestyle, especially obtaining the diplomas ("or else you are a failure"), necessary prerequisites for social mobility. The Creole's entrance to Dutch culture is thus facilitated by a usually greater knowledge of language and custom than Hindustani or Chinese compatriots have. Creoles thus more readily understand, accept, and comply with Dutch rules. Controllers described Creole businessmen as "docile and obedient." Creoles told us they "obeyed the law to be rid of controllers, who were just doing their job."

Hindustani entrepreneurs had a different attitude. Some pretended they had just learned about certain regulations from us. Later they would ask us if they needed a license. They gave us the impression that they would comply if the fines became heavier and more frequent. Moreover, they were able to "arrange" a great deal through their larger network of relations. Brought up in self-employed families and often with considerable personal experience, Hindustanis, more often than the Creoles, were "operators" who played the system. There are indeed a number of techniques and measures that can be used to survive, quite successfully, in spite of the law.

One of the successful semiformal entrepreneurs, Felix, explained some of his survival techniques to us.

Felix produces and sells beautiful leather clothing, trousers, jackets, and accessories. He calls himself "small" because he has no personnel, and "big" because of his turnover. Last year he sold 80,000 belts. "I continually change my products. That is my strength. Eight years ago I went bankrupt for the first and last time. The tax people took everything, even my stock. I had to begin again from scratch." Since then he keeps no stock, "nothing but my skill."

"Of course I registered my firm with the Chamber of Commerce—I think under the "art" section, or something. What I do remember is that for my leather business I needed a certificate of technical competence. Friends told me that. But I didn't have one. For an art business you need nothing. I have a marvelous atelier. But in fact I own nothing. Do you understand? Everything I own is listed in someone else's name. I learned that as a little man in Holland you really can own nothing."

He recently bought a new car, a Suzuki, for 12,000 Surinamese

[237]

guilders cash. "I don't need credit because as a black I wouldn't get it anyway. I don't need government support either, because if things go badly. . . . Look, I don't pay taxes anymore. Because if you require nothing you need pay nothing. I live comfortably, but I want to take care of myself and not trouble the government for subsidies. In exchange they don't have to bother me."

He does his own "bookkeeping." He pulled out his wallet and took out a long slip of paper. On one side he had listed tobacco, coffee, etc., and on the other side was his income from the sale of his products. "In this land of blossoms and barbed wire, you have to look after yourself, otherwise you get hurt."

There are thus a number of survival techniques. To begin with, it is possible to manipulate various certificates—for example, one can formally register the enterprise in a name of a person who does have the required license or diploma. It is also possible to register the enterprise as one that is license-free, as Felix did. Other informants provided further examples:

> To open a garage you must have licenses and certificates of competence. On the other hand, you need none to sell new cars. Furthermore, you need no certificates to become a car breaker. Thus, you can open a garage as long as you make sure you have no formal roof over your head. You can also repair bicycles without a license, but you can't sell new parts—although you can get away with it if your books "show" that you use these parts for your repairs. If you want to become a jeweler—which requires certificates—you register as a tinsmith. For that you don't need diplomas. If you repair one pan a year you meet the formal requirement!

Other survival techniques include telling the judge your son is studying hard for his diploma, or one can even rent or borrow a diploma from an acquaintance who ostensibly forms part of the enterprise. These are some of the techniques used to solve the problem of missing certificates and licenses.

To avoid tax assessment, which in the case of a newly established enterprise takes place only after the first five years, a number of entrepreneurs "terminate" their activities after four years. They drop out of the register and start up elsewhere under a new name. This is why small catering establishments change hands so frequently, police-controllers told us, but the technique is apparently not used too often by the Surinamese. The enterprises we examined that suddenly ceased operation after the first five years were usually genuine bankruptcies. The most frequent cause of bankruptcy was the extraordinarily heavy tax assessment brought on by ignorance of the tax obligations. Some were able to stave off bankruptcy by working out a program of repayments. We found that most entrepreneurs engaged professional bookkeepers specifically to avoid tax problems. Those who had encountered severe tax problems had been able to avoid bankruptcy by drawing on the help of relatives and friends. Our entrepreneurs considered bankruptcy a scandalous, dishonorable event to be avoided at all costs. A number of informants told us that by keeping a double set of books it is possible to avoid paying 'too much' tax. One observed, "Half your bookkeeping should be white and the rest black. You cannot do everything black, or they'll catch you and you'll lose everything."

In order to avoid heavy personnel costs, many informants used casual labor prepared to work flexible hours for flexible wages. Quite a number disapproved of using illegal labor that worked below minimum-wage levels, and those who operated in this manner are feared. By taking greater risks, they are able to compete more aggressively, because by cutting overhead costs they can sell their goods more cheaply.

Another factor that contributes to informal activities is the 1954 Business Establishment Act, which creates severe problems for many entrepreneurs, and especially craftsmen. Their informal entrepreneurship is largely involuntary. Dutch laws do not take into account the specific nature of their activities, and many goldsmiths and barbers are unable to meet the conditions of the act. On the one hand, they are generally poorly informed as to the precise details of the regulations. On the other hand, many of those who are well informed have had their applications for exemption rejected. A good example is the case of Fa, a goldsmith.

> Fa, a Surinamese Chinese, took over a jewelry shop from a compatriot. He also bought the inventory, which included a number of pieces made of gold of less than 14 carats. According to Dutch law, all gold objects must be at least 14 carats. Fa was not aware of this. When his stock was inspected many pieces were impounded. Moreover, he did not have a license to operate. He thought that with his twenty-five years experience as goldsmith in Surinam he had complied with all requirements, but he learned from the inspectors that this was not the case. His petition for exemption on the basis of his experience was denied—his technical knowledge was deemed insufficient, and he was told he also had to be able to work in silver. The fact that in Surinam only goldsmiths were in demand and his customers in Am-

sterdam were interested only in gold jewelry was regarded as unimportant. Fa, accompanied by an interpreter, failed his technical test for working silver jewelry, but he is still making jewelry. He is sure that because he now conforms to Dutch regulations regarding the gold content of his jewelry he will be exempted from the requirement to have a certificate of competence in silver.

We are considerably less optimistic than Fa is, given the inflexibility of those who administer the regulations.

Fa's colleague On was also refused an exemption. On and his brother were operating a snack bar. When he wanted to establish himself as a goldsmith, a craft at which he had worked for many years in Surinam, On applied for an exemption from the required certificates. Although he had a Surinamese goldsmith's certificate, his application for exemption from the Dutch diploma regulation was turned down because he was already able to provide for himself with his snack bar so his case provided no "extenuating circumstance." When we told an official the facts in On's case, the official told us that if On had filed an appeal against the ruling he probably would have been successful. But On was unaware of his right to appeal, and equally ignorant of the way to get through the maze of red tape required to file such an appeal.

The extent to which the actual needs and problems of the entrepreneurs provide the raison d'être of the Business Establishment Act is an open question, although extensive lip-service is paid to this principle (Ministerie van Economische Zaken 1981). From our point of view as researchers, and certainly from our informants' point of view, the people interpreting and enforcing the regulations seemed more intent on applying the letter of the law rather than its spirit. They seemed more concerned about protecting the vested interests of established entrepreneurs than in helping the newcomers.

Surinamese barbers and hairdressers have also been adversely affected by the exemption procedures of the Business Establishment Act. Recently the under-secretary for small and medium-sized business stated: "It is absolutely shocking the way barbers working without correct papers are damaging the established hairdressers. We must put an end to this sort of fly-by-night bungling" (Bouwman 1983:9). While all may agree on the negative consequences of unprofessional informal activities, Surinamese hairdressers are more or less obliged to become fly-by-night operators (cf. Bovenkerk 1983), because those who established businesses around 1975 to straighten their compatriots' hair were unable to qualify for exemption. Although many have had years of experience in Surinam, they are still obliged to attend Dutch technical schooling, which has only theoretical instruction in hair-straighting (ibid.). Exceptions to this regulation are not permitted. Nevertheless, those who follow this instruction are given no practical training, we were told, because models for practical demonstration are not available. Thus, those who have taken the course and obtained a certificate of competence are expected to be able to straighten hair on the basis of theoretical instruction only. Surinamese hairdressers, and particularly their clients, find this highly questionable, and the latter are not prepared to experiment.

In short, it is difficult for many Surinamese craftsmen, in spite of their experience, to qualify for exemption from the required Dutch certificates of competence. An informant told us that the Central Industrial Board, which grants the exemptions, maintains that "only the preparation of Afro hairstyles presents a few problems. For everything else customers can be helped by Dutch hairdressers." The board also demands that Surinamese goldsmiths be able to work for Dutch clients, just as Dutch jewelers are able to work for Surinamese. All craftsmen must be treated alike, whether Dutch or immigrant. The extent to which Dutch goldsmiths would be able to provide the *mattekloppers, taratee, lontai,* and other specialized jewelry that Surinamese customers demand is an open question, of course. Surinamese goldsmiths continue to practice their craft in the Netherlands, but they must do so informally. In Surinam the law concerning crafts was applied flexibly; in the Netherlands this flexibility is largely absent.

In spite of the experience of a number of craftsmen to the contrary, many informal entrepreneurs are in time able to adjust to the requirements of Dutch law. As noted, various inspectors and controllers stimulate this, as do urban renewal programs. Small self-employed operators who do not meet all formal requirements risk missing out on various subsidies that would compensate for their past investments. The municipality recently appointed a specialist to advise ethnic entrepreneurs about their rights. Transition from informal to formal entrepreneurship is in fact a dynamic and differentiated process. Many entrepreneurs have found ways to comply with the regulations and have become completely formal.

The Impact of the Surinamese on the Law

Dutch law has had an impact on Surinamese entrepreneurs, but the entrepreneurial activity of the Surinamese has also ensured that Dutch law accommodates a number of Surinamese customs. One way to effect this is to influence Parliament. A second way is to fight arbitrary application of the law. Researchers working with ethnic groups are often used in this process.

Parliament

During the passage of the 1971 Retail Establishment Act, it was noted that the law could create problems for entrepreneurs from neighboring Common Market states that applied for Dutch establishment licenses. According to the under-secretary at the time, discrimination against foreigners in 1971 was "a fairly academic question, because today *no foreign entrepreneur has actually attempted to establish himself* in the retail trade" (Menger 1980:35ff.; emphasis added).

The problem has now been resolved for citizens of Common Market countries. Common Market entrepreneurs obtain exemption in Member States on the basis of certification by their own Chamber of Commerce that they have actually been active as entrepreneurs for a number of years. The under-secretary, however, had been poorly informed. At the time, many Indonesian immigrants owned *tokos*, and many Surinamese established businesses in the 1970s. Formally, however, they were not considered foreigners because as colonial subjects they had Dutch nationality. In Surinam they were governed by laws that had been specially adapted by Dutch legal experts, but in the Netherlands the regulations governing the establishment of businesses differed.

In the meantime, the Council for Small and Medium-Sized Business questioned whether the minimum level of profitability according to Dutch standards should be applied without further adjustment to ethnic minorities. Entrepreneurial activity, the council argued, is sensitive to cultural background and depends on the cultural norms and customs of people (RMK 1983a:150ff.); it made the same point in a parliamentary submission in 1981. The under-secretary replied that in "exceptional cases" and if "important interests were at stake," solutions could be found in the law's provision for exemptions (Ministerie van Economische Zaken 1981). We have seen that these "provisions" are unable to resolve the problems of goldsmiths and hairdressers. It is our impression that as a matter of principle all self-employed craftsmen are subjected to these objective qualitative criteria and that they are strictly administered. Yet when government established these criteria, there were virtually no foreign-trained immigrant craftsmen and businessmen to take into account. The criteria were intended for ordinary Dutch entrepreneurs catering to Dutch consumers, so no attention was given to the specific skills and qualifications of hairdressers and goldsmiths required by immigrant consumers. On the other hand, the specific needs of and demand for Muslim butchers did receive attention.

Muslim Butchers

Muslims are forbidden to eat meat from certain animals, such as pork, and meat that has not been ritually slaughtered. Most Muslims objected that Dutch butchers did not slaughter ritually and that they prepared and sold pork products too. The meat they sold was therefore unclean.

One Surinamese entrepreneur, Ben, established a Muslim association in 1969 when he was forbidden to continue slaughtering ritually. His initiative was followed in many cities. In 1975 the Federation of Muslim Organizations in the Netherlands was founded. The federation became a spokesman for all Muslims in the Netherlands, and it finally scored on the question of ritual slaughtering. In 1977 the government decreed that ritual slaughtering could be carried out in a number of large slaughterhouses. This put an end to the clandestine slaughtering that had been taking place and also met the wishes of the federation. Muslims got permission to open butcher shops if they passed a simple practical examination. Thus, the government was willing to make an exception for problems arising from religious beliefs. The precedent for this had been complaints of Orthodox Jewish poulterers after introduction of the Meat Inspection Law of 1922. They too had been granted an exemption.

The Industrial Board for Trades further refined the exempt status of Muslim butchers. To assure a reasonable turnover and to meet customer needs, one Muslim butcher was authorized for every 1,000 single Muslims and heads of families (about 1,600 Muslim residents). Some officials are unhappy about the way the regulation has been applied—"How do you determine that there are more than 1,600 Muslims resident in an area?" Second, the budding butcher remains completely dependent on the board, which grants the exemptions. Without an official butcher's diploma, a person does not have the *right* to a license. In the meantime, supplementary vocational training courses for butchers have been organized for people more than twenty-eight years old who do not yet have their certificate of competence.

It is interesting to note that the "need" factor—abolished during the 1930s—has been reintroduced to meet the needs of Muslim customers for ritually clean meat. It is ironic that the government has refused to accept the need element when considering the special needs that Surinamese have for their own hairdressers and goldsmiths. Ethnic spokesmen attribute government support of diploma requirements to its wish "to protect existing enterprises" (Leeuwen 1984:32). It appears that established businesses are being protected against newcomers. It is important to note that the only exemption granted on a statutory basis (other than ad hoc exemptions) has to do with religious belief. The structural permutations that stem from diverse beliefs are fundamental political principles in the Netherlands that are also reflected in policy regarding broadcasting and education.

There are also many active Muslim butchers who have not been granted formal exemptions, and this has antagonized Dutch butchers who must comply with strict requirements. Moreover, many question the authenticity of the ritually slaughtered meat, their concern being shared by some of the authorized Muslim butchers. As Ben put it: "I had to wait six months before I could open my business. I had to be able to prove that I had worked in Surinam as a butcher. The others begin just like that. They are even open on Sundays." Another observed: "When they run into problems in a year or two and have to pay tax and get inspectors on the doorsteps, they will simply stop. The shop gets a new owner."

It is possible that in the future legally established Muslim butchers will organize to fight competition from informal rivals by demanding stricter government control. This would not be the first time immigrant entrepreneurs resorted to such measures. In the late 1930s, Italian ice-cream sellers multiplied so rapidly that they successfully petitioned the government to limit their number (Bovenkerk, Eijken, and Bovenkerk-Teerink 1983:168). Turks engaged in the rag trade have organized themselves for other reasons. They have attempted collectively to strengthen the position of their enterprises by arranging for a training course that takes their specific problems and cultural background into consideration (Tap 1983). It is clear that national and interethnic Muslim organizations have made an impact on the law.

Salt Beef

The interpretation of laws often presents a problem. It is not always possible a priori to determine whether something is legal. Recently arrived immigrant entrepreneurs do not protest too much the comments of officials or the fines they levy. This can change as they gain experience and are continually obliged to defer to the wishes and interpretations of the officials, "who are well aware that we work this way." One way to determine which interpretation is legal is by means of a court case.

Shopkeepers long ran the risk that if they sold salt beef to their clients they could be fined for cutting it up. Salt beef, a Surinamese staple, is imported in large chunks in vats of brine. The shopkeeper chops these chunks into smaller pieces according to the needs of his customer. This operation is similar to the way a grocer slices ham or sausage. The Meat Inspection Service classified salt beef as processed meat and saw nothing illegal in shopkeepers carving it up but the Economic Control Service disagreed.

> Lo, who had been running a grocery shop for eight years, was inspected by the Economic Control Service. The inspector saw him preparing salt beef and regarded this as "the unauthorized exercise of the butcher's profession." The Economic Control Service ruled that because Lo was operating as a butcher he had to have a special permit or an exemption. He had neither. In 1981 Lo was fined to a total of 750 guilders for acting as a butcher. The Economic Police judge charged the magistrate to carry out further research. Lo, who spoke only broken Dutch, hired a lawyer, who pointed out to the magistrate that the Meat Inspection Service had classified the beef as processed meat. The Economic Control Service finally accepted this. It advised the police in writing that the "suspect" in fact did not have to possess a butcher's permit or exemption. Lo was acquitted by the judge, who ordered reimbursement of his fine. He had to pay the 1,200 guilders lawyer's fee out of his own pocket.

If influencing the interpretation and implementation of laws is an indication of social power, then the salt-beef affair can be viewed as a slight shift in favor of ethnic entrepreneurs. In general, the inspection services maintain a reserved policy toward "unknown" or "cultural" products. As long as there is no direct threat to public health, they pay little attention to articles in the so-called "gray zone"—products that are not specifically listed in the law and are sold only to a restricted clientele. We found that older inspectors generally stressed information and were more prepared than their younger colleagues to warn and advise entrepreneurs who were in danger of being fined.

Sometimes threats help to keep inspectors at a distance. The immigrants' lack of information about the manner in which inspectors and quality-controllers operate, and the ignorance of the latter with regard to the culture and customs of the former, cause frequent clashes. Moreover, there is no uniform local or even national policy. This lack of a uniform policy was seen as a problem by many of the inspectors and it causes considerable confusion among entrepreneurs, especially those who have branches in different municipalities. One informant gave us an example of his frustration: "We even had weekly inspections! It became so bad that the girl behind the counter, who had been with me for years, finally had enough. She grabbed the meat cleaver from the chopping block and waved it at the inspector: 'Just you come back here once more!' He naturally ran off. I had to appear before the regional director, but there I was finally able to unburden myself. Now we are inspected only once a year."

Inspectors told us that businessmen from other ethnic groups occasionally threatened violence. Some Dutch shopkeepers also threatened to close down and fire all their workers if violations were reported—a severe threat in these times of economic recession. Sometimes inspectors take such threats seriously and are lenient, for they realize that heavy fines can indeed bankrupt a small business. Thus, threats occasionally have the desired effect.

A final factor contributing to the (re)interpretation of law is the activity of researchers. When the entrance of immigrants into the market became socially relevant—because of its employment potential and its assumed positive impact on increasingly racist public opinion—the government became interested in ethnic entrepreneurship. Although the Ministry of Economic Affairs ultimately financed our research, we proposed it, and the research drew the government's attention to a number of problems. Some steps have been taken—for example, we noted that while Dutch consumers paid only a 5 percent value-added tax for staples, Surinamese consumers were obliged to pay a 19 percent tax because their staples were classified as "exotic" and "unknown." The Dutch Ministry of Finance is now taking steps to resolve this discrepancy. We also pointed to the inadequate operation of the government's advisory services. Advisory pamphlets for starting entrepreneurs were subsequently prepared in several languages (though not in Chinese), and a special minority adviser was employed. At Lo's request we advised his lawyer about the Meat Inspection Service's classification of salt beef as "processed meat," which was instrumental in winning the case. The minority bill of 1983 also included a paragraph on ethnic entrepreneurs. Finally, the Ministry of Economic Affairs sent banks a copy of our report, in which we noted that Surinamese entrepreneurs believed that they were being discriminated against when they applied for loans.

Surinamese Commercial Interest Groups

In principle, Surinamese entrepreneurs should be able to influence the law and its interpretation through political parties and trade organizations. A necessary condition for this is that first-generation entrepreneurs be prepared to cooperate. Most of our informants said they would like to be able to cooperate and were certainly in favor of a pressure group. But they also observed that their relations were determined by the fact that they were not only compatriots but also rivals. They did not cooperate. The very limited cooperation beyond the family level, especially among Hindustanis, was reminiscent of "amoral familism" (Banfield 1958). There was trust among the family members, but suspicion and distrust of nonrelatives. Rivalry is likely to increase, for the number of *tropicas* and snack bars is multiplying, although the number of ethnic consumers has stabilized, since immigration has virtually ceased.

Shopkeepers also challenge the right of others of sell certain products. One *tropica* owner remarked: "I cannot follow government policy. When you go to a *tropica*, you find *bakkeljouw*, dried fish. The proprietor also sells records and hair cream. He also sells medicine and cooked food. There is also a restaurant. Under which regulation does he fall? Is it a *tropica*, a restaurant, or a drugstore?" In fact, it is all three. Nevertheless, Surinamese businessmen do not believe it is possible to come together to discuss such problems—or for that matter other problems, such as housing. There is much jealousy and backbiting. A Hindustani businessman (not the only one who expressed a similar opinion) told us: "The Hindustani is asocial. He would rather go to a Dutchman, where he has difficulty being understood, than to a compatriot. He may stumble, but because of status, jealousy, and envy of others, he still goes. Hindustanis are more prepared to accept something from a Dutchman than from one of their own people." One of his colleagues observed that the best mediator would be the municipal government. "We need the strong hand of government to solve these problems." The reluctance of small businessmen and the self-employed to cooperate is certainly not limited to Surinamese. It is a general characteristic of small entrepreneurs (Boissevain 1981:136ff.).

Conclusion

The widely held view that ethnic entrepreneurs operate informally, cheat, avoid the rules, and pay no taxes is not supported by the facts.

[247]

Although not everyone conforms to all provisions of the Business Establishment Act, this cannot and must not be generalized. In fact, it is surprising that so many do conform to the regulations. In Surinam, after all, lack of a license was hardly a problem. The essential requisites for those who wanted to secure a license were, among other things, the right connections and money. In the Netherlands the Surinamese were confronted with a totally different situation: extensive and complicated regulations, an efficient registration system, and strict supervision and law enforcement. Unquestionably many Dutch self-employed businessmen do not conform to all the regulations of the laws either, but little has been written about them. Therefore, informal entrepreneurship is not static or uniform—it is a dynamic and varied process.

Inspectors play an important role in the process of formalization. They explain to the new entrepreneurs that all entrepreneurs in the Netherlands have a *right* to a license if they comply with the requirements. The difference between informally and formally established enterprises is only partly a result of the length of time spent in the Netherlands. The longer an enterprise operates, the more often the entrepreneur will have been in contact with inspectors.

A more flexible policy regarding exemptions would solve the problems of such craftsmen as goldsmiths and hairdressers and would entail measures similar to those that were implemented for Muslim butchers. Those measures were the result of pressure groups operating at the national level, which arose because immigrants had to defend themselves against powerful associations of Dutch businessmen that apply constant pressure on the government to enforce regulations in order to keep the outsiders at a distance. The Muslim butchers were regarded as competitors. Exemptions were finally granted some Muslim butchers on religious grounds—a fundamental political principle in the Netherlands. Whether Surinamese entrepreneurs will succeed in establishing an interest group that is able to influence legislation is uncertain. For the time being, each attempts to solve his problems individually. This sometimes involves a direct and not always unsuccessful confrontation with the law.

In the decade or so that they have been active in Amsterdam, 250 Surinamese entrepreneurs have managed to survive in spite of the extensive Dutch laws "regulating" their activities. Most seek to conform to the law insofar as they are able. Many lack the necessary qualifications, though most are willing to acquire these once they are pointed out to them. A few seem to have chosen to remain partly or largely informal.

[248]

Most comply in time. Some with sufficient self-confidence and financial backing have, as individuals, brought about a more favorable interpretation of existing regulations. Lo, the salt-beef champion, brought the Economic Control Service to its knees, thereby benefiting all *tropicas*, but it is equally obvious that the Surinamese commercial community is weak, because members refuse to or are incapable of organizing themselves to apply pressure to government or to mobilize public opinion. While an individual may force reinterpretation of existing regulations, it appears that laws can be changed only by collective efforts. Ethnic entrepreneurs in the Netherlands are individualists and face a well-organized structure of small and medium-sized Dutch businessmen, professional associations, semigovernmental industrial boards, municipal and national inspection services and controllers, and a conservative Ministry of Economic Affairs. This solid edifice has a vested interest in maintaining the status quo and will not easily be eroded by the occasional individual chipping away at its foundation.

Acknowledgments

This chapter is based on Boissevain, Choenni, and Grotenbreg (1984), esp. chap. 6. The research was carried out in 1983 by the authors and August Choenni, assisted by Mariette Meester and financed by the Netherlands Ministry of Economic Affairs. Altogether, we interviewed one hundred people, some at great length. Besides our fellow researchers, we are grateful to R. Fetter, Paul van Gelder, J. Godschalk, A. W. Van der Haas, A. L. Mok, G. Roorda, and Jojada Verrips for their helpful criticism.

Shorter, preliminary versions of this chapter were published in *Migrantenstudies* 1 (1986):2–24 ("Ondernemerschap en de wet: Surinaamse zelfstandigen in Amsterdam") and in *Revue Européenne des Migrations Internationales* 3 (1987):99–222 (Département de Géographie, Université de Poitiers) ("Survival in Spite of the Law: Surinamese Entrepreneurs in Amsterdam").

REFERENCES

Banfield, E. C. 1958. *The Moral Basis of a Backward Society.* Glencoe, Ill.
Begeer, W., and H. K. van Tuinen. 1984. "Statistische operationalisering van het begrip informele economie." In *De informele economie: Vereniging voor de Staatshuishoudkunde Preadviezen*, pp. 37–39. Leiden.

Boissevain, J. 1981. *Small Entrepreneurs in Changing Europe: Towards a Research Agenda*. Maastricht.

Boissevain, J., A. Choenni, and H. Grotenbreg, assisted by M. Meester. 1984. *Een kleine baas is altijd beter dan een grote knecht: Surinaamse Kleine Zelfstandige Ondernemers in Amsterdam*. Amsterdam.

Boissevain, J., and H. Grotenbreg. 1986. "Culture, Structure, and Ethnic Enterprise: The Surinamese of Amsterdam." *Ethnic and Racial Studies* 9(1):1–23.

Bonacich, E. 1973. "A Theory of Middleman Minorities." *American Sociological Review* 38:583–594.

Bouwman, M. 1983. "Alles liever dan eeuwig werkloos." *Intermediair* 19(48):3–11.

Bovenkerk, F. 1982. "Op eigen kracht omhoog: Etnisch ondernemerschap en de oogkleppen van het minderhedencircuit." *Intermediair* 18(8):1–11.

———. 1983. "Zelfstandig ondernemerschap van minderheden." Lecture delivered at the Ministry of Economic Affairs Conference, Rotterdam, September 7.

Bovenkerk, F., A. Eijken, and W. Bovenkerk-Teerink. 1983. *Italiaans ijs: De opmerkelijke historie van Italiaanse ijsbereiders in Nederland*. Meppel.

Brana-Shute, G. 1979. *On the Corner: Male Social Life in a Paramaribo Creole Neighborhood*. Assen.

Breman, J. 1976. *Een dualistisch arbeidsbestel? Een kritische beschouwing van het begrip "de informele sector."* Rotterdam.

Broeksma, C. A., H. Hennes, and A. C. M. Jansen. 1981. "De kleine ondernemer buiten beeld." *ESB* 66:284–288.

Budike, F. 1982. *Surinamers naar Nederland: De migratie van 1687 tot 1982*. Amsterdam.

Buenk, B. W. 1980. *De Kamer van Koophandel in de Praktijk*. Deventer.

Dijk, M. P. van. 1980. *De Informele sector van Ouagdougou en Dakar: Ontwikkelingsmogelijkheden van kleine bedrijven in twee Westafrikaanse hoofdsteden*. Ph.D. thesis, Free University, Amsterdam.

Ellemers, J. E. 1984. "Etnische verhoudingen in Nederland—de behoefte aan een differentiele zienswijze." *Maatstaf* 32(9):47–57.

Gelder, P. van. 1984. *Werken onder de boom: Dynamiek en informele sektor: de situatie in Groot-Paramaribo, Suriname*. Ph.D. thesis, University of Amsterdam.

Gershuny, J. 1978. *After Industrial Society: The Emerging Self-Service Economy*. London.

Gershuny, J., and R. E. Pahl. 1980. "Britain in the Decade of the Three Economies." *New Society*, January 3, pp. 7–9.

Godschalk, J. J. 1985. *De informele economie: Report for the Council for Small and Medium Sized Business*. Amsterdam.

Heilbron, W. 1982. *Kleine boeren in de schaduw ven de plantage: De politieke ekonomie van de na-slavenijperiode in Suriname*. Ph.D. thesis, University of Amsterdam.

Kroniek van het ambacht/klein-en middenbedrijf. 1983. Special issue: *Conferentie Vestigingswetbedrijven*, vol. 37.

Kruijer, G. J. 1977. *Suriname: De problemen en hun oplossingen*. Utrecht and Antwerp.

Leeuwen, M. van. 1984. "Minderhedenbeleid, discussie en knelpunten." *Kroniek van het ambacht/klein- en middenbedrijf* 38:30–34.

Lier, R. van. 1971. *Frontier Society. A Social Analysis of History of Surinam*. The Hague. First published 1949.

Menger, P.J.P.T. 1980. *Vestigingswet Detailhendel*. Zwolle.

———. 1983. *Vestigingswet bedrijven 1954: Vestigingsbesluiten Bedrijfsvergunningenbesluiten*. Zwolle.

Ministerie van Binnenlandse Zaken. 1983. *Minderhedennota*. Parliamentary Document 102(20–21).

Ministerie van Economische Zaken. 1981. Kamerstuk 17, 100 hfdst. 7 (nr.38). "Vragen gesteld door leden van de Kamer, met de daarop door de Regering gegeven antwoorden."

———. 1982. Kamerstuk 17, 553 (nr.13). "Het midden- en kleinbedrijf in hoofdlijnen: Beleid inzake het starten van een eigen bedrijf."

———. 1983. Toespraak van de Staatssecretaris van Economische Zaken. P. H. van Zeil, Rotterdam, September 7.

———. 1984a. "Voorlichting, financiering en inkomenshulp t.b.v. adspirant-ondernemers: Brief aan de Voorzitter van de Tweede Kamer der Staten-Generaal" (784/2/211/HAD10), May 30.

———. 1984b. *De kleine onderneming en de Nederlandse overheid: Informatie over wetten, regelingen en adviesmogelijkheden*. The Hague.

Ministerie van Sociale Zaken en Werkgelegenheid. 1983. *Het Arbeidsbesluit Jeugdigen*. The Hague.

Nicholls, W. M., and W. A. Dyson. 1983. *The Wealth of Families: How Canadians Are Responding to Economic Crisis by Tapping Our Base Economy*. Montreal.

Pompe, J. H. 1984. "Over Italiaans ijs en Turks textiel." *Kroniek van het ambacht/klein- en middenbedrijf* 38(1–2):7–21.

Reubsaet, T.J.M. 1981. *Surinamers in Nederland, een momentopname*. Nijmegen.

———. 1982. *Surinaamse Migranten in Nederland: De positie van Surinamers in de Nederlandse samenleving*, vol. 2. Nijmegen.

Riel, J. W. G. van. 1961. *De Vestigingswet in de praktijk*. Utrecht and Antwerp.

RMK (Raad voor het Midden- en Kleinbedrijf). 1983a. *MKB-Voorlichtingsinstrumentarium*. The Hague.

———. 1983b. *Bedrijfsgeorienteerde Stadsvernieuwing*. The Hague.

Sampson, S. L. 1983. "Rich Families and Poor Collectives: An Anthropological Approach to Romania's Second Economy," pp. 1–25. Paper presented at the Institute for Ethnology and Anthropology, Copenhagen.

Tap, L. J. 1983. "Het Turkse Bedrijfsleven in Amsterdam." Rapport naar aanleiding van een afstudeeronderzoek. Groningen.

Tillaart, H. J. M. van den, H. C. van der Hoeven, F. W. van Uxem, and J. M. van Westerlaak. 1981. *Zelfstandig Ondernemen: Onderzoek naar de problemen en mogelijkheden van het zelfstandig ondernemerschap in het midden- en kleinbedrijf*. Nijmegen.

Vermeulen, H. 1984. *Etnische groepen en grenzen: Surinamers, Chinezen en Turken*. Weesp.

[10]

Interpreting American Litigiousness

Carol J. Greenhouse

Sooner or later any discussion of the role of law in the United States turns to the question of the litigiousness of Americans. Litigiousness is widely held to be an American trait, not only by allegedly less litigiousness foreigners but also among Americans themselves. This chapter is about Americans' concerns with litigiousness. I treat these concerns as a cultural self-representation of American society. Litigation is an important activity in its own right, but it is the concerns of Americans about litigiousness that is the subject of what follows. My starting point is in the observation that many Americans are ready to believe in, almost to the point of insistence, their own allegedly litigious national character, even when evidence for this characterization is absent, ambiguous, or contradictory.[1]

[1]Galanter 1983 persuasively reviews this evidence. He questions the widespread criticism that Americans express for "hyperlexis"—excessive use of the law. Engel's study of "Sander County" begins with the observation that "although it is generally acknowledged that law is a vital part of culture and of the social order, there are times when the invocation of formal law is viewed as an *anti*social act and as a contravention of established social norms" (Engel 1984:549; emphasis in the original). Engel suggests that popular concern with litigation "can . . . draw our attention to important underlying conflicts in cultural values and changes or tensions in the structure of social relationships" (ibid., p. 550). This chapter pursues that theme.

Talking about Litigiousness

How do Americans talk about litigiousness? How does this term convey meaning? How are the meanings of litigiousness learned? Who is their audience? A first step toward addressing these questions is in examining the discourse surrounding litigiousness, a discourse widely shared by American academics, practitioners, and laypeople alike (Galanter 1983:5–11).[2] Its features can be summarized in the following way:

1. *Scale.* The adjective "litigious" is generally applied to groups rather than individuals; it is used in reference to a collective phenomenon. Thus, an ordinary usage would be "Americans are litigious," not "my neighbor is litigious." One's neighbor might be a troublemaker or a bad neighbor, but not, in ordinary American speech, litigious. The referents of this adjective are virtually always the third-person plural. The open-ended, collective referent of the term suggests that its scale is that of American society itself, or the American social fabric. This scale suggests that when people express concern about litigiousness they are concerned that some defect exists in American culture or social structure.

2. *Value.* Litigiousness carries negative connotations. Why this should be so is part of the subject of this chapter; that it is so is widely understood. Later we will be exploring two features of this negative value: the connection between litigiousness and disputing, and the connection between litigiousness and appeals to authority.

3. *Orientation.* Concern with litigiousness is process-oriented not result-oriented. Thus, while opening floodgates for new classes of litigation might result in positive social change, the talk about litigiousness focuses instead on the use of the legal process itself, as if use equals abuse.

4. *Temporality.* "Litigiousness" carries with it an adverbial aura, because those who comment on it generally make assumptions about the

[2]Some examples of the extensive commentary on litigiousness include the following: "[Americans have] an almost irrational focus—virtually a mania—on litigation as a way to solve all problems" (Chief Justice Warren Burger, quoted in *Newsweek,* November 21, 1983). (Litigation seen as abnormal.) "We've gotten to the point where there are just plain silly suits" (John Cibinic, Jr., Professor of Law, George Washington University, quoted in *Business Week,* May 28, 1984). (Litigation seen as parody.) "While something intractable in the American character may make us such a contentious lot, the national obsession with litigation has clearly reached ridiculous proportions. Court suits are increasing six times faster than the population, and each year state courts alone report more than 13 million new civil cases" (*Washington Monthly,* June 1983). (Litigation seen as unnatural.)

direction of social transformation with respect to court use. People who worry about litigiousness worry about its increase; the mythology holds that Americans were once able to resolve disputes without major recourse to courts but can no longer manage to accomplish the business of personal life without judicial intervention (e.g., Nelson 1981).

5. *Textuality*. Finally, litigiousness seems to be understood as constituting social commentary. Talk about litigiousness centers on how to "read" it for messages about the state of society. Engel's (1984) study suggests that Americans "read" different categories of litigation differently. Ethnographic evidence (developed below) from the United States shows that litigiousness is popularly understood as a symbol of important social characteristics. These interpretive efforts are at the heart of the larger problem this chapter addresses.

These five dimensions help focus the following discussion on a few interrelated problems that converge in the question of how and why litigiousness functions so effectively as an element of the semiotics of social experience in the United States. Specifically, what relationships does litigiousness symbolize? And how is it that, in the eyes of so many Americans, litigiousness signals something negative about American society?

We begin with ethnohistorical data from the United States. The case study is built around an ethnographic problem: In the American town I call "Hopewell," Baptists express a strong aversion not only to litigiousness but also to litigation and every other adversarial form of dispute-processing. Southern Baptists in Hopewell are by no means an extreme sect; they are sophisticated suburbanites who in most ways live much like their neighbors. (This fact distinguishes Hopewell's Baptists from the Amish, who proscribe litigation for other reasons; see Hostetler 1984.) The Hopewell Baptists are white, educated, and affluent. Like most Americans, they do not use the court, which is readily accessible, Hopewell being the county seat. Unlike the majority of Americans, however, Baptists in Hopewell explain their avoidance of the court and of disputing altogether in religious terms, which are explained in the next section (for a full account, see Greenhouse 1986a).

The heart of the following case study involves a comparison between Hopewell's Baptists and another dominant local social faction during the middle third of the nineteenth century. At the time, Baptists were forming a symbolic equation between harmony and Christianity. The other faction, meanwhile, was developing new uses of the judicial system. Specifically, while the Baptists were framing their proscriptions of

conflict in terms of the contradictions between appeals to human authority and Christian faith in Jesus, the local judicial system was increasingly
monopolized by relatively few actors. Both processes reached a climax
between 1858 and 1868. I must stress the local aspect of this discussion,
because the connection between these two groups had to do with local
responses to the vectors of political controversies in the state, the region,
and the nation.

Attitudes toward Conflict in Hopewell

My fieldwork, from 1973 to 1975 and again in 1980, was in the small
metropolitan suburb I call Hopewell, Georgia. I shall summarize the
findings of that research (Greenhouse 1982a, 1982b, 1983, 1986a, and
1986b).

Baptists in Hopewell place special importance on the inappropriateness of disputing for Christians.[3] Their rejection of disputing is based on
scriptural exhortations to "turn the other cheek," to yield what is demanded, and most important, to leave all judgments to Jesus. The result
of this ethic is a pattern of conflict resolution that centers on indirection;
prayers, jokes, narratives, or simple avoidance hint obliquely at the
issues that divide people. Local Baptists place a great deal of importance
on the spiritual significance of their restraint as well as on the significance of its absence among non-Baptists, whom they assume to be
contentious and litigious—and damned.

The proscriptions—felt and urged, more than enforced—against
overt adversarial conflict have a particular character—for example,
church members encourage one another to abjure only some conflicts,
conflicts within the circle of the church membership, family, and friendship. Feelings of conflict with non-Christians (i.e., the unsaved) are not
exactly encouraged, but they are actively relevant to Baptists' sense of
their distinctive social and moral identity. For example, Baptist teen-
agers in Hopewell are urged to avoid their peers' habits of drinking,
dancing, and—until they are deemed ready for serious courtship—
dating as couples. The effect is that friendship networks among youth

---

[3]At several points in this chapter, I stress the local nature of my findings. This must be
one of them. Baptist communities elsewhere have been described by Batteau 1982,
Bryant 1980, and Peacock 1975; these do not show the same aversion to confrontative
interaction that I describe here. This chapter is in part an attempt to show why Hopewell
used a religious idiom to address fundamental political questions.

tend to be based in Hopewell and to center in the Baptist church, even if the young people attend school or work elsewhere. This segregation is viewed positively.

While feelings of conflict can have this morally and socially positive side, Baptists draw a sharp line between such sentiments and overt disputing. In Hopewell, many Baptists explained to me that disputing is a profoundly unchristian act because the Bible states clearly that Jesus is the judge of all people. The implication seems to be that to enter into a dispute is to stand as judge over another person, and to do so not only reveals lack of faith in Jesus, but preempts Jesus' power ("All vengeance is mine . . . saith the Lord"). Another related dimension of this pro-scription is the Baptists' premise that Christians have no need to press their own interests in any context because God has all human needs in mind. A frequent theme in sermons was that of proper Baptist prayer—which should always give thanks, rather than make requests or offer contracts in the form of vows. Finally, since Baptists are convinced that non-Baptists live lives of constant carping and turmoil, they extend their own principle of the "life of good witness" (the preferred form of evan-gelism in Hopewell) to their abstinence from disputing. All these factors lead Baptists in Hopewell most frequently to withdraw from conflict situations that seem likely to result in a dispute.

On another dimension, Baptists acknowledge that disputing and "making a case for oneself" is a strong temptation in everyday life, and they present their own assiduousness in avoiding disputes as the product of concerted effort buttressed by prayer. That Baptists see the tempta-tion to dispute as one component of their continuing need for salvation is some measure of the large role they give prayer in ordering their private lives. Indeed, prayer is a vital part of private and public life among Baptists in Hopewell. In church, among friends, at the dinner table, on the telephone—prayer is public. In addition, an individual's private prayer life is potentially virtually constant. A housewife may recount having knelt alone by a chair or by the bedside for a moment of prayer, but prayer does not require any physical interruption of the day's ac-tivity. Prayer is a form of narrative that accompanies the performance of everyday activities or, more accurately from the Baptist perspective, inserts some textuality into the looming chaos of "the world" ("the world" refers specifically to a society dominated by the unsaved, until the Day of Judgment). Prayer is verbal and is addressed directly to Jesus ("So I said to the Lord, 'Lord . . .'" was the beginning of many prayer narratives I heard in conversation). The most frequent themes of prayers narrated to me were pleas for Jesus' support in refraining from disputing and from having feelings of conflict within a family or friendship group, and prayers for the salvation of some particular individual. Prayers for interpersonal harmony consist of potentially lengthy explanations, spoken aloud or verbalized silently, of the history of the conflict.

While prayer is held to be adequate for the faithful as a means of achieving order in their personal lives, Baptists acknowledge the difficulties of accomplishing harmony for people with stunted, misdirected, or absent "prayer lives." The law, they say, helps these people live in peace. It is only in this sense—of making the world of the unsaved safe— that the Baptists in Hopewell concede any valid place to the law. Man-made law (they stress "man-made") is by definition a conceit, because it is not the law of God. It is important to note that Hopewell's Baptists do not conceive of God's law as a set of rules (Greenhouse 1982a); they do, however, understand man-made law as rules. God's law—the central tenets of the Christian life—are individually *felt*. This is part of the significance of the Baptists' insistence that the Scriptures are accessible to all Baptists by virtue of their faith, but that the "Christian life" is reason itself. The contrast to the world of rules, lawyers, judges, and (in Baptist eyes) the exaltation of contention could not be clearer: where God's law is felt, man's law is imposed; where God's law is reason itself, man's law is artificial; where God's law promises eternal life, man's law thrives on enmity and conflict; where God's law is expressed in prayer, man's law is expressed in rules. Under God's law, all people are equal— all people *become* equal, shedding the inequalities (particularly the ultimate vanity of basing status on material possessions) that Baptists see in the non-Baptist world.

Thus, like other Americans, Baptists in Hopewell see their own way of life as by definition legal, although they carefully locate its legality in reason, the source of which is God, and in nature, which is understood as God's dominion.[4] The Baptists' vision of social order, which comes about by extending God's word to the unsaved, is a vision of a society at peace because each individual "does right" and "knows right in his heart." Authoritative intervention is not necessary to the achievement of this order, although Hopewell Baptists do concede a role for the law in the interim period before Judgment Day. In this world view, litigiousness is

---

[4]Hopewell's Baptists reject both the asceticism of the Primitive Baptists and what they see as the sensual excesses of the unsaved on these grounds; both rejections are based on the principle of the healthy normality of physical appetites, within reason.

a sign of "the world," proving the need for salvation again and again on a large scale.

While Hopewell's Baptists might resist the drawing of parallels between their stance toward the world and that of other Americans, those parallels are apparent. First, it is important to note that, like the Baptists, most Americans have no experience with litigation. While most adult Americans have consulted a lawyer once, the vast majority of those consultations are over the administration of a mortgage or a will; although I had no means to gauge the recourse of Baptists to lawyers for these purposes, I never heard them proscribed.[5] Second, Baptists' attitudes toward the legal quality of society are not substantially different from those of other Americans, although the social maps of Baptists might differ. (This point will be taken up in a later section.) Hopewell Baptists "read" litigiousness as an index of society's ultimate formation; they feel that use of the official law violates an ordained equality among citizens and believers. Like other Americans, Hopewell Baptists share in the consciousness of the liberal state and its long heritage in Western culture. Baptists are not ambivalent about official law and its relationship to the "natural" legality of social life, but this is a difference only of degree from the more general attitude outlined earlier.

Conflicting Signs

Modern Baptists in Hopewell are confident in their rejection of conflict, disputing, and litigiousness on theological grounds, but while deeply held, their beliefs appear to be the product of a very different stance in the early days of the county's history (Greenhouse 1986b). In the years between the first organization of the Baptist church in Hopewell (1824) and the Civil War (1861), the local Baptist leadership actively sought to eliminate conflict from the churches by interpreting it as unchristian. It is interesting to know why and how they accomplished this strategy. Briefly, they sought to eliminate the church's role as a forum for disputing so that the church could survive the deep political divisions of the day—states' rights, Cherokee removal, and abolition. The church in Hopewell was apparently deeply divided over these questions, and at one point its membership may have fallen to as low as seven. At this period in Hopewell's history, survival of the order de-

[5]There is recent documentation of Americans' uses of the law in Curran and Spalding 1974 and in Galanter 1983.

manded that the church somehow transcend, or at least contain, politics. It finally did so by stressing its theological objections to the human authority that would be inescapably constituted in any overt dispute. By reiterating the contradictions between God's law and human authority over a period of twenty or more years, the local Baptist church association was finally successful in symbolically linking conflict with the unsaved. The Civil War marked an end to any mention of disputing in the church record, and the life of good witness became doubly that of the aspiring Baptist and the defeated Southerner.

But then as now, Hopewell was a diverse community, by no means entirely Baptist and by no means controlled by the Baptist world view. The withdrawal of Hopewell Baptists from conflict situations was above all a strategic local response to the political crosscurrents of their times. Baptists were not only a religious minority in Hopewell, as they are now, they were also a political minority on every significant issue of the day. The county applauded Cherokee removal; the Baptists lamented it. The county was strongly populist; the Baptist leadership, locally, came from the more aristocratic regions of Georgia. The South generally built its cause on antiabolitionism and states' rights; the local Baptists (but not, it is important to note, the Southern Baptist Convention) supported states' rights only. Against this shifting background of opposing and realigning forces, the Baptists in Hopewell forged their new semiotics of Christian harmony out of a combination of scriptural symbols and American political logic.

It would be an error to suppose that in signaling human authority as the agency of the undoing of God's law, Hopewell Baptists were responding in purely theoretical terms to a problem of theology. For them, human authority had faces and names over and above its generic meanings. Who were the Baptists' neighbors, and can we find a seam connecting the emergent Baptist symbolism and the responses of non-Baptist Hopewell to the same issues? Let us turn to the institution that was the object of the Baptists' reproach—the court. If we can discern who was using it, and how, perhaps we can sharpen the sense of context surrounding the question of how local Baptists interpret law use, and why.

Hopewell acquired three courts when the county of which it is the seat was founded in 1858. The area had been settled by whites since the 1820s, but it was incorporated as Hopewell, seat of the new Hopewell County, in the later year. The Court of Ordinary (for probate matters) and the Inferior Court had strictly local jurisdiction, but the Superior Court formed part of a judicial circuit that included several other counties to the north, west, and south. It is interesting to note that the boundaries of the circuit, established by the Georgia legislature in 1833 and expanded with the establishment of contiguous counties, followed the same boundaries as the voting blocs in the legislature that had formed over the establishment of Hopewell County. The establishment of Hopewell County had been proposed by J. T. Smithson (another pseudonym), of neighboring "Lynette" County (to the west). His bill passed by a comfortable margin, but the nay votes clustered together in the wide swath of aristocratic counties to the east. (Phillips [1968] offers a clear description of Georgia state politics at this period.) Thus, it appears that the legislature took political alliances into account in forming the judicial districts.[6]

The setting of the boundaries around the Superior Court circuit united Hopewell County with its populist parent county, from which it had been formed. The political elite of Lynette County moved to Hopewell, where they continued in prominence as state senators and representatives and as founders of the Methodist church, among other activities. The Baptists in Hopewell, who had settled in the area earlier, came from "Harold" County to the east. Harold County, Hopewell's other "parent," was on the western frontier of the aristocratic counties; its dominant political party, plantation agriculture, slaveholding, and higher levels of affluence tied Harold to its lowland neighbors to the east. The net effect of the Superior Court's jurisdictional boundaries, then, was to divide local Baptists from their closest kin and friends. It is perhaps significant that the local Baptist church association included both Hopewell and Harold counties. In short, the Superior Court circuit was constituted geographically in a way that might predictably alienate Baptists, not on any doctrinal grounds but on grounds of origins and sympathies.

In 1858 the Superior Court met twice a year in each county of the circuit. Judges were required under the state constitution to be resident in the circuit, but during the period of concern at this point in our discussion (1858–68), the local circuit chief judges do not appear to have been resident in Hopewell County.[7] It seems likely that the local Supe-

---

[6]An alternative would have been to follow congressional districts, which put Lynette (populist, to the west), Harold (aristocratic, to the east), and Hopewell (between them) in one unit. This grouping may explain why nineteenth- and early twentieth-century elections were often extremely close—a "seesaw" in the word of one Hopewell citizen.

[7]It is difficult to know the residence of the judges, but my extensive collection of local genealogies does not include the names of the Superior Court judges. The Inferior and Ordinary Courts, on the other hand, draw entirely on local families.

rior Court judges were literally outsiders, as well as political outsiders from the Baptists' perspective.

Finally, Superior Court judges were elected under the state constitution for three-year terms. In 1861 a new constitution gave the power of appointment to the governor, and terms were extended to four years. Georgia's governors were Democratic after 1857, when J. E. Brown was elected, but the war years and the early years of reconstruction were a turbulent period for the governor's office. The state constitution of 1877 partially returned the selection of judges to the people (by having the state legislature elect them), but in the interim Georgia's governors were highly compromised in the eyes of those who had been loyal to the Southern cause. During the years when the Superior Court came to Hopewell and the power of appointment was most concentrated in the governor's hands, the Baptists in Hopewell conclusively defined impositions of human authority as alien to God's kingdom.

People in Hopewell would have been well aware of these developments in the judiciary, because each political party had its own local partisan newspaper. Other sources indicate the extent to which the local population were engaged in politics—for example, one minister complained in his diary that the congregation was too involved in debate on the church lawn to come inside for the sermon. Election-day riots were regular occurrences. It certainly was a turbulent period.

Even if the structure, composition, and selection of the Superior Court did not directly concern local people, the way their neighbors used it did. One modern commentator from Hopewell lightheartedly described the continual striving between the "ins" and "outs" as a seesaw, as closely matched forces battled for office at the local level. Close elections were the norm, and his evidence suggests that party faithful used whatever means they could to secure the ballot. Among these means was the Superior Court, where local political contests often had their last round, as one side or the other would have the other arrested on riot charges and brought to trial. Indeed, during the period before the Civil War, the docket of the Superior Court reads as a local roster of politically active men, all locally prominent.

Because the court sat only twice a year, it is not surprising that local people developed their own patterns of self-help. The court's role seems to have been one of validation, affirming the self-appointed efforts at social control from one side or the other. In a very different urban and historical context, Merry (1979) shows that modern Americans' use of the court in contexts of dispute is similarly directed largely at attempts to validate or authorize self-designed solutions to conflict. The contributors

[261]

to Tomasic and Feeley's (1982) volume on "neighborhood justice" amplify a portrait of Americans using the court and other public agencies as instruments of self-help. Later we will consider the possible significance of this apparent continuity in the way Americans use the official law.

After the Civil War, patterns of court use in Hopewell did not change dramatically, except for a notable increase in cases of debt. One strategy to avoid the court's collection efforts was first developed by J. F. Smithson (this man was politically active, regionally prominent, and an experienced litigant from several charges of riot). Smithson failed to appear, he explained persuasively to the court later, because the presence of federal troops in the area and the general destruction around Hopewell had led him to believe that the court would not sit. Similar strategies were used later by Smithson's friends and eventually by clients of Smithson's law practice. Smithson was one of the two wealthiest men in the county in 1860, when the census reported property, and his successful attempts to avoid paying local creditors after the war probably met with mixed reaction.

While the Superior Court was used to validate self-help solutions to problems among relatively few "repeat players" (Galanter 1974) in Hopewell, the Court of Ordinary provided a stark contrast. While it is possible that "settlements" there had been negotiated in advance, the refrain of those records in this period is "There being no disagreement . . ." or "There being no dispute . . ." to questions of the administration of wills, guardianship, and the distribution and sale of estates. The transfer of property from one side of a family to another and from one generation to another occurred publicly and smoothly through this court. It was a forum not only for men, who are the sole recorded Superior Court litigants in this period, but also for women and children to make their pleas concerning the disposition of a dead kinsman's affairs.

The contrast to the Court of Ordinary suggests that if the emergent doctrine of Hopewell Baptists had secular referents in the judiciary during this period, they were in the Superior Court (the Inferior Court was largely concerned with county administration). While the evidence is indirect to varying degrees, we can see that the public role of the court was to provide a forum for local political confrontation and, if Smithson's litigation is indicative, for personal gain. This is not to say that the court itself was corrupt, but its use was monopolized by litigants who designed a participatory role for the institution by manipulating complaints and defenses in strategic ways. Indeed, Baptists today condemn not the courts but the plaintiffs, although none of these historical developments is remembered. For Hopewell's Baptists a century ago, it is plausible to conclude that they saw the court as an arena in which the faction with which they were most at odds performed political dramas before strangers, for their own ends.

This section has given some faces and social identity to the institutional forms and authoritative agents whom the Hopewell Baptists conclusively rejected as being unchristian. The crucial period is the decade before, during, and after the Civil War, when the regional issues and divisions (Cherokee removal and other sectarian conflicts) gave way to the national issue of the Union's survival. The church records never name or otherwise identify the sources or issues of the disputes they were so concerned with effacing; their consideration of conflict is in purely "generic" terms. By rejecting disputing as a genre, the church leaders were able to replace it with another one: the genre of God's law. In establishing these genres of social discourse—the one to be rejected and other to endure—the local Baptists drew on the symbols they had available to them: the imagery of the American Revolution—individualism, equality, and freedom—and the imagery of the Bible. They did not have to reach very far to find their symbolism; it was all around them in the Protestant idiom of the American philosophical mainstream (see, e.g., Wills 1979) with its strong natural-law bias.

Litigants were moved by other strains of the same general philosophy. They had every reason to identify with the courts. In Hopewell the group most frequently in court was precisely the same group that had been instrumental in the establishment of the county in 1858 and had gerrymandered its boundaries to include the residences of leading members. Their control of the political process, in the legislature, in the courts, and in more private settings, made litigation an effective and predictable course of action for them. They too demonstrate their natural-law bias in merging the judicial branch with the legislative and using both as arenas for long-standing political contests. These were populists who drew heavily on the imagery of democracy and local control.

Law as a Cultural Category in the United States

The case study of emerging meanings of litigation and litigiousness in Hopewell in the nineteenth century illustrates the nature and context of one group of Americans' concern with litigiousness. This context was one of developing factionalism in a community profoundly, if ambiguously, divided on major contemporary controversies. While the populists were cementing their local position by creating Hopewell County, controlling its temporal affairs, and monopolizing the judicial system in strategic ways, the Baptists were articulating and defending an ideology that equated harmony with Christianity. In Hopewell, these two positions referred both to each other and to the wider philosophical currents of the time. The case study suggests that the position of the local Baptists, who equated litigiousness with the very undoing of God's order, was constructed of signs that pointed to the community of Hopewell. The local Baptist view of conflict and conflict resolution was thus directly tied to the local situation, in which the populists threatened—in the Baptists' eyes—an unwarranted hegemony, or at least an unwanted confrontation. Hence, the Baptists focused on the adversarial nature of conflict, on devaluation of plaintiffs' stances, and above all, on the inappropriateness of interventions of human authority in relationships that are supposed to be between equals.

The argument so far is not that the Baptists "invented" a legal ideology to separate their forces from those of the litigious group, for whom they felt distrust or antipathy on various grounds. The problem is constructed the other way around: in experiencing a need for social distance, Baptists focused on litigiousness and the problematic aspects of human authority as a symbolic resource. Why? This resource was available to them in practice (in the institutionalization of the local courts) in the mid-nineteenth century. Furthermore, this was a time of great local tension and widening distance among local factions. But these factors alone could not have shaped local Baptist political discourse; the wider cultural context made that discourse available. Specifically, the antiauthoritarian sentiment enshrined in the American Revolution channeled questions of difference and distance into questions of conflict, control, and hierarchy. The Baptist prescriptions for avoidance can be read as prescriptions for egalitarianism; this is one example of the impact of revolutionary logic on American social thought.

To generalize from this case study, therefore, we should look not to other Baptists' ideas about law, but to modern Americans' patterns of rejecting forms of discourse that illuminate the potential for hierarchy in relationships presumed to be equal. In their lamentations about litigiousness, Americans resist the capacity of the law to create these forms of discourse. Let us shift now from Hopewell's Baptists to the United States more generally.

Anthropological research on the United States suggests two approaches to the question of how litigiousness acquires its significance as a cultural sign. The more general suggestion comes from Schneider (1968, 1977) and Perin (1977), who interpret American concepts of law as cultural references to a whole, ordered social life. Schneider's analysis of American kinship is built on cultural categories elicited from interviews: blood (descent) and law (marriage) are the warp and weft of the familial fabric. In placing the marrige promise—a contract—at the foundation of the family, Americans also provide the foundations of society itself, since, as Tocqueville observed (1945, 2:104–106), Americans perceive their society as built *up* of family units. In this sense, Americans define their society as a collection of voluntary social contracts, a natural law of sorts. In the conclusion to his study of American kinship, Schneider (1968:109) develops an equivalence between Americans' sense of law and the anthropological concept of culture—both reveal "the outcome of the action of human reason on nature" and resolve "the contradictions between man and nature."

In identifying Americans' view of society as a "legal" view, it is important to qualify (as Schneider does) the sense in which it is legal. It can be called a legal vision *if* law is, in fact (which is to say, in theory), the sum of private contractual promises. It can be called a legal vision *if* the law is what the people say it is—"what the most do" (Hoebel 1968:15). It is a legal vision *if* law and custom are held to be one and the same, and *if* the population is egalitarian, homogeneous, or at least capable of consensus. The vision of the law that Schneider shows Americans to hold assumes that all people are equals, agents of the law by their very actions in relation to other people, through the media of their respective social roles. This view of law turns simultaneously toward both nature and society, as Unger (1975:19) elucidates in his essay on the consciousness of the liberal state:

> The dominant consciousness in the liberal state includes a characteristic view of the relation between man as an agent or a thinker and the external world, between man and his fellows, and between man and his work or social place. With respect to the first, it emphasizes the subjection of nature to human will as the idea of action and the choice of efficient means to given ends as the exemplary procedure of reason. With regard to the second, it underlines the separateness of person, the artificial character of society, and the ties of reciprocal need and hostility among individuals. As to the third, it focuses on the ambivalent value of work as both a manifestation and a surrender of personality.

Unger's analysis suggests that if Americans view "law" as the name of some aggregate contractual connection among themselves, it is a contractual connection mandated by nature—and exalted in its domination of human nature.

A popular attitude in the United States holds that ordinary life is "legal"—in that it is ordered or to the extent that it is ordered (or presumed to be). It is important to note that this externalization of the reciprocal, contractual aspect of social relations implies that order is never implicit in relations, but always applied to relationships as a form of self-control or control over others. Hopewell's Baptists ascribe this order to God's word, but other populations bring secular concerns to their images of social order. In his community study, Engel (1984) shows some of the practical consequences of this attitude in the everyday process of social classification: people in Sander County see troublemakers and litigious groups as people for whom the ordinary bonds of the natural legal order are not effective or not sufficient. Specifically, it is personal-injury disputes that generate anxieties over litigiousness in Sander County, not contract disputes (ibid., p. 575): "Duties generated by socially imposed obligations to guard against injuring other people were seen as intrusions upon existing relationships, as pretexts for forced exchanges, as inappropriate attempts to redistribute wealth, and as limitations upon individual freedom." Engel's study suggests that, in the eyes of Sander County residents, concerns about litigiousness channel diffuse anxieties about the community's increasing pluralism. Hopewell Baptists show a similar response in somewhat different terms; they see disputing and litigation as defining characteristics of the unsaved (Greenhouse 1982a and 1982b).

Given Americans' popular understanding of the law as the sum of their society's functional and organic qualities, it is not surprising that Americans should perceive conflict with some apprehension, as a sign of social dissolution. In this sense, the Hopewell Baptist imagery of damnation differs from that of others neither by kind nor by degree, but only in its religious referents. Yet if this is so, how does court use acquire its exceptional, even "antisocial" (Engle 1984:549), status? Why are courts seen as inappropriate remedies for social conflict? This attitude would seem paradoxical. The Baptists addressed this paradox by pointing to Jesus' sole authority. What concerns structure the secular variant of their thinking?

Litigiousness as a Cultural Sign in the United States

The source of the paradox appears to lie in a central tension in Americans' long-standing conception of official law, and that is its competitive relationship with the unofficial natural law described above. It is as if courts do not augment society's inherent legality, but violate or preempt it. Society may be legal by definition, but this legality somehow excludes the bench and the bar. What constitutes this abrupt shift away from natural-law imagery when Americans face their own legal institutions? Miller (1965:104) suggests it is the scholasticism of the law, its "beguiling *mystique*" that (in a popular view) severs the law from the society it claims to serve. Miller's observation is helpful in sharpening the sense in which the redundancy of legal institutions is negative rather than positive, competitive rather than supplementary. His reference to the subversive "sophistication" of the official law suggests the terms in which Americans view the law's "textuality"—that is, the textual aspects of the law. Because most Americans never experience litigation, this textuality is somewhat hypothetical, a fact that gives its terms a certain arbitrariness and breadth. Is one source of Americans' traditional ambivalence about the law to be found in their rejection of the law's textual character? Some contrastive consideration of the narrative discourse of everyday life suggests that this is the case.

In everyday life, social roles are essential, not only in organizing society but also in giving it its legal quality (Schneider 1968; Warner 1962). In the United States the discourse of everyday life is performed in a rather formal sense—that is, it is the form of life that has public meaning.[8] Indeed, the colloquial question "What are you going to be when you grow up?" is readily understood even by small children as an inquiry about their occupational goals. Doing and being merge. In some general sense, it seems likely that part of Americans' resistance to the idea of law in their everyday lives is a response to the insertion of the law's sophisticated textuality in the performance of society itself, a society organized by the harmony of nature and reason. Why, however, is the law's textuality unacceptable in ways that other forms of textuality (e.g., prayer, to take an example from the ethnographic discussion) are not?

Here the work of anthropologists concerned with language is particularly helpful. If ongoing social life is conceptualized (as ethnographers suggest it is) as a system of performed roles, it is important to observe that, as performances, roles have genres, points of view, and audiences. Such "generic" social roles can accumulate in a single individual (e.g., mother, wife, and lawyer), but they do not merge there.

---

[8]I borrow the distinctions between discourse and narrative, performance and text, and form and substance from Chatman 1978:26.

The individual is crosscut by their multiplication.[9] Hence, Americans worry about family obligations conflicting with the requirements of the workplace, or ethnic identity competing with national identity, and freedom compromising equality. These are competing genres that are felt as challenges to individuals and to society. Individuality itself, however, is not a generic role in this sense. Individuality defines the relationships between a person and his own generic attributes. An individual is in that sense unique, but individuality also entails identifications with others whose roles are counterparts. Varenne's (1984:242–243) analysis of pronouns in American English leads him to conclude that the use of "we" expresses the politics of identification with a speaker's audience. Because personal identity is a cluster of generic roles, uses of "I," "you," and "we" elide fairly easily, as Varenne shows.

Varenne's discussion of the first person (singular and plural) involves at one point a contrast to what he calls "bureaucratic" speech—the third-person singular and plural that marks a political distinction between the speaker and his subject. This is the third person of administration and the law: "May it please the court . . ." or "Yes, Your Honor." The impoliteness of "I–you" forms in legal contexts emphasizes the extent to which "you" is the implied audience in ordinary narrative discourse, as well as the extent to which "I–you" involves a relationship that is qualitatively different from "I–he" (for example). Varenne (ibid., p. 244) concludes: "Western ideology . . . is best characterized not so much by its 'individualism' as by the institutions that it constructs as it tries to deny the relevance of a holism that it is in fact experiencing." The relevance of this important observation to the subject of this chapter is in its suggestion that the experience of authority is an experience of hierarchy and that, while authority/hierarchy can be canceled or denied in the performance of ordinary formal discourse, appeals to the law make that denial problematic. Litigious Americans, who invoke and invite the intervention of a third party into the "I–you" discourse of everyday life, violate the unspoken proscription against introducing hierarchy into private relationships.

Arno considers another aspect of the capacity of legal language to

[9]Parsons (1970:142–143) offers a vivid example of the way social roles divide an individual into conflicting components in his discussion of the traditional ambivalence Americans express concerning married female schoolteachers: "If the differentiation between what may be called *the maternal and the occupational components of the feminine role* is incomplete and insecure, confusion between them may be avoided by insuring that both are not performed by the same persons. The 'old maid' teacher of American tradition may thus be thought of as having renounced the maternal role in favor of the occupational" (emphasis added).

reorder social relationships. He analyzes official law as a "conflict discourse" (Arno 1985:42), and his discussion maps the impact of the law's "control communication" on the "structural communication" of everyday life. The language of the law is not only a different text, it actively transforms the structure of ordinary life (ibid., p. 45): "By bringing the problematic relation within its own terms of reference, control communication [brings] about substantive ordering, and that is precisely its overt function."[10]

These linguistic analyses suggest that a central dimension of the competitive stance of the official law is its authority. It is not that the law has an illegitimate authority, or that some other institutional arrangement might be preferable; as for Hopewell's Baptists, it is the *fact* of human authority that is at issue.[11]

In effect, Americans seem to hold two views of the law. The ethnographic and historical literature suggests that Americans hold a natural-law philosophy (described above) when the question is the functioning structure of society itself, but when the question turns to the nature of official law, Americans are positivists. To put this another way, Americans may see society as intrinsically ordered by collective contractual arrangements (hence its legal quality), but they simultaneously see official law as rules imposed externally by elite institutions. (For a succinct contrast of these two philosophies, see Unger 1975:72.) The natural-rights theorizing of Americans suggests that Americans identify with the law and view its use in a positive light. On the other hand, their positivist theorizing suggests that confrontations with the law are likely to be risky encounters on almost literally unfamiliar territory—in a strange language, around strange principles devised by strangers. Indeed, statistical and ethnographic studies of Americans' use of the courts reflects this ambivalence, as disputants either litigate or avoid confrontations altogether (Buckle and Thomas-Buckle 1981; Nader 1980; Merry 1982). The important point for the purposes of this chapter is that Americans hold these two views simultaneously and apply them to two

[10]For a sociolinguistic analysis of a religious institutional setting, see Zaretsky 1974: 166–219.

[11]Americans' ambivalence on authority is an old theme in social commentary on the United States. See, e.g., Tocqueville 1945 and Kammen 1973:157–165, and for a modern ethnographic perspective see Fitchen 1981:67 on the attitudes of rural white men toward responsibility on the job: "To accept a position of authority over others is thought to invite jealousy, resentment, and certain criticism. [Quoting an informant]: 'My husband wouldn't want to be in the middle that way. He'd catch heck from his boss above him and he'd catch heck from the guys below him. No, he'd rather be one of them [the crew of laborers], even if he has to pass up a higher salary.'"

different populations: the regular folk who "get along" and "litigious Americans."

This ambivalence is expressed in the discourse of authority and its place in social relations. As we have seen, to the extent that Americans resist the law in personal affairs, one aspect of the resistance is linguistic. Specifically, this resistance is aimed at the intertextuality of the official law and everyday life; it is a resistance that would cancel the discourse of official law altogether (indeed, in 1810 the Georgia legislature entertained a bill to prohibit the practice of law). The embedded imagery of the law as a genre of discourse is helpful to our discussion, because it sheds light on how litigiousness acquires some of its negative value in the cultural complex at issue here. To continue the notion of legal discourse in a metaphor, litigation is a form of apostrophe,[12] a diversion of ordinary dyadic exchanges to some third party, an interruption of context. Culler's (1981:135) discussion of apostrophe focuses on the awkwardness of such obtrusive appeals: "[Apostrophes] may complicate or disrupt the circuit of communication, raising questions about who is the addressee, but above all they are embarrassing." Culler goes on to discuss the status of the voice in written literary forms, but a close analogy to his observation highlights the specific crisis of litigiousness: as apostrophe, its embarrassment is political. In turning aside to voice an appeal to agents who stand outside the problematic relationship, the plaintiff sets the outsider—the lawyer, the policeman, the judge—above his neighbor. The embarrassment of apostrophe in social relations deemed to be already legal is the sudden overturning of a supposed relation of equality by a relation of hierarchy and authority. From this perspective, it is the possibility of equality's transformation into hierarchy that makes litigiousness seem to be the very unmaking of the Revolution.[13]

[12]Culler (1981:135) credits Quintilian with the definition of apostrophe as "a diversion of our words to address some person other than the judge." In my application of the term to ordinary conversational contexts, the "judge" would refer to one's conversational partner.

[13]Gorer (1948:39–40) also recognized the obtrusiveness of the invocation of norms in ordinary social relations, but he expressed what I am calling their apostrophic nature in terms of gender: "The idiosyncratic feature of the American conscience is that it is predominantly feminine. . . . Duty and Right Conduct become feminine figures. . . . The fact that rules for moral conduct are felt to emanate from a feminine source is a cause of considerable confusion to American men. They tend to resent such interference with their own behavior, and yet are unable to ignore it, since the insistent maternal conscience is a part of their personality." Unless research demonstrates that concern with litigiousness is more prevalent among men, I prefer to read Gorer's analysis as a commentary on the ways in which his male informants symbolized otherness.

What are the connections between the case of Hopewell's Baptists and other Americans? Drawing on an interdisciplinary literature concerning American patterns of disputing, the politics of identity, and culture, we can point to some parallels: their shared sense (expressed by Schneider) of the definition of society as a set of legal contracts. These contracts, or this legality, is not intrinsic to relationships, but is brought to them—perhaps by virtue of citizenship, or by salvation, or by some other attribute. On this particular point, we might expect considerable diversity. There is also a second obvious parallel in the extent to which Hopewell's Baptists and those Americans who decry litigation by others condemn litigiousness as both a cause and a sign of social disintegration. Third, the negative valuation of disputing and litigation that both Hopewell Baptists and other (though certainly not all other) Americans express resides in the formal aspects of their discourse—in the creation and reproductions of generic categories of others, sometimes named, sometimes not, whose social predations are served by their allegedly inappropriate use of courts. The Baptists of Hopewell have used generic classifications to convey the meaning of litigiousness across the generations since the mid-nineteenth century; they remain in form but have changed in content. Today's concerns in Hopewell focus not on the anti-Cherokee, hard-line Democrats but on godless businessmen or self-absorbed city people, and so on. These categories reiterate the generic forms of the outsider and the power elite, as well as the futility and sacrilege of confronting them.

The Baptist church is thriving in Hopewell, where the new temptations of affluence in the Sunbelt fuel a continuing felt need for salvation. This observation leads to a concluding point: to the extent that Americans worry about litigiousness, they share with Hopewell's Baptists a cultural vision that reveals at once a cultural model of society and a portrait of its enemies. The cultural model of society is, as we have seen, a harmoniously functioning web of contractual relationships among equals. The portrait of the enemy lacks a face—he might be one's neighbor, one's customer, one's client, or one's patient—but (and on this the portrait is clear) he has stolen the mantle of the king.

Acknowledgments

This paper is based on two years of research conducted in "Hopewell," Georgia, from 1973 to 1975, and a short stay of several weeks in 1980.

Carol J. Greenhouse

The original research was funded by a National Institute of Mental Health Traineeship to Harvard University's Department of Anthropology; my return was funded by a Faculty Research Grant from the College of Arts and Sciences, Cornell University. I am very grateful to these sources, and to Paul Meade, for research assistance on the present chapter. I also express my appreciation to the sponsors and members of the Wenner-Gren Symposium, for which the first version of this paper was written. Special thanks are due to the conference organizers, Jane Collier and June Starr, for their constructive comments on that version.

REFERENCES

Arno, Andrew. 1985. "Structural Communication and Control Communication: An Interactionist Perspective on Legal and Customary Procedures for Conflict Management." *American Anthropologist* 87(1):40–55.

Batteau, Allen. 1982. "Mosbys and Broomsedge: The Semantics of Class in the Appalachian Kinship System." *American Ethnologist* 9(2):445–466.

Bryant, Carlene. 1980. *We're All Kin*. Knoxville, Tenn.

Buckle, Leonard, and Suzann Thomas-Buckle. 1981. "Doing unto Others: Dispute and Dispute Processing in an Urban American Neighborhood." In R. Tomasic and M. Feeley, eds., *Neighborhood Justice*, pp. 78–90. New York.

Chatman, Seymour. 1978. *Story and Discourse*. Ithaca, N.Y.

Culler, Jonathan. 1981. *The Pursuit of Signs*. Ithaca, N.Y.

Curran, Barbara A., and Francis O. Spalding. 1974. *The Legal Needs of the Public*. Chicago.

Engel, David M. 1984. "The Oven-Bird's Song: Insiders, Outsiders, and Personal Injuries in an American Community." *Law and Society Review* 18(4):549–579.

Fitchen, Janet M. 1981. *Poverty in Rural America: A Case Study*. Boulder, Colo.

Galanter, Marc. 1974. "Why the 'Haves' Come Out Ahead." *Law and Society Review* 9(1):95–160.

———. 1983. "Reading the Landscape of Disputes: What We Know and Don't Know (and Think We Know) about Our Allegedly Contentious and Litigious Society." *UCLA Law Review* 31(1):4–71.

Gorer, Geoffrey. 1948. *The Americans*. London.

Greenhouse, Carol J. 1982a. "Looking for Rules, Looking at Culture." *Man*, n.s. 17:35–53.

———. 1982b. "Nature Is to Culture as Praying Is to Suing." *Journal of Legal Pluralism* 20:17–35.

———. 1983. "Being and Doing: Competing Concepts of Elite Status in an American Suburb." In George Marcus, ed., *Elites*. Albuquerque.

———. 1986a. *Praying for Justice*. Ithaca, N.Y.

———. 1986b. "History, Faith, and Avoidance." In H. Varenne, ed., *Symbolizing America*. Lincoln, Nebr.

[272]

Hoebel, E. A. 1968. *The Law of Primitive Man*. Cambridge, Eng.

Hostetler, John A. 1984. "The Amish and the Law: A Religious Minority and Its Legal Encounters." *Washington and Lee Law Review* 41(1):33–47.

Kammen, Michael. 1973. *People of Paradox*. New York.

Merry, Sally E. 1979. "Going to Court: Strategies of Dispute Management in an American Urban Neighborhood." *Law and Society Review* 13:891–926.

Miller, Perry. 1965. *The Life of the Mind in America*. New York.

Nader, Laura, 1980. *No Access to Law*. New York.

Nelson, William E. 1981. *Dispute and Conflict Resolution in Plymouth County, Massachusetts, 1725–1825*. Chapel Hill, N.C.

Parsons, Talcott. 1970. *Social Structure and Personality*. New York.

Peacock, James L. 1975. *Consciousness and Change*. Oxford.

Perin, Constance. 1977. *Everything in Its Place*. Princeton.

Phillips, Ulrich B. 1968. *Georgia and State's Rights*. Yellow Springs, Ohio.

Schneider, David M. 1968. *American Kinship: A Cultural Account*. Engelwood Cliffs, N.J.

———. 1977. "Kinship, Nationality, and Religion in American Culture: Toward a Definition of Kinship." In J. L. Dolgin, D. S. Kemnitzer, and D. M. Schneider, eds., *Symbolic Anthropology*, pp. 63–71. New York.

Tocqueville, Alexis de. 1945. *Democracy in America*. 2 vols. New York.

Tomasic, Roman, and Malcolm Feeley, eds. 1982. *Neighborhood Justice*. New York.

Unger, Roberto M. 1975. *Knowledge and Politics*. New York.

Varenne, Herve. 1984. "The Interpretation of Pronominal Paradigms: Speech Situation, Pragmatic Meaning, and Cultural Structure." *Semiotica* 50(3/4):221–248.

Warner, W. Lloyd. 1962. *American Life: Dream and Reality*. Chicago.

Wills, Garry. 1979. *Inventing America*. New York.

Zaretsky, Irving. 1974. "In the Beginning Was the Word: The Relationship of Language to Social Organization in Spiritualist Churches." In I. Zaretsky and M. Leone, eds., *Religious Movements in Contemporary America*, pp. 166–219. Princeton.

PART IV

Constructing and Shaping Law

[11]

History and the Redefinition of Custom on Kilimanjaro

Sally Falk Moore

Local customary law "systems" within present African states are referred to from time to time in legislation and in the courts. These references read as if preserved parts of previous traditions actually existed intact. In Tanzania the Primary Courts are specifically given jurisdiction over cases arising under customary law (*sheria ya mila*) (*Maelezo* 1964). Yet it is obvious that in practice the congeries of custom that do survive enjoy their continued life in profoundly altered political and economic environments and have themselves changed in a variety of ways. The "customary rules" that do remain in use are not necessarily Tylorian "survivals," anachronistic fragments of the past that are neither part of nor appropriate to a contemporary world (Tylor 1958:70). Instead, they must be seen at this moment as integral elements in an ongoing political order. In Africa the invocation of tradition can be as much a way of resisting the government as a means of cheating one's brother.

Present-day clusters of local legal "traditions" therefore require interpretation in at least two apparently contradictory dimensions—the dimension of formal continuity over time and the dimension of sequential transformation. Emphasis on the sameness of form over time has often been important both in the strategies of individuals and in the policies of governments. The very concept of "customary law" has legitimating implications.

However, "custom" also means current local practice that may or may not be tied to the deep past. As a legal scholar of the Middle Ages named Azo (d. 1230) said a long time ago, "A custom can be called *long* if it was introduced within ten or twenty years, *very long* if it dates from thirty years, and *ancient* if it dates from forty years" (Plucknett 1956:308). Tradition as it was and practice as it is are not necessarily the same. Context, content, and meaning shift, even as familiar forms are repeated for new reasons.

This chapter is an attempt to communicate a sense of the practical facts and theoretical significance of a historical instance of such metamorphoses—the past one hundred years of legal change among the Chagga of Mount Kilimanjaro.[1] If law in such a setting is analyzed over time, situated in the life of a particular community, then it follows that the changing circumstances of that community are part of the content of its legal system. To abstract legal ideas from the operating community in which they are "used" generates the kind of categorical and semantic analysis recently produced by Geertz (1983:167). That kind of approach may tell us about ideological forms, but such "linguistic" or "literary" analyses of the conceptual elements in a legal order do not take one very far in understanding what people actually do on the ground or why they do it at particular times and places. I agree with Geertz that it is essential to know in what terms people think about basic moral and legal issues. Yet, however elegantly such ideas may be described, presenting the "traditional" categories of legal discussion without the context of discourse offers statements without speakers, ideas without their occasions, concepts outside history.

Instead, the two case histories of land disputes below, both chosen from the 1969 period, provide time-grounded instances of the use of "customary law" on Kilimanjaro in Tanzania. These stories make it clear that certain basic ideas with their source in the culture of a century ago are still current on the mountain and that they inform practice. But there is no way to read these microhistories without also noting that a cash crop is grown on the land that is often piously talked about in terms of the buried bones of the ancestors, that interests in the same land were recently being bought and sold, that some of the players in the local drama are salaried teachers as well as landholders, while others are solely farmers, and that down the road there are courts and officials who

[1]For a much more detailed historical account of the transformation of "customary law" on Kilimanjaro, see Moore 1986, which had not been published at the time the paper that is the basis of this chapter was presented.

are local agents of the central state. What is visible in the case histories is the surface of the complex intertwining of "old" and "new," of "customary law" and the coffee connection, of present relationships and old cultural forms.

That this product of history cannot be satisfactorily accounted for solely through a description of its interwoven present is evident. Anthropological fieldwork necessarily relies heavily on exploring what people understand their situation to be at the time they are observed. Yet close synchronic description, for all its irreplaceable value, necessarily limits analysis through enlarging the importance of the observed moment. Fieldwork being what it is, anthropologists are almost methodologically committed to overvalorizing what they observe and are told. That is the way the experience of others becomes part of their own. Yet where a longer historical background is known, awareness of that deeper past can change the way the observed present is analyzed. The present can be reconceived as the product of a sequence and as the moment before the future, as a scene in motion. Inquiries can be made into the conditions that have formed, transformed, and propelled these elements of which the present is constructed through given trajectories into their current combinations. Thus, after sketching the facts of the local case histories from the 1969 period below, I shall turn to the larger-scale historical background. Some conclusions about the concept of customary law itself follow.

Anticipated Inheritances: Two Case Histories from the Late 1960s

The Locale

On Kilimanjaro, in one of the Catholic districts past magnificent waterfalls bounded by steep ferny cliffs, lies the little subparish (*mtaa*) of R——. It is a maze of gardens interplanted with bananas and coffee bushes and vegetables. One neatly hedged garden is immediately next to another. Between them, a living fence of dracaena marks the boundary. Looking through the plants from the paths that wind in and out of the homestead plots, one can glimpse the outlines of dwellings. There, in the middle of the plantings, lives a Chagga household, and sometimes more than one. Contiguous gardens often belong to agnatically related men, so a subparish is composed largely of localized patrilineal clusters, with some scattered individual households interspersed among them.

This green, leafy haven with gently flowing irrigation canals looks like a rural paradise. But it is not a paradise. An acute shortage of land disturbs all relationships, and a more difficult future hangs over the present. Men with enough cash are always looking for ways to buy a little more land for themselves. They want it for their own purposes now, but later for their sons. However, most men do not have enough cash to buy land. Only those who have salaried employment or small businesses or other access to money besides coffee find it possible to buy land. Most men acquire their land from kinsmen in the normal course of allocation and inheritance and have no means of acquiring more through purchase.

The "customary law" rule is that a father should provide his eldest son with a banana grove of his own on marriage, and that the youngest son should live in his mother's (or parent's) compound for life and bring his wife there and raise his children there and eventually inherit the parental house and land. Middle sons are supposed to look after themselves and go cultivate new plots in the bush. But that last rule cannot be obeyed. On Kilimanjaro there is no bush to cultivate, so when there are middle sons there is a serious problem of providing for them. In fact, even when there are only two sons, the paternal *kihamba* (banana) garden often is not large enough to divide for the support of two, let alone three, households.

For as long as anyone has known anything detailed about Chagga horticulture, the Chagga have relied primarily on their permanent, well-manured, and often irrigated banana gardens high on the mountain. Annual crops of maize, beans, and millet have also been cultivated on auxiliary plots in the lower areas to enlarge the food supply. In the old days, and in some places today, those maize lands toward the foot of the mountain were not held permanently and were farmed in a form of shifting cultivation, reallocated annually by the chiefs. These annual-crop lands were soon exhausted and had to lie fallow. At that point, a new area would be designated for cultivation and divided by the chief or his deputy. As population increase has forced the Chagga to spread down-mountain, and as further irrigation and fertilizers have made some lower areas more habitable than they once were, some of these lower area *shambas* have come to be permanently occupied.

In families with severely inadequate amounts of land, married sons without plots of their own sometimes build dwellings in the compound of their father and seek work as occasional laborers in the gardens of others. Life is difficult and impoverished for them. Only the households of shopkeepers and salaried persons are securely well-off. For every such prosperous household in a localized lineage, there are many others that are poor. Many live exclusively on the products of the small plots of land they have inherited.

This is the general setting in which the following case histories were collected. Both involve allusions to "customary law" rules as used in and out of the courts. The stories of the specific fortunes and misfortunes of these particular families demonstrate clearly enough the general persistence of a nexus of rule-statements and practices that historical evidence connects with the deep cultural past of the Chagga. They also sharply attest to the modernity of these uses of the "traditional."

Case 1: Bounded Lands and Limitless Hatred

In the parish of R——— there was a father with two sons. As they reached adulthood and married, the father divided his banana/coffee garden into two parts and gave each son half. He did not stay to live out his years in the half of the younger son, as custom dictated. He had the resources to make other arrangements for himself and went to live permanently in a *shamba* he had in the lower area.

The two sons were very different, and the course of their lives differed almost from the beginning. The firstborn son was a good student and eventually became a teacher. His respected, salaried job and his education made him one of the well-to-do men in the parish of R———. He married and had children, and for a long time all was well with him and his household. The younger brother did not fare as well. He never got past "standard four" in school and was functionally illiterate. He had no job to supplement the meager subsistence he and his wife scratched out of their land. Worse still, his wife bore him no children. This barrenness went on for so many years that it became plain there never would be any children from that household.

In such situations among the Chagga, suspicion inevitably develops between the wives of the brothers. The wife with children is likely to be suspected of having caused the barrenness of the wife without children. In this family there was no doubt that, in the absence of male issue in the younger brother's line, the elder brother and his line would eventually inherit all the land. Whether the wife of the elder brother had used witchcraft materials or was a witch, or whether she had simply cursed her sister-in-law, invoking the power of the Christian God, was not clear. But that she had used some such illicit means to achieve her ends was the talk of the neighborhood.

[281]

Now it happened that the teacher was posted to a school in another place and came home to the village of R—— only during the holidays. Gossip in the village had it that on one occasion, just before leaving, he told his wife that she should pull up the boundary plants that marked the border between their plot and that of his younger, childless brother. He was said to have told her to "make herself at home" there and to plant vegetables. She did so in an area that was roughly ten paces by five in what had been the banana garden of her husband's brother. She also planted a new boundary at the edge of the area she had cultivated. The brother whose land had been encroached on was enraged and complained to their father.

The father returned to R—— to try to make peace between the households of his two sons. With his own hands he pulled up the dracaena that had been placed at the new boundary, and he restored the old boundary and marked it with new plantings of dracaena. This he did before witnesses. The wife of the teacher was very angry about this and took her revenge. She went to the courthouse and complained to the magistrate that her father-in-law had violated Chagga "customary law" by entering her compound in the absence of her husband, his son. There is indeed a rule of customary law that a father-in-law should not approach his daughter-in-law, or enter his married son's compound, unless the son is present. The magistrate decided that the case was one that would more suitably be heard by lineage elders than by the court. Not long afterward, the elders convened and heard the dispute. The wife of the teacher not only lost her case, but was fined one *pipa* and eight *debe* of beer for violating the dignity of her father-in-law, to whom she owed respect. He was said to have been grievously and unforgivably insulted by being taken to court in this manner and on this charge.

The wife of the teacher did not brew the beer that she was fined and never paid it. Instead, she once again pulled up the boundary plants and placed them where she had put them before, and once again began planting in the area she had staked out. Her father-in-law again assembled witnesses and pulled up the dracaena. The daughter-in-law returned to court and this time was more successful. The father-in-law was put in the lockup for three days for having broken the peace and trespassed on his daughter-in-law. When he emerged from the cell, the father-in-law prayed to God to curse the disputed land and the woman who had created such disorder.

Not too long after, the wife of the teacher fell ill and went to the hospital. She returned home, but she never recovered from her illness.

After a time she died. After her death, the father-in-law went to the banana garden of his son the teacher and said that it was now finished, that what he wanted had happened. Then he told his son the teacher that if he took the land of his brother without paternal permission all his children would die. The teacher was obdurate and told his father he would not return the piece of land taken from his younger brother unless and until the father brought back to life the wife he had caused to die.

Neither the father nor the younger brother would speak to the teacher thereafter, and the father provided the younger brother with another place to live near him in the lower area. The teacher was left in possession of the cursed piece of land in addition to his own plot, but it was said in the neighborhood that he did not dare eat any food that had been planted in that land for fear he would die. Nor could he go to his father to ask his pardon because of a conditional curse he himself had brought forth. During his wife's illness, when the teacher accused his father of bringing sickness to his wife, he also had sworn a mighty oath that should he ever ask his father's pardon the father should quickly follow the deceased wife into the hereafter. No doubt he had hoped thereby to frighten his father and save his wife. But his efforts were to no avail, and he was left a widower who could not beg his father's pardon. All the same, it seemed clear that he and his sons would inherit the cursed banana garden after all.

Case 2: The "Kidnapped" Heir

Under "customary law," a man who wanted to alienate a piece of land and give it to a nonkinsman could do so legitimately only after obtaining the consent of his agnates. That rule was of urgent interest to a well-to-do man named Antoni of the lineage of N——, who wanted to buy a small banana garden next to his own that was about an acre in size. Antoni had a salaried job at the mission, and his wife was a teacher, so he was a comparatively rich man. The plot he coveted was encumbered in a complex way. It had been the property of old man Salewi of the K—— lineage, who had died a few years earlier. One of Salewi's wives had lived there with her two sons, Paul and Jacob, as they grew up.

In terms of Chagga customary law of yesteryear, her banana garden might have been expected ultimately to become the property of their youngest son, Jacob. But land shortage has produced revisions of practice. Now it is just as much a matter of practical custom for a father to divide the plot of his wife between her two sons as to leave it all to the younger in the traditional manner. The legal question at issue in this case history has to do with whether Paul, the elder son, had a right to a share of his mother's land. In 1969, only Jacob, the younger son, and his household lived in his mother's plot and used the proceeds from its produce. Both Paul and Jacob were entirely dependent on farming for their living. Neither had any additional source of income.

The elder son, Paul, did not live in the parish of R—— at all. His father, Salewi, had given him a bigger piece of land in one of the lower areas, near Himo, a market center on the main road. Paul worked the land his father had given him and lived in the lower area with his wife and son. At first they occupied a rented house, but in 1969 Paul decided to build his own house in his own lower-area plot and started to do so, but to complete the house he needed more cash. At that point Paul decided he wanted to sell what he claimed was his rightful share of his mother's plot in the parish of R——. He was in need of money, and this seemed the only way to raise enough cash. He went to the sub-village head to tell him about his plan to sell the land to Antoni, as required by law. (The sub-village head happened to be a lineage relative of Antoni.) Paul told his own agnates about his plan and gave his kinsmen an opportunity to buy. This right to first refusal was the modernized version of the consent of agnates required by Chagga customary law. None of the lineage kinsmen came forward with an offer, so after a few weeks Paul posted the necessary formal notice in the local court announcing his intention to sell. At that time the notice had to be posted thirty days before the sale to give anyone who might have claims an opportunity to come forward. At first, no one made any objections known.

Antoni (the unrelated neighbor) went ahead and paid Paul 1,500 shillings toward the purchase price. However, in Chagga law the right to land does not pass until the full purchase price has been paid. The deal was by no means complete. This, of course, was known to several of Paul's kinsmen. They did not tangle directly with Paul, but went to his house near Himo and persuaded his sixteen-year-old son, Donasia, to come with them to R—— to claim that the land was not his father's but his own. The implication of such a claim was that Paul was trying to alienate property that did not belong to him, and hence that he had nothing to transfer. Toward making this case, Paul's kinsmen brought young Donasia to R—— and placed him in the protective care of the senior elder of their lineage, the lineage of the K——s. The senior elder is the ceremonial head of the localized lineage. His authority rests on his position as the ritual intermediary between living agnates and the lineage ancestors. To offend him carries significant risks, this-worldly and other-worldly. Paul was enraged, but there was not much Paul could do because young Donasia had been persuaded that his father was doing him out of his rightful property. The K——s also whispered in Donasia's ear that if he ever showed his face in Paul's house again Paul would kill him. Donasia became the instrument of his relatives' intentions.

The claim of the K——s was that Salewi had left what might have been his eldest son's share of land directly to his *grandson* Donasia. There is in Chagga "customary law" a rule that a grandfather may skip a generation in his allocations to leave land to the firstborn son of his firstborn son if the son is already well provided for. That the firstborn son had land was clearly the case in this instance. What was not so clear was whether Salewi had in fact made such a generation-skipping allocation.

Meanwhile, Paul's younger brother Jacob was living on and using the very land that Paul and Donasia each claimed. In June 1969, Jacob took Antoni, the prospective buyer of the disputed plot, to court and alleged that Antoni had uprooted nine coffee trees in Jacob's property. The disputed plot was contiguous to Antoni's and had a common boundary with his. Jacob alleged furthermore that Antoni had thrown stones at Jacob when Jacob passed on the path in front of Antoni's compound. Antoni managed to get the case dismissed. He contended that Jacob and Paul had themselves uprooted the trees to frame him and to prevent him from completing the purchase of the land.

After winning that victory, Antoni lost the next round. The K——s appealed to the village executive officer and managed to persuade him to stop the sale. The executive officer was taken to the garden in question and shown the place where the bones of the K—— ancestors were buried. This was proof that this was patrimonial property and according to Chagga tradition should not be sold without the consent of all. But the village executive officer also told Donasia that if he wanted to keep the land he would have to find a way to pay back the 1,500 shillings Antoni had already invested. Donasia had no idea where he could get the money. He feared his father too much to approach him, and evidently with good reason.

Donasia's father, Paul, was known to be a very excitable and violent man. I was told that his sibling, Jacob, took the precaution of putting a spell on him to try to keep him calm through this period of altercation. It seemed very desirable to do so, as suddenly there was another bidder who offered to pay even more than Antoni for Paul's share (or Donasia's, as the case may have been). The person who came forward with the more

[285]

tempting alternative offer was none other than the teacher in Case 1, a neighbor of all these contenders. There would be no end to the story.

Interpreting the Two Case Histories

This account of the two disputations has mentioned certain large-scale circumstances that lie behind the pressure on the land: population increase and the cash-cropping of coffee. The logical link between land shortage and bitterly disputed claims is not too difficult to find. Without land there is neither enough produced food nor enough coffee cash to buy food. Unless a landless man manages to get a wage-paying job (and those are few) or already had an income-producing business (and those are still fewer), landlessness can bring the poor perilously near to death. It can be physical death from hunger, or social death from the need to leave the community in search of a better situation elsewhere. The other form of social death is to be without offspring—at the end of the line. If you have male children, you need land for them; if you have no male children, it must mean that your agnates covet your land.

Belief in the potentially lethal repercussions that follow from oaths and curses are part of Chagga cultural cosmology. These misfortune-causing consequences of human words and occult acts are as consistent with present versions of Christianity as they are with precolonial Chagga ideas about the power of the dead over the living and the nature of "witchcraft" and "magic." The cases present word-caused homicide as a fact. Whether what is said is so or not is generally regarded as contingent, as possible. There are often differences of opinion. This is the way it comes up in conversation. Land shortage is death-dangerous in more than one sense.

Submerged in these two stories as well is the march of an unrelenting process, the process by which the better-off Chagga men try to do their poorer relatives and neighbors out of their land. In both these cases, we see that it is the salaried men (the salaried teacher in the first case, and the salaried mission-employee, Antoni, in the second) who are energetically on the road to acquiring more land. In both stories these acquisitive men or their wives are accused of offenses, and their antagonists use other legal maneuvers to try to foil their plans. The ultimate outcome of these particular struggles had not emerged at the time this material was collected. Indeed, in a sense, such struggles are unending. Nor is the outcome fully predictable in any particular instance. There are many

[286]

possible reversals of fortune that even a relatively prosperous man may suffer. But in the long run it seems clear that the better-off, the more literate, the more able to get along in the modern sector will be able to outdo their less fortunate agnates and neighbors in the competition for resources. Even so, their accumulations will soon be subdivided among many offspring. Demography keeps wealth in check.

Thus, the case accounts only hint at economic differentiation and asymmetry of power, because these are not matters open to verbal disputation; they are incontestable circumstances. Instead, the discourse in and surrounding the cases goes to some lengths to present the normative rationales the claimants made for their arguments. That is where "customary law" enters the picture. Presumably some of the factual claims were fabricated. What is not individually constructed is the culturally embedded legal rationale. That commonality can be verified from other case histories by the dozen. (See Moore [1986] for an extended description of the content of "customary law.")

The two land case histories are classical instances of recent situations that the Chagga themselves characterize as "customary law" cases, instances involving the *mila*, the customs of the Wachagga. Both involve practices and ideas that refer to the past but that are closely woven into the present fabric of rural Chagga life. It goes without saying that the Chagga know as well as anyone else that there are occasions when it is convenient to invoke tradition to obtain property. For other purposes, the very same people are likely to say that times have changed and new ways of doing things are more appropriate. The choice of the "modern" perspective or the "traditional" is often clearly a matter of strategy.

But the availability and the plausibility of the particular traditional arguments is not to be explained solely by the way they figure in the strategies of individuals. To take the actor's perspective in that narrow sense ignores the larger-scale conditions that determine the limits of individual choice. The parties to such legal disputes are not fully free to constitute their own reality. To a great extent they operate constrained by general circumstances that they do not control, and they are often subject to quite specific limitations set by more powerful others. These kinds of contextual constraints and asymmetries of power are the preoccupation of much current social theory (Lukes 1986). The problem is to keep a balance between the task of uncovering determinants and the task of identifying possibilities. What Bourdieu has proposed, both with his concept of the *habitus* and in his books on education and on taste, and what Willis has argued even more forcefully in *Learning to Labor*, is that even what is experienced by the actors as purely strategic, innovative, or rebellious choice-making ultimately has, on the large scale, the effect of "reproducing the system" (see Bourdieu 1977, 1984; Bourdieu and Passerson 1977; Willis 1981). No one would argue that there are no continuities in categorical hierarchies and the various asymmetrical relationships they spawn, but the "reproduction" model is rigidly static as a total framework of analysis and it leaves a huge question unaddressed— How then do systems change? Neither Bourdieu's model nor Willis's interpretations fully addresses that question. How is an anthropologist working at the micro-social scale, nose-to-nose with the protagonists, to distinguish the process of change from the process of reproduction if both present themselves as change?

The solution is difficult and not always practical. Whenever possible, the local, small-scale, actor-centered materials of fieldwork must be reinserted into the long story of historical transformation. It is only because he knows what happened *afterward* that Sahlins can make what he does of the misadventures of Captain Cook (Sahlins 1981, 1987). Only because I know what happened *before* can I see Chagga "customary law" of the 1960s and 1970s as something very different from the late nineteenth-century body of practices to which "customary law" implicitly refers both for legitimation and for some of its specific cultural content. There is an impoverishment of understanding when an ethnographic situation is stripped of its deeper temporality. For the Chagga the question why certain traditional legal claims, arguments, and ideas have remained viable while others vanished is in large part answerable, but to answer it properly requires attention to history. Part of that story can be told succinctly.

Reorganizing the Chagga as a Project of Governments

For a century governments have been telling the Chagga what they may and may not do and what parts of their system of "customary law" were acceptable and enforceable by the state and what parts were not. Colonial governments, first German (1886–1916), then British (1916–61), had a variety of plans to reorganize, control, and reshape Chagga life. (The missionaries and settlers who arrived with them had their own agendas too.) Since 1961 the postcolonial government, with its program of African socialism, has undertaken new reforms under very different ideological banners, but independence from colonial rule for the nation has not meant independence from central government directives for Tanzania's peoples. Dictation of change from above continues.

Given such a past and such a present, developments in the local system of "customary law" over the century can be seen as taking place in what is officially regarded as a residual category. At first, "customary law" was that part of an earlier way of life with which colonial government institutions either deliberately chose not to interfere, which they could not easily alter, or which were left in existence because they fell outside the locus of administrative attention. The distinction between "customary law" and government-made law was originally a product of the colonial encounter, but that encounter did more than create two parallel legal categories, one new and one old. It determined what part of the old would be preserved—or rather, it determined that part of the old would *not* be preserved. The rest—the residual category that did not offend against colonial definitions of morality and that was not inconsistant with colonial law and policy—was permitted to continue. Over time, substantial changes appeared in the content of that "customary law" sector. That is not surprising. The most important formal change in the place of traditional Chagga "customary law" which also affected its content is the fact that from the beginning of the colonial period to the present it has been harnessed to political and economic structures that are entirely different from those existing in the late nineteenth century.[2]

Direct state interventions in Chagga affairs, and their legal consequences, could be illustrated in a number of different ways, but none more telling than the history of Chagga formal organization. A knowledge of the drastic reorganizations worked by governments puts in proportion the other half of the story: the fact that the localized patrilineages of precolonial times sought to preserve a degree of autonomy and succeeded in remaining significant entities in the allocation of property.

Much of what was transformed on Kilimanjaro in this century was changed through the agency of three major organizations of European provenance introduced on Kilimanjaro during the colonial period. All three are still there, and still very important, though they are now present in mutated forms. One was the Christian church, in Lutheran and Catholic versions, together with their mission schools and hospitals. The second was the national, provincial, and district administrative

[2]And the late nineteenth century undoubtedly was very different from the early nineteenth century. See Stahl 1964 and Iliffe 1979.

structure now run through the national party (first called TANU, now CCM). The third was the coffee cooperative through which all Chagga have sold their coffee since the 1920s. In one sense, because the indigenous system of localized patrilineages has persisted, these other organizations of European origin might appear to be merely additions to, rather than replacements of, the most basic indigenous arrangements. But the powerful presence of these ubiquitous organizations worked deep alterations on every imaginable aspect of Chagga life and thought. They were inside the rural Chagga neighborhoods, not outside. Virtually every Chagga household belonged to all the organizations and was directly affected. As universal membership organizations to which virtually every household "belonged," they transformed economy, politics, religion, and knowledge.

The nineteenth-century Chagga chiefdom, as it had been, has utterly vanished. The precolonial chiefdom had a closed constitutional framework that permitted only certain kinds of groups to be formed. Chagga chiefdoms were a variant on a familiar East African pattern, with entities defined by *kinship* (exogamous segmented patrilineages and their member households, chiefship descending in one of the lineages), political entities defined by *community, geography,* and *authority* (subdistricts, districts, and chiefdoms), and crosscutting structures of mobilization defined by *age* (formal male age-sets and age-grades, and a less frequently activated and more generalized classification of women by age category). Military service and corvée labor were exacted through the male age-sets. In addition, there were *irrigation canal users groups* (groups of men whose household gardens shared the same man-made watercourse). The "canal users group" was sometimes coincident with the subparish, sometimes not. New groups were constantly being formed, but they were constituted within the framework outlined. There were new groups, but not new *kinds* of groups.

This system of chiefdoms, districts and subdistricts, lineages, age-grades, and water-sharing groups constituted the total formal corporate organizational structure of the Kilimanjaro area in the late nineteenth century (see Gutmann 1926; Moore 1986; Stahl 1964). People could be mobilized for collective action through each of these entities. Each kind of group had not only an important productive role in the economy, but also substantial powers of control over its members. For males, they were what I have called "universal membership organizations" (Moore 1986:310–317)—all men belonged to all of them. The achievement of self-acquired social position took place largely within these milieus, as did transmission of property and position from one generation to the next. Each level and type of organization had its own internal means of enforcing its control over members and of hearing and closing episodes of dispute that arose among them.

There was, in practice, a degree of fluidity in the alignments and numbers of the collectivities that made up a chiefdom, and a degree of flexibility in the choice of leadership. Chiefs routinely stepped down in middle life in favor of their sons. The succession could be accelerated or decelerated as the political situation required. Chiefs could also be deposed and replaced. Households could move from one chiefdom to another. The chronic raiding and fighting both among the Kilimanjaro chiefdoms and with "outsider" chiefdoms, which characterized late nineteenth-century life, provided many opportunities to rearrange Chagga political affairs (and even to do away with incumbents in office) or forcibly to persuade chiefdoms to change their alliances or to become tribute-payers and clients of those who threatened them most. The control over regional and long-distance trade must have been a major factor in all this turmoil. The monopoly of chiefs over the most important items in the trade, especially over ivory, captured cattle, and other trade goods, gave chiefs a strong hold over the key people in the chiefdom. The chief, through redistribution, could offer incentives as well as deploy threats in relation to subordinates.

Once the colonial period began, all the balances in this political arena changed, even though some of the basic constitutive elements of its *form* continued in being. Warfare ended, the military aspects of the age-grade system were abolished, and the long-distance trade completely changed its character. Chiefs lost their acquisitive and redistributive monopolies, and Europeans took over the marketing of significant commodities. What had been independent chiefdoms became subordinate administrative units in a colonial state. The cash-cropping of coffee was introduced, and eventually coffee was planted by virtually every household in its own land. The Chagga continued to grow subsistence crops as well. Most families were converted to Christianity. Schools and shops sprang up. The population doubled and doubled again, going from 100,000 in 1900 to almost 500,000 in 1978.

All the while, in form, many of the major local organizational units of precolonial times were maintained. Chiefdoms, districts, lineages, and the water-sharing groups persisted. Some became larger, some smaller, some new ones were founded, some old ones abolished. But each type of entity continued, many just where they had been before. In 1961 chief-

[291]

ship was abolished once and for all, and a new formal division of administrative units was brought into being. But they were for the most part composed of the same old basic subdistricts and other low-level organizational entities that existed before. These continue in metamorphosed versions to this day. However, though locally conceived in terms of their continuity, the content and milieu of these organizational frameworks has continuously shifted and changed.

From the 1890s to 1961, each chief became more and more an agent of the administrative apparatus of the colonial state, collecting taxes, enforcing regulations, and presiding over a court—the jurisdiction of which was carefully limited by the government. With warfare gone and the long-distance trade in other hands, political rivalries shifted their focus. The colonial administrations, both German and British, gradually reduced the number of chiefdoms by half. Thus some chiefdoms became subordinate to others and lost their chiefly office. The manipulation of choice in this matter was not without input from the Chagga chiefs themselves. Politics became focused on position in relation to the colonial authorities.

Continuing a process of consolidation begun earlier, the British completely reorganized the structure of local government, creating new levels of administration and a type of centralization that had no foundation in the Chagga past. They united all the Chagga chiefdoms. By 1929, all the chiefs were grouped together in a single council, and that council not only became a legislative body through which many colonial ordinances were promulgated, but also was constituted as a court of appeal. The power of the chiefs in their local chiefdoms was gradually diminished. In place of the earlier almost complete judicial separateness of each chiefdom, the chiefdom courts over which they presided had become the lowest judicial bodies in a local hierarchy. By the late 1920s the chiefs had been put on salaries paid out of tax funds, and their tribute-demanding powers were curtailed. After independence, in 1961, though chiefship was abolished, most of the local courts the chiefs or their delegates had presided over for most of the century were continued in the same sites. Their place in the national hierarchy of courts was changed (Moore 1986:159–160). They were renamed Primary Courts and presided over by an appointed "magistrate." It was to such a court that our protagonists in the land cases went with their various tales of woe.

A process of economic reorganization parallel to the administrative consolidations of the chiefdoms and to the creation of the judicial hierarchy was undertaken. In the 1920s, at the instigation of a colonial officer in the district, the coffee cooperative was begun in order to centralize coffee sales and regulate production. The parallel between administrative centralization and the concentration of economic control is striking, as was the use of the law to effectuate this coordinated development. The cooperative came to be extremely successful, but that was a matter neither of accident nor of local popularity. A law was passed that in effect made it illegal for the Chagga to sell their coffee to anyone other than the cooperative. There was to be no competition. Consequently, regulation and taxation of the coffee crop became much easier for the administration. Thus, supralocal centralized organizations to oversee the political and economic goings-on in the chiefdoms were in place more than fifty years ago.

Meanwhile, on the ground the localized patrilineages continued to control most transfers of land between kin, but it was not for want of trying to bring all land matters under central administrative control that the colonial government failed to do so. In 1930, to this end, the government proposed that a system of land registration would be beneficial. This was met with strong demonstrations of protest from the Chagga. Any intimation that the existing system of land tenure might be interfered with in any way was unacceptable. Although in 1930 land was beginning to be bought and sold, the colonial government could not take the political risks involved in tampering with the "traditional" system of land tenure. The reaction had been too strong. The Chagga were extremely wary on this point. It remains to be seen whether now, more than fifty years later, the independent government will fare any better if it undertakes fundamental interventions.

This cursory review of governmental, economic, and judicial reorganizations on Kilimanjaro, while lamentably limited as historical narrative, illustrates certain unstated but implicit definitional boundaries of the residual category "customary law." As perpetuated by colonial and postcolonial governments, the category obviously excluded most of those aspects of traditional law that had to do with political organization. Even where political offices were nominally continued, their attributes were carefully redefined by administrative fiat and legislation. Virtually all supralocal organization, political and economic, has been firmly under the control of regional and central authorities from the start of the colonial period to the present. By these means, political challenges to the state have been contained and certain local affairs have been directed from above. "Customary law," if understood as allowing local people to do their own cultural "thing," should also be understood to have been a carefully restricted fragment of "tradition."

As it turned out, the control of political affairs and of the coffee crop did not preclude leaving the allocation of individual rights in local land to the patrilineages. Thus the principal productive resource, the land, has remained in the domain of "customary law" to this day. As might be expected, however, the new product, the coffee, is governed by a new set of "customs."

Changes in the Content of Customary Law

Many *stated norms* of kinship tradition remain as they were, however the milieu has changed. With new kinds of property and a new environment, many new norms have also been generated to keep company with the old ones. Some examples of these changes follow.

Land Rights Conveyed from Fathers to Sons

The two case histories at the beginning of this chapter show plainly that, these days, the "customary law" rule that the youngest son should inherit his father's homestead and garden is often honored in the breach. In conditions of land shortage, other considerations prevail. The Chagga make the moral assumption that some land should be available to any decent married man. Where there is no one else to provide it, since there is no virgin land to pioneer, a father should try to provide some of his own land for each of his sons. If a father has several plots in scattered parts of the mountain, he may divide his holdings, sending one son away from the lineage cluster and keeping the other, or he may move himself. As indicated earlier, where the only solution available is to divide his own garden, a father may well do that, or if the father does not divide the land before his death, his kinfolk may do so after he dies. But a father may choose not to divide his land, and a son may find himself obliged to enter the migrant labor force or volunteer to be a pioneer in one of the new cooperative villages.

Whatever the pragmatic outcome in any particular instance, the "customary law" rules continue to be restated, and from time to time they actually do guide behavior. What are we to make of this? Is the "customary law" of succession and inheritance in existence or not? And is such a rule a law if, though a son may make claims on his father and may legitimize his claims by invoking customary rules, the son still cannot force his father to provide for him in the customary way? Could he ever do so? Today if the son makes his claims before a group of lineage elders, he may or may not succeed in getting them to decide in his favor. And even if they do side with him, the father may or may not heed their directives. Fathers had the right to disinherit sons in the customary system, and there is every evidence that they still claim this right and sometimes exercise it. When land questions get to the courts, the outcome may depend not on who is right but on who controls the key witnesses.

It is probably fruitless to speculate on whether the practice of dividing land represents a dynamic direction that might eventually end in an explicit change in the customary rules. It is clear that "customary law" statements can coexist as cultural artifacts contemporaneously with contradictory practices and contradictory norms. The Chagga emphasis on the existence of customs that only they are competent to administer is part of their use of tradition in their present political situation. Under these circumstances, there may be value for them in refraining from explicitly acknowledging change in the system to the extent of describing new practices as new rules. The definition of "customary law" that was a product of the colonial period has had substantial effects on the Chagga conception of the scope and nature of custom, and the scope and nature of their domains of autonomy.

Recently announced plans for projected changes in rural land law will, if implemented literally, generate profound new disruptions. Yet the plans may be adapted to local conditions. The government notes in its announcement of the new village plan that local custom should be respected as much as possible (*Agriculture Policy* 1983). Chagga peasants in the rural areas may know nothing of the plans as announced, but they have almost a century of experience in using "customary law" arguments to minimize official intervention in the sphere of their control. They are likely to continue.

Coffee Rights and Cash Rights: The Relative Position of Women and Men

The general adoption of coffee as a cash crop on Kilimanjaro generated many rules and practices concerning the new kinds of property. These are now explained as analogies to customary rules or extensions of them to new items. So, for example, coffee bushes, being attached to the land

and grown by the Chagga in their individually held banana gardens, have always been considered the property of the male household head, just as the bananas had been and still are. Most of the annual vegetable crops grown in the same gardens by the women of the household were regarded traditionally as female property and remain so today. Women also have rights in the crops of the *shamba* lands they cultivate on the plain.

It is the duty of the woman of the house to feed the family, so she cannot sell very much of her crop in the women's markets that dot the map of Kilimanjaro, but she may sell some of it. Sometimes she sells bananas, but does so legitimately only after obtaining her husband's permission because the bananas, like the cultivated land, belong to him. A widow may acquire the temporary use of the banana rights until she dies, provided she continues to reside in the plot she occupied during her husband's lifetime. The coffee rights are usually given to a male relative of her deceased husband. These he holds as a sort of trustee and guardian of the widow and her children. He should spend the monies for their benefit to the extent that the husband would have done, but these successor-guardians often keep most of the proceeds themselves. If the widow has an adult married son residing in her compound, he often has this role. When the widow dies, all rights in the land, the bananas, and the coffee revert to the male line.

The amount of cash a woman can obtain from her market sales is minute, compared with the cash a man is paid for the coffee he sells to the cooperative for processing and sale. The labor of women—indeed of men, women, and children—is mobilized in season to pick the coffee and to do preliminary processing. However, the women have no *right* to any share of that income. It is considered a male obligation to provide a wife and children with clothing, but that duty does not mean he has any obligation to supply her with cash as such. He may give her some cash specifically to buy a piece of cloth or a piece of meat, but he does not give her cash to spend as she likes. Thus, the rule that the coffee bushes and the coffee cash belong to men has meant that women have had much more limited access to the cash economy than their husbands have had.

A seemingly contradictory rule is that the coffee rights can be separated from the rights to bananas and land. Should the male landholder choose, he can allocate land and banana rights and keep the coffee rights. Many men do this. Thus a father who has only one plot of land may have his youngest son and the son's family residing with him in his compound. The father may be quite willing to give the son a corner of the compound in which to build his house, and he may designate a small area in which the son's wife may plant her crops. He may even give his son the full rights to the bananas in some part of the garden. Yet the father can retain the coffee rights to bushes growing on the same land for himself. If the son dares pick the coffee in these circumstances, he is guilty of a theft.

The legal idea of divisible and concurrent interests in the same property existed among the Chagga long before there was coffee on the mountain. Such interests existed with regard to land, crops, and cattle. The complex of rights in coffee and cash may be built on these old ideas, but the change in the economy has been so fundamental that these traditional analogies mask real innovations: the changed basis of the relative economic position of men and women, and the changed basis of the economic differentiation between households.

The Buying and Selling of Land

Rights in land on Kilimanjaro probably began to be available for cash around 1930. This inference is based on the fact that in 1927 the chiefs expressed strong disapproval and petitioned the governor to forbid the buying and selling of land (Griffiths 1930:60,88). Before that, "traditionally," land is said to have been transferred for a conventionalized payment of a cow and a goat. Land-plot histories suggest that many "traditional" transfers took place long before cash payment was a common possibility. The time at which cash became an issue was also the time at which a serious land shortage was beginning to be felt in some localities.

One suspects that the reason the chiefs opposed sales for cash is that it threatened to reduce their prerogatives. In the customary system, all unused land in theory reverted to chiefly control. There was no land shortage in the nineteenth century. Political control over people and their labor was undoubtedly more important than control over land. Land had no value without labor to work it. The land was there for the asking. In the British colonial period, as before, the native authorities, the chiefs, and their appointees, and the district heads controlled the allocation of undeveloped land, or lands that had been "abandoned." (The latter differed from the land of people who were temporarily absent, who retained the right to reclaim previously held land when they returned.) In this period, the chiefs and their subordinates received substantial "gifts of thanks" for assigning these empty plots to others; they also often gave them to their own relatives. During the colonial

[297]

period, chiefly consent came to be required for all land transfers. This was an expansion of administrative power. The chiefs disapproved of the buying and selling of land because they did not want to give up their reversionary claims or their controls.

The chiefs did not succeed in their plan. The buying and selling of land was not forbidden, and if anything it was encouraged. Ultimately even the buying and selling of land worked in favor of the chiefs. Because they were relatively rich men they were able to afford to buy land, which most Chagga could not do. This meant that they accumulated more lands than most others and enjoyed a continuing enhanced income from their scattered plots.

There was another category of people who had enough cash to buy land—the salaried men, and those with small businesses—a category that has grown enormously since 1950. Such men stood ready to buy land from anyone who was in debt or who because he had too small a plot to make a living was ready to leave and settle elsewhere. This does not mean that such buyers have become great landholders. On the contrary, the rise in population has been such that allocations to their many sons and grandsons has redivided the land again and again.

The purchase and sale of land has been conceived locally as an analogue of the former transfer in exchange for a cow and a goat. Indeed, when Chagga speak of past times when such transfers did take place, they often refer to them as sales, laughing at the "low price." Today, as a matter of law, the state holds all title to land in Tanzania, and rural people hold only the usufruct. A variety of national party guidelines about egalitarianism make multiple plot-holding more difficult than it used to be. Present party policy is that land should go to the tiller, but the buying and selling of the right to possession, and the right to beneficial use, continues on Kilimanjaro. Furthermore, the ingenious Chagga find many ways to place surrogates who are clients, or other dependent people, in their auxiliary plots so that the appearance of things will conform to party policies. Besides, the government policy that land belongs to those who work it says nothing about what happens when the tiller dies. On Kilimanjaro, "customary law" still reigns in such matters. Inheritance is a question of kinship. The rules, as I have shown, are subject to a great deal of situational amendment and negotiation, and probably always have been. Manipulation of this kind makes adjustments in conventional rules that are consonant with changing conditions. In name and in a certain sense in practice, much land law is still conceived of as "customary." But land law as it was no longer exists.

Conclusions

The two case histories from 1968 and the highly condensed description of a century in the life of the Chagga show that what is now
considered "customary law" on Kilimanjaro has undergone many metamorphoses. Radical changes in local and larger-scale asymmetries of
power and in the economic milieu have made that inevitable. The
apparent continuities of customary law have changed in semantic content. The relationships and resources to which "customary law" refers
are not as they were. Rights in land in 1880 and rights in land in 1980,
however similarly stated normatively, are not rights in the same kind of
entity, nor are the claimants in the same situations.

The answer to the question of what the category "customary law"
means in these circumstances depends on who is using the concept and
when it is being used. The courts have their own way of dealing with the
issue. Both in the colonial period and now, local courts were and are
specifically granted jurisdiction over questions of customary law. Because "customary law" is a residual category, and because it may be
different in each locality, there is no specific legislation on the point of
substantive content. On Kilimanjaro, "customary law" rules are to be
determined case by case in the Primary Courts (as they were in the
predecessor chiefly courts during the British colonial period). Two senior local laymen, the assessors, sit with each magistrate and are to be
consulted on all points of customary law. The venerable assessors are
assumed to have special knowledge of local norms and practices by
reason of their standing in the community.

Within this law-finding structure, at least three possible meanings are
conflated. One is that custom is a set of traditional rules handed down
from generation to generation. A second is that custom is a matter of
present general practice. A third is a more formal judicial meaning—
that custom is the residual category of local norms claiming tradition as
legitimation that pertain to matters on which there has been no legislation or binding judicial rulings by the central state, yet which the state is
willing to acknowledge and enforce. The actual content of such rules and
practices are different from one place to another and change from one
period to another.

The very idea of "customary law" implies that there is a different kind
of law with which it can be contrasted; so the concept itself is the ongoing
product of encounters between subordinate local political entities and
dominant overarching ones. Those encounters and the *legal* distinction

between law and custom have a long history in the West. In Tanzania the colonial state (and now the postcolonial state) has had reason to allow certain kinds of limited local autonomy to be perpetuated. What is left of locally specific legal custom is the result of that political decision. A variety of governments and several generations of rural people have, for very different reasons, collaborated to encode the division between the central state and its subordinate peoples in this legal duality. All anthropological studies of African law must be read in this light, and not simply as accounts of traditional thought.

Today, "customary law" on Kilimanjaro is as much a creature of the present state and the present economy as it is a link with a past cultural heritage. The theoretical implication is plain: the unit of analysis in the study of such interdigitations must encompass both local and supralocal entities, and it must do so within a historically conceived framework. Contextualization has always been the principal method of social anthropology. But there is disagreement about the nature of the context. I argue that the analytic context is not only a legal cultural system in the Geertzian (1983) sense. The shifting political and economic milieus in which the cultural elements are used are an integral part of the anthropo-logic of such cultural forms.

REFERENCES

The Agricultural Policy of Tanzania. 1983. Dar es Salaam. March 31.
Bourdieu, Pierre. 1977. *Outline of a Theory of Practice.* Cambridge, Eng.
———. 1984. *Distinction: A Social Critique of the Judgment of Taste.* Cambridge, Mass.
Bourdieu, Pierre, and Jean Claude Passerson. 1977. *Reproduction.* Beverly Hills, Calif.
Geertz, Clifford. 1983. *Local Knowledge.* New York.
Griffiths, A. W. M. 1930. "Land Tenure Report, Moshi District." Copy in the Manuscript Collections of Africana, Rhodes House Library, Oxford, MSS. Afr. s. 1001.
Gutmann, Bruno. 1926. *Das Recht der Dschagga.* English translation by A. M. Nagler, "Human Relations Area Files" (New Haven, Conn.).
Iliffe, John. 1979. *A Modern History of Tanganyika.* Cambridge, Eng.
Lukes, Steven, ed. 1986. *Power.* New York.
Maelezo ya Mahakama za Mwanzo. 1964. Dar es Salaam.
Moore, Sally F. 1986. *Social Facts and Fabrications: "Customary Law" on Kilimanjaro, 1880–1980.* Cambridge, Eng.
Plucknett, Theodore F. T. 1956. *A Concise History of the Common Law.* Boston.

Sahlins, Marshall. 1981. *Historical Metaphors and Mythical Realities*. Ann Arbor, Mich.

———. 1987. *Islands of History*. Chicago.

Stahl, Kathleen M. 1964. *The History of the Chagga People of Kilimanjaro*. The Hague.

Tylor, Sir Edward B. 1958. *The Origins of Culture*, Part I: *Primitive Culture*. New York.

Willis, Paul. 1981. *Learning to Labour: How Working Class Kids Get Working Class Jobs*. New York. First published 1977.

[12]

Islamic "Case Law" and the Logic of Consequence

Lawrence Rosen

Social scientists have frequently asserted that the conjuncture of cultural concepts and social relations can be seen with great clarity in even the most arcane aspects of religious, economic, and political life. Whole visions of the world view of a people have been found in an isolated rite de passage, an entire ethos in the complex exchange of shells, and complete cosmologies in the struggle for transient elective office. Yet with few exceptions the operations of formal courts of law have been treated by anthropologists either as peculiar domains whose untypical language, rules, and procedures somehow remove them from the mainstream of cultural life, or as microcosmic realms beyond which one need seldom stray in order to understand how conflicts may be authoritatively composed. The tendency by anthropologists to avoid formal courts of law in the societies they study may be due in part to the distance with which courts and lawyers are viewed in Western culture—a domain seen to be fraught with professionally skewed assumptions and far from disinterested goals—or with an antiquated desire to show, contrary to colonial ideology, that native peoples possess law in every bit as refined a sense as Western societies do. The result has been a valuable acknowledgment of the nonjudicial modes of dispute management, but a sometimes inappropriate avoidance of the courts themselves.

But the modes of thought or forms of interaction found in courts are not necessarily any less culturally characteristic of the broader societies than the modes of thought or forms of interaction found in a monastery, a market center, or a men's club—all of which anthropologists readily enter without further specialized study or fear of professional disapproval. Therefore, in what follows I want to consider a distinctly legal topic—the nature of case law in the courts of modern Morocco—and use this as a vehicle to show how in this society law pervades culture and culture informs law. Like a single ritual, a network of exchange, or a contest for political leadership, one cannot hope to see all of a society through such a limited focus. But such an example can show us what it means to speak of law as culture and to trace out some of the implications this approach may have to offer.

The Collections of Islamic Judicial Opinion

Earlier in the twentieth century a difference in interpretation arose between two of France's foremost scholars of Islamic law.[1] The dispute centered on a body of writings, collectively known as the 'amal literature, which consist of the opinions of Islamic judges on a wide variety of issues they have been called on to decide. On one side stood Louis Milliot, the dean of French Islamic law scholars, who first brought to Western attention the 'amal collections that formed a part of the legal literature of Morocco and who argued that these opinions constitute a set of doctrinal propositions that function like a body of positive law. Some years later, Jacques Berque, a former Affaires Indigènes officer and later professor at the Collège de France, suggested that the collections of judicial practice, far from being the functional equivalent of a code of law, might operate instead as a kind of case law, a series of opinions used to guide rather than settle certain cases coming before a court. The issue has considerable significance for the study of Islamic law not only in North Africa but also elsewhere in the Islamic world where scholar and judge, legal doctrine and judicial practice, may compete for authoritative voice. But beyond the historical and practical concerns the 'amal literature provides for Islamic law studies, a larger set of questions that is relevant to the compartive study of legal development arises.

What, we may ask, does it mean to speak of a body of writing as

[1]The key sources in this discussion are Berque 1944 and 1960, Milliot 1918:13–21, and Milliot and Lapanne-Joinville 1952:v–xix. See also Toledano 1981.

constituting either a codelike set of rules or a system of particularizing
case-law when participants in the system have not themselves clearly
calculated the respective importance of general rules and individual
cases? How, in the absence of historical or anthropological examples,
may we envision the use of actual court decisions in the Islamic law
development of North Africa, and against what broader cultural features
may we interpolate their role? Indeed, in what ways do the construction
and implementation of doctrine and practice become clear when viewed
in the light of those cultural assumptions that appear to suffuse the entire
process of judicial reasoning and judicial fact-finding in the context of
modern Islamic law?

In order to answer these questions, it may be helpful to describe
briefly the nature of the ʿamal literature and the specific ways in which
Milliot and Berque came to interpret it. Then, standing back from the
ʿamal itself, it will be necessary to indicate how the larger background of
cultural assumptions and modes of reasoning inform Islamic law and the
uses to which actual judicial opinions are put by contemporary judges.
Finally, a particular interpretation will be offered of the role and meaning of case law in the Moroccan context, and of the role it may play in the
development of Islamic law in a modern nation-state.

The collection of writings called the ʿamal that Louis Milliot first
described in his Démembrements (1918) consists primarily of a series of
works drawn up in the fifteenth through seventeenth centuries. Unlike
some other sources of Islamic law—particularly the Quran and the
traditions concerning the Prophet's utterances and acts—or the treatises that set forth the approach of notable scholars around whom particular schools of thought developed or that constitute later commentaries on them, the ʿamal rest on the actual practice of judges of Islamic
law. Some, such as the Lamiyya of Ali al-Zaqqaq, were composed as
procedural guides that judges could consult to see how earlier jurists
approached issues that came before them, while others, like the ʿAmal
al-Muṭlaq, encouraged judicial use by presenting their materials as
mnemonic poems or practical manuals. In each instance the approaches
of named jurists are mentioned in the context of a series of distinct
issues, though neither the details of particular cases nor the factual bases
for distinguishing one type of case from another are elucidated. Rather,
the presentation of opinions turns on the nature and range of acceptance
of one approach over another. Because this rather technical factor is
important to the relationship Moroccan culture has to Moroccan law, it
is worth noting how this form of presentation and legal reasoning operates.

[304]

Faced with an issue not squarely covered by Quranic injunction, the
'amal authors instructed judges to follow what is called the dominant
opinion (*mashhur*)—the approach taken by most jurists in a given area
and incorporated as such in most collections of judicial practice. However, a preferred approach (*rajih*), one based on what is socially desirable or customarily done, or even an isolated approach (*shadd*), one
based on necessity, custom, or the approach of a well-known jurist,
could be used in place of the predominant approach. While no specific
techniques were established for distinguishing precisely when each of
these approaches could be invoked, much less for distinguishing cases
by their facts, it is clear that the overall orientation implied by the *'amal*
is itself entwined with the added concepts of public welfare and custom,
ideas that are themselves grounded on a series of broader cultural
assumptions.

Although classical Islamic law allowed no specific place to custom as a
source for judicial decision-making, the existence and shape of the
opinions collected in the *'amal* writings clearly demonstrate that these
collections themselves served as a vehicle for legitimizing local custom.
Not only do preferred opinions appear to acquire their status because
numerous judges have taken the same approach, but also their wide
acceptance is often based directly on local practice. Working from the
tradition that "what the faithful regard as good is good in the sight of
God," Islamic judges have long incorporated the actual practices of those
they serve as legitimate in the sight of the law. Indeed, preserving
existing practice has long been recognized as one of the indispensable
necessities for the preservation of communal harmony against that chaos
and strife (*fitna*) that hang as an ever-present threat over human society.
Yet instances may arise in which even the approach preferred by many,
if not indeed the most distinguished, judges may need to give way in the
face of a broader harm that may result from a strict application. In such
an instance, a judge may turn to the concept of the public interest
(*istislah*) or to the idea of a solution appropriate to the circumstance
(*istihsan*) to resolve the issue at hand. Whether it be a case in which the
law requires a custodial parent to remain near her former husband yet
the court rules that it is unfair to make her move as frequently as the
soldier/husband is required to move, or a case in which the judge grants
the wife of an imprisoned man an irrevocable divorce because the sole
form of divorce to which she is legally entitled would allow her husband
to recall her to a life of continuing hardship, judges have available to
them techniques articulated and legitimized in these early collections of
judicial practice that allow both custom and circumstance to inform

[305]

specific judgments. But to understand the way the choice of approaches and rationales operates at present and may have operated when these practices were themselves being collected, we must have recourse to that larger set of cultural circumstances on which the actual practice of Moroccan law so clearly rests (see Rosen 1984).

The Cultural Context of Islamic Legal Thought

For Westerners first coming in contact with Moroccan society—or for that matter, societies throughout the Arab world—the institution of the bazaar marketplace often serves to establish a general perception of the culture. It is there that one encounters a domain where prices are not fixed and bargaining is ever-present, where the absence of clear indicators of quality, quantity, and availability leads to a constant quest for information or for personally reliable suppliers, and where the lines of competition run less between one seller and another than between any given seller and the buyer who stops for a moment before a shop or stall. If one were then to extend this image beyond the marketplace to the broader realm of social relations, one can grasp certain essential features of Moroccan social and cultural life. Just as in the bazaar, it is through a constant process of negotiation and contracting that Moroccans form relationships with one another. Family, tribe, or neighborhood may offer bases from and within which to fashion one's affiliations, but it is only through a constant process of constructing a network of obligations that each person can seek relationships in which security may be found. And just as in the marketplace, where conventions and institutions, shared concepts, and recognizable tactics give shape and order to the constant process of negotiation, so too in the realm of constructing one's social ties, wherever they may prove most desirable, individuals act against and through a set of common assumptions and institutions. For our purposes, three such sociocultural constellations are important.

The first relates to the central importance of the individual in Moroccan life. For Moroccans each individual stands at the center of a web of obligations and incorporates, in his or her own set of characteristics and network of ties, the features of social background (*asel*) and situated encounters (*ḥal*) by which they will be known to others. As each person tries to predict how another will act, and how he or she may fit in to their own network of affiliations, attempts will be made, as in the marketplace, to find out things about the other's associations and personal characteristics. A wide range of cultural concepts is geared to this emphasis on knowing another's situated ties. Thus, if one looks at Moroccan narrative styles one sees that the constant emphasis is on knowing the host of situations in which one has encountered others. Because people do not fashion their individuated selves any more than humanity may fashion the moral precepts by which it must live, emphasis is not on the individual as the possessor of a psychic structure that generates a self that is, whatever its overt manifestations, most authentic where it is most private, but rather on the person as the embodiment of traits and ties that are discernible and subject to incorporation in one's own realm of affiliations. The narration of a story thus focuses on the situated encounters of the individuals involved rather than on inner states or implacable forces of nature or circumstance. Even time is seen less as the movement of events in conformity with an underlying design or revelatory direction and more as the encapsulation of affiliations as they may exist at any given instant. A believable account therefore relies not on chronological ordering but on seeing the person through the various encounters they have with others. Understanding a person is like understanding a gem not by its geological history but by the features it reveals as it is turned around in one's hand.

This stress on the contextualized person is itself connected to the Moroccan concept of truth, for truth is seen not as something that inheres in an utterance or an act, but as a process by which human beings bring otherwise neutral statements into the realm of human relationships and consequence. Just as a price mentioned in the marketplace is not true or false until an agreement—a relationship—is formed with reference to it, so too in the realm of social relations a statement about an attachment to another does not become subject to evaluation as true or false until it has been validated. Such validation may occur by using an oath, by marshaling public opinion to one's own view of the asserted relationship, or by confirming the relationship by acting as if it were indeed so. Thus, just as one keeps bargaining options open in the bazaar until an agreement receives accepted confirmation, so too one keeps open the possibility to form ties wherever they may prove most advantageous by not holding another's statements about his relation to you to its normal consequences until an institutionalized mode of validation brings it into the realm of the true, where it may be subject to the criteria and sanctions of the true.

If the situated individual and the validated utterance are two key ingredients of the Moroccan vision of reality, a third aspect is bound up

[307]

in the idea of consequence. In the Moroccan view, one can identify and assess a person, an utterance, or an act only by their consequences in the world of human relations. Thus it is not a person's inner state separate from his or her overt acts, or that person's claims to reciprocity apart from their validated status, that matter; it is the impact each person has on various networks of obligation that serve to place and measure him. And because the repercussions of one person's acts may differ markedly from those of another, the assessment of a person's deeds is an integral feature of determining that person's importance and reliability. So, for example, it is believed that a rich man can have a greater impact on relationships than a poor man, or a learned man can have a greater impact than one whose ignorance is less likely to make him a model to be followed or an ally to be sought out, and therefore that the harm that people of various categories may do suggests the standard of responsibility to which they should be held. An elaborate calculus of consequence thus serves to place actors and their attendant acts in context and to render them subject to evaluation as members of various social networks.

Each of these factors—of person, truth, and consequence—takes particular shape and implication in various situational and institutional settings. Because truth must be personal to have any consequence in the world of relations, it is to the reliable witness that one turns for authentication of a tradition of the Prophet, a claim to the occurrence of an act in the world, or the existence of a legally cognizable relationship. Just as it is the person who makes the assertion believable, so too it is the consequences a person may have in the world that makes the weight of that person's claim assessable. Just as it is the repercussions of one's acts that do not simply reveal but actually comprise the qualities associated with character and background, so too it is only within their personalized embodiment that significant social features possess meaning in the world. And just as one can trace the implications of this dynamic—of the individual unit set in an organizing but not governing framework—in the realm of social relations, artistic production, and religious rite, so too one can discern its role in the structure and process of Islamic adjudication (see Gittes [1983] on the Arabic frame tradition).

Islamic law courts in contemporary Morocco are characterized by several distinctive institutional features. As in earlier times, it is still the single judge, the *qadi,* who decides each case, and though his jurisdiction has been circumscribed by the creation of other courts within the unified legal system, and his place has been settled within the hierarchy of a national bureaucratic structure, it remains true that his is a very traditional court both in the law it applies and in the process by which his judgment is brought to bear on individual cases (see also Rosen 1980–81). Briefly, it is to the *qadi* that cases are brought that involve matters of personal status or property matters in which the basis of one's claim is a document made out by notaries of the court. This latter feature would appear to suggest that written documents are the central form of proof in the *qadi*'s court, when in fact quite the reverse is true. Oral evidence is what really counts, the personal presentation before the court or its personnel of an individual's asserted claim. The notaries (' *adul*) are simply the institutionalization, within the legal setting, of those reliable witnesses who, as in any social relationship, can serve to validate an utterance by the force of their own reputation as reliable actors in a network of consequential ties. It is before such notaries—who always work in pairs—that a litigant will therefore appear, often with a significant number of fellow witnesses, to make assertions that can be assessed as true or false only when the court personnel have transformed mere utterances into legally cognizable claims. In the role of notaries and in the emphasis on oral testimony we thus see in the domain of the law the centrality to Moroccan concepts of reality and credibility of the person and the impact of speech as acts affecting relationships. But the notaries are not alone in shaping issues for adjudication; courts also use various experts who come from the local area and who have been engaged in the craft or trade in which their expertise lies. At the judge's direction they may be sent to determine boundaries, the quality of construction, the costs of living for wives and children, and the like. Through them important apects of local standards are brought before the court by people designated as personally knowledgeable about such matters.

When, therefore, a case actually comes up for a hearing, the mode of fact-finding and the form of judicial reasoning employed by the *qadi* reveal that they are closely related to the patterns of thought and action found in the culture at large. For example, at the outset of each case the *qadi* is very careful to determine the social background (*asel*) of each of the parties, for such information offers him, as any Moroccan, a clue as to the customary ways that such people enter into relations with one another and their most likely ties to one another. Moreover, he requires oral testimony, either by the parties or by their spokesmen, since it is only by such statements that one can probe for another's believability. Considerable discretion is involved in drawing bounds of relevance around the issue presented, and it is not uncommon for the *qadi* to consider a wider range of relationships and issues when rich or important people, or populous or prestigious groups, are involved simply because the repercussions of such people's acts are regarded as more critical to the preservation of social harmony. But perhaps the most striking features of the *qadi's* proceeding are the emphasis on local circumstances and the style of judicial reasoning.

As already suggested, the *qadi* relies heavily on the notaries and the experts for determination of facts. Indeed, it can be argued that unlike many complex legal systems that propel investigation and decision-making up to the higher reaches of the legal order, in Morocco the process of adjudication continually pushes matters down and away from the *qadi*—down to the level where local custom and circumstance can become most significant. The use of multiple witnesses appearing before the notaries for certification of their oral claims, the frequent recourse to those who are experts on local matters, and a legal order in which the rules set down by authoritative sources are few and the scope for local practice is explicitly sanctioned—all contribute to the centrality of local customs and standards in the process of ajudication. The emphasis on the local is also evident in the judge's evaluation of oral evidence. For example, if the oral or notarized testimony of witnesses conflicts, the *qadi* will often turn to assumptions about what people of a given background or personal circumstances are most likely to be knowledgeable about or, as a matter of human nature, what they are most likely to have done. Thus, it is generally assumed that neighbors are more reliable than witnesses living at a greater distance, that relatives are more likely to lie on behalf of kinsmen than strangers are, and that a transaction is most likely to have occurred if people have operated as if it had existed for some time. Even when the evaluation of oral testimony or the discernment of local facts by experts cannot resolve a matter, a strong element of the rational and customary enters into the use of the ultimate vehicle of fact-finding—the decisional oath.

Oath-taking in Moroccan law, like the remnant still found in some European systems, allows the defendant to swear to his or her statements and thus bring the case to an end favorable to the oath-taker. However, the defendant may choose to refer the oath back to the plaintiff, who can successfully conclude the case by then swearing to his or her claims. Whoever takes the oath first wins. Where the element of rational, local practice enters is in the designation of the plaintiff and the defendant for purposes of oath-taking. It is not necessarily the one who files the case or answers it who plays each of these roles when oath appointment is at issue. Rather, the defendant is whichever party the court believes is most likely to possess knowledge of the issue at hand and thus most able to swear to the matter. For example, a husband who sues his wife for return of their household goods may be designated the defendant when the question as to who owns articles that are normally associated with a man can be resolved by no other means than a decisory oath. If one traces the presumptions built into this system of oath-taking, it is clear that, far from being an "irrational" mode of proof, the process incorporates a broad range of cultural assumptions about who is most likely to know what, and thus have the first right—and the initial burden should they swear falsely—to conclude the case with an oath.

Similarly, the modes of legal reasoning employed suggest similar attention to local detail and broadly shared assumptions. Consider, for example, several elements of Moroccan judicial reasoning. There exists in Islamic law, not only as practiced in Morocco, the idea that positive assertions should take precedence over negative ones—that is, that (all other things being equal) testimony about something having occurred should be favored over testimony that it did not occur. Thus, testimony that a sale occurred is seen as positive, and a claim that nothing has occurred to alter prior circumstances is designated negative, while testimony impeaching another's character is taken as positive, and testimony tending to support one's character is demarcated negative. The law therefore seems to recognize that shifts in the balance of obligations among people are indeed the normal course of things and that such alterations should be given judicial sanction. So sales are taken as probable occurrences, disputed marriages are confirmed, and the likelihood acknowledged that a man who has not been able to establish his reputation for credibility before a dispute arises will be of poor moral character and an unreliable witness to events.

Judges may also draw together a series of features about background and circumstances to draw conclusions of legal import. Knowing that a person is from a given social background, that one is a man or a woman, or that one is learned or illiterate often implies, for judges as for others, a set of entailments that are taken as predictive of the impact of one's actions. In Morocco, the reference point in judicial logic, as in cultural logic, is therefore not so much to an antecedent set of rules or stereotyped categories of role or social position. Rather, the focus is on what John Dewey (1924) once called a "logic of consequence," in which the effects of another's acts are of central concern and prior data is marshaled toward the evaluation of one or another action in the world rather than to the application of a set of rules. Thus, in the Moroccan case, knowledge about others cumulates into a conception of what a particular person is likely, by acts or utterances, to bring about in the world. It is not a system either of social or of legal perception that concentrates on judging individuals by standardized behavior or idealized roles, but one that assesses individual impact as a result of individuated circumstance. And it is against this background that the last feature of legal reasoning, and the one that will lead us back to an understanding of the literature on judicial practice, comes into play—namely, the role of analogic reasoning.

Qiyas, or analogic reasoning, is one of the acknowledged sources of law in Islam, a vehicle by which extensions could be made from the limited number of Quranic rules and Prophetic traditions to those circumstances that had never been addressed. Although individual authority to engage in extensions of the Sacred Law through such analogic reasoning was ostensibly circumscribed in the early centuries of Islam through the formation of specific schools of thought and the closure of "the gates of independent reasoning," analogic reasoning has in fact continued to develop, often in arcane and scholastic ways, to present times. For our purposes, two points need to be underscored.

The first point concerns the materials used in constructing analogies. Traditionally, litigants submitted to the judge the opinions of scholars who themselves developed analogies that were proffered as solutions to the case at hand. These scholars distinguished cases not by reference to one another but against a general proposition embodied in a concrete circumstance. Thus, an argument in favor of holding a son to the payment of bridewealth when only his father had contracted for the payment would be analogized to the kind of unjust enrichment involved in loaning money for interest. Analogic reasoning thus worked through broad concepts exemplified by specific situations, rather than by eliciting detailed rules from acknowledged rules or by recourse to a logical principle by means of which a series of individual instances would have to be regularized in order to maintain doctrinal consistency (On analogic reasoning, see Makdisi 1985; Schacht 1964; Yamani 1968). The second point to underscore is that analogies are, as we implied earlier, framed in terms of repercussions instead of antecedent precepts. Thus, a judge will compare outcomes rather than prior rules, results rather than causes. To decide that reopening a long-closed passageway is like perpetuating avenues of trade and intercourse, or that stopping an ongoing injury by granting an irrevocable divorce where only a revocable one is allowed, is to focus one's comparisons on a local outcome and repercussion rather than on the refinement of a creed or code.

It is here, then, that we can recapture the role of the literature on judicial practice and the debate over its role as positive law or case law. The collections of *'amal* writings depend, both in their structure and—we may conjecture—their acceptance, on many of the social and cultural features to which we have been referring. As one analyzes these collections, it becomes evident that the judicial choice among conflicting scholarly opinions is itself informed, through the principle of the socially useful, by the articulation to the court of local practice. Examples of this process abound. For instance, one can point to *'amal* interpretations that say that even though the clause in a marriage contract allowing a woman to initiate a divorce is granted by the husband voluntarily, it should receive the stricter enforcement of an agreement that was actually bargained for because local custom regards it as something given in exchange for a lower brideprice. Or one could point to modern usages where the *qadi* refuses a rural woman's claim against her former husband for the cost of hospital delivery of their child because birth at home is customary for such women even though most commentators include all birth expenses among those to which a woman is entitled.[2] In each instance the focus of judges, both historically and at present, is not on principles or doctrines as such, or on the factual differentiation of cases, but on an assessment of consequences, on the repercussions for the networks of ties that people possess, or should be free to contract, in face-to-face dealings. Just as the thrust of judicial organization and the determination of facts constantly involves the tendency to propel matters down to the locally defined and locally derived, so too the mode of judicial reasoning represented in the *'amal* as in current practice channels the judge's thinking not to the level of ever more refined doctrinal analysis or to the elaboration of legally distinct modes of reasoning, but to filling up propositions with local meaning.

Indeed, the study of contemporary judicial decision-making suggests that the goal of the law, now as at an earlier time, contributes greatly to the way it is formulated and implemented. It can be argued, accordingly, that the primary goal of the Islamic law judge is to put people back into a position of negotiating their own arrangements within the broad bounds laid down in the canon of Islamic law. If we look at Islamic law as

[2]These and many similar examples, as found in the writings of Sijilmasi, are elaborated in Toledano 1981.

a whole, as well as at collections of early and recent judicial practice, we can see that most critics are wrong when they claim that Islamic law, unlike other highly developed systems, lacks doctrinal refinement and consistency (see Schacht 1964:199–211). Such a criticism misses the point that Islamic law is consistent with those very relationships and assumptions that inform local society and that the court is seeking to reinforce, not with some internally refined set of principles. The role of the *qadi*, rather like that of Islam in general, is thus to set the general parameters of conduct but not to govern every detail of daily life. Just as in Islamic architecture, music, mathematics, and social organization, the law forms an organizing framework, not a governing force, and harmony lies in allowing such lines of individual-centered affiliation to work themselves out by the free arrangement of units according to local circumstance. That is why, in the context of the literature on judicial practice, one finds an early jurist emphasizing local consequences over the retention of doctrinal consistency when he says: "Once the argument of the opinion adopted in judicial practice becomes clear to you (O judge!) it becomes your duty to issue judgment in accordance with it, for adjudicating contrary to the judicial practice leads to civil strife and great corruption" (Toledano 1981:167).

Case Law, Code, or Cultural Process?

Interpolating from contemporary social, culture, and legal features to the meaning and role of the practice contained in the ʿamal writings thus leads to a view of this literature that is slightly different from that offered by either Milliot or Berque. Milliot (1920:15–21) saw in the collections of judicial practice the articulation of specific ways of resolving concrete situations. He distinguished these writings from form books and the opinions of scholars and equated the function of the ʿamal with that of legal opinions as used by lawyers in France. By seeing the ʿamal as tantamount to positive law, however, Milliot mistook a result for a process. He saw these opinions as a source of filling the lacunae in the Sacred Law rather than as an example of a mode of reasoning by which custom is drawn into the law not to develop a body of doctrine but to allow local circumstance judicial legitimacy. And by not probing for the highly personalistic way in which the opinion of one person may take precedence over another, he gave insufficient attention to how particular opinions have widely different effects when they might otherwise

[314]

seem to be on an equal footing. Thus, while Milliot was able to see that Islamic law was not the functional equivalent of the French code, he mistakenly believed that a rulelike set of propositions emanates from Islamic judicial practice and that the publications of contemporary opinions would succeed in establishing a new body of positive law that, under the French protectorate, would allow Islamic law to cope with modern circumstances.

By contrast, Jacques Berque has never felt that our understanding of the ʿamal allows for a definitive evaluation of its role. However, he has on several occasions suggested that the ʿamal appears to have functioned more as a set of specific solutions that could be adopted or rejected in case-law fashion by subsequent jurists: He has found no evidence that the ʿamal was meant to yield a set of rulelike propositions. In order to constitute positive law, the ʿamal would have to be based on a stable set of underlying precepts, when in fact, Berque argues, it has no such normative reference point. Instead, he characterizes Islamic judicial practice as pragmatic case-law.[3] But Berque is not entirely clear about what he means by case law. If he means that the ʿamal—or any modern Islamic law judgment—is used as French lawyers use cases, he would be suggesting that while such cases lack any precedent value and may even not be frequently cited by judges in subsequent cases, they do suggest concrete solutions to cases that possess some authority for having been used by well-known judges or in important jurisdictions. By his reference to case law, Berque presumably does not mean that opinions in Islamic law operate as they do in Anglo-American law, where, to borrow Edward Levi's formulation, categorizing principles develop out of the factual circumstances of one case and are extended or distinguished by application to the facts of new cases that come before the courts. Such a formulation would, of course, be inappropriate in Islamic law, whereas Berque's vision of judicial practice as pragmatic guidance appears to be closer to the mark. What is, I believe, necessary in order to see more fully the role of the ʿamal literature—and to offer a more accurate interpretation of its role in the past—is to see how this pragmatic tool operated in the larger pragmatic context of Moroccan social and cultural life.

Seen from this vantage, decisions in prior cases replicate a process of fact-finding and reasoning whose goal is to put litigants back in a position

[3]See Berque 1944:33–50 and 1960. See also the discussion of Islamic case-law in Coulson 1959.

of negotiating their own ties. Islamic courts have the broad duty of retaining control over the practices specifically addressed by the Quran and of fulfilling, on behalf of all, those duties incumbent on the community of believers if it is to remain a moral body in the eyes of God. By constantly drawing the local into the ambit of the judicial, and by emphasizing the perception of social utility as seen by a judge who, like others in society, can make his the accepted view not by force alone but by conducing acceptance by those affected by his judgment, the pattern of Islamic judicial decision-making replicates social practice and thereby adds legitimacy to judicial practice. Prior decisions thus do not work like European positive law in their orientation toward the formation of a body of doctrinally consistent rules, nor are they isolated practices that should be treated as discrete artifacts, the traces of the passing of the law. Instead, the 'amal and contemporary Moroccan opinions partake of a common process and by the different ways they are applied in the ongoing nature of that process they can be attended to or ignored or adduced or avoided, with the same force and in the same manner as any other human view. Because the law is regularized by reference to local practice rather than to doctrine, the 'amal and current opinions make sense only as seen in light of the local. And because local law is itself not a body of artificial reason or professionalized doctrine so much as it is the articulation of the accepted, Islamic law makes sense, in turn, only as part of a larger social and cultural scheme.

Such an interpretation of Islamic law in Morocco, in the past as in the present, finds confirmation in the course of legal development in recent decades. In the first years following national independence in 1956, the Moroccan government formulated a new Code of Personal Status. This code, which remains very close to the traditional Islamic law, states that in the event that judges do not find guidance for a particular issue in the statute they may turn to local custom and the 'amal writings. Indeed, there is some indication that the authors expected the code would contribute to the development of a new body of 'amal writings.

But during the two decades since the code was adopted this has not proved to be true. The reason for this may be, first, that there is now an appellate hierarchy, which did not exist in precolonial times. In classical Islamic practice the idea of an appellate structure was contrary to the idea that no one could claim to speak definitively for the Sacred Law and, as our earlier analysis would suggest, the use of appeals might contradict the emphasis on local practice over the establishment of universal rules. And while appeals could certainly be used to create a body of substantive national law, the appellate courts have not proceeded in this direction, but have acted like de novo review boards rehearing many facts and directing attention to code provisions that lower court judges may have missed. Thus we see that opinions in specific cases have not changed their role, even with the introduction of a national code or appellate structure.

But the existence of the code has changed something else. In the past, *qadis* seem to have set the general terms of many issues, while local practice set the particulars, but now the code has taken on some of the functional role of general guidance, and *qadis* appear less ready than some of their precursors to enunciate broad standards. Moreover, there has been a significant increase in the number of lawyers in Morocco, and their role may ultimately affect the use of judicial opinions too. So far, however, it is my impression that lawyers are not so much bringing to the attention of *qadis* the decisions of other courts—as the *'amal* and scholary briefs did—as they are serving to regularize and facilitate the production of evidence to the court. Berque's (1944:28) suggestion that progress in Islamic law would come not through the perfection of positive law but through greater efficiency in the procedures and techniques employed in adjudication remains insightful if as yet unproved. What does seem clear thus far is that the process by which Islamic judicial decision-making has been characterized up to now—with its emphasis on reconstituting interpersonal negotiation and its orientation to the consequences of individual's acts—continues to play a conservative role in Moroccan legal development. Instead of becoming a vehicle for social reform by particular interest groups or an instrument for limiting or extending government control, case law represents instead the replication of local standards, at least as articulated by those chosen to give them voice, and thus it repeats, rather than challenges, existing patterns.[4] Regularity in Islamic law, at least as presently practiced in Morocco, lies not in the similarity of results in cases that appear to be similar, but in the constancy of the mode of analysis—of employing reliable witnesses, focusing on oral testimony, weighing the social interest, and relying on local experts. The logic of the case is the logic of one of various alternative ways of reading local consequence, and an array of cases proves the array of possible alternatives. Moroccans can therefore see in the range of judicial decisions what they are wont to see in their

[4]Compare this interpretation with the image of Islamic law as a patrimonial system in Weber 1967. See also the discussion of Weber's interpretation in Turner 1974:107–121.

general lives—that consistency and harmony are not to be found in reducing differences to single propositions, or varied judgment to uniform antecedents. Rather, the appreciation of security and the avoidance of chaos will be further assured by cases that bespeak a common goal and a common process more than a common result, for that way lies conformity to the way people truly are and how God intended they should conduct themselves. It is therefore very likely that, short of a major upheaval in the body politic, Islamic law in Morocco will continue its conservative course and that individual opinions will contribute not to the development or regularization of doctrine but to the mutually reinforcing legitimization of interpersonal negotiation within a framework that partly for that very reason is regarded as authentically Islamic.

Law is, of course, only one domain in which a culture may reveal itself. But like politics, marriage, and exchange, it is an arena in which people must act, and in doing so they must draw on their assumptions, connections, and beliefs to make their acts effective and comprehensible. In the Islamic world, as in many other places, the world of formal courts offers a stage—as intense as ritual, as demonstrative as war—through which a society reveals itself to its own people as much as to the outside world.

REFERENCES

Berque, Jacques. 1944. *Essai sur la méthode juridique maghrébine.* Rabat.
———. 1960. "'*Amal.*" *Encyclopedia of Islam,* new ed., vol. 1, pp. 427–428.
Coulson, Noel. 1959. "Muslim Custom and Case-Law." *Die Welt des Islams* 6(1–2):13–24.
Dewey, John. 1924. "Logical Method and Law." *Cornell Law Quarterly* 10:17–27.
Gittes, Katherine Slater. 1983. "The *Canterbury Tales* and the Arabic Frame Tradition." *PMLA* (Publications of the Modern Language Association) 98:237–251.
Makdisi, John. 1985. "Legal Logic and Equity in Islamic Law." *American Journal of Comparative Law* 33(1):63–92.
Milliot, Louis. 1918. *Démembrements du Habous.* Paris.
———. 1920. *Recueil de jurisprudence chérifienne,* vol. 1. Paris.
———. 1953. *Introduction à l'étude du droit musulman.* Paris.
Milliot, Louis, and J. Lapanne-Joinville. 1952. *Recueil de jurisprudence chérifienne,* vol. 4. Paris.
Rosen, Lawrence. 1980–81. "Equity and Discretion in a Modern Islamic Legal System." *Law and Society Review* 15(2):217–245.
———. 1984. *Bargaining for Reality: The Construction of Social Relations in a Muslim Community.* Chicago.

————. 1989. *The Anthropology of Justice: Law as Culture in Islamic Society.* Cambridge, Eng.

Schacht, Joseph. 1964. *An Introduction to Islamic Law.* Oxford.

Toledano, Henry. 1981. *Judicial Practice and Family Law in Morocco.* Boulder, Colo.

Turner, Brian. 1974. *Weber and Islam: A Critical Study.* London.

Weber, Max. 1967. *Max Weber on Economy and Society.* New York.

Yamani, Ahmad Zaki. 1968. *Islamic Law and Contemporary Issues.* Jidda.

[13]

The Crown, the Colonists, and the Course of Zapotec Village Law

Laura Nader

Early in the twentieth century, much of ethnographic analysis in anthropology was dominated by structural-functionalism. Such studies were often ahistorical, generally focused on artificially bounded communities, and tended to use the equilibrium or harmony model to describe social relations. In the ethnography of law, the longitudinal method was rarely used. In fact, Llewelyn and Hoebel (1941), who might or might not be considered structural-functionalist, took cases spanning a seventy-year period and compressed them into an ethnographic present time dimension. In our critiques of these earlier works, the nonuse of history and the equilibrium or harmony models have become theoretical obstacles to be overcome.

More recently, anthropologists have recognized the importance of history for ethnographic understanding and have expanded the scope of their studies to encompass external social and cultural forces that, in addition to internal forces, have shaped local communities. In doing such work I became interested in the order of legal change (Nader 1978), while others, such as my colleague Elizabeth Colson (1974), explored questions dealing with the politics of legal change. Anthropologists are now developing ethnohistorical models that combine historical, sociological, and cultural analyses within the framework of a power structure. Such approaches enable us to understand the dynamics of legal change caused by shifting political alliances between nomadic and settled peoples, between religious, customary, colonial, and nation-state law, between all these laws and the international and multinational structures (Attia 1988; Hammoudi 1985; Moore 1986), or as in this chapter, between the Crown, the Colonists, and the indigenous villagers. The harmony model takes on a new dimension within this broader context.

An examination of village social organization and the workings of village law courts among the mountain Zapotec of Mexico reveals the link between social organization and harmony as a political strategy, on the one hand, and between the data and structural-functionalist analysis on the other. The relative influence of internal and external forces operates through community social organization and active disputing processes that are governed by the ideology of harmony. The central focus of this chapter rests on attempting to explain the production of harmony as ideology and the way in which this ideology influences the development of anthropological theory.

My students and others have observed that in many societies it appeared as if the harmony model was being replaced by the adversary model as the new nation-states developed (Nader and Todd 1978). On the other hand, in 1969, Aubert reported that Norway had moved toward the harmony model and away from the adversarial one, while ten years later the harmony model had also taken off in the United States (Nader 1978; Abel 1982). An analysis of the uses of harmony or adversariness as political tactics in the community and in individual action reveals that legal changes are not sheer happenstance, but represent part of a common order of happening (see Nader 1986).

In the ethnohistorical example that follows, the focus is on harmony as ideology. I am concerned with the way political alliances of the colonial period have influenced the course of village law. My analysis of this process is based on fieldwork in a mountain Zapotec village in southern Mexico and on historical records. The colonial policy established by the Spanish Crown in the sixteenth century still informs Indian village courts. The relationship that the Crown created between itself and its colonists, both Spanish and Indian, led to the semiautonomous village communities that Wolf (1959) found described in colonial records as *la república de indios*. Crown policy left room for a range of political maneuvers.

Crown Policy and *la República de Indios*

The Spanish Crown's policy of creating Indian communities emerged from maneuvers over issues of relative power between the Crown, the colonists, and the Indians. According to Wolf (ibid., p. 190), Crown policy was formed:

> to guard against the rise of combinations of power that could rival the authority of the crown, the king divorced the right to receive Indian tribute from the control of Indian labor. If Indian labor made the wheels turn in this New Spain, then whoever was lord and master of the Indians would also be lord and master of the land. With unlimited access to Indian energy, the colonists would soon have no need of Spain or king; hence the crown had to limit this access, supervise it, curtail it. . . . The Indians were thus declared to be direct vassals of the crown, like the colonists themselves. . . . No private person could lay hands on Indians without prior license from the crown.

After the first half of the sixteenth century, the Indians were royal wards responsible to royal officials and supervised by the Crown. By the seventeenth century there was an economic depression, a decline in mining and food production resulting from depopulation (Borah 1951). As Wolf (1959:202) observed, the century was characterized as a "retreat from utopia," whereby Middle America retreated into its countryside as in previous times of social and economic difficulties. Wolf describes two patterns that emerged in the course of this retreat: the *hacienda* (a landed estate privately owned by the colonist) and the tightly knit community of the Indian peasantry, *la república de indios.* One was to become the instrument of the conquerors, the other the instrument of the conquered. The unit of Indian life was to be the concentrated small community rather than the individual or the city. The Crown underwrote the legal identity of each Indian community as a check on colonists and as a way to maintain their exclusive control over the Indians. Each Indian community was to be:

> a self-contained economic unit, holding a guaranteed 6.5 square miles of agricultural land, land which its members could sell only after special review by the viceroy. . . . Communal officials were to administer the law through the instrumentality of their traditional custom, wherever that custom did not conflict with the demands of church and state. The officers of the crown retained the privilege of judging major crimes and legal cases involving more than one community; but the Indian authorities received sufficient power to guarantee peace and order in the new communes. The autonomy which the crown denied to the Indian sector of society as a whole, it willingly granted to the local social unit. (Ibid., p. 214)

[322]

This system allowed the indigenes a good deal of room to maneuver to their advantage. Nevertheless, the ensuing diversity among communities was developed within a common frame, resulting in communities that had much in common, although what they had in common they used differently. The core of this community was its political and religious cargo systems, which rotated among adult males the responsibilities for religious organization and operation of the *municipalidad* or town hall, where the town courts are located. By means of this Mesoamerican political and religious system, power and responsibility are allocated and reallocated at intervals to the men in the community. It is through them that ritual and economic life is organized. The Indian community (if we can use the term) has been further described as one where the group is more important than the individual, where people are suspicious of conflict, where conflicts are adjusted, where economic differences are redistributed, and where status is linked to the number and quality of office-holding experiences. The community defends its land against outsiders by prohibiting the sale of land to nonmembers and by marrying within the community.

The differences between communities are usually characterized as open or closed villages, traditional or progressive villages, homogeneous or heterogeneous villages, peaceful or divided villages, or belligerent or passive villages. These categories reflect the transformative elements in such communities: the innovators, the power-seekers, the proselytizing missionary, the political activist, the developer. As Wolf (1959) and others have observed, these communities have never evolved in a single direction; they oscillate, fluctuate, and change in fits and starts, never independent of the larger society to which they send their excess population and to which they are bound by a series of interlocking interests (Hirabayashi 1986).

A Mountain Zapotec Village: Talea de Castro

Early reports by Spanish friars describe the southern part of Mexico, now politically united as the state of Oaxaca, as a land of diverse peoples, languages, and cultures. The Zapotec have lived in the area for more than 2,000 years before the Spanish Conquest. The conquest and then colonization brought dramatic changes: the *encomienda* system, the heavy use of taxation, the use of workers in the mines and fields, which changed the traditional division of labor between men and women, the

[323]

concentration of Indians in larger compact settlements. Later changes favored the Indian economy and the developing mestizo and creole classes. New crops were brought in from Europe and other parts of the New World (wheat, sugar, and fruits of various kinds), new tools (the wooden plow and the horizontal loom), and arms (the steel machete and axes). All these innovations spawned new developments.

The Zapotec I write about are mountain people (Nader 1964b). They live in an area known as the Rincón, located approximately 200 kilometers northeast of Oaxaca City. The Rincón is a home of rivers and mountains, and as the label suggests, settlements are located between the peaks, cornered by mountains on three sides. The Indians are primarily farmers. Their land provides a livelihood through the staples of corn, beans, and sugarcane. Coffee, the principal cash crop, was introduced around the turn of the century. Other vegetables and fruit are planted, and a wide variety of wild plants are gathered for food, decorative, and medicinal purposes. The specialties of each village provide a variety found in local markets, producing a lively trade within the area and between the Rincón and other areas.

The oldest route from the Rincón to Oaxaca City runs straight south to Solaga, Tlacolula, or Mitla, and then to Oaxaca City. Until October 1959, this was the route by which coffee, loaded on donkeys, was shipped out of the region. Now, however, the impassable mountains that had previously "cornered" the Rinconeros have been opened to connect the Rincón with the valley of Oaxaca. Until 1959 there was no vehicular road into the Rincón. Traders had to walk into the region from the Sierra Juárez by way of Calpulalpan and Maravillas, a path that was cut off for weeks during the rainy season. By virtue of its geography, the Rincón has been a refuge area.

For the most part, the people of the Rincón live in clustered mountain villages. One village I studied was Talea de Castro, said to have been founded in 1525 when Fray Bartolomé de Olmedo came from Mexico City to baptize and preach Christianity among the Zapotec of the Rincón. Local historical documents record that the respected elder statesmen from various pueblos of the Rincón had gone to Mexico City in the previous year to request that the new king, Cortés, send ambassadors of the new religion. Even in the early sixteenth century the area, although difficult to reach, was neither isolated nor out of touch with the happenings in central Mexico.

In the sixteenth century, Talea was probably smaller than the surrounding towns of Yatoni and Juquila; the history in the town archives showed only a handful of houses on the accompanying maps. Unfortunately, information is scant on Talea and the region in general from the time of founding until the last century, but every Indian village in the area was affected by the arrival of the Spaniards and the ensuing growth of Mexico as a country separate from Spain—in religion, in economic and political institutions and technologies, and in patterns of exploitation. Contact by choice and by conquest may have come swiftly and directly, or slowly and gradually. Yet even in the more remote and inaccessible corners of the Rincón, contact was in good part linked to economic exploitation and the introduction of cash crops.

During the colonial period, the district of Villa Alta was famous for its riches, particularly in the areas of cotton production and gold and silver mining. Spanish administrators clamored to be sent to this area (Hammett 1971:16–17,36). Political control of the area was obtained primarily through Spanish colonial organization. Each village was to be a self-contained autonomous unit (Gerhard 1972:14). The mines and cotton production that declined after Mexican independence from Spain in the second decade of the nineteenth century were revived in the middle of the same century when Don Miguel Castro, lawyer and politician, came to the vicinity of Talea to rebuild the gold and silver mining industry (Pérez-García 1956, 2:129). Talea became a town of importance in provisioning the miners. There was enough variety of work so that some 200 people could engage in nonagricultural pursuits as miners, blacksmiths, carpenters, carbon makers, brickmakers, butchers, bakers, candlemakers, weavers, tortilla producers, and more.

Around 1905 the mines at the hacienda in Santa Gertrudis closed permanently, and many of the miners from a variety of villages came to settle in Talea, where they began farming for a living. Following this migration of miners from Santa Gertrudis to Talea, the market was gradually moved there as well. After the closing of the mines, Talea was to become the most important commercial center in the Rincón region. Older informants remember Talea at the turn of the century as having a population of about 1,000. By the 1960s the population had more than doubled. Since its founding, Talea has probably changed its size and composition more than any other Rincón village. It was fortunate and probably not an accident of history that Talea became a center of commerce, for with this sudden influx of people from the mines, the gradual accretion of lands from neighboring villages was not rapid enough to provide all these new citizens with land. Many turned to commerce as an adjunct to farming, and to cash cropping as an adjunct to subsistence farming. Talea was the first Rincón town to grow coffee, and in all probability this was related to the advantages that coffee production has for a town suffering from land shortage. Coffee provided Taleans with cash and changed the relationship that Talea had with the surrounding towns. Apart from the prestige from cash wealth, Talea became more dependent on the surrounding towns for subsistence crops.

A more recent event in the transformation of Talea occurred in 1946, when approximately thirty Talean men left to work for one or two years in the United States as part of migratory labor teams imported from Mexico. Many changes came with the return of these guest workers, who brought back "progressive" ideas and savings, which they invested in coffee plants. Many more Taleans were to follow their lead and leave Talea to seek work in the urban areas of Mexico and in the rural areas of the United States (Hirabayashi 1981).

A final important occurrence was the introduction of the Papaloapan Development Plan, through which the Mexican government hoped to integrate the Sierra Juárez and the regions beyond the sierra with the rest of Mexico. Again there was an economic boom, which was temporarily set back by the drop in coffee prices at the end of the 1950s and early into 1960. But the Papaloapan Commission was responsible for the completion of a road, which provided an opening for manufactured goods of the state and of the nation to compete with regionally produced goods (Berg 1976:109–110).

Each economic fluctuation has left its mark on Talea de Castro. Sometimes this results in the town's collaboration with outside forces, and sometimes there is resistance. Powered by common interests and antagonism to forces outside their small *república*, the Taleans are forever aware of the fragility of their situation—one that accompanies power differentials. Without the Crown, the Indians face the colonists who are now Mexicans, but the Crown left them with an organization that could be used to their advantage.

Social Control through Interlocking Aspects of Social Organization

> If it is true that the imperialists study their colonial charges, it is equally true that the charges study their masters—with great care and cunning. Who shall say which understands the other more? (Borah 1983:226)

The Rincón Zapotec villages have been organized as politically independent, self-reliant, endogamous places that remain free to determine their lives only to the extent to which they can manage themselves successfully. Villages with feuds that divide them, or problems that escalate to the district seat in Villa Alta, to the state government, or beyond, are more vulnerable to national state interference. For the Taleans, their ability to manage the wider world impinging on them depends on how well they can manage their internal world.

Earlier in the chapter I mentioned some of the cultural patterns that have been described as characteristic of Middle American Indian communities: the way such communities distribute power and wealth through the political-religious system, the rotation of responsibility among adult men rather than a concentration among a few over time, the observation that wealth is not allowed to accumulate among individuals but distributed through the institution of ritual feasting, the strong tendency to practice endogamy, and the maintenance of land sale within the village. All these patterns are also true of Talea and certainly operate to control the behavior of members because conformity is expected in these arenas. Instead of focusing on how the political-religious organizations work as social control, I would like to condense my understanding of Talean Zapotec social control by examining some of the major principles that serve to govern life in the village. These principles of social organization are deeply embedded in social activity, as described above, but are neither coterminous with any one sphere of social activity nor stable through time. They are based on the dimensions of hierarchy, symmetry, and cross-linkage, which operate to stratify, level, and integrate the whole village. All three dimensions are found at all levels and in every domain of village social organization, although over time they carry different weight.

In Talea as in most indigenous Middle American communities, all groups, whether governmental, religious, or kin, are hierarchically organized on the basis of sex, age, wealth, and/or experience. As a man moves up the social ladder, he assumes a great amount of responsibility, authority, and respect. Although how far a man climbs and the number of positions in which he serves before retirement vary with the size of the town and qualifications of the candidate, the system is always hierarchical. In work relationships, depending on the task at hand and the availability of land, one is either a boss or a worker, although who is the boss or the worker has varied through time with changing circumstances. Family relations are also hierarchically ranked by generation and age, and each role is defined as subordinate to the one above. The leveling dimension, the value placed in egalitarian relations, may be seen as contradictory or complementary.

[327]

The concept of leveling, of balanced proportions, operates in many of the same social settings in which hierarchy is found. Leveling mechanisms mediate the harsher aspects of hierarchy in superordinate/subordinate relationships and challenge the high value accorded such relationships. In the family, for example, older brothers have authority over younger brothers, and to some extent brothers have authority over sisters. Yet ideally all children are supposed to inherit equally. In the celebration of fiestas, those who can afford the financial burden are expected to bear the costs. Although this is a leveling device, wealthy donors gain prestige and respect. Moreover, participation in town meetings by all adult men allows citizens to question the actions of those at the top of the ladder. Symmetry is also very much a part of the aesthetic sense of these mountain Zapotec people. It is unappealing to be too rich or too poor, too fat or too thin, too pretty or too ugly. Asymmetry is often the underlying cause of envy, witchcraft accusations, or disputes in courts.

The dimension of cross-linkage is found at the level of village organization and structure, unlike the dimensions of hierarchy and leveling, which permeate the daily round of activities. Cross-linkage as a principle of organization brings people together as groups or individuals, while at the same time dividing them by linking some of them with different groups. The degree to which intergroup relations cross-link affects the development of opposition groups or factions in the town. People who belong to the same musical organization do not belong to the same savings and loan association. People who reside in the same sections share membership in a particular savings and loan association with people from other parts of town. When we examine Talean organization in its entirety, the membership crosscuts, and the result is what Kroeber (1917:86–87) in another context called a "marvelous complexity guaranteed to guard against segmentation, rift, or fission." In Talea the savings and loans associations, the musicians groups, and the division between employers and workers would all be dividing agencies if their boundaries coincided. But they do not. As between individuals, cross-linkage strengthens relations between social groups at the expense of individual ties. One might therefore expect to find a higher proportion of disputes between individuals than between groups.

Even before the rapid changes that followed the opening of communication routes during the 1960s and 1970s, one could see how the weight of these principles of social organization was beginning to shift. In the family, relations between husbands and wives have become increasingly hierarchical, a change generally attributed to Westernization. Male dominance is noticeable in Talea among those who have had a great deal of contact with the external Western world; it contrasts with neighboring villages, where authority is shared more equally between husbands and wives. On the other hand, relations between parents and children are becoming increasingly egalitarian—also something that is attributed to contact. In the realm of symmetry there were also signs of transformation as early as the second or third decade of the twentieth century. Traditional leveling devices, such as loading the heaviest religious obligations on the richest men, have shifted from individuals to the group through creation of savings and loan associations called *barrios*. In the domain of ritual kinship, which also operated as a leveling device, the rich still have more godchildren to care for than the poorer families do. But this too is beginning to change, as the institution of godparenting alters its pattern of linkage by showing preference to family members or members of the same social grouping. It can be said that in Talea, leveling devices have given way to stratifying devices and that the social order has been maintained by ensuring that citizens share multiple memberships in a variety of organizations. As Taleans have felt the outside as threatening, their cross-linkages have increased through the proliferation of committees and commissions to deal with whatever they perceive as a threat—usually something that weakens village unity or independence.

As I have said, the exact manner in which hierarchy, symmetry, and cross-linkage operate as ordering and controlling processes to maintain the autonomy of the village is affected by internal and external changes. For a number of reasons, stresses, strains, and fissive activity end up in court when hierarchy, symmetry, and cross-linkage are not sufficient to control behavior: (1) where behavior slips between social fields, (2) where standards are not homogeneous or universally shared, or (3) because the court is an important institution for reaffirming and re-negotiating the ideology of order.

The Village Court: Disputing, Ideology, and Autonomy

> The struggle to restrict the impingement of superordinate power is carried out . . . consciously. Aside from outright resistance, those involved in the struggle have two principal means at their disposal: an appeal to tradition and rigorous attention to legality. (Colson 1974:76)

Today the state of Oaxaca is divided into districts. Each district is divided into a number of *municipios*, or townships, which vary in land and population size. These townships administer their own affairs through elected town members and are also responsible for smaller villages and dispersed settlements (*rancherías*) located nearby and referred to as *agencias*, which also elect their own leadership. In a political sense, several agencias lie within each township, several townships lie within each district, and all the districts combine to form the state of Oaxaca. Geographically, however, these subdivisions do not lie within one another because both agencies and townships have their own territories with established boundaries that in some cases may date from before the Spanish conquest. Talea lies in the district of Villa Alta and has jurisdiction over three *agencias*. In the decade of the fieldwork reported on here (1957–69), these communities had a combined population of approximately 2,400 people. The municipal building in Talea is the largest in the Rincón. In this building are located the three courts of Talea, which for the purposes of this chapter will be referred to as "the village court."

Some initial observations about the village court are important at the start. This court is a place where Taleans have been hearing their own cases at least since the founding of the village in the sixteenth century. It hears all cases—family cases, land cases, slander cases, debt cases, and so forth—and with the exception of cases where blood has been drawn, the village has the right to conclude the case if the litigants so wish. It deals mainly with cases involving individuals, but also with matters of dispute between both intravillage and intervillage groups if brought before the court by the litigants. It is a place where traditional ideas are formulated and expressed. It is also a place where legal ideas introduced by the state are applied. It is a place where conformity is promoted and rewarded, where local values are expressed, where images of the external world are built, and where village autonomy is declared. Dispute-handling processes, like endogamy and the prohibition of the sale of land to nonvillagers, contribute to village autonomy.

In my previous research on the Talean village court (Nader 1964a), I analyzed the work of the court, which is both administrative (managing the physical plans of the town as well as events of the life cycle, such as birth, marriage, sickness, and death, and also managing relations with the outside—*relaciones exteriores*) and judicial (having to hear and handle disputes). I studied the users of this court—the plaintiff, the defendant, and the court officials—who they are, what they expect from a hearing in court, and the degree to which they reflect the dispersal of power blocs in the village. But studying what people do to resolve problems and what officials do about disputes is only a small fraction of what the study of disputing should encompass. The disputing process is neither merely solving problems nor just a study of the manner in which problems are addressed. As described elsewhere (Nader and Todd 1978; Nader 1984), it is a political process whereby divisions are created or overcome and ideologies are formed. It is also a study of why there is any disputing process in the village or why it is that village conflicts have been left to the inhabitants to handle themselves. In what follows, I shall address some of these important aspects of disputing as they relate to the ideology of harmony in relation to village autonomy.

In a paper entitled "Scarcity and Disputing: Zeroing in on Compromise Decisions," Starr and Yngvesson (1975) suggested that anthropologists have made more of the argument that disputants with multiplex ties will try to compromise their differences than their own published data warranted. After examining the work of three anthropologists, two of whom worked in Africa, they concluded:

> Gluckman in *The Judicial Process among the Barotse* (1955), Gulliver in *Social Control in an African Society* (1963), and Nader in "Styles of Court Procedure: To Make the Balance" (1969) emphasize the compromise or reconcilatory nature of the processes they studied among people in multiplex relations. . . . However, some of their case outcomes cannot be described as compromises between competing claims, some settlements to disputes did not reconcile the disputants, and when an outcome of a reconciliatory process was not to the disputant's liking, he frequently took his complaint elsewhere, sometimes to several different dispute handling forums in order to seek a decision in his favor. We began this inquiry by seeking an explanation for these discrepancies between descriptions of the process and the ethnographic data. (Starr and Yngvesson 1975:562)

As partial explanation they observed:

> The literature . . . reflects a bias. . . . A Durkheimian emphasis on harmony or interests and shared goals has heavily influenced our thinking and seems to have shaped the ways in which anthropologists have perceived the handling of disputes. . . . It is important to separate the objectives of the disputants from those of the third party, whose interests most frequently will be in maintaining the status quo. (Ibid., pp. 559–560)

At the time, I wrote Starr a letter in which I remarked that they had still not adequately explained why so many anthropologists had emphasized harmony and compromise as dominant characteristics of the disputing process, despite evidence to the contrary in their published data.

In my article "Styles of Court Procedure" (1969), to which Starr and Yngvesson refer, I had described the main feature of style in the Talean court as one that values the achievement of balance between principals in a case. I had also completed a documentary film and used the title "To Make the Balance" (1966). Specifically in reference to Talean court styles, I said: "It is compromise arrived at by adjudication or, in some cases, adjudication based on compromise. . . . The aim is to rectify the situation by achieving or reinstating a balance between the parties involved in a dispute" (1969:69). After presenting cases taken from the 1966 documentary, I added: "The judge is a warden of order and fair play among peers. He resolves conflict by minimizing the sense of injustice and outrage felt by parties to a case. . . . He is expected to render a verbal and written agreement for each case—an agreement that *consensus would label equitable*" (ibid., p. 85; emphasis added).

In the same paper I had tried to separate the specifics of the cases as they varied, from case features found to be continuous: "The substantive aspects of procedure which vary from case to case are determined principally by the type of case and type of participants. The continuous features that permeate court activities and constitute the form and manner of the court give the preceedings their style (Kroeber 1957)" (ibid., p. 70). Close observation of courtroom encounters led me to argue the particular settlement to a given dispute may be designed to fine, jail, ridicule, or acquit the principals, but that the desired outcome is rectification. It seemed that outcome rather than decision was the important dimension for style. Outcome centers attention on the desired result of harmony. As Taleans observe: "A bad agreement is better than a good fight." I also said that although the decision must be agreed on by both parties, the "compromise" is not always a result of mutual concessions because it is the judge, rather than the litigants, who after listening to the case decides where the middle ground is or encourages them to make their own agreement. And the decision is often the judge's understanding of what is best for "making the balance," which often means restoring relations to a former condition or to an ideal condition where conflict is absent. Some years later (Nader 1985) I analyzed the cross-sex cases in this village court for the value they have in perpetuating the compromise ideology. Cases between women and men predominate in this court, and the most prevalent decisions associated with such cases— when they involve plaintiffs accusing a man of physical abuse, lack of support, or abandonment—is some sort of compromise (although the plaintiff is rarely seeking compromise). I argued then that users of the court influence the eventual direction of the law over time, in this instance in the direction of harmony.

An analysis of interviews with former court officials further obscures the picture of what really is going on. I was curious about what the officials thought "justice" was. One judge listed the following types of "justice": judging well, not judging or fining, good justice, bad justice, agreement or resolution, or finding guilt. On "bad justice," the same court official said: "For example, he [the judge] could be drunk and a case come up and he would ignore it. Or he could fine the defendant and the plaintiff without thinking. Or he would take money and not give it to the treasurer but put it in his pocket—all this is bad justice." Or on the subject of judging: "Say you did something, or you're not certain that you hit so-and-so . . . not certain if you hit or didn't hit. Nothing more is said, but you are going to pay a fine. They fine without knowing anything, whether you're guilty or not guilty. That is bad justice." And on the question of how the court officials are held responsible: "Police, *regidores*, and even the *presidente*; if he commits a wrong then the *síndico* fines the *presidente*, and if the *síndico* commits a wrong then the *presidente* fines him or puts him in jail."

So it is possible that a judge is not always a "warden of order and fair play resolving conflict by minimizing the sense of injustice and outrage," as I suggested earlier, but he should be. At the same time, when looking at the whole picture, I could conclude that Talea is a highly ordered town that has a large and active court participation pattern, both at the village level and in the district court. Taleans are low on violent crimes, compared with the Oaxacan average, but active in asserting themselves in order to find remedies for wrongs. It is not so much that these Zapotec like to litigate, but rather that they do not like problems to grow, fester, or escalate. Their presentation of self is associated with balance and equality.

Present court styles in Talea have emerged from the aesthetic and emotional values placed on balance and on equality, the particular activities of this small society that necessitate cooperation, and the requirements of a social organization directed toward village independence and autonomy and away from dependence on the state. These styles also stem from the types of cases brought to the courts, whether they deal simply with human conduct or with the distribution of scarce resources. My mode of analysis was internalist.

[333]

At the core, the harmony style and its associated ideology, as I described them for the Zapotec, are internal accommodations to conquest and domination. It is the Crown that presented indigenes like these Zapotec with the semiautonomy that both grows out of and supports Talean values of mutual aid, social order, equity, prevention, and village solidarity. As Wolf (1982:145) reports, "In setting up these units, the Crown followed a double purpose: to break up the pre-Conquest apparatus of power, and to ensure the separation and fragmentation of the resulting jurisdictions." But many indigenous communities like Talea utilized the separation of jurisdiction to promote autonomy, although from the Spanish point of view, dominant ideologies, as with liturgy, were "joined to local belief and practice by missionaries attempting to anchor an ideology in local understandings and by local practitioners, striving to render this ideology expressive of local interests. The outcome was religious structures that varied from community to community and that paralleled in their ideological localocentrism the political separateness of communities" (ibid., p. 148). Taleans see themselves as peaceful, and present themselves as such in public and to outsiders, because keeping the peace, or at least the illusion of peace, is crucial to the maintenance of their autonomy.

In the literature on disputing, theories explaining style or dominant tendencies in this process have been accumulating along the lines of single variables such as the nature of relations between the litigants (Gluckman 1955) or situations where scarce resources form the basis of a dispute (Pound 1959:70; Starr and Yngvesson 1975). Such theories are limited to the internalist perspective. If we look at style as a component of a political ideology, however, we come closer to understanding that the Talean harmony model is a tool for restricting the encroachment of external, superordinate power.

Why have I stressed harmony or balance in my work on the Taleans? In spite of my observations and interviews, which revealed considerable discord in Talean social life, I emphasize the importance of harmony and balance not only because I read Durkheim and the structural-functionalists, but also because I learned from the Taleans that they themselves prefer that disputes be settled on the basis of these principles. Even when one becomes more of an insider and hears of many instances of conflict and division, Taleans still present themselves as peaceful and harmonious. Harmony, they argue, is what differentiates them from others—the people of the sierra or the Valley of Oaxaca or the Cajones, where people are not peaceful. We are thus more in the domain of

[334]

ideology than of observational reality. Taleans strongly believe that if they were not living peaceful, harmonious lives the state would interfere in their business. It is also their theory about how their society related first to the Crown and later to the Mexican state. The image of harmony thus dominates how they present themselves to outsiders in what they like to describe as *relaciones exteriores*. As they state: "We are peaceful in this village, and by being peaceful and minding our own business we keep control of our village. We keep it in local hands, and by so doing we can maintain a relative autonomy." And as we shall see, this attempt to present a united front in response to external contact is not an uncommon reaction to colonization and what Wolf (1982:148) called "the tug of war between conquerors and conquered."

The political effectiveness of the Talean court depends on democratic participation, whereby it disperses power and reinforces community solidarity. In the name of harmony the court can hold private power accountable for the general good of the village. In the name of autonomy the court encourages decision-making that is accountable. In the name of solidarity it makes decisions reflecting concerns about long-term consequences. Through its legal processes the court expresses and ranks social values that are important to the village and to its relationship with the outside world. The village court can compete effectively with the district court, for villagers generally opt for local dispute-handling processes (Parnell 1978a, 1978b). The courts are the expression of political interest pursued through democratic legal procedures that are governed by the concepts of harmony and balance. These concepts enable conflicting interests to be accommodated in dispute settlement. In terms of actual case-handling, the harmony model reflects less attention to the facts of specific cases than to the language of disputing in the village court as opposed to that used in state courts. Through their ideology of harmony, villagers create an image of their society as cohesive and independent and thus fend off the outside world.

In earlier writings on the Talean Zapotec (Nader 1964a, 1964b), I sought an explanation for their harmonious relationships through village social organization based on cross-linkage. This mode of social organization promotes order by preventing fragmentation or rifts in individual and group relations. Yet this cross-linked pattern of social organization is also part of the same cultural ideal of harmony. We need to examine the phenomenon of Talean harmony within the broader context of village relations with the Mexican state in order to account for this particular ideology and social organization as resulting from villagers' interactions

[335]

with the outside world—Spaniards, Mexicans, and the various "developers" that each epoch has brought them. A straightforward Simmelian analysis might argue that external threat brings internal order, but in the Sierra Juárez and in the district of Villa Alta, not all villages respond to external threat as the Taleans do. The people of Yalalag, a large town also located within the jurisdiction of Villa Alta, are divided and fragmented, with a high incidence of violence (Fuente 1949). According to Kearney (1972), the village of Ixtepeji, located in the district of Ixtlán in the Sierra Juárez, is historically not a village thought of in terms of order or disorder, but a village that achieved unification through belligerence and from raiding other communities. Resistance and collaboration are diverse and inconsistent in these mountains, but members of all these communities agree on one thing: danger comes from the outside. Lack of an integrated Zapotec indigenous policy has left people with various options for response, and different options have been adopted over the years. The terms "closed" and "open" for communities reflect two such responses (Wolf 1959), while the terms "traditional" and "progressive" are sometimes one and the same with "closed" and "open." But these four terms do not express the crucial issue of autonomy, for autonomy is directly related to ideologies and social structures of unity or division.

It is well known that the divided village is more susceptible to external domination. Thus, general awareness of this fact would encourage those who want to maintain some degree of autonomy to develop the means to promote internal cohesion. The Taleans are explicit on this point. In divided villages, other values override the value villagers place on autonomy. Yet in communities like Talea the strategy is twofold: managing the internal world of the village through systems of social and cultural control, and developing through the court, and more broadly through town meetings as participatory democracy, the ways to maintain communal loyalty and instill a unifying ideology. Jane Collier (1973) provides a vivid description of this strategy in her study of Zinacantan, where villagers and the state struggle for control over domains of relative power. She concludes: "Zinacanteco law will survive as a system apart from Mexican law only so long as Indians continue to use native ideas of cosmic order to justify procedures and outcomes" (ibid., p. 264). With regard to Talea, I argue that Talean Zapotec law will survive as a system separate from Mexican law only as long as village law, rather than Mexican law, is perceived as meeting village needs, *and* only as long as the Mexican state (like the Spanish Crown previously) continues to regard local rule as in its best interests. As long as the Mexican state can continue to regulate the economy (labor, resources, consumption) outside of law, and as long as local disorder is not a threat to the state, local village law will continue in its present manner, fluctuating around changing issues but ever mindful of the connection between harmony and autonomy.

Zeroing in on Compromise Again

It is worth reiterating that the features of Talean court style have something in common with models presented by anthropologists and sociologists for people in other parts of the world, despite great organizational and cultural differences. While Starr and Yngvesson (1975) argue that the anthropologists were seeing compromise because of a Durkheimian bias, a closer look might suggest that compromise and, more generally, the harmony model are political strategies commonly used by indigenous groups either to protect themselves from encroaching superordinate powerholders or as defense against organized subordinates.

Ethnographies on Africa, as Colson (1974:86–87) has pointed out, report cases of societies managing to maintain local autonomy in face of colonial incursion by using local law. Among the many examples of such societies are the Barotse studied by Gluckman (1956) and the Arusha studied by Gulliver (1963). In describing the Shona administration of justice, Holleman (1974:18) states: "Justice aims at *solving* the conflict between the parties rather than *deciding* its legal aspects in terms of law. Justice . . . then becomes a process of persuasion with the accent on the reasonable behavior of all concerned in a spirit of give and take. . . . The successful end of a tribal process is a judgment which both parties formally agree to accept and observe." This quotation comes from a book that deals with African law as it faces changes in personal and group aspirations and in obligations and loyalties. Much more is at stake than "a personal search for suitable compromises between the conflicting values of a new and complex world. The legal basis of marriage and legitimate offspring, the respective responsibilities of husband and wife, of parent and child, the nature and strength of their wider kinship affiliations and obligations, in short, the very structure and coherence of corporate kin-groupings, are being affected in the groping search for new norms" (ibid., p. 18).

Compromise is the politics of adjustment, but it becomes a politics of

[337]

survival when indigenous communities are threatened by more powerful societies. Community courts become the places where colonials
imposed indirect rule that gave the colonized people a degree of local
autonomy. Compromise can also serve as a political strategy under quite
different conditions. Haley (1982, 2:125–147) describes Japan's decision
to introduce mandatory conciliation in landlord-tenant, family, and
other disputes between the first and second world wars. In this case, it
was the Japanese elite who pressed for conciliation as a political strategy
to safeguard family and other traditional Japanese institutions from the
impact of litigation under the new civil code. Similarly, some scholars
view the alternative dispute-resolution movement over the past decade
in the United States as a political strategy to stem the tide of litigation
that expanded during the 1960s as a result of the civil rights movement
(Abel 1982; Auerbach 1983; Nader 1980, 1984). It is noteworthy that the
movement toward the harmony model in the United States is compatible with the concomitant increased popularity of fundamentalist Protestant beliefs about handling and avoiding conflict (Greenhouse 1986).
And from the strategists' viewpoint, it does not matter whether this
move toward harmonious dispute resolution affects behavior or actually
enhances conciliation, equilibrium, or rectification. What is important
in this aversion to discord is the ideology. We are dealing with a rhetoric
of harmony and compromise—principles extolling the general virtue of
"give a little, get a little" over zero-sum win-or-lose adversary strategies,
which appear more confrontational.

Groups that support a harmony ideology usually share the belief that
the forces of disorder lie outside their group. In fact, it is the recognition
of external threat that mobilizes religious-based beliefs in the harmony
model. In seventeenth- and eighteenth-century Protestant New England villages, the inhabitants carried unanimity to an extreme in order
to maintain harmonious relations that would enable them to remain
independent from the influence of the Boston colony leaders (Lockridge
1970; Zuckerman 1970) or to control discord within the group (see
Auerbach 1983:23).

One could also make a comparable argument for the rise of the
adversary model—for the use of confrontation as a political or economic
strategy. The point here is to acknowledge and examine the ideological
components of dispute-processing independent of particular cases and of
the degree of satisfaction obtained by disputing parties. In sixteenth-
century Castile, compromise was the ideal and preferred means for ending disputes (Kagan 1981:18). Kagan reports that lawsuits were thought

to be at odds with Christian belief. Rapid changes—demographic, economic, social, legal, and political—came to be linked to an increase in adversarial behavior and presumably a decline in religious fervor. The medieval tradition that allowed a magistrate to base his decision not on the law but on his own estimation of what was correct was altered to a more formal legal system in which litigants could win cases (ibid., pp. 22–23).

In the United States during the 1960s, adversarial law was highly valued as the means for attaining civil rights. At that time this legal model was broadened to include attainment not only of rights but also of remedies in such domains as civil rights, consumer rights, environmental rights, and the rights of women, Native Americans, and the elderly. Opponents of the adversarial model moved with surprising speed to supplant it within ten years by a harmony model that has been translated into action and institution-building (Abel 1982; Nader, 1986). Again, I believe the rapidity with which the change in styles of dispute-resolution was accepted can be attributed to the growing movement in Christian fundamentalism in the United States. This example of the shift from adversary to harmony models in the United States, as fundamentalism has gained new strength, inspires me to consider the spread of Christianity around the globe as a possible source of the harmony model in reality and in anthropological theory.

In New Guinea, both the spread of Christianity and the absence of colonial courts with indirect rule determine the manner in which indigenous communities handle contention and disputes in contact situations. Reay (1974:219–220) makes explicit reference to the impact of religion:

> With the spread of Christianity, a greater proportion of councillors . . . were now directly affiliated with some mission or other, [and] these introduced a new style of court hearing. Often the councillor . . . would rebuke people who spoke angrily, saying that anger belonged to Satan and that God was watching. He placed more emphasis on the restoration of friendly relations than on the allocation of *kumap*, on the principle that all men were brothers in the eyes of God.

Epstein (1974:31) does not attempt to trace the source of the idea of amity, but he does remark that living in amity is a social value to which different societies attach varying importance: "Amity as an ideal is likely to be more strongly emphasized where people find it important, for whatever reasons, to remain together in relative and stable residence." And in New Guinea some peoples find peaceful separation more advan-

[339]

tageous than village unity—or at least they did so until colonial contact changed the social and cultural ecology. On the other hand, the colonial policies of the Australian administration prevented the development of either village autonomy or village courts. The Australian administration, Epstein reminds us (ibid., pp. 35–36),

> consistently refused to recognize or set up "native courts" on the African model, and most disputes could only be legally handled in the first instance by administrative magistrates, . . . Reluctance to accord legal recognition to the work of indigenous dispute settlers has rested on the assumed incapacity of New Guineans to handle disputes with the required degree of impartiality . . . many of the current difficulties relate to the failure to integrate local procedures for settlement into the wider judicial system.

If the Spanish Crown had not developed a policy for the creation of semiautonomous Mexican Indian villages, and if there had not been a powerful policy of converting the Indians to Christianity beginning 400 years ago, there might not be any Zapotec village law today, or any ideology emphasizing harmony and compromise. Colson (1974:87) describes the contrasting situation for North American Indians:

> The denial of any local autonomy to Native Americans on their reservations gave them less reason to update their traditions of law and order and so connect past with present. . . . Instead, they were forced to defend themselves in alien courts which were governed by legal rules stemming from another tradition. They could neither withdraw from close supervision by their agents nor use the power of numbers to gain the political power that would affect . . . legislation.

The emphasis on harmony and compromise, whether viewed as philosophy or as ideology, becomes part of the discourse of those "colonies" that were governed by indirect rule. This discourse is useful because of the inherent ambiguity and elasticity of such terms as "compromise." After initial encounters with European colonists and their missionaries, village law becomes the product of current social conditions and disputes resulting from routine village activities. Village law thus goes beyond being a mere creation of the Crown policies that gave villagers their original options for maneuver. The inhabitants of Talea de Castro have managed to maintain strong local control over both their land and their own problems, and many Taleans feel their justice is evenhanded. Over the past several hundred years, this community has been able to incorporate external economic and political pressures without losing its local integrity and autonomy.

Anthropologists, Their Informants, and Anthropological Theory

This chapter has addressed two issues: (1) the close relationships over time between disputing processes, the political conduct of governments and religious institutions, and the people over whom they exercise power; and (2) the more general question of where anthropologists get their ideas. We now look at why anthropologists have sometimes insisted that disputing among non-Western peoples aims to restore harmony to social relations, that harmony is either functional in face-to-face societies or the product of their specific social organization. Because anthropologists are so deeply involved in empirical analyses, they are heavily influenced by what their informants tell them. If the structural-functionalists argued that dispute settlement is aimed at restoring social harmony, it is probably because that is what their informants told them. And in good empirical tradition, the telling that was part of their data became part of the analysis as well. In the case of Talea, harmony is part of the people's ideology—their theory of how they can maintain some autonomy from the state. The ideology of harmony thus becomes transformed into the image of themselves that Taleans present to outsiders, and it may reflect to some extent what missionaries have preached to them over 400 years—that harmony is the Christian way. This ideology and image of Talean social life has not only been approved by outsiders, but also helped maintain village solidarity.

Anthropological theory is shaped by the ideologies presented to them by informants, as well as by the Western world and such social philosophers as Emile Durkheim. That this ideology may have had Western origins makes it even more interesting as we attempt to trace the origins of anthropological ideas and to determine why Taleans employ the principles of harmony and balance in dispute settlement and in dealings with outsiders. Although I have focused here on how the "natives" use the harmony model, this issue has brought me closer to understanding how anthropologists use the natives' harmony model and how anthropological theory has been shaped both by colonial policies and by Christianity as preached to indigenous peoples. It thus appears likely that structural-functionalists have influenced colonial policy and been influ-

[341]

enced by colonial policies through the resulting indigenous harmony ideologies. In the history of anthropological theory, structural-functionalism becomes more understandable when we realize how our informants have used colonial policies and how these people and their ideology have been reflected in our analyses. Fact, indigenous ideology, and anthropological theory thus become part of a common temporal perspective on law. If the early functionalists were internalist in their analyses focused on structure, continuity, or equilibrium, while contemporary anthropologists are more interested in transformations and in the role of external forces of change, both periods contribute to the understanding of continuity and transformation in law.

What is currently exhilarating about research in the anthropology of law is that we are becoming more critical of certain intellectual paradigms and of the truths that anthropologists construct from such paradigms. We are developing a good number of social scientists who study legal phenomena and who produce a diversity of data. These analyses cover a wide variety of circumstances, some of which are contradictory. Furthermore, we are living long enough to experience enormous change in the societies being studied. The current speed of change makes it possible for us to recognize better the relationship between local cultures and larger external social forces (neglected in earlier studies). These reflect asymmetrical power structures that overlap in interesting ways. As this chapter on the production and dissemination of the harmony model demonstrates, the temporal dimension in anthropology is further complicated because the anthropologist is both instrument and analyst of the people studied. Anthropology was never meant to be only the study of others. It is also meant to provide a mirror for the observers.

Acknowledgments

I am grateful to the following friends and colleagues for their perceptive and critical readings of this chapter: Elizabeth Colson, Suzanne Bowler, JoAnn Martin, Bjorn Clausen, and Norman Milleron. In addition, I thank June Starr and Jane Collier for having stimulated my thoughts and giving me the opportunity to put them down on paper.

REFERENCES

Abel, R. L., ed. 1982. *The Politics of Informal Justice*, vol. 1: *The American Experience;* vol. 2: *Comparative Studies*. New York.

Attia, H. 1985. "Water Sharing Rights in the Jerid Oases of Tunisia." In A. Meyer, ed., *Property, Social Structure, and Law in the Modern Middle East.* Albany, N.Y.

Aubert, V. 1969. "Law as a Way of Resolving Conflicts: The Case of a Small Industrialized Society." In L. Nader, ed., *Law in Culture and Society.* Chicago.

Auerbach, J. 1983. *Justice without Law?* New York.

Berg, R. L. 1976. "The Zoogocho Plaza System in the Sierra Zapoteca of Villa Alta." In S. Cook and M. Diskin, eds., *Markets in Oaxaca.* Austin, Tex.

Borah, W. W. 1951. *New Spain's Century of Depression.* Iberoamericana No. 35. Mexico.

————. 1983. *Justice by Insurance: The General Indian Court of Colonial Mexico and the Legal Aides of the Half-Real.* Berkeley and Los Angeles.

Collier, J. 1973. *Law and Social Change in Zinacantan.* Stanford, Calif.

Colson, E. 1974. *Tradition and Contract: The Problem of Order.* Chicago.

Epstein, A. L. 1974. *Contention and Dispute: Aspects of Law and Social Control in Melanesia.* Canberra.

Fuente, J. de la. 1949. *Yalalag: Una Villa Zapoteca Serrana.* Serie Científica. Mexico.

Gerhard, P. 1972. *A Guide to the Historical Geography of New Spain.* Cambridge, Eng.

Gluckman, M. 1955. *The Judicial Process among the Barotse of Northern Rhodesia.* Manchester, Eng.

Greenhouse, C. J. 1986. *Praying for Justice: Faith, Order, and Community in an American Town.* Ithaca, N.Y.

Gulliver, P. 1963. *Social Control in an African Society: A Study of the Arusha.* Boston.

Haley, J. O. 1982. "The Politics of Informal Justice: The Japanese Experience, 1922–42." In R. L. Abel, ed., *The Politics of Informal Justice,* vol. 2: *Comparative Studies.* New York.

Hammett, B. R. 1971. *Politics and Trade in Southern Mexico, 1750–1821.* Cambridge, Eng.

Hammoudi, A. 1985. "Substance and Relation: Water Rights and Water Distribution in the Dra Valley." In A. Mayer, ed., *Property, Social Structure, and Law in the Modern Middle East.* Albany, N.Y.

Hirabayashi, Lane Rio. 1981. "Migration, Mutual Aid, and Association: Mountain Zapotec in Mexico City." Ph.D. diss., Department of Anthropology, University of California at Berkeley.

————. 1986. "The Migrant Village Association in Latin America." *Latin American Research Review* 21(3):7–29.

Holleman, J. F. 1974. *Issues in African Law.* The Hague.

Kagan, R. L. 1981. *Lawsuits and Litigants in Castile, 1500–1700.* Chapel Hill, N.C.

Kearney, M. 1972. *The Winds of Ixtepeji: World View and Society in a Zapotec Town.* New York.

Kroeber, A. L. 1917. *Zuni Kin and Clan.* Anthropological Papers 18. New York.

————. 1957. *Style and Civilization.* Ithaca, N.Y.

Llewelyn, K. N., and E. A. Hoebel. 1941. *The Cheyenne Way.* Norman, Okla.

Lockridge, K. 1970. *A New England Town: The First Hundred Years.* New York.

Malinowski, B. 1922. *Argonauts of the Western Pacific.* London.

Moore, S. F. 1986. *Social Facts and Fabrications: Customary Law on Kilimanjaro, 1880–1980.* New York.

Nader, L. 1964a. "An Analysis of Zapotec Law Cases." *Ethnology* 3(4):404–419.

———. 1964b. *Talea and Juquila: A Comparison of Zapotec Social Organization.* University of California Publications in American Archaeology and Ethnology 48(3):195–296.

———. 1966. *To Make the Balance.* Distributed by University of California Extension, Berkeley, Calif.

———. 1969. "Styles of Court Procedure: To Make the Balance." In L. Nader, ed., *Law in Culture and Society,* pp. 69–91. Chicago.

———. 1978. "The Directions of Law and the Development of Extra-Judicial Processes in Nation-State Societies." In P. Gulliver, ed., *Cross-Examinations: Essays in Memory of Max Gluckman,* pp. 78–95. Leiden.

———. 1980. *No Access to Law: Alternatives to the American Judicial System.* New York.

———. 1984. "From Disputing to Complaining." In D. Black, ed., *Toward a General Theory of Social Control,* pp. 71–94. New York.

———. 1985. "A User Theory of Legal Change as Applied to Gender." In *The Nebraska Symposium on Motivation: The Law as a Behavioral Instrument,* 33:1–33.

———. 1986. "Some Notes on Alternative Dispute Resolution: A Bifurcate Perspective on the Making of an Ideology." Lecture delivered at the University of Florida Law School.

Nader, L., and H. Todd, eds. 1978. *The Disputing Process: Law in Ten Societies.* New York.

Parnell, P. 1978a. "Conflict and Competition in a Mexican Judicial District." Ph.D. diss., Department of Anthropology, University of California at Berkeley.

———. 1978b. "Village or State: Competitive Legal Systems in a Mexican Judicial District." In L. Nader and H. Todd, eds., *The Disputing Process: Law in Ten Societies,* pp. 315–350. New York.

Pérez-García, R. 1956. *La Sierra Juárez.* Vols. 1 and 2. N.p.

Pound, R. 1959. *An Introduction to the Philosophy of Law.* Rev. ed. New Haven. First edition 1954.

Reay, M. 1974. "Changing Conventions of Dispute Settlement in Minjarea." In A. L. Eptstein, ed., *Contention and Dispute: Aspects of Law and Social Control in Melanesia.* Canberra.

Starr, J., and B. Yngvesson. 1975. "Scarcity and Disputing: Zeroing in on Compromise Decisions." *American Ethnologist* 2(3):533–566.

Wolf, E. 1959. *Sons of the Shaking Earth: The People of Mexico and Guatemala: Their Land, History, and Culture.* Chicago.

———. 1982. *Europe and the People without History.* Berkeley and Los Angeles.

Zuckerman, M. 1970. *Peaceable Kingdoms: New England Towns in the Eighteenth Century.* New York.

[14]

The "Invention" of Early Legal Ideas: Sir Henry Maine and the Perpetual Tutelage of Women*

June Starr

Every age has it own gestalt. Sometimes authors use ideas and relationships from earlier times and cultures as implicit contrasts to their own society, but using the past for allusions to the present is hazardous, because everyone has a limited view of the rate of change in the modern era. We now know that the person who in 1909 remarked, "The world changed less since Jesus Christ than in the last thirty years" (quoted in Durant and Durant 1968:12), was quite mistaken.

In addition to a foreshortened sense of history, false analogies, and too much importance attributed to one's own times and values, other problems arise when authors use the past to illuminate the present. The most formidable obstacle is perhaps shallowness of insight into a former time. Asking "Do we really know what the past was," what "actually happened," or is history "a fable" not quite "agreed upon?" historians Will and Ariel Durant (ibid., p. 11) caution us about the interpretative task of historical analysis: "History as usually written . . . is quite different from history as usually lived: the historian records the exceptional because it

*The "perpetual tutelage of women" is a phrase used by Maine (1977:90). Under the *XII Tables* and in classical Rome, a woman of any age who was *sui iuris* needed a guardian, called a "tutor." In his will a man appointed a guardian for any woman under his *manus* or *potestas* (protection), who would become *sui iuris* at his death. No woman could be a guardian. See Jolowicz and Nicholas 1972:121.

[345]

is interesting—because it is exceptional" (ibid., p. 41). Anthropologists and historians use history differently because anthropologists are generally more concerned with uncovering, describing, and analyzing the normal processes of social life and of change, rather than the exceptional processes. And legal history differs from both in its attempt to reconstruct the laws and legal systems of a particular period and their uses in society.

The Durants were raising phenomenological questions concerning the study of history in the late 1960s, about the time the questioning of the "scientific objectivity" of ethnographic writing by social anthropologists intensified. Some anthropologists challenged the authority and "objectivity" of ethnographic reporting, while others raised it to a creative art form, pointing out that "writing" is central to what anthropologists do both in the field and thereafter (Clifford and Marcus 1986:vii–viii). Ethnographic writing is creative writing, not simply a reporting of *transparent representations and immediate experiences*. When ethnographic experiences are seen as "something made or fashioned," ethnographies become part of the "worldly work of writing" (Clifford 1986:6).

The above is relevant to this chapter for four reasons. First, in an attempt to understand better how anthropologists of law had conceptualized power relationships and the control of resources, I began in 1981 to reread Sir Henry Maine's *Ancient Law* (1977), published in 1861. Sir Henry Maine had profoundly influenced a number of social anthropologists, and even in the mid-twentieth century his formulations of social and legal evolution continued as a touchstone for new integrative theories (Fried 1967; Gluckman 1965:113; Nader 1965:25, 1978; Colson 1974; Moore 1978:63). I sought to understand Maine's conceptualizations of social change by reviewing his ideas about the influence of changing gender relationships on law in early and classical Roman society, but on rereading Maine I continually felt uneasy. My previous understanding of his ideas was at odds with the multiple and complex view of patriarchal family life I had seen through field research in several different patrifocal cultures.

Second, in Marcus and Cushman's article "Ethnographies as Texts," I recognized a similarity between their analytical stance and mine, especially when they described "experimental ethnographies" (1982:25). Experimental ethnographies integrate the textual representation of native life and thought with the ethnographers' reflections. If contemporary ethnographies are to be treated as creative texts that express the times and thoughts of their authors, the writings of earlier social thinkers

[346]

should be treated the same way. Ideas from literary criticism, such as deconstructionism, also suggest how we might read texts as "cultural artifacts of an age" (see Derrida 1976; Culler 1982).

Third, the current anthropological enthusiasm for self-scrutiny of field research, field-workers, and their written products (see Marcus and Cushman 1982) was just beginning to be extended to nineteenth-century writers. Lively debates in the 1960s and 1970s about Marx and "Marxisms" had raised certain issues. For example, Leacock's (1972) introduction to a new edition of Engels's *Origin of the Family, Private Property, and the State* (1884) called for Marxist anthropologists to rely less on "idealism" and to separate materialistically conceived structures and actions from the subjectively held views of members of the societies being studied. This meant that an enormous amount of reinterpretation needed to take place (Leacock 1972:65,66). But most non-Marxist anthropologists used nineteenth-century writers in a literal manner or simply ignored them. The attempt to see "representational forms," "fictional" aspects, and "cultural intrusions" in the work of influential nineteenth-century theorists—Bachofen, McLennan, Fustel de Coulanges, Maine, Spencer, Engels, Weber, and Durkheim—has not yet had a major impact on social anthropology. Kuper's work reevaluating the ethnographic evidence concerning the lineage (1982) and on contextualizing Sir Henry Maine in his times (1985) are major exceptions.

Fourth, the uses made of nineteenth-century theory were even more striking in the anthropology of law. Evolutionary frameworks were mostly passé, and ideas considered false were ignored. But other ideas were appropriated in "unreconstructed" theoretical formulations. With some anthropologists of law turning to analyze how power shapes cultural and historical relationships among groups, it seemed time to bring contemporary scholarship on classical times to the study of the texts of earlier anthropological theorists.

The effectiveness of this unity between classical scholars and social anthropologists in reviewing nineteenth-century thinkers has been demonstrated in the new introduction to Fustel de Coulanges's *Ancient City* (1980). Momigliano and Humphreys boldly state that Fustel de Coulanges was in favor of private property and that throughout his life he engaged in a polemic against socialism, which led him to posit private property as *the original* human institution. They are quite critical of his major theory, remarking: "The reader of *The Ancient City* must be on guard at every step about what Fustel states as given in his sources. For instance, the notion—essential for the validity of Fustel's theories and presented by him as a fact—that the Greeks and Latins buried their dead in family tombs within their own estates is simply not supported by the evidence he produces (or by any evidence discovered subsequently)" (1980:xi).

My attempt to view the writings of the nineteenth-century writer Sir Henry Maine as "texts" is thus part of a new evaluative and interpretative stance occurring in anthropology. By contextualizing some of Maine's published work within his historical period, I demonstrate that the same philosophical energies used by social anthropologists to analyze the ethnographic writings of contemporary times might be brought to bear on the great formative ideas of our discipline. The gain would be a more powerful understanding of past societies. This chapter will add to anthropological conceptualizations of changing power relationships and the control of persons and resources in early and classical Roman societies. Once we began to inquire into the ability of women to hold property in classical Roman times, we will have to change our anthropological ideas of Roman property and kin relationships. Thus, the study of gender relations adds greater depth to our understanding of all societal relations.

This chapter first analyzes Sir Henry Maine's use of the *Institutes* of Gaius in writing *Ancient Law* in 1861. These fragments served as a touchstone for Maine's general theory concerning the direction of legal change from legal fictions through equity to legislation. Then we shall reexamine women and property relationships in early and classicial Roman society from the point of view of Gaius and other sources. And finally, we treat *Ancient Law* as a "cultural text" that reflects some of the great ideas and controversies of the nineteenth century. Like many others who trace secondary sources back to the original, I discovered that a literal reading of the data did not permit all the conclusions drawn by Maine. Maine's ideas, like those of other eminent essayists, evolved during his lifetime. His views changed between the publication of *Ancient Law* in 1861 and the publication of *The Early History of Institutions* in 1875. But *Ancient Law* is the text of primary concern because it has most influenced social anthropologists and is the one most often cited. In it Maine was "liberal," "evocative," and sometimes mistaken in his extrapolations from Gaius's text.

Writers and intellectuals in each age reinterpret past times, and some social and cultural groups even rewrite or invent their histories (Hobsbawm 1983:7). Thus, we can no longer take literally even what the historians of an age say about their own period. As Giddens states so clearly, "The production of a society . . . is always and everywhere a skilled accomplishment of its members" (1976:126).

Maine's Ideas Presented and Critiqued

Sir Henry Maine stated that the process of change within the structure of elite Roman families resulted from lawyers' ability to influence judicial decision-making in civil litigation and from judges' use of the rules of equity. This supported his generalization that the law evolved from legal fictions, through equity to legislation. The time period Maine considered was from 451 B.C., the time of the *XII Tables* (what Maine called the "ancient codes" or "ancient law"), to the second century A.D., the period of Gaius's *Institutes*. My use of Gaius and other sources provides a view of Roman society that is an alternative to Maine's and that is supported by current legal and historical scholarship concerning Roman law (see Crook 1967; Honore 1962, 1981; Watson 1968, 1975).[1]

"Ancient law," wrote Sir Henry Maine, "knows next to nothing of Individuals." It is concerned with Families, not with single human beings, but groups" (1977:152).[2] "The Roman distinction between the Law of Persons and the Law of Things . . . though extremely convenient, is entirely artificial" (ibid.). Maine continues: "The separation of the Law of Persons from that of Things has no meaning in the infancy of the law . . . it is more likely that joint-ownership, and not separate ownership, is the really archaic institution" (ibid., pp. 152–153). Maine sums up his theory when he states later, "On a few systems of law the family organization of the earliest society has left a plain and broad mark in the life-long authority of the Father or other ancestor over the person and property of his descendants, an authority which we may conveniently call by its later Roman name of Patria Potestas" (ibid., p. 80).

Thus Sir Henry Maine, who was to hold the first professorship in Roman law at Oxford University and who is considered the father of comparative legal studies,[3] launched his theory of patriarchy. Many

---

[1]Literary sources also discuss a woman's place in elite Roman family structures. See Cantarella 1987, Hallett 1984, and Lefkowitz and Fant 1982.

[2]Maine is referring to the time the *XII Tables* were compiled—under the Roman Republic, 451–450 B.C.

[3]Sir Fredrick Pollock, in the introduction to the tenth edition of *Ancient Law*, credits Maine with creating the natural history of law (1930:xvi). Maine "showed . . . that legal ideas and institutions have a real course of development as much as the *genera* and species

legal scholars did not take *Ancient Law* seriously in its day (Kuper 1985:24). In the same year a Swiss jurist, J. J. Bachofen, had published *Das Mutterrecht* (1861), a widely acclaimed book based on Greek and Roman sources. Bachofen's theory was that early societies were based on matrilineal inheritance and maternal authority. Thus, already there is a contested view of the interpretation of the original Greek sources. Maine's successor to the Oxford Chair of Jurisprudence had this to say of Maine's work in his inaugural speech in 1892: "It is not unusual nowadays to talk in a rather supercilious manner of the lack of erudition and accuracy, of the allusiveness and vagueness of Maine's writing. Those who indulge in such cheap criticism should rather try to realize what accounts for his having been a force in European thought, a potentate in a realm where parochial patronage and a mere aptitude for vulgarization are not recognized as titles to eminence" (Vinogradoff 1904:2). Some critics of Maine have viewed *Ancient Law* as a bold attempt to gain the coveted post of "legal member" in the viceroy's council in India. In fact, Maine was appointed to this position in 1862, one year after *Ancient Law* was published. He held the post for seven years (Kuper 1985:279).

Although Maine's formulations of legal change in *Ancient Law* had little impact on comparative law scholars and Roman historians (ibid., p. 24), these ideas were later taken up by social anthropologists (see Fried 1967; Gluckman 1965; Nader 1965, 1978; Colson 1974; Moore 1978). A critical issue in anthropological theory, for instance, has been the transformation from kin-group ownership of land to private control of estates. Maine's concept of social change has influenced the evolutionary thinking of Morgan (1877), Engels (1884), and more recently Morton Fried (1967).[4]

The appeal of Maine's formulations to continuing generations of social anthropologists lay in the usefulness of the dichotomies he proposed, which provided a model of change from preindustrial societies to complex, stratified states. In *Ancient Law*, Maine consistently discussed the movement from early Roman society to the classical Roman Empire as a change from a kinship-oriented society to one based on common ter-

---

of living creatures," but he "made it clear that these processes deserve and require distinct study and cannot be treated as mere incidents in the general history of the societies where they occur" (ibid.).

[4]Fried was as influenced by Hobhouse, Wheeler, and Ginsberg (1915) as by Maine. Fried suggested that political society evolved through the distributive role of leaders instead of by changing systems of landownership. His concern was with the systematic emergence of social stratification in previously egalitarian societies and how systems of stratification related to political and economic control.

ritoriality. According to Maine, under the ancient Roman codes property was held in kinship groups. In classical times it was held in private ownership. Roman law evolved from laws relating to commonly held land by kin groups to laws regarding individual people. In kinship-organized society, social relations and rights were based on status in a kinship group. As societies changed, kin-based organizations gave way to individual relationships based on contractual agreements.[5]

These assertions are not supported by scholars of Roman law however. There is a marked paucity of evidence when one tries to reconstruct a "gentile" stage of society in Italy (Watson 1974, 1975:67). Watson (1977:40) states that at the time of the *XII Tables* (Maine's "ancient codes"), "the *gentes* had for centuries ceased to have much real significance. Who can doubt that for hundreds of years the propertied Roman would have preferred close relatives to succeed rather than the distant— and, in fact, very shadowy—*gentiles?*" Second, the era of the *XII Tables* is dominated by private ownership and wills. Land could be acquired and held as private property, private property that was different from inherited property (Jolowicz and Nicholas 1972:139). Third, the *XII Tables* stipulated that privately owned lands should be inherited by someone in a *potestas* (protected) or *manus* (literally, under the hand) relationship (i.e., a son, wife, or daughter) who became "freed" (*sui iuris*) by the death of the patriarch. (A wife or a daughter who became freed was given a guardian, called a "tutor.") If no son, wife, or daughter survived, the nearest agnate should inherit. Only if he refused did the inheritance go to the *gentiles* (gens). This situation is not one of "common agnatic kin rights to land." Finally, the beginning of Roman contracts drawn up between individuals has been traced to the era shortly *before* the *XII Tables* (Watson 1985:4–11).

This difference of opinion between accumulated Roman law scholarship during the last hundred years and the "received wisdom" of social anthropology suggests that we should bring our ideas concerning property relationships in early and classical Roman society up to date. To do so, we need to review a critical juncture in Maine's theory—the opposition between *res mancipi* and *res nec mancipi*. Maine explained these Latin terms, but he never clearly glossed them.[6] But for a clear under-

---

[5]For a summary of Maine's theory of the evolution of law as developed in *Ancient Law*, see Newman 1983:6–12. For an analysis of how Maine's research dovetailed with his political ambitions, see Kuper 1985. For Maine's influence on the work of other evolutionists, see Kuper 1982.

[6]In fact, Maine's original edition lacks citations, bibliography, and footnotes, as do the later editions. These terms, still in their Roman gloss and untranslated, were later

standing of women's status and rights to control property in ancient Roman society, we need to deconstruct the meaning of these terms in denoting property relationships, and we need to understand Roman marriage forms.

Fragments of manuscripts by a second-century A.D. Roman lawyer, Gaius, stimulated Maine's ideas.[7] The fragments, discovered in 1816 by Barthold Niebuhr in the cathedral library at Verona, have provided the European world with information concerning early Roman law which, according to Maine, "had disappeared" from the "mature Roman jurisprudence" of the sixth century known in Justinian's Code (Maine 1977:90). Maine asserts (although it is not true) that "a considerable part of Gaius's volume" is taken up with descriptions of the numerous expedients, some of them displaying extraordinary ingenuity, which the Roman lawyers had devised for enabling women to defeat the ancient rules" (ibid.).[8] According to Maine, "led by their theory of Natural Law, the jurisconsults had . . . assumed the equality of the sexes as a principle of their code of equity. The restrictions which they attacked were . . . restrictions on the disposition of property, for which the assent of the woman's guardians was still formally required. Control of her person was apparently quite obsolete" (ibid., pp. 90–91).

The above quotation from Maine obscures the existing situation.[9]

---

appropriated by Gluckman (1965:113) and also by Laura Nader (1965:25) for theory-building.

[7]Gaius became famous as a legal scholar only in the fifth and sixth centuries, but he may have been writing the *Institutes* as early as A.D. 161 (see Jolowicz and Nicholas 1972:386–387, n. 2). The *Institutes* is three books that formed the basis of the first year of legal education in Byzantine schools. Justinian and the compilers of his codes single him out by calling him "Gaius noster," an important honorific title (Honore 1962:xi). Because Gaius's manuscripts were subsequently lost, everything the legal world knew of Roman law came from the codes of Justinian, published between A.D. 529 and A.D. 530 (Harris 1875:2–3). When Niebuhr discovered them, they were immediately recognized by the great legal scholar (and Niebuhr's contemporary) Savigny as containing original work (Jolowicz and Nicholas 1972:389). The manuscript is a palimpsest and probably dates from the fifth century A.D. Some works of Saint Jerome had been written over the original text. It is difficult to read because of "the numerous mistakes made by the copyists and the free use of abbreviations" (ibid.). In some places two inscriptions had to be removed. Harris stated: "In consequence of the economy of parchment, about a tenth . . . is wholly lost or illegible" (1875:1).

[8]For a basic historical treatise on Roman law, see Jolowicz and Nicholas 1972.

[9]A fourth fragment of Gaius's *Institutes* was found in 1927, as well as a few fragments from a papyrus of about A.D. 250 and part of a magnificent parchment codex of the late fourth or early fifth century. Taken together, these help clarify the meanings in Gaius's manuscripts and "enable us to follow in detail the famous three-fold arrangement of the subject-matter of the law as it concerns 'persons,' 'things,' and 'actions'" (Jolowicz and Nicholas, 1972:389).

Women were both freer in some contexts, and more controlled in others, than Maine claimed they were. For instance, women were free to sell and buy all kinds of property that was not *res mancipi*. This included sheep, goats, poultry, pottery, jewelry, clothes, furniture, houses, and land outside Italy (Gardner 1986:18). In terms of women's personal freedom, however, Crook has aptly said, when commenting on the alleged freedom and independence of Roman women, that this view is generalized from "the antics of Roman 'night-club' society" and tends to be much exaggerated (1967:103–104).

Maine's reading of Gaius assumed that women had already gained "control of their person" when in fact this was still at issue. Women were under either their father's, husband's, or guardian's protection. Women with living fathers could marry only in the first two marriage forms (for the marriage forms, see later in this chapter), and neither form allowed them free choice of a husband. Women whose fathers had died might engage in legal maneuvers to marry the male guardian (i.e., husband) of choice, but this limited his status and that of her male children. This marriage form created problems if the husband or male children born of such a union should later aspire to the high-priestly office.

If a woman was *sui iuris* (i.e., if her father had died and she had not yet married), then at the time of the *XII Tables* and for a long time afterward she needed a guardian (Jolowicz and Nicholas 1972:121). As Crook comments in his *Law and Life of Rome*, "women were never released" from guardianship, and "subjection of women's legal acts to some male authority was virtually universal in antiquity. . . . This life long guardianship was whittled away by legal devices, though as a formality it hung grimly on" (1967:114).

A detailed study of Roman law relating to women begins: "With few exceptions, all Roman women were for their entire lives subject to some degree of limitation on their capacity for independent legal action" (Gardner 1986:5). All action depended on male permission—women needed to obtain consent from fathers, husbands, or guardians. The few exceptions were six in number—the six vestal virgins. In *Ancient Law*, Maine misinterpreted the transfer of women's subordination from father to husband as a growth in freedom, saying: "Ancient law subordinates the woman to her blood relations, while a prime phenomenon of modern jurisprudence has been her subordination to her husband" (1977:91). Twenty years of female agitation in England led Maine to recant this position later, but most anthropological theories emanating from his views are based on the earlier work, not on the later work. In a lecture delivered at Birmingham on March 25, 1873, "The Early History of the

[353]

Property of Married Women, as Collected from Roman and Hindoo Law" (later published in nearly the same form in *The Early History of Institutions* [1875]), Maine stated that women should be equal to men: "It has been said that the degree in which the personal immunity and proprietary capacity of women are recognized in a particular state or community is a test of its degree of advance in civilization" (1873:21).

Ancient Law, however, makes it clear that Maine viewed the lawyers' manipulation of the legal system to transfer control of an adult female from father to husband as a growth of women's rights. Although some elite women were able to use lawyers to plead their property cases on grounds of equity, women of poorer ranks did not have access to lawyers. Furthermore, case-to-case argumentation is an indication that new legislation protecting female equality was not in place. Appellate cases argued under rules of equity instead of from existing legislation indicate that the subject was still controversial.

Three legal documents from the second century A.D., cited in Crook (1967:114), provide further proof that a Roman woman still needed permission from her guardian to engage in commercial transactions regarding land or money. The scholarship of Crook, Gardner, and Honore (discussed more fully below) provide deeper interpretations of law in the classical period of Roman society. Because the written law demonstrates only what people may or may not do, not what actually happened when cases were brought to trial, selected cases from Honore's text (1981) are briefly discussed later in the chapter.

Maine's Theory of *Res Mancipi* in Contrast to the Views of Gaius

Before turning to Roman law cases, it is necessary to establish the original meaning of the legal concepts of property and ownership denoted by *res mancipi* and *res nec mancipi* as used in Gaius's fragments. Here interpretations by professors of Roman law are helpful in clarifying what Gaius meant, especially with regard to women's ability to own and control property in Rome in the second century A.D. To fully understand the *context* in which female autonomy was limited in law and in practice, we need to know the three prevailing forms of marriage and their consequences for the woman in terms of her status, autonomy, and legal rights. Several law cases examined below, in combination with the legal rules provided in the text of Gaius, and interpreted by Roman law

[354]

scholars in the twentieth century provide an alternative view of the degree of women's emancipation in classical Roman society, the period considered by Maine.

To develop an image of Maine's views of the Roman law of property, we have to piece together different sections of his book. Maine did not present the material consecutively, because he felt there was a confusion in the Roman classifications of property, that Romans did not recognize the natural distinction between movable and immovable property. The "*Res Mancipi* of Roman Law included not only land, but slaves, horses and oxen" (Maine 1977:161). Maine also believed that "the classifications of Ancient Law are classifications implying superiority and inferiority" and that "*Res Mancipi* . . . did certainly at first enjoy a precedence over the *Res nec Mancipi*" (ibid.).

Reading further in Maine, we discover that *res mancipi* is a type of property for which "mancipation" is required. Maine continues: "By their side there may have existed or grown up a class of objects, for which it was not worth while to insist upon the full ceremony of Mancipation. It would be enough if, in transferring these last from owner to owner, a part only of the ordinary formalities were proceeded with, namely the actual delivery, physical transfer" (ibid., p. 163). These commodities were *res nec mancipi* of ancient jurisprudence —"things which did not require a Mancipation" (ibid.).

From Gaius's text we learn that the ritual for *res mancipi* (the ceremony of emancipation) included five witnesses, the saying of a formula spoken by the person giving up rights to the property, and symbolic actions denoting weighing (Gaius, translated by Zulueta 1953:59). In a footnote by Gaius's translator, we learn that because until the fourth century B.C. the medium of exchange was uncoined bronze, weighing had been essential, and it continued still in the symbolic form of the ritual emancipation (Zulueta 1946:58–59).

Maine's belief in "natural law" led him to find confusions in the Roman classifications of property, because Romans classified some movable property with immovable property (Maine 1977:160–161). According to Maine, this confusion retarded the development of European law of property until well into the Middle Ages. In Maine's view the "history of Roman property law is the history of the assimilation of *Res Mancipi* to *Res nec Mancipi*" (ibid., p. 160)—that is, the two classifications of property merge into one, a property that does not entail a ritual to be alienated from its owner but that can be transferred by mere conveyance. Jointly held property, which included all aspects of the productive resources (land in Italy, slaves, and beasts of burden) required a special ritual when sold. Maine's point is that this requirement disappeared because joint agnatic ownership gave way to individualized ownership.

But legal commentaries on the text of Gaius stress an interpretation that Maine glossed over. Most twentieth-century commentators have suggested that the distinction between *res mancipi* and *res nec mancipi* bore some resemblance (but not a complete similarity) to the earlier distinction in Roman law between *familia* and *pecunia*. Watson attempted to solve the puzzle about the different meanings ascribed to these words in several different Latin texts (1975:57). He suggests that *pecunia* means property and that *familia* means "a man's property considered as a unit." This view is supported by another scholar, who points to the *original* concern of Romans to control the movement of property *between* families as the meaning of these distinctions (Kaser 1980:46). In other words, it is to prevent a few families from gaining control of most of the land in Italy (ibid.). According to Roman tradition, the *XII Tables* came about as a compromise in "the class struggle" between plebeians and patricians (Watson 1975:177). Whether "tradition" is accurate or has been created as hindsight, it allows an explanation of the development of written law as a mechanism to limit property accumulation in the hands of an emerging elite.

The classifications of property—*res mancipi* and *res nec mancipi*—are important points of departure for Maine's theory of the evolution of legal forms. Although Maine introduced considerable complexity into his theory, and even separated European continental law from developments in property law in England, he maintained the cultural idea of the progressive evolution of legal forms. Of course, he recognized that English law was also constantly changing, but because of his evolutionary theory he distorted the underlying intent of the Roman distinction between *res mancipi* and *res nec mancipi*. This was necessary to show the progressive nature of law from ancient codes through earlier Roman law to the mature Roman law of Justinian's Code and its current manifestations in the Scottish law of inheritance (Maine 1977:161).

The Argument Summarized

Elite women were neither as dependent nor as independent as Maine suggested. By the "ancient rules" of the *XII Tables*, all women (except the vestal virgins) were dependent. In the time of Gaius, elite Roman women were struggling to find ways, with the help of lawyers, to circumvent these rules, but the struggle remained individualized, on a case-by-case basis. The emancipation of women was not an accepted principle. Control of landed property in Italy pertained only to upper-class women, who *won* their cases. But even when they won, it was difficult to dispense with a guardian, who managed the property (Jolowicz and Nicholas 1972:116–117,121).

This chapter, therefore, aims at solving two problems. The first is to provide a more convincing interpretation of the older texts and a better understanding of selected aspects of the writings of Gaius. The second relates to the emancipation of Roman women, especially with regard to their ability to control property. Thus, this chapter also contributes to the study of property relations.

Roman Marriage Forms

Maine discussed "the peculiar contrivance of archaic jurisprudence" which retained a female in bondage in her family for life (1977:90). His description of the *patria potestas* sounds like the archetype of the patrilineal, patriarchal family. The female is not able to communicate any rights of agnation to her descendants, although she is included in the agnatic bond. Maine's enthusiasm for the manuscripts of Gaius lies in part in his attributing to them the disclosure of the legal concept "perpetual tutelage of women" at the time it "had fallen into complete discredit and was verging on extinction" (ibid., pp. 80,90). The "ancient rules" of the *XII Tables* of Rome were still in effect when Gaius was a Roman lawyer. These gave fathers tremendous rights over sons, daughters, and wives. Codified in 451–450 B.C., they allowed a father to sell a son into bondage twice and forced all females (except for the vestal virgins of Rome) to remain for life under the control of a male guardian (Hallett 1984:22–23; Watson 1968).

In describing these ancient rules and contrasting them to those of his own time, Maine stated: "Ancient Law subordinates the woman to her blood-relations, while a prime phenomenon of modern jurisprudence has been her subordination to her husband" (1977:91). Yet, a reading of the *Institutes* of Gaius makes it clear that the legal status of women is much more complex. Why would Maine overstate the situation to such an extent, saying on the one hand that "control of [a woman's] person was apparently quite obsolete" and on the other hand that Roman women

[357]

were free when control of them passed from their fathers to their husbands (ibid., pp. 90,91)?

One answer, suggested earlier, is that the book was written hastily in order to gain a coveted position in the Indian civil service. A second answer may be Maine's immersion in the ideas and assumptions of his own culture. In 1871, English women were very much under the control of their fathers and husbands.[10] In an admittedly ambiguously titled final chapter, "The Emancipation of Roman Women," Gardner traces the restrictions on elite women in English society from 1857 to 1935 (1986:257–266). Then, referring to Dale (1894), another nineteenth-century writer, Gardner concludes: "It is no wonder that to a late-Victorian writer Roman women seemed unrestrained to the point of license" (1986:257–258).

A third explanation may be that in 1861 Maine was less interested in the rights of English women to hold property than he was in 1875. In the United States of the 1840s and in Great Britain by the 1860s, women were involved in a social movement that was to attain new legislation allowing married women to make contracts and purchase, sell, and hold property (Basch 1982; Holcombe 1983; Rabkin 1980). In fact, much of the impetus for women to gain voting rights in Great Britain and the United States grew out of the laws that restricted married women from controlling their inherited property (see Rabkin 1980:10; Holcombe 1983).

Turning to the writings of Gaius, we find that before marriage a Roman woman in the second century was under her father's *manus* (literally, hand, i.e., control, protection). She entered into marriage in three ways: by *usus*, *confarreatio*, and *coemptio*. *Usus* was a situation in which a woman cohabited with a man for a year without interruption, whereupon she passed unceremoniously into his family, came under his *manus*, and gained the rank of daughter (Gaius, translated by Zulueta 1946:35). Any woman who did not want to come under her husband's *manus* must stay away from his house three nights a year, thus interrupting *usus*. Gaius suggests that this marriage form (*usus*) had in his time been partly abolished by statutes and partly obliterated by disuse. Un-

---

[10]Before 1881, British women could hold property only in the form of a trust, so that male trustees and guardians had the true decision-making power concerning sale, investment, and so on. Thus, in Great Britain in that period there were certain parallels to times in classical Rome. Between 1881 and 1887 the Married Women's Property Act became law in Britain, giving female British citizens the right to hold property directly in their own names and to make decisions concerning sale, alienation, purchases, and the like.

doubtedly it began to disappear because in order to hold public office a male, and sometimes his parents, had to be married more formally (described below as the second marriage form).

The second marriage form, *confarreatio*, was entered into through a civil ceremony that took place in front of ten witnesses in which specified words were spoken formally and a "spelt" cake was offered to the god Jupiter Farreus. This was the most formal marriage mode, and men who wanted to hold higher positions as *flamens* (a priestly office) had to have been born of parents married in this manner or be himself so married (ibid.).

The third form of marriage, *coemptio*, was used when a woman's father had died. It allowed the woman to gain the guardian (i.e., husband) of her choice through a legal maneuver and took the form of a "mancipation." Mancipation was a symbolic sale performed in the presence of five Roman citizens and a sixth citizen who held the bronze scale. The person now giving up his *manus* over the other says, while holding a bronze ingot, "I declare that this slave (or son, or person in my guardianship) is mine by Quirtary right, and he is purchased by me with this bronze ingot and bronze scale." He then strokes the scale with the ingot and gives a symbolic price to the person he is mancipating. But this ceremony did not free a woman; it acted to transfer her from her father or guardian to her husband's authority. She passed into the *manus* of the man in whose presence this ceremony was performed (ibid.).

By the time of Gaius, this third form of marriage allowed a woman to be transferred to the guardianship of a stranger, who then transferred her to the guardian (i.e., husband) of her choice. Gaius is explicit: "A woman wishing to get rid of her existing guardian and to obtain another enters into the third marriage form with a stranger" (ibid., p. 37). After that she could be mancipated to "the person of her own choice." This was also the legal device used in a period when women did not have the right to make wills. A *coemptio* marriage with a stranger allowed a woman to be "remancipated" and "manumitted" to the person of her choice, who then became her guardian. In that way he acquired rights over her property. This was not a will on parchment, like a Roman male could make, but it had legal status. In all the marriage forms it was the accepted view that a wife always acquired the position of a man's daughter and that any marriage form gave her a daughter's rights.

With a father alive, a woman could leave her father's guardianship only by marriage. And the first two marriage forms placed her under the control of her husband (ibid., p. 45). Parents appointed guardians for

[359]

both male and female children, but at puberty the male child ceased to have a guardian, while the female needed to continue in guardianship all her life. If adopted, a daughter could not compel her father to perform a ceremony of mancipation to her husband for her.

A woman in any marriage form could compel a husband to allow her to leave him if she sent him notice of divorce (ibid., p. 47). But divorce did not free a woman of male guardianship, only of guardianship by a particular male. The classical Roman lawyers (who, as we saw, found ways for unmarried women to marry the man of their choice after their father's death) held that a female must stay in guardianship. Only vestal virgins were free of guardianship, because of their religious office. Those for whom no guardians were appointed would have, under the laws of the *XII Tables*, their agnates as guardians (ibid., p. 51).

Any person under a father's guardianship (*patria potestas*) could own no property; it belonged to the *familia* (Jolowicz and Nicholas 1972:121–125). When married according to the second or third marriage form (available when a father had died), a woman brought some property from her father's household, which in Gaius's time or shortly thereafter was called *dos* (Zulueta 1953:39). The husband was manager of the *dos*, and during the marriage he had the right to control it as a *patria potestas* and to enjoy its income, but his rights did not allow him to sell or mortgage it. At his death or at divorce, the *dos* had to be returned to the wife, but he was allowed to make certain deductions from it, such as for wifely misconduct.

In later Roman law the wife became the preferred creditor for her husband's general estate (ibid., p. 40). This meant that the husband could spend and lose all his own property and then borrow all his wife's property, while the law gave her no remedies. Roman lawyers began developing wives' rights to change guardianship of their property by arguing through case law and not attempting to change the existing legislation.

Roman Women's Lawsuits Challenging
the Structure of Property Relations

From Gaius's writing we find elite women in second-century Rome developing legal mechanisms to free women from the continual status of a minor. But even when individual women gained majority status they were not given the rights their brothers enjoyed. Recently translated

[360]

law cases from third-century Rome provide glimpses of the process of females gaining control over their inheritance (see Honore 1981). The cases rank as "true law reports" because "they report not merely the facts of cases and the course of judicial proceedings but the points of law at issue and the arguments addressed to them" (ibid., p. 15). According to Honore, twenty-six cases are reported in reasonable detail, dating from the reigns of the Roman emperor Severus, who ruled from A.D. 193 to A.D. 211 and the emperor Caracalla, who ruled from A.D. 211 through A.D. 217 (Crook 1967:337). Of all the cases, nineteen concern private law, thirteen involve inheritance, seven concern trusts (*fideicommissa*), and one is the division of an inheritance. This "confirms that upper-class Romans were more inclined to litigate about succession and inheritance than anything else" (Honore 1981:16). Four of the cases published by Honore (1981) involve women.

These cases demonstrate that even in the century after Gaius the position of women was not clearly established in legislation, so that it could be taken for granted, as Maine has asserted. Of course, the principle of the equality of adult women could have been established and then canceled, but scholarship on Roman law does not support a cyclical view of the evolution and decline in the laws governing property relations. Roman women did not find it easy to gain the freedom to change managers of property that they had purchased or inherited. It was a long struggle because each case had to be heard individually. The four cases (translated by Honore 1981) discussed below were taken on appeal to the highest legal resource, the emperor. Like the other evidence presented here, these four cases, heard on appeal, illustrate the existence of different opinions about the legal rights of adult women in managing resources.[11]

Case 1: Cancellation of a Sale

By the terms of the sale under review in this first case, the seller could cancel if the balance due was not paid within a certain period. Before the due date the buyer died, leaving an underage daughter as heir. Her guardians did not pay the balance when it was due, although the seller pressed them to pay. In the end he sold to someone else. When the daughter became of age, she claimed restitution—that is, claimed to be

---

[11]All law cases cited here are in Honore 1981: case 1, pp. 17–18; case 2, p. 18; case 3, pp. 18–19; case 4, pp. 19–20.

able to tender the price and obtain delivery of the property from the seller. Her claim was rejected by both the urban praetor and the urban prefect, judges who heard such lawsuits.

The case then went to Severus's council, which had a split vote on the issue. Paul, a member of the "literal-minded, strict-constructionist" group agreed with them on the grounds that the daughter was claiming restitution under a contract made by her deceased father and not by her (Honore 1981:17–18). But the emperor felt it was important that the installments came due when she was in tutelage. Paul argued against the emperor Severus, saying that restitution should be granted only on the grounds that the seller, by calling on the buyer to pay the price after the due date had passed, had renounced the right to cancel the sale. However, the emperor granted restitution "because he disliked the provisions for cancellation" and because the tutors had failed to pay on the due date and had been accused of defaulting (ibid., p. 18).

This case demonstrates that a woman who had reached majority was granted restitution because her guardians had mishandled her property. The case was heard at three hierarchically ordered legal institutions before being resolved by the emperor.

Case 2: A Daughter's Right to an Inheritance

In a second case Paul, the literal-minded conservative, once again argued against the emperor and had his view rejected. In this instance a testator appointed his son heir to two-thirds of his estate, and his daughter to one-third. If the son died without children, he gave his daughter certain other property through a trust (*fideicommissum*). By a codicil, the testator gave his daughter specified other lands and told her to be content with these in lieu of the inheritance and of everything left her in the will. The son died, and the son's property was forfeited to the tax collector.

The issue was whether the daughter could accept the trust. Paul argued that the codicil clearly stated the daughter could take nothing but the specified lands, so she could not take the trust. But the emperor Severus decided, on the basis of a more humane interpretation, that she could, saying that the codicil deprived her only of what she was to receive under the will during her brother's lifetime, not what she was to take on his death. A second issue was whether the father intended his property to go to his daughter if his son died. The emperor decided that the father did intend that, and thus awarded the trust to the adult female over the claims of the state tax collector. The trust was to be administered by her guardians.

Case 3: The Testator's Intentions
Toward His Friend's Daughter

The testator appointed as heir the daughter of Pactumeius Magnus and substituted her father for her because all women were still in male guardianship. Magnus, consul in A.D. 183, was killed by or at the insistence of Commodus, and Pactumeia, his daughter, was rumored to be dead. The testator then changed his will and named as heir Novius Rufus "because I could not have as heirs those whom I wished." Pactumeia, the daughter, turned up safe later.[12] The emperor Severus awarded the woman the inheritance on the grounds that this was what the testator intended, but he imposed on her the legacies prescribed by the testator in his second will in favor of Novius.

Case 4: A Testator's Intention

A testator who had a son and a daughter made his daughter heir, but in his will he instructed her not to make her own will unless she had children. She succeeded him, but died without children. The crucial issue became: could her brother claim the estate by way of a trust (*fideicommissum*)? Severus decided that the brother could. The only point of telling the daughter not to make a will until she had children was that her father wanted her brother to inherit the estate if she died without heirs. Hence, a trust in favor of her brother is implied.

This case demonstrates that a father could choose to give his property to one child only, in this case a daughter, instead of his son, and that such a wish would be respected in courts of law. This case went to the emperor on appeal because of the need to interpret the intent of the deceased in the will.

[12]A strict interpretation of Roman law in this case would be that "when a false reason" is given for instituting someone as heir that reason should be disregarded because it expresses the motive, "he could not have those he intended" (ibid., p. 19). He intended Pactumeia to be his heir and she was awarded the inheritance. Note that until the time of Augustus, and often thereafter, "a Roman woman was called by the feminine form of her father's family name, from the cradle through however many marriages to the grave" (Hallett 1984:67 and n. 7).

Conclusions

Today in social anthropology many of our "accepted verities" are being rethought under the impetus of interdisciplinary scholarship. This chapter uses Roman law scholarship and analytic modes of analysis from "deconstructionism" to contextualize the writings of Sir Henry Maine and the sources he used in discussing change in Roman society. In returning to legal research on Rome, I provide a fresh view of the status of upper-class Roman women, their ability to control property, and the use of this data in Maine's book, *Ancient Law*, which is still an important text for social anthropologists.

Yet, Roman law specialists are not the only ones who are critical of Sir Henry Maine. A social anthropologist recently remarked: "Although it is clear that early Roman law reflected a society deeply rooted in ownership of private property and practising contract and testamentary disposition," Maine rejected his main source of information—Justinian's Code of the sixth century—as "contaminated" (Kuper 1985:278). Had Maine extended his historical vision to the sixth century, as twentieth-century Roman legal scholars have, he would have recognized that Justinian's Code was an authentic view of the degree to which concepts of private property had developed by the second century A.D.

In following Max Gluckman's dictum to confine an anthropological study within certain narrow limits (Devons and Gluckman 1964:16–17), I have considered here only tenets of Roman law that related directly to Maine's arguments. A close examination of some of the laws in Gaius's *Institutes*, and explications by Roman law scholars other than Maine, have demonstrated that females were not free of paternal and male guardianship. They did not have control of their property or even of their own persons in the second century A.D., as Maine had asserted.

A woman with a living father could marry in one of two ways, both of which required paternal consent. If a father had died and a woman had not yet married, she might engage in the third marriage form: first she need assume a stranger for a guardian, who then passed her on in a simple ceremony to the guardian (i.e., husband) of her choice. Thus, only women without living fathers could marry whom they chose, and to do this they needed to engage in legal maneuvers that deprived them of the higher-status marriage ceremony. When parents married in less formal ways, both the husband and the male children were prevented from seeking the prestigious priestly offices. Every form of marriage deprived females of rights accorded their adult brothers. By the second century A.D., however, the favored form of marriage, the second form, gave a wife more status because of its public nature and the religious ceremony. In classical Roman society, no woman could ever be a guardian, and the status of a wife was unequal to that of her husband or her adult brother.

A return to the Latin texts that inspired Sir Henry Maine helps us to determine the actual meaning of the terms *res mancipi* and *res nec mancipi*, which Maine used but never appropriately glossed. The interpretations offered by Roman legal scholars helps us place these legal concepts of property in their context—that is, in relation to Roman attitudes toward state formation and state control. Contrary to Maine, the terms did not denote kinship-held land versus privately held land, but expressed a principle in classical Roman law that protected productive farmland in Italy from being amassed by a few families. Watson's extensive search of Roman legal and literary sources led him to refute Maine conclusively on the topic of the kinship organization of Roman society into gens at the time of "the ancient codes" (1977:40; see earlier in this chapter).

The nineteenth-century social movement in Great Britain that worked for the rights of married women to hold, buy, and sell property explains the changing political climate in which Maine worked and which led him between 1861 and 1873 to change his views concerning what constituted full equality for women. That he knew of the agitation for the passage of "the married women's property act," and approved of it, is clear from a reference in a lecture Maine gave in Birmingham, England, in 1873 (Maine 1873:3).

Our inquiry into the "perpetual tutelage of women" in Roman society and women's ability to hold property has changed our anthropological ideas about Roman property relationships. In other words, a study of gender relationships is a study of societal relationships writ large. Recent scholarship in Roman law helps clarify legal ideas and principles relating to Roman property relationships. Anthropologists should never have let the ancient Romans speak to us for so long in the accents of nineteenth-century Europeans.

Acknowledgments

I thank Tony Honore, professor of Roman Law at Oxford University, for encouraging me to read Gaius's *Institutes* and for giving freely of his

time in several discussions about the Romans. My thanks go also to
Renée Hirschon for discussions about women and property, to the
Oxford Women's Social Anthropology Seminar, where this chapter was
first presented as a paper, and especially to Rose Coser, who sharpened
the argument and encourged me to critique a scholar as eminent as
Maine. The critiques of earlier drafts by William Arens, Jane Collier,
Elizabeth Colson, Sally Falk Moore, June Nash, and Lawrence Rosen
were also helpful and gratefully received.

REFERENCES

Bachofen, J. J. 1861. *Das Mutterrecht*. Basel.
Cantarella, Eva. 1987. *Pandora's Box: The Role and Status of Women in Greek and Roman Antiquity*. Baltimore.
Clifford, James. 1986. "Introduction: Partial Truths." In J. Clifford and G. E. Marcus, eds., *Writing Culture: The Poetics and Politics of Ethnography*. Berkeley and Los Angeles.
Clifford, James, and George E. Marcus, eds. 1986. *Writing Culture: The Poetics and Politics of Ethnography*. Berkeley and Los Angeles.
Colson, Elizabeth. 1974. *Tradition and Contract: The Problem of Order*. Chicago.
Crook, John. 1967. *Law and Life of Rome*. Ithaca, N.Y.
Culler, Jonathan. 1982. *On Deconstruction: Theory and Criticism after Structuralism*. Ithaca, N.Y.
Dale, M. 1894. "The Women of Imperial Rome and the English Women of Today." *Westminster Review* 141:490–502.
Derrida, Jacques. 1976. L'Archéologie du Frivole. Paris.
Devons, Ely, and Max Gluckman. 1964. "Introduction." In Max Gluckman, ed., *Closed Systems and Open Minds: The Limits of Naïvety in Social Anthropology*, pp. 13–19. Chicago.
Durant, Will, and Ariel Durant. 1968. *The Lessons of History*. New York.
Engels, Frederick. 1884. *The Origin of the Family, Private Property, and the State*. 1944 ed. New York.
Fried, Morton. 1967. *The Evolution of Political Society: An Essay in Political Anthropology*. New York.
Fustel de Coulanges, N. 1980 (1864). *The Ancient City: A Study of the Religion, Laws, and Institutions of Greece and Rome*. Baltimore. Originally published 1864.
Gardner, Jane F. 1986. *Women in Roman Law and Society*. Bloomington, Ind.
Giddens, Anthony. 1976. *New Rules of Sociological Method: A Positive Critique of Interpretative Sociologies*. New York.
Gluckman, Max. 1965. "Immovable Property and Chattels in Social Continuity." In *The Ideas in Barotse Jurisprudence*, pp. 113–139. Manchester, Eng.

Hallett, Judith P. 1984. *Fathers and Daughters in Roman Society: Woman and the Elite Family*. Princeton.

Harris, S. 1875. *The Elements of Roman Law Summarized: A Concise Digest of the Matter Contained in the Institutes of Gaius and Justinian*. London.

Hobhouse, L. T., G. C. Wheeler, and M. Ginsberg. 1915. *The Material Culture and Social Institutions of the Simpler Peoples: An Essay in Correlation*. London School of Economics and Political Science, Monographs on Sociology 3. London.

Hobsbawm, Eric. 1983. "Introduction: Inventing Traditions." In E. Hobsbawm and T. Ranger, eds., *The Invention of Tradition*. Cambridge, Eng.

Hoebel, E. A. 1954. *The Law of Primitive Man: A Study in Comparative Legal Dynamics*. Cambridge, Mass.

Holcombe, Lee. 1983. *Wives and Property: Reform of the Married Women's Property Law in Nineteenth-Century England*. Toronto.

Honore, A. M. 1962. *Gaius*. Oxford.

————. 1981. *Emperors and Lawyers*. London.

Jolowicz, H. F., and Barry Nicholas. 1972. *Historical Introduction to the Study of Roman Law*. Cambridge, Eng.

Kaser, Max. 1980. *Roman Private Law* (Romisches Privatrecht). Trans. Rolf Dannenbring. Pretoria, South Africa.

Kuper, Adam. 1982. "Lineage Theory: A Critical Retrospect." *Annual Review of Anthropology* 2:71–95.

————. 1985. "Ancestors: Henry Maine and the Constitution of Primitive Society." *History and Anthropology* 1:265–286.

Leacock, Eleanor Burke. 1972. "Introduction." In Frederick Engels, *The Origin of the Family, Private Property, and the State*, pp. 7–67. New York.

Lefkowitz, Mary R., and Maureen B. Fant. 1982. *Women's Life in Greece and Rome: A Source Book in Translation*. Baltimore.

Maine, Sir Henry. 1873. *The Early History of the Property of Married Women, as Collected from Roman and Hindoo Law*. Lecture delivered at Birmingham, England, March 25, 1873. Manchester, Eng.

————. 1875. *Early History of Institutions*. New York.

————. 1977 (1861). *Ancient Law*. London. Reprinted from the 1917 edition. First published 1861.

Marcus, George E., and Dick Cushman. 1982. "Ethnographies as Texts." In B. J. Siegel et al., eds., *Annual Review of Anthropology*, pp. 25–69.

Momigliano, A., and S. C. Humphreys. 1980. "Foreword." In N. Fustel de Coulanges, *The Ancient City: A Study of the Religion, Laws, and Institutions of Greece and Rome*. Baltimore.

Moore, Sally Falk. 1978. "Archaic Law and Modern Times on the Zambezi: Some Thoughts on Max Gluckman's Interpretation of Barotse Law." In P. H. Gulliver, ed., *Cross-Examinations: Essays in Honor of Max Gluckman*, pp. 53–77. Leiden.

Morgan, Lewis H. 1877. *Ancient Society*. New York.

Nader, Laura. 1965. "The Anthropological Study of Law." *American Anthropologist* 67(6, pt. 2):3–32.

————. 1978. "The Direction of Law and the Development of Extra-Judicial Processes in Nation-State Societies." In P. H. Gulliver, ed., *Cross-Examinations: Essays in Honor of Max Gluckman*, pp. 78–95. Leiden.

Newman, Katherine S. 1983. *Law and Economic Organization: A Comparative Study of Preindustrial Societies*. Cambridge, Eng.

Pollock, F. 1930 (1906). "Introduction." In Sir Henry Maine, *Ancient Law*, 9th ed. London. First published 1906.

Rabkin, Peggy A. 1980. *Fathers to Daughters: The Legal Foundations of Female Emancipation*. Westport, Conn.

Vinogradoff, Paul. 1904. *The Teaching of Sir Henry Maine*. London.

Watson, Alan. 1968. *The Law of Property in the Later Roman Republic*. Oxford.

———. 1974. "*Enuptio Gentis*." In A. Watson, ed., *Daube Noster*, pp. 331–341. Edinburgh.

———. 1975. *Rome of the XII Tables*. Princeton.

———. 1977. *Society and Legal Change*. Edinburgh.

———. 1985. *The Evolution of Law*. Baltimore.

Zulueta, F. 1946. *The Institutes of Gaius*, Vol. 1: *Text with Critical Notes and Translation*. Oxford.

———. 1953. *The Institutes of Gaius*, Vol. 2: *Text with Commentary*. Oxford.

Index

[369]

Index

Library of Congress Cataloging-in-Publication Data

History and power in the study of law : new directions in legal
  anthropology/June Starr and Jane F. Collier, editors.
      p.   cm.—(Anthropology of contemporary issues)
  Includes index.
  ISBN 0–8014–2113–6 (alk. paper).   ISBN 0–8014–9423–0 (pbk. : alk.
paper)
    1. Ethnological jurisprudence—Congresses.   2. Law and
anthropology—Congresses.   I. Starr, June.   II. Collier, Jane
Fishburne.   III. Series.
K190.A3 1985
340′.115—dc19   88–30258